EDUCATION AND SOCIAL CHANGE: *Themes from Ontario's Past* brings together some important trends in contemporary historical writing, among them the renewed interest in the history of education as a field of study, the awakening interest of Canadians in the social history of their country, and the international movement known as the "new social history" — an attempt to use quantitative means to analyze systematically the development of social patterns, structures, and institutions.

In EDUCATION AND SOCIAL CHANGE: *Themes from Ontario's Past* a number of young scholars, familiar with the newest techniques of historical scholarship, focus upon English-speaking Canada and assess its educational development in terms of the country's institutions and culture. Their provocative essays include a section of fresh interpretations of important issues in the history of public education: the relationship between the school, the child and the state; the origins of juvenile delinquency; the perception of the family; the support for educational innovation and the origins of different forms of higher education. Another section of the book offers a series of essays which explore methodological questions. Combining considerations of the general problem with specific examples from the Canadian Social History Project, Professors Mattingly and Katz present here the social and family basis of school attendance, the relation between the residential patterns of the city and the provision of public institutions and, finally, the extent and sociological distribution of literacy. In addition, this collection of essays gives specific attention to the impact of the nineteenth century phenomena of "the city" in terms of changes in public literacy to provide a measurable index of school performance.

This edition provides a new perspective, not only for the origins and development of Canadian educational institutions, but for the development of Canadian society as a whole. At the same time, they offer stimulating ideas and concrete illustrations of new

EDUCATION

research directions which will also be of interest to students of social history abroad. For the educational as well as the social historian, the essays integrate the new demographic methodologies with sensitive interpretations of the texts and the rhetoric of policymakers and reformers alike.

Taken as a group, these essays present the most authoritative analysis available of subjects and methodologies in Canadian educational history. No other study or collections offers such a rich and definitive perspective. For college courses in Canadian society, in social and educational history, in urban geography, demography, and professional development, this edition represents the most current and innovative analysis of a developing culture and its schools.

PAUL H. MATTINGLY is Associate Professor of Education and Chairman of the Department of History and the Philosophy of Education at New York University. He was educated at Georgetown University and the University of Wisconsin and has contributed to numerous scholarly journals including *History of Education Quarterly, The American Educational Research Journal, The Journal of American History, Educational Studies* and *Teacher's College Record.* He is the author of "The Classless Profession: American Schoolmen in the Nineteenth Century," a recent NYU Press publication and is editor of the NYU Press series, *Education and Socialization in American History.*

MICHAEL B. KATZ is Professor of History at York University, Toronto, Canada. He is a graduate of Harvard University and is the author of a number of books on the history of education, notably, "Education in American History," and "Class, Bureaucracy and Schools: The Illusion of Educational Change in America." He is the current President of the History of Education Society, 1974-1975.

EDUCATION AND SOCIAL CHANGE

Themes from Ontario's Past

Edited by

Michael B. Katz and Paul H. Mattingly

New York • NEW YORK UNIVERSITY PRESS • *1975*

Copyright © 1975 by New York University
Library of Congress Catalog Card Number: 74-21635
ISBN: 0-8147-5372-8

Library of Congress Cataloging in Publication Data

Main entry under title:

Education and social change.

Includes bibliographical references.
1. Education—Ontario—History—Addresses, essays,
lectures. I. Katz, Michael B. II. Mattingly, Paul H.
LA418.06E38   370'.9713   74-21635
ISBN 0-8147-5372-8

Manufactured in the United States of America

MICHAEL B. KATZ

PREFACE

IN THE LAST FEW YEARS Canadians have begun to rediscover their educational past. For the most part the movement to revitalize the history of Canadian education has been the work of younger scholars, and the results of their thought, energy, and research are just now reaching the point of visibility. The purpose of this collection is to make some of that work more public.

This collection of essays makes no attempt to survey comprehensively the development of education in Ontario. Rather, I asked a number of people to contribute to a special issue of the *History of Education Quarterly* solely because of the interest and importance of what they have to say. For at this stage in the development of Canadian educational historiography, it seemed of most significance and utility to put together a series of probing and suggestive interpretive essays. The reception of the special issue generally was favourable enough to encourage me to add some other good pieces and bring out the collection as a book. It is my hope that this volume will prove useful to students and teachers of Canadian history and heuristic and informative as well to students of social history in other countries. Despite its limitation generally to Ontario, and its selection of only a few of many important topics, this group of essays does offer, I believe, a unique and insightful examination of a number of the most interesting issues surrounding the origins of Canadian public education.

In the Introduction Neil Sutherland explores in some detail the relationship of this collection to the historiography of Canadian education. He makes it clear that a number of common themes run through these articles. The first section, "The Origins of Public Education," investigates the connections between culture, social and political conflict, and the founding of school systems. R. G. Gidney begins with a reassessment of the provision of educational facilities in early Upper Canada (Ontario) and a suggestive interpretation of the relation between schooling and rural communities in the early nineteenth century. In the next chapter Susan Houston isolates both the social and political conflicts that were central to the

official establishment of an educational system. Finally in this section, Peter Ross shows that even the passage of legislation did not
still educational controversy, which continued to reflect both social
and political divisions.

The second section, "The Child, the Family and the State,"
illustrates the manner in which the perception of problems related
to the nature of the family and the condition of children has inter-
twined with the formulation of educational policy. Susan Houston
begins by exploring the centrality of anxiety about vagrant and
delinquent lower-class children to the origins of the reform school,
the definition of adolescence, and the creation of public educational systems. Alison Prentice locates a shift in the conception of
the ideal family within the same period, which she relates to a
debate about the provision of educational facilities. Both authors
point to the way in which conceptions of the family act as paradigms
in the reform and creation of other social institutions. Neil Sutherland, examining events in a later period, analyses the manner in
which concern for the health of children, interacting with scientific discoveries and the development of professions, contributed to
the assumption of new responsibilities by the state.

Professor Sutherland's emphasis on the relationship between
scientific advance and public policy highlights themes that run
through both of the articles in the second section of this collection,
"Science, Professionalism, and the Higher Learning." In the first
essay, Douglas Lawr focuses on the way in which problems of
institutional role definition combined with the development of
agricultural science to create both a new profession and a highly
successful way of assisting farmers. The problem of defining the
connection of formal learning to the advancement of science, Peter
Ross shows, also permeated debates over the development of graduate work at the University of Toronto. In his discussion of this
theme Dr. Ross provides an example of the way in which the characteristic Canadian ambivalence toward the United States expressed
itself in the creation of educational institutions.

The last group of essays, "Approaches to Research," provides
three illustrations of analytical research strategies applied to problems of very great importance to historians of education in all
countries. Each article combines a general discussion of a research
problem with an illustration of the application of a particular

methodology to its analysis. Haley Bamman discusses the way in which policy decisions about the location of schools have reflected educational purposes; his essay underlines the potential approach of the urban geographer for understanding the relation between social policy and institutional function. Harvey Graff treats the neglected question of literacy, demonstrating the use of manuscript census material for its analysis. He offers, as well, some suggestions about the relations between literacy and social structure based on his own research. I take up the problem of school attendance and try to show its historical importance; how it may be studied; and what one quantitative analysis suggests about the relations of school attendance to questions of family and class. Finally, Ian Davey demonstrates another mode of studying school attendance historically and illustrates, once again, the close connection between school reform, social class and the family in nineteenth-century cities.

The chapters by Graff, Davey and me, it might be pointed out, all utilize the data-base assembled for my on-going study of the impact of modernization on social and family structure. That project uses Hamilton, Ontario, in the nineteenth century as a case study and rests on the computer-assisted analysis of the manuscript census, assessment rolls, city directories and other sources which contain listings of individuals who lived in the city. These lists are analyzed separately and, where possible and appropriate, joined together to permit the reconstruction of individual life histories and social patterns over time.[1]

One theme that unites all of these essays remains largely implicit. It is the question of the comparability of educational development in Canada and other countries, particularly the United States. It is clear from these essays that the relation between Canadian, British, and American educational history is highly complex. Simple notions of direct borrowing will not suffice any more adequately than naive assumptions about cultural isolation. It is quite clear that similarities in social forces, in economic development, and in political and cultural values produced educational systems with many of the same underlying features in both Canada and the United

[1] The first major result of the project is my book, *The People of Hamilton, Canada West: Family and Class in a Mid-nineteenth Century City,* Cambridge; Harvard University Press and Toronto: McClelland and Stewart Limited, 1975.

States. There is no doubt, likewise, that Canadians have participated in a trans-Atlantic intellectual community that has debated important educational questions for more than a century and a half. At the same time, Canadians have always been keenly aware that their society and their cultural traditions differed from those of both Britain and America in critical ways. Thus from one point of view the history of Canadian education reveals a continual and self-conscious adaptation of internationally shared assumptions and theories to a very particular context. The same, of course, might be said of America or Britain. Only through understanding this process of adaptation in other countries can the historian of Canada, Britain, or America fully comprehend what has happened in his own.

CONTENTS

NEIL SUTHERLAND

INTRODUCTION TOWARDS A HISTORY OF ENGLISH-CANADIAN YOUNGSTERS *

EACH HUMAN BEING who survives for an appropriate number of years takes a unique but tightly circumscribed route along the broad path from birth to maturity. Our genetic inheritance, our physical and mental characteristics, the attitude of our parents towards children, learning, and working, and their need for our time and energy, determine much of the form our individual journeys will take. The intertwining of our class, religious, and ethnic identities tightens the limits of how, how far, and in which direction we proceed. What those who establish, manage, and man the various institutions in which we may spend parts of our lives want of and for us, and how they look upon and treat us governs much of what these places will give to and take from us. Other such time- and place-bound circumstances as the size of our cohort in relation to those preceding and following it, standards of health, the way that the economy is organized, and the nature and availability of work within it, further constrict the amount of choice that we may exercise and the amount of influence that we may have over the forming of our own adult selves. It is to the relationship amongst these factors, or to some selection from them, that the historian of childhood must address his attention.

The historiography of childhood, family life, and education in Canada has also been tightly bound into time and place. Contemporary concerns and academic fashions have shaped professional interest in continuities and changes in the ways Canadians grow up. Naturally caught up in the persistent Canadian need to explain how their nation was created and preserved, most Canadian historians have ignored children, families, and education. Some have, of course, written about schools and even about youngsters. Given our over-riding interest in our political evolution, most of

* I am in debt to a number of scholars for guidance and stimulation, especially Marvin Lazerson, Michael Katz, W. A. Bruneau, and Paul H. Mattingly.

these efforts have dwelt on those occasions when educational issues have obtruded into politics. Historians have focussed their attention on the effects that debates over educational policies—and especially those dealing with religion and language—have had on provincial and national politics rather than, say, on what these quarrels have done to the families, pupils, teachers, or schools involved in them.[1] A few historians have also shown an interest in the history of those institutions, especially schools, that deal with young people and how such places have changed certain of their practices over time.[2]

Here it is worth noting a major difference between the way in which American and Canadian historians have approached both the history of institutions and of the practices that characterize them. Until quite recently American historians have customarily written within an intellectual context that saw the United States as somehow called to perform a special mission in the world. Thus most historians examining the role of American institutions have emphasized what might be described as the "favourable difference." What Americans did, runs this sort of explanation, was generally right and good, and certainly better than anything prevailing in Europe.[3] Canadian historians, on the other hand, perceiving their emerging nation to be tightly bound into the web of the North Atlantic triangle, have noted and even emphasized how much of what Canadians do has been derived from elsewhere.[4]

Until quite recently, too, Canadians who addressed themselves to educational issues have generally written "teleological" history. Without really examining the notion, these historians assume that schooling—and especially public schooling—is a "good thing" and the more widely and thoroughly Canadians distribute this good thing, the better their society will be. Thus, as they moved towards nationhood and independence, Canadians created the institutions— including the schools and universities—necessary for a mature society. In the most common and popular version of this story, to establish their school system Canadians had to overcome such conditions as the harsh climate, sparcity of settlement, poor transportation, religious controversy, and so on.[5] In another rendition, a conservative elite controlling Canada only grudgingly provided a most meagre form of schooling, or no schooling at all, for the vast majority of Canadian youngsters.[6] In both accounts, however, the "reform" view is seen as the correct one. Advocates of public education, goes the story, tried to persuade their fellow citizens to set up a school system that would provide equal educational opportunity to all children. Most historians also see the reformers as succeeding in this task.[7]

The essays in this book, representing new approaches in the history of Canadian childhood, family life, and education, are attempts to revise traditional views. They are rooted in three distinct but closely related developments. First, they are part of a recent and wide-ranging effort by Canadians to explain their national condition more completely. Historians who share in this popular concern have begun a more systematic study of Canadian social and intellectual history.[8] Second, critics have attacked modern Canadian child-rearing and educational practices. For two decades or more, many articulate people have drawn attention to what they describe as the mediocre intellectual product of mass education.[9] More recently, other Canadians have expressed their dismay at the inhumanity and other faults that they see built into the public school.[10] In its effort to account for what it dislikes, each group has naturally turned to history for part of the explanation.

The third development is perhaps the most intriguing: the central role that informal "networks" of historians had in shaping the way that Canadians have tackled the reinterpretation of their past. Elsewhere, I have tried to show that the change Canadians made between the 1880s and the 1920s in the ways in which they treated youngsters were neither independent Canadian creations nor copies of what was going on in Britain and the United States.[11] In the late nineteenth century members of the new professions in public health, social welfare, and education began to form themselves into what the literature calls "transnational" communities.[12] As members of these bodies, the Canadian reformers who appear in my own essay in this collection both drew from and contributed to the expanding pools of knowledge and practice in each of these fields. In a very similar way, as historians of public health, of social welfare, and of childhood, family life, and education, the Canadians writing in this volume and many of their colleagues both draw on and contribute to the efforts of transnational networks of historians to devise more complete ways of explaining what went on in the past. Thus, although their reasons for writing revisionist history are strongly rooted in Canadian developments, the way that Canadian historians do their revising is intimately related to what is taking place elsewhere. The fact that most of this collection first appeared in *The History of Education Quarterly,* an American journal with broad international coverage and readership, is physical evidence of this situation. A brief examination, then, of appropriate networks and other international connections will show how the essays below relate both to each other and to their contexts.

Although the notion of networks is both commonsense and commonplace, it is important to identify certain characteristics that they generally share. Networks are not formal organizations. They customarily form themselves when certain historians conclude that an issue—such as the function that education serves an industrial society—or a technique—such as nominal record linkage—is worth systematic examination. Although the ones we will examine did not do so, sometimes networks—such as those now writing and rewriting the history of women—put themselves together very quickly.[13] As in the world they describe, certain persons usually play key roles in laying out or indicating the routes that other network members follow. More important than leadership, however, is the fact that members of networks are actively and self-consciously involved in each other's work. They often share the same ideology. They use, extend, clarify, and question each other's conceptual frameworks and research findings.[14] Their writing displays a sense of community that is much stronger than that shown by historians who merely share similar interests and who customarily read each other's work. Given these circumstances, networks are naturally informal and often temporary groupings that exist not so much to create or sustain a shared identity as to ease the flow of ideas.

Two of the most important networks in educational history—those of the moderate and the radical revisionists—clearly exemplify these characteristics.[15] Moderate revisionism had its start in the 1950s in the Committee on the Role of Education in American History.[16] Bernard Bailyn's *Education in the Forming of American Society* is this group's most widely-read work and Lawrence Cremin's magisterial *American Education: The Colonial Experience* is its most important product.[17] Defining education as "the deliberate, systematic, and sustained effort to transmit or evoke knowledge, attitudes, values, skills, and sensibilities," Cremin draws attention to "the multiplicity of institutions that educate—families and churches, schools and colleges, museums and libraries, summer camps and settlement houses." He also explains that such institutions relate to one another in what he calls "configurations of education." Further, both the institutions within a configuration, and configurations themselves, interact with each other and "with the larger society that sustains them and is in turn affected by them." [18]

No historian in this network handles this complex and subtle model—only very briefly sketched in here—with anything like Cremin's skill. Indeed, most who belong have done their work in the context of Bailyn's less precise definition of education ("the entire process by which a culture transmits itself across the generations") and of Cremin's earlier, less all-encompassing history of Progressive education.[19] While not obliged to accept either Bailyn's or Cremin's conclusions, most Canadian and American and many English historians who have written on the history of education since the last 1950s have been careful to distinguish between schooling and education, and to make a self-conscious effort to interweave changes in both with changes in the wider society in which they are taking place.

Moderate revisionism characterizes some recent writing on Canadian history. Although not always successfully realized, moderate revisionism is the thread that is supposed to tie together the essays that comprise the most recent survey of Canadian educational history.[20] In one of the best sections of the book J. Donald Wilson "demythologises" Egerton Ryerson. Wilson clearly shows that Ryerson's efforts were not unique but very much in the mainstream of educational changes of time. Nor did Ryerson single-handedly put together Ontario's universal, free, and compulsory system of education. Nonetheless, Wilson looked shrewdly but not basically unfavorably upon most of what he describes as the "accomplishments" of the Ryerson era.[21] In a recent article R. M. Stamp has suggested that federal intervention in vocational education is best understood in the context of the "National Policy." [22] W. A. Bruneau has argued that the earliest examples of formal learning were a product of economic surplus and urbanization.[23] John Calam has carefully examined and explained the failure of the Society for the Propagation of the Gospel to fulfil its expectations in Colonial America.[24]

Three essays in this collection are also examples of Canadian moderate revisionism at work. Douglas A. Lawr shows how the notion of formal agricultural education, "one of the most persistent ideas of the nineteenth century," eventually found in the Ontario Agricultural College an appropriate institutional home. Peter N. Ross examines the intellectual and social context that prompted the University of Toronto to institute the Ph.D. degree. In my own paper I try to show how and why the Canadian public health movement chose school children for a major and sustained effort at preventive medicine.

Both Bailyn's and Cremin's definitions are comprehensive enough for us to put most of the historians mentioned in this essay into a single network. Each operates in the context of notions that Bailyn and Cremin pushed into the historiographical mainstream. Each relates changes in his or her speciality with those in the wider society. Further, most are conscious of how the work of colleagues in intersecting networks of historians help one lay bare the precise nature of the connections between their special interest and its context. In a major sense, then, most of us who have written on the history of education since the early 1960s *do* belong in a single grouping: we are bound to each other in our mutual rejection of the simple view that public education has been getting better and better with each passing generation, a view that Lawrence Cremin has aptly called "the wonderful world of Elwood Patterson Cubberley." [25]

Despite this common ground, the radical revisionists clearly constitute a distinct network. The most obvious reason for separating them from the first is the existential one; the second group so clearly differentiates itself from others in the field. More important, since the two groups have profoundly different attitudes towards education and society in general, in their research and writing they ask very different sorts of questions. Bailyn, Cremin, and their American and Canadian colleagues are, at heart, Whig historians. They are not, I hasten to add, believers in the blatant "all history is progress" idea that characterized some of their intellectual ancestors. Although likely skeptical of what human institutions have accomplished and can accomplish, the work of members of this network limns in both an affirmation of much of the human experience in modern Western society, and, more important, an affirmation of what impact "configurations" in education have had in moving society forward.

In particular, the work of moderate revisionists often displays an acceptance of what the distinguished Canadian sociologist John Porter describes as the liberal as opposed to the radical view of equality of educational opportunity. In this formulation, society is merely obliged "to provide opportunity for those with ability, industry and motivation." [26] As expressed in patriotic rhetoric, in school textbooks, and in the work of professional historians, equality in North America—for the idea also appeared in Anglophone Canada—came to mean, as David M. Potter put it, "parity in competition." Equality "had no intrinsic value but only a value when used." Further, the United States "has had a greater measure of social equality and social mobility than any highly developed society in human history." (To this the Canadian parenthetically and characteristically adds: "And we are number two!") Finally, in North America, "education has been more available to people with native ability; professional and business opportunities have been more available to people with education; wealth has been more available to people who excelled in business and the professions; and social fortresses have yielded to the assaults of wealth more readily than in any other country." [27]

Moderate revisionists believe that, despite many flaws, education in modern society has generally "worked." They are therefore interested in such questions as how the "configurations of education" have provided opportunity for upward mobility, how they have met the need for a literate citizenship, how they have assimilated so many nationalities, and so on. Educational failures stem partly from the way that certain individuals manage certain parts of the system but mostly from a failure to make an appropriate "fit" between institutions and the society of which they are a part. Moderate revisionists look for ways to make public education function more effectively.

Radical revisionists reject this cluster of assumptions. North American society, they argue, has not and does not offer equality along these or any other lines. Even the fruits of industrialization, in which the promise of abundance and consequently equality for all could most likely be realized, did not bring about any more egalitarian a society than the agricultural and commercial one that preceded it. Schools have not and do not offer "parity of competition." On the contrary, mass education has ensured—some say deliberately—that the old divisions of power and resources were maintained and extended into nineteenth and twentieth century urban and industrial society. Family and other class factors govern what use youngsters will make of the school. Thus the passive liberal version of educational equality is merely a device to permit those who already have the advantage to use for their own benefit a system that the rhetoric says was designed for all.

Further, in the radical revisionist view, to effect equal educational opportunity the school must take an activist stance. As Porter puts it, it is "the school's responsibility to create achievement, . . . to assume responsibility to do something for those coming from inhospitable cultural environments." [28] But schools are integral parts of the whole social system. Reformers therefore cannot hope to change schools in any significant way without first changing the total system. Since radical revisionists tend to be pessimistic about the possibility of such fundamental social change, they are also pessimistic about the chances of effecting any real changes in the school system.

Michael Katz is the most important and influential radical revisionist historian.[29] In *Class, Bureaucracy, and Schools,* he summarizes a position that has received widespread attention if not always complete acceptance. By 1880, he explains, American education had become "universal, tax-supported, free, compulsory, bureaucratic, racist, and class-biased." [30] Although acutely aware of the differences between the Canadian and American experiences, Katz's research in the history of Canadian education leads him to believe that the main outlines of his interpretation apply to Canada as well as to the United States.[31] Moreover, despite the many changes that both Canadians and Americans have wrought in education since the systems were put together, in both countries the form and purpose of education have remained essentially as they were when mass public education came into existence.

Katz also argues that each of the seven characteristics he identifies was and is an integral part of the whole. By thus binding qualities that we customarily and perhaps unthinkingly favour—schooling that is universal, tax supported, free, and compulsory—with those that we customarily abhor—schooling that is bureaucratic, racist, and class-biased—Katz is not conducting a Cremin-like enrichment or extension of what we only partly knew. On the contrary, he is self-consciously trying to destroy both the traditional and moderate revisionist interpretations of the role of education in American and Canadian societies. If their work is to be taken seriously historians of education are obliged to give serious attention to Katz's propositions regarding social class and educational change, the professionalization of teaching, the use of the school to defer social reform, and so on. Indeed, while not necessarily coming to the same conclusions as Katz, both radical revisionist and other recent research into the history of American education wrestles with these and related questions.[32]

There is at least the suggestion of a paradox in the radical point-of-view. Perhaps because they believe that mass public education has had such negative effects—that formal schooling has shown itself to be a strong social force, at least in the area of "social control"—radical revisionists are sometimes also more optimistic than others about what might be possible in the future. Indeed, some project the feeling that they would like to become real, old-fashioned Whigs. Although the possibility is remote, if Canadians or Americans did fundamentally re-order their society—perhaps along socialist or social democratic lines—then they could fashion an educational system that would truly transform the notion of human progress from rhetoric to actuality. In light of their general pessimism regarding human motivation, radical revisionists with this turn of mind should perhaps subject this view of a possible future to the sort of skeptical analysis that they apply to reformers of the past.

Canadian members of this network have naturally taken a keen interest in the origins of mass education in Canada. Since Ontario's highly centralized system apparently served as a model for other parts of Anglophone Canada, they have concentrated much of their attention on events in that province. These historians—some of whom were Katz's students at the Ontario Institute for Studies in Education and the University of Toronto—confront both the traditional mythology and the notions of the moderate revisionists. Three essays by R. D. Gidney—one in this collection—set the stage for a radical reinterpretation.[33] Gidney shows, and Harvey Graff confirms that, contrary to the melancholy refrain of the educational

"revivalists," Upper Canadian society in the 1830s and 1840s provided, without an elaborate bureaucratic or coercive apparatus, such
schooling as parents wanted for their children at a price most could
afford.[34] Here we must underline the difference between education
and schooling. As with all education, that of Upper Canada at this
time had a strong moral core. However, the responsibility for providing for the moral growth of youngsters rested with the parents
who customarily discharged their duty within the household. Most
schools were set up to teach the three r's.

Gidney's description of a varied, voluntary, and parentally-
directed pattern of education indicates that, for a time, Canada
possessed a version of the organizational model for education that
Katz calls "democratic localism." [35] Gidney's research also suggests
that, in this informally organized system of education, Canadians
had a real alternative to the bureaucratic form of educational organization that they eventually put into almost universal practice.[36]

If it was neither an inevitable nor necessarily worthwhile development, then how and why did Canadians come to adopt
bureaucratic education? A radical revisionist answer to this question can be found by examining the essays of Gidney, Alison Prentice, Susan Houston, and that of Peter Ross on Toronto, as a
single unit. Taken together, these writings indicate that a socially-
conservative urban middle class imposed the new system on its
fellow citizens. Its members were moved to do so for a number of
reasons. In what they saw as rapidly-changing times they were
concerned for the position of their families, and especially for the
future of their youngsters. They worried about the threats to a
supposedly tenuous social order posed by Americanization, pauperism, crime, vice, and ignorance. They hoped to ensure continued prosperity, especially for themselves and their families, with
a labour force that was docile and productive. In common with
their counterparts in other countries they saw the school and other
institutions as the appropriate mechanisms to deal with present or
potential social problems.

Thus middle class "reformers" transformed public schooling into
public education. They made moral development, and especially
the moral development of the poor and the immigrant, into the
central purpose of the common school. To ensure that the school
carried out its task effectively, they embedded it into a bureaucratic

—meaning centralized, hierarchical, professionally-administered, rule-governed, and victim-seeking—organization. Elsewhere, T. R. Morrison has endeavoured to extend this analysis to the present. He asserts rather than shows that, when combined with compulsory attendance, the bureaucratization of education ultimately made the Canadian school into a "total" institution with all the undesirable characteristics associated with such places.[37]

In addition to his pivotal role in radical revisionism, Katz is a key figure in an historiographical and methodological network. In showing relationships amongst such variables as household size, ethnic identity, parental occupation, school attendance, and so on, Katz has made effective use of quantitative techniques. Here we must emphasize two important characteristics of this sort of research. First, methodological change is ideologically neutral; historians can employ cliometric techniques to strengthen traditional interpretation as well as to create new ones. Second, when an historian decides to put census or other data through a computer, he is not doing something that is fundamentally different from what his colleagues do; he is merely extending the range of the data that every historian has at his disposal.[38] Katz's real strength as a quantitative historian lies in the careful and imaginative questions that he puts to all the data that he has stored away. He saw, for example, that presently-used occupational classifications may not necessarily describe the structure and mobility of the Canadian work force in the middle of the nineteenth century.[39] Again, while historians are not obliged to accept Katz's ordering of nineteenth century working people, they must try to come to grips with the questions he raises about applying present notions in this field to past conditions.

Four essays in this collection suggest the range of tasks that historians may tackle with quantitative techniques. Haley P. Bamman applies them to the spatial questions asked by historical geographers. His work enables us to peer down on the school; to look upon it in its physical and social setting almost in the way that we knew or know so much about the neighbourhood of the schools we attended or those that our youngsters attend. So too does the work of Cole Harris and Bamman help provide Canadians with an extra dividend.[40] Quantitative techniques add to the ways in which Canadians can continue to indulge the immense popular and in-

tellectual interest that they have always displayed in the continuities and changes in their landscape.[41]

Harvey J. Graff, Katz and Ian Davey show how quantitative
techniques enable historians to sort out and examine the significant
characteristics of such previously undifferentiated data as rates of
literacy and school attendance. If the published census abstracts
distort the original manuscript, as David Roberts puts it, "by tear-
ing the aspects of an individual away from him," then the computer
permits us to restore them to him in a way that enables us to relate
him to others in an almost infinite number of ways.[42] Davey's
article nicely illustrates the utility of an often neglected source,
school registers, while both Graff's questions and techniques bind
his work to that of historians elsewhere who are grappling with the
measurement of literacy and its wider individual and social implications.[43] Taken together, these four essays provide a significant
substantive and methodological addition to the small but growing
body of quantitative research into Canadian social history.[44]

Canadians have also joined the growing band of historians who
are reconstructing the history of childhood and the role of children
in family life.[45] Since the work of this network overlaps and inter-
weaves with that of many other historians—some of whom are
bound together in other networks—it is a looser association than
those revising educational history.[46] Its members have bonds with
historians such as Edmund Morgan, Philippe Ariès, Bernard Wishy,
and Daniel Calhoun who work in what is really the intellectual
history of the concepts of "child" and of "family." [47] They have
connections to those such as Ivy Pinchbeck, Margaret Hewitt, and
Julius Carlebach in Britain, Robert H. Bremner and Robert M.
Mennel in the United States, and Richard Splane and Judith Fingard in Canada, who are examining or re-examining the history of
social welfare, especially as it applies to children and families.[48]
They have associations with historians like John Demos, David
Hunt, and Lloyd deMause—some of whom are coming to call themselves psychohistorians—who apply theories drawn from the behavioral sciences and psychiatry to the past.[49] They have obvious
and close relations with historical demographers, especially those,
like Peter Laslett, who deal with family reconstruction and others,
like Stephan Thernstrom, who deal with social mobility.[50] Again,
Katz plays a central role in this work. His Canadian Social History

Project is the most ambitious and influential extension of these networks into Canada.[51] As an examination of our texts and footnotes will reveal, Alison Prentice, Susan Houston, and I also have ties to one or more of these sources.

This collection only touches lightly on the role that historians of ethnic and religious groups, and of the process of assimilation, have in writing a new history of childhood and education. In both Canada and the United States, historians are approaching cultural pluralism from two different perspectives. "Non-denominational Protestantism," Susan Houston explains, "could provide a common faith on which to rest the shared loyalty basic to a national consciousness." Timothy Smith has shown how a similar faith evolved in the United States in the first half of the nineteenth century and how intimately contemporary beliefs about education were bound into this dimension of popular culture.[52] One thrust of historians with such interests is to explore the ways that the "host" societies in Canada and the United States tried to employ educational and other strategies to incorporate first the Roman Catholic Irish and later other "alien" immigrants into either British-Canadian or American national identities.[53] Their second thrust is to show how various groups in what Canadians now call the "third force" in their society—which may include the indigenous Indian and Inuit populations—employed family, congregation, ethnic association, and the schools, sometimes to preserve old identities as intact as possible in the new setting or circumstance but, more often, to create new sorts of people who were both Ukrainian and Canadian, or German and American, and so on.[54]

The work of those examining both processes suffers from the fact that such historians have not really come together in a readily identifiable network. Although some Canadian historians are, for example, familiar with what Timothy Smith has done in both aspects of this work, others seem unaware of what their American colleagues are doing.[55] In turn, most Americans are unfamiliar with Canadian research in this field.[56] Few historians on either side of the border, therefore, are able to exploit the strong comparative and analytic possibilities inherent in both the great similarities and sizeable differences between the two national experiences. In his investigations of what he describes as "the pioneer who arrived in Canada considerably freighted with cultural baggage" Jorgen

Dahlie suggests how notions taken from Rudolph Vecoli, Timothy Smith, and Silvano Tomasi can be applied, extended, and revised by testing them against Canadian experiences.[57] Allan Smith, writing within the network of modern Canadian intellectual historians, provides a framework in which we can examine the ways that Canadians came to use American concepts and ideas to explain their own experience.[58]

Like any metaphor, that of the network—transnational or otherwise—can be pushed beyond useful limits. Some historians are doing interesting and significant work without apparently belonging to any closely-knit group. Extending notions that have been applied elsewhere, Michael Bliss has taught us much about the sexual ideas which were inculcated into generations of Canadian youngsters.[59] Judith Fingard, who shares much of the skepticism of the radical revisionists, has immensely broadened our understanding of the life of the poor child in his family, at school, and with great effect, in throes of a Canadian winter.[60] Richard Allen has explained that Christian "social passion" moved many reformers to work to improve the lot of their fellow citizens.[61]

S. D. Clark is a particularly interesting "outsider." Anticipating many of the radical revisionists, as early as 1956 he wrote that educational reform—which he defined as "whatever is directed towards the object of adapting education more fully to the needs of present-day society"—may mean "little more than making education serve better the interests of dominant cultural groups in society." [62] Clark also clearly demonstrates one of the less desirable features of some networks; the work of those who belong to none is sometimes ignored. Since Clark swam against the stream in sociology and was interested in topics then of concern to only a very small group of Canadian historians, for a long time his writings in Canadian social history received far less attention than they deserved.

This collection is directed to both Canadian and to non-Canadian readers. Certain parts of this introduction will therefore be redundant—even gratuitous—to some in each group. Most of us, however, can learn something from the essays themselves. For their substantive contribution to the history of childhood, families, and education, the reader must now turn to examine each separately. Here we may conclude by tying together some of what, as a group, they may suggest about the conduct of historical research. The collection shows how historians can effectively use historical ideas and historiographic techniques that they draw from the transnational pool. I would emphasize, parenthetically, that the volume is also a major contribution to that transnational pool. The collection also indicates that, despite some losses, self-conscious networks of historians can be extremely useful devices for forwarding historical explanation. To carry this particular notion a step further, it is fair to suggest that some historical research may be unnecessarily weakened because those conducting and reporting it do not bind their efforts to that of others. The history of medicine and other health services in Canada, for example, is still very much at the "Cubberleyian" stage; that is, it is a history that exists to create and to sustain the myths of its professions.

Finally, an examination of these essays in their many contexts strongly suggests that other historical topics might well benefit from the formation of networks that will wrestle with important but as yet only imprecisely put and only partially answered questions. The apparently unrelated efforts of Frank Musgrove and of Charles Burgess and Merle Borrowman indicate that the size of one group in the population in relation both to other cohorts and to such other circumstances as technological change may be more critical in governing the lives of youngsters than the more obvious factors to which we customarily give our attention.[63] Again, their suggestive but incomplete examination of the topic provides but one example of an area where historians may advantageously conduct systematic transnational research. There are many others.

NOTES

1. See, for example, the essays and bibliographic note in Craig Brown, ed., *Minorities, Schools, and Politics,* Canadian Historical Readings No. 7 (Toronto: University of Toronto Press, 1969).
2. Traditional materials on the history of Canadian education are conveniently summarized in Willard Brehaut, "Some Approaches to Research in the History of Canadian Education," Canadian Association for Foundations of Education, Annual Meeting, 1967, and Alan H. Child, "The History of Canadian Education: A Bibliographical Note,"

Histoire Sociale/Social History, 8 (November, 1971): 104–117. An excellent introduction to Canadian social history may be found in the essays and bibliographic note in Michiel Horn and Ronald Sabourin, ed., *Studies in Canadian Social History* (Toronto: McClelland and Stewart, 1974).

3. I first noticed this characteristic way of looking at the American experience when I read the popular text by Carl N. Degler, *Out of Our Past: The Forces That Shaped Modern America* (New York: Harper, 1959). Despite his recent call for a comparative approach to the history of education, I would argue that R. Freeman Butts' most recent article clearly belongs in this tradition. Only historians with a sense of national mission, it seems to me, could view their craft as "the Progress of the Pilgrim called Historian." See his "Public Education and Political Community," *History of Education Quarterly,* 14 (Summer, 1974): 180.

4. This is a central characteristic of J. Donald Wilson, Robert M. Stamp, and Louis-Philippe Audet, *Canadian Education: A History* (Scarborough: Prentice-Hall, 1970).

5. The major work in this genre is Charles E. Phillips, *The Development of Education in Canada* (Toronto: Gage, 1957). The view is also implicit in many general works in Canadian history. See, for example, Gerald M. Craig, *Upper Canada: The Formative Years, 1784–1841,* Vol. 7 of *The Canadian Centenary Series,* ed. by W. L. Morton and D. G. Creighton (17 vol.; Toronto: McClelland and Stewart, 1963–), pp. 181–7, and J. M. S. Careless, *The Union of the Canadas: The Growth of Canadian Institutions, 1841–1857,* Vol. 10 of *The Canadian Centenary Series,* pp. 213–8.

6. Marxist historian Stanley B. Ryerson gives the clearest statement of this minority opinion. See his *Unequal Union: Confederation and the Roots of Conflict in the Canadas, 1815–1873* (New York: International Publishers, 1968), pp. 281–6. See also Howard Adams, *The Education of Canadians, 1800–1867: The Roots of Separatism* (Montreal: Harvest House, 1968), and his "The Roots of Separatism," *History of Education Quarterly,* 8 (Spring, 1968): 35–43. Adams' view is vigorously rebutted in J. Donald Wilson, "Canadian Historiography," *History of Education Quarterly,* 9 (Spring, 1969): 88–96.

7. Of the historians already cited only Adams dissents from this opinion. Successful reform is also a central theme of F. Henry Johnson, *A Brief History of Canadian Education* (Toronto: McGraw-Hill, 1968).

8. Listings in the "Recent Publications Relating to Canada," that appears in each issue of *The Canadian Historical Review,* clearly indicate this shift in emphasis. Easily the best effort so far to integrate these new interests with perennial Canadian concerns is Robert Craig Brown and Ramsay Cook, *Canada 1896–1921: A Nation Transformed* (Toronto: McClelland and Stewart, 1974), Vol. 14 of *The Canadian Centenary Series.*

9. The most influential criticism was Hilda Neatby, *So Little For the Mind: An Indictment of Canadian Education* (Toronto: Clarke, Irwin, 1953). It is still in print.

10. See Douglas E. Myers, ed., *The Failure of Educational Reform in Canada* (Toronto: McClelland and Stewart, 1973); Terence Morrison and Anthony Burton, ed., *Options: Reforms and Alternatives for Canadian Education* (Toronto: Holt, Rinehart, 1973); and George Martell, ed., *The Politics of the Canadian Public School* (Toronto: James, Lewis, and Samuel, 1974).

11. Neil Sutherland, *Children in English-Canadian Society* (Toronto: University of Toronto Press, 1975), ch. 14.

12. While research into "transnational" networks in health, education, and social welfare is not very far advanced, three recent essays sketch in the context in which they might be investigated. See James A. Field, Jr., "Transnationalism and the New Tribe," in *Transnational Relations and World Politics,* edited by Robert O. Keohane and Joseph S. Nye, Jr. (Cambridge: Harvard University Press, 1972), pp. 3–22; Kjell Skjelsbaek, "The Growth of International Non-governmental Organization in the Twentieth Century," ibid., pp. 70–92; Diana Crane, "Transnational Networks in Basic Science," ibid., pp. 235–51.

13. See, for example, the special issue "Reinterpreting Women's Education," *History of Education Quarterly,* 14 (Spring, 1974); D. Suzanne Cross, "The Neglected Majority: The Changing Role of Women in 19th Century Montreal," *Histoire Sociale/Social History,* 6 (November, 1973): 202–223.

14. Radical revisionists—discussed below—provide in their reviews and review articles a nice example of a network conducting this sort of task. To sample, see Carl F. Kaestle, "Social Reform and the Urban School," *History of Education Quarterly,* 12 (Summer, 1972): 211–28; Marvin Lazerson, "Revisionism and American Educational History," *Harvard Educational Review,* 43 (May, 1973): 269–83; Michael B. Katz, "The Origins of Urban Education," *Reviews in American History,* 2 (June, 1947): 186–92.

15. In his "Public Education and Political Community," Butts sorts out roughly the same groups into "cultural revisionists" and "radical revisionists."

16. Paul H. Buck, Clarence H. Faust, Richard Hofstadter, Arthur M. Schlesinger, Richard J. Storr, *The Role of Education in American History* (New York: The Fund for the Advancement of Education, 1957).

17. Bernard Bailyn, *Education in the Forming of American Society: Needs and Opportunities for Study* (Chapel Hill: University of North Carolina Press, 1960); Lawrence A. Cremin, *American Education: The Colonial Experience, 1607–1783* (New York: Harper and Row, 1970).

18. Lawrence A. Cremin, "Notes Towards a Theory of Education," *Notes on Education,* 1 (June, 1973): 4.

19. Lawrence A. Cremin, *The Transformation of the School: Progressivism in American Education* (New York: Knopf, 1962).
20. Wilson, Stamp, and Audet, *Canadian Education: A History.* For a shrewd but sympathetic assessment of this volume see the review of it by John Calam in *The Journal of Educational Thought,* 5 (April, 1971): 58–62.
21. Wilson, Stamp, and Audet, *Canadian Education: A History,* ch. 11.
22. Robert M. Stamp, "Technical Education, the National Policy, and Federal-Provincial Relations, 1899–1919," *Canadian Historical Review,* 52 (December, 1971): 404–423.
23. William Arthur Bruneau, "Literacy, Urbanization and Education in Three Ancient Cultures," *Journal of Education,* 19 (Spring, 1973): 9–22.
24. John Calam, *Parsons and Pedagogues: The S.P.G. Adventure in American Education* (New York: Columbia University Press, 1971).
25. Lawrence A. Cremin, *The Wonderful World of Ellwood Patterson Cubberley: An Essay on the Historiography of American Education* (New York: Teachers College, Columbia University, 1965).
26. John Porter, "Equality and Education," Canadian Society for the Study of Education, *Proceedings/Compte Rendu,* 1974, 9.
27. David M. Potter, *People of Plenty: Economic Abundance and the American Character* (Chicago: University of Chicago Press, 1954), pp. 92; 95–6.
28. Porter, "Equality and Education," 9.
29. Lazerson, "Revisionism and American Educational History," esp. 271–4.
30. Michael B. Katz, *Class, Bureaucracy, and Schools: The Illusion of Educational Change in America* (New York: Praeger, 1971), p. xx.
31. Michael B. Katz, "Class, Bureaucracy and Schools," in *The Failure of Educational Reform in Canada,* pp. 15–28.
32. See Marvin Lazerson, *Origins of the Urban School: Public Education in Massachusetts, 1870–1915* (Cambridge: Harvard, 1971); Joel H. Spring, *Education and the Rise of the Corporate State* (Boston: Beacon, 1972); Clarence J. Karier, Paul C. Violas, Joel Spring, *Roots of Crisis: American Education in the Twentieth Century* (Chicago: Rand McNally, 1973); Stanley K. Shultz, *The Culture Factory: Boston Public Schools, 1789–1860* (New York: Oxford University Press, 1973); Carl F. Kaestle, *The Evolution of an Urban School System: New York City, 1750–1850* (Cambridge: Harvard, 1973); David Tyack, *The One Best System: A History of American Urban Education* (Cambridge: Harvard, 1974); Diane Ravitch, "Local Control in the New York Public Schools, 1842–1896," *Notes on Education,* 6 (January, 1975): 1–5.
33. In addition to the essay in this collection, see R. D. Gidney, "Upper Canadian Public Opinion and Common School Improvement in the 1830's," *Histoire Sociale/Social History* (April, 1972): 48–60; R. D. Gidney, "Centralization and Education: the origins of an Ontario tradition," *Journal of Canadian Studies,* 7 (November, 1972): 33–48.

34. For a less favourable portrait see J. Donald Wilson, "The Teacher in Early Ontario" in *Aspects of Nineteenth Century Ontario: Essays Presented to James J. Talman,* ed. by Frederick H. Armstrong, Hugh A. Stevenson, and Donald Wilson (Toronto: University of Toronto Press, 1974).

35. Katz, *Class, Bureaucracy, and Schools,* pp. 15–22.

36. Gidney, "Centralization and Education," esp. 46.

37. T. R. Morrison, "The Illusion of Education: Learning and Bureaucratized Schools," in Morrison and Burton, *Options,* pp. 234–49.

38. A case can be made that there is a major difference between those who use the computer for such tasks as linking people on one list to those on another in order to sort out more data about them—really, an extension of counting—and others who use advanced statistical techniques, especially multivariate analysis. In each case, however, the historian must be judged as he always is: according to the effectiveness with which he handles this or any other sort of evidence. The two approaches, of course, are not contradictory.

39. Michael B. Katz, "Occupational Classification in History," *Journal of Interdisciplinary History,* 5 (Summer, 1972): 63–88.

40. Cole Harris, "Of Poverty and Helplessness in Petite-Nation," *Canadian Historical Review,* 52 (March, 1971): 23–50.

41. Stephen Leacock long ago observed that what "the English feel about the Armada and the Scottish about Bannockburn, the Canadian . . . feels about the vast geography of Canada." *Funny Pieces: A Book of Random Sketches* (New York: Dodd, Mead, 1936), p. 290.

42. David Roberts, "Social Structure in a Commercial City: Saint John, 1871," *Urban History Review,* 2 (October, 1974): 15.

43. See especially Lawrence Stone, "Literacy and Education in England, 1640–1900," *Past and Present,* 42 (February, 1969): 69–139; Michael Sanderson, "Literacy and Social Mobility in the Industrial Revolution in England," ibid., 56 (1972), 75–104.

44. The Canadian Population Studies Group was formed in 1973. For a cumulative bibliography and current research projects, see Herbert J. Mays, "Canadian Population Studies Group: Report of Research in Progress," *Histoire Sociale/Social History,* 13 (May, 1974): 165–73. See also Frank T. Denton and Peter J. George, "Socio-Economic Characteristics of Families in Wentworth County, 1871: Some Further Results," *Histoire Sociale/Social History,* 13 (May, 1974): 103–11; Frank T. Denton and Peter J. George, "Socio-Economic Influences on School Attendance: A Study of a Canadian County in 1871," *History of Education Quarterly,* 14 (Summer, 1974): 223–32; see also Michael B. Katz, "Reply," ibid., 233–4.

45. Although I think his classification is open to argument, C. John Sommerville has written the best bibliographic essay on this topic in his "Bibliographic Note: Towards a History of Childhood and Youth" in *The Family in History: Interdisciplinary Essays,* ed. by Theodore K. Rabb and Robert I. Rotberg (New York: Harper, 1973): pp. 227–35;

see also Philip Stewart, "Toward a History of Childhood," *History of Education Quarterly,* 12 (Summer, 1972): 198–210.

46. While its impact on this field so far has been slight, undoubtedly the sharply-growing interest in women's history will do much to enrich our knowledge of childhood as well.

47. Philippe Ariès, *Centuries of Childhood: A Social History of Family Life* (New York: Knopf, 1962); Edmund S. Morgan, *The Puritan Family: Religion and Domestic Relations in Seventeenth Century New England* (New York: Harper, 1966); Bernard Wishy, *The Child and the Republic: The Dawn of American Child Nurture* (Philadelphia: University of Pennsylvania Press, 1968); Daniel Calhoun, *The Intelligence of a People* (Princeton: Princeton University Press, 1973).

48. Ivy Pinchbeck and Margaret Hewitt, *Children in English Society, Volume I: From Tudor Times to the Eighteenth Century; Volume II: From the Eighteenth Century to the Children Act 1948* (London: Routledge, 1969 and 1973); Julius Carlebach, *Caring for Children in Trouble* (London: Routledge, 1970); Robert H. Bremner, ed. *Children and Youth in America: A Documentary History, Volume I: 1600–1865; Volume II: 1866–1932* (Cambridge: Harvard, 1970 and 1971); Robert M. Mennel, *Thorns and Thistles: Juvenile Delinquents in the United States, 1825–1940* (Hanover, N.H.: University Press of New England, 1973); Richard B. Splane, *Social Welfare in Ontario, 1791–1893: A Study of Public Welfare Administration* (Toronto: University of Toronto Press, 1965). For Fingard, see footnote 60 below.

49. John Demos, *A Little Commonwealth: Family Life in Plymouth Colony* (New York: Oxford University Press, 1970); David Hunt, *Parents and Children in History: The Psychology of Family Life in Early Modern France* (New York, 1970); Lloyd deMause, "The Evolution of Childhood," *History of Childhood Quarterly,* 1 (Spring, 1974): 503–575. Michael Katz was one of a number of historians who was asked to comment on this article; ibid.: 600–3.

50. Peter Laslett and Richard Wall, ed., *Household and Family in Past Time* (Cambridge, Cambridge University Press, 1972); Stephan Thernstrom, *Poverty and Progress: Social Mobility in a Nineteenth Century City* (Cambridge: Harvard, 1964).

51. Michael B. Katz, *The People of Hamilton, Canada West: Family and Class in a Mid-Nineteenth Century City* (Cambridge: Harvard University Press/Toronto: McClelland and Stewart, 1975).

52. Timothy L. Smith, "Protestant Schooling and American Nationality, 1800–1850," *Journal of American History,* 53 (March, 1967): 679–695.

53. See, for example, Cornelius Jaenen, "Ruthenian Schools in Western Canada, 1897–1919," *Paedegogica Historica,* 10 (1970); Cremin, *Transformation of the School,* pp. 66–75.

54. See, for example, Elizabeth Wangenheim, "The Ukrainians: A Case Study of the 'Third Force' " in *Nationalism in Canada,* ed. Peter Russell (Toronto: McGraw-Hill, 1966).

55. Timothy L. Smith, "Immigrant Social Aspirations and American Education, 1880–1930," *American Quarterly*, 21 (Fall, 1969): 523–43.
56. See, for example, Frank G. Vallee, Mildred Schwartz, and Frank Darknell, "Ethnic Assimilation and Differentiation in Canada," *Canadian Journal of Economics and Political Science*, 23 (November, 1957); Kenneth Duncan, "Irish Famine Immigration and the Social Structure of Canada West," in Horn and Sabourin, *Canadian Social History*, pp. 140–63.
57. Jorgen Dahlie, "Learning on the Frontier: Scandinavian Immigrants and Education in Western Canada," *Canadian and International Education*, 1 (December, 1972): 56–66.
58. Allan Smith, "Metaphor and Nationality in North America," *Canadian Historical Review*, 51 (September, 1970): 247–75.
59. Michael Bliss, " 'Pure Books on Avoided Subjects': Pre-Freudian Sexual Ideas in Canada," in Horn and Sabourin, *Canadian Social History*, pp. 326–46.
60. Judith Fingard, "Attitudes towards the Education of the Poor in Colonial Halifax," *Acadiensis*, 2 (Spring, 1973): 15–42; ———, "English Humanitarianism and the Colonial Mind: Walter Bromley in Nova Scotia, 1813–25," *Canadian Historical Review*, 54 (June, 1973): 123–151; ———, "The Winter's Tale: The Seasonal Contours of Pre-Industrial Poverty in British North America (1815–1960)," *C.H.A., Historical Papers*, 1974.
61. Richard Allen, *The Social Passion: Religion and Social Reform in Canada 1914–28* (Toronto: University of Toronto Press, 1971).
62. S. D. Clark, *The Developing Canadian Community* (2nd ed.; Toronto: University of Toronto Press, 1968), p. 200.
63. F. Musgrove, "Population Changes and the Status of the Young," in *Sociology, History and Education: A Reader*, ed. by P. W. Musgrave (London: Methuen, 1970), pp. 36–57; Charles Burgess and Merle L. Borrowman, *What Doctrines to Embrace: Studies in the History of American Education* (Glenview, Ill.: Scott, Foresman, 1969), ch. 5.

LIST OF ILLUSTRATIONS

(pages 162–166)

Part I

The Origins of Public Education

R. D. GIDNEY

1. ELEMENTARY EDUCATION IN UPPER CANADA: A REASSESSMENT

There was both a pessimistic and an optimistic view of the state of education in Upper Canada. This article offers an assessment of those views and suggests first, that there was far more schooling available than has generally been recognized, and thus the optimists were closer to the truth than the pessimists; secondly, that judgments about the quality of schooling must be made within the context of contemporary educational expectations; and third, that the pessimistic viewpoint tells us far more about the expectations of the school reformers of the 1830s and '40s than it does about the expectations of those who actually created and maintained the schools.

IN HER BOOK on Upper Canada published in 1838, Anna Jameson was sharply critical of the state of education in the colony. Ignorance and indifference to educational improvement, she asserted, were rampant. Many members of the assembly "could not read, and many more could not spell"; she was informed, moreover, that "in the distant townships, not one person in twenty or thirty could read or write, or had the means of attaining such knowledge." Her own small attempt to change things met only rebuff; "cold water was thrown upon me from every side—my interference in any way was so visibly distasteful, that I gave my project up . . . ." [1]

Mrs. Jameson's opinions on the state of education in Upper Canada were neither new nor singular. The literature of the period is crowded with familiar comments to the same effect. In the early 1820s, E. A. Talbot had claimed that "the great mass of the

R. D. Gidney is a faculty member at the Ontario Institute for Studies in Education, Toronto. This article is reprinted with permission from Ontario History *(September, 1973).*

people . . . are completely ignorant even of the rudiments of the most common learning." [2] A year after Mrs. Jameson's book was published, Lord Durham wrote that "even in the most thickly peopled districts there are but few schools, and those of a very inferior character; while the more remote settlements are almost entirely without any." [3] Many contemporaries agreed. The witnesses who appeared before Mackenzie's committee on grievances were nearly unanimous on the inadequacy of the common schools.[4] The sorry state of education was a frequent subject of discussion in the newspapers.[5] And more than one serious critic argued that between 1815 and 1839 the condition of the schools had actually become worse rather than better.[6]

Such pessimism about the state of education in Upper Canada was common enough; but it was never a unanimous verdict. Indeed, it was contested by a variety of observers throughout the colony's history. As early as 1810 a correspondent to the *Kingston Gazette* had declared that schools "are numerous in every part of the country." [7] Writing at the same time as E. A. Talbot, John Howison, a British visitor, thought that while provision for higher education was sadly lacking, "schools, at which the essential branches are taught, exist in the most secluded parts of the Province . . . ." [8] In the early thirties, Isaac Fidler, an English clergyman living near Thornhill, remarked that "education in country places is not so far advanced as in towns . . . yet I am greatly mistaken if there are many persons in Canada who cannot read and write, if we except poor immigrants from Europe." [9] The *Kingston Chronicle* agreed: "there is scarcely a hamlet in Upper Canada where the schoolmaster may not be found . . . ." [10] In 1839 the same newspaper flatly rejected the charges made by Mrs. Jameson,[11] as did a correspondent in the *Brockville Recorder:*

verily, Mr. Editor, our sympathising neighbours across the St. Lawrence have their Mrs. Trollope, and we good ignorant souls, have our Mrs. Jameson. . . . I assert, and I have some means of knowing . . . that even in the "distant townships" there is not one in five who cannot read and write, and in my own township of Augusta there is not one in ten, who cannot read fluently and write legibly; and if there are exceptions, they are, as the *Kingston Chronicle* justly observes, composed of persons not born in the Province.[12]

There was, then, both a pessimistic and an optimistic view of the state of education in Upper Canada. Over the years, however, it has generally been the pessimistic version that has found its way into the historical literature. Even when historians have rejected the extreme claims of Talbot or Mrs. Jameson, they have still tended to agree with contemporary critics that the provision of basic education in the colony was inadequate and needed to be improved. It is the purpose of this article to offer a reassessment of that interpretation, and to suggest first, that there was far more schooling available than has generally been recognized, and thus the optimists were closer to the truth than the pessimists; secondly, that judgements about the quality of schooling must be made within the context of contemporary educational expectations; and third, that the pessimistic viewpoint tells us far more about the expectations of the school reformers of the 1830s and '40s than it does about the expectations of those who actually created and maintained the schools.

Upper Canada possessed a variety of ways for passing on literacy and learning from one generation to the next. The most familiar means was through the schools that received financial aid from the government under the terms of the Common School Act of 1816—schools that, to borrow an English phrase, I shall call "grant-aided." Because the trustees were required to report regularly to the legislature, we have been left with a substantial body of sources on the grant-aided schools, including the school reports and statistics published in the Legislative Journals—sources that were often reprinted in the newspapers and quoted in speeches and books by contemporaries.

These sources, it must be emphasized, refer almost exclusively to the grant-aided schools; but they have too often been used as though they account for all of the basic schooling available in the colony. Though the grant-aided schools are obviously an important component in any evaluation of the availability of elementary education, they were only one of the means of obtaining literacy and learning. There were also a large number of common schools not recorded in the government statistics because they did not receive the government grant—schools I shall call "non-aided." And the day school, aided or non-aided, was only one of the ways in which children acquired the rudiments of an English education. Neither the non-aided schools nor the other institutions of basic education have received the attention they deserve.

There is no means of measuring in any exact way the number of non-aided schools. But there is a substantial amount of evidence to suggest that, from 1816 until the early 1840s, the non-aided schools were as numerous, or nearly so, as those that received government aid. The information contained in the returns to Robert Gourlay's questionnaire to the people of Upper Canada is particularly valuable. Gourlay's informants were requested to provide statistics on the number of schools in their townships. In some cases their replies can be matched up with complete school reports for the same year, from the District Boards of Education. Where this is possible, far more schools turn up in the former lists than the latter. In the London District, for example, nineteen schools received the government grant, but thirty-six are listed in the Gourlay returns; in the Gore District it was nine as opposed to thirty-seven; in Niagara, thirty as opposed to forty-six; in the Western District, ten as opposed to forty. The same discrepancies appear in other parts of the colony.[13]

A variety of sources confirm the existence of this gap between the total number of schools and the total number of grant-aided schools, not only for the early years of the Act of 1816, but throughout the period it was in force. John Strachan, a close observer of the colony's educational development, noted the discrepancy repeatedly. In 1819 he remarked that some thirty-five hundred children were in grant-aided schools "besides a great number of schools of a similar description to which the bounty of government cannot be extended." [14] In the mid-twenties he wrote that "the Schools supported by Subscribers are perhaps not fewer in number than those established by Law." [15] A remarkable number of more specific examples support Strachan's view. The Home District Board of Education reported in 1819 that twenty schools had received the grant and "many others . . . from various irregularities have not yet been recognized." [16] The township and town of Sandwich reported in 1829 that it had two grant-aided schools; but in a select committee report of 1830, a witness mentioned that the town had five schools, with three more in the rural parts of the township.[17] Toronto provides an extreme example. The city had only one school listed in the returns for 1838; yet three years later *The Church* estimated that Toronto had some forty non-aided schools.[18] As late as 1846, Egerton Ryerson claimed that only half the children attending day schools in Toronto were in government-aided schools.[19]

The existence of these non-aided schools is also confirmed by the large number of teachers who at one time or another registered complaints about being excluded from the government grant. In 1841, for example, a teacher in the Home District petitioned the legislature for redress, declaring that he had taught school for several years but had not received his share of the grant because he was not a British subject.[20] In York, Thomas Appleton and Alexander Stewart, both of whom had their grants cut off in the early twenties, continued to teach in the town until at least the end of the decade.[21] Such examples can easily be multiplied.[22]

The difference between the number of grant-aided and total common schools has also been noted by students of local history. J. A. Bannister, for example, in his careful study of the schools of Norfolk County, found that "the location of each of the schools [reported to the government during the 1820s] can be fixed with tolerable accuracy. . . . Yet there is no reference to any [grant-aided common] school in the vicinity of Vittoria though for a decade it had been the judicial centre of the London District, and was by far the most important town at that time." But there are, he adds, local records that give scattered evidence of schools in Vittoria throughout the 1820s. "Dover Mills [Port Dover] was another of the thriving centres of population for which no school is mentioned in the reports"; yet here again there were schools in existence from 1810 onwards.[23]

At a time when many communities were new and poor and thus in need of the government grant, the existence of so many rural non-aided schools calls for some explanation. In part it was due to the terms of the Act of 1816 itself. Grant-aided schools were required to remain open for six months of the year and to have at least twenty children in attendance. Some schools could not meet one or the other of these conditions and were consequently refused the grant by the boards of education.[24]

More important in limiting the number of grant-aided schools than the Act itself, however, was the way in which it was administered. The government had imposed a maximum grant for each

district, and an upper limit on the amount to be paid to any one
teacher. Beyond that, distribution policy lay with the District Boards
of Education. For years in the Home District it was a matter of
policy to restrict the number of grant-aided schools on the grounds
that a few well-paid teachers would produce better schools than a
multitude of badly-paid and hence incompetent ones.[25] The Western
District Board of Education followed a somewhat similar policy,
giving the maximum individual grant the law allowed to a relatively
small number of well-paid teachers. Inevitably such policies meant
a limited number of grant-aided schools, and a large number of
precariously-financed, non-aided schools, especially in the back
townships.[26] In other parts of the colony, the grant was divided,
increasingly minutely, among all the teachers who applied for it,
and this too contributed to the number of non-aided schools. After
1820, when the total government grant was reduced by two-thirds,
individual payments might amount to as little as five pounds or
less annually. To receive their grant, teachers had to appear before
members of the district boards. And since it was often a long way
to the district town, and many of the boards met on rare, irregular,
and frequently unpublicized occasions, some teachers simply never
bothered to make the effort required to receive such small sums.[27]
There were, as well, teachers who failed to obtain their grants
through ignorance of the law or misadventure of various kinds.[28]
For a variety of reasons, then, there were always a substantial
number of schools in the rural areas of the colony that existed
without the government grant and thus do not show up in the
colony's school statistics.

The presence of non-aided schools in the towns and villages is
easier to explain. A larger and more compact population, and the
availability of hard currency, attracted a steady flow of teachers
prepared to risk opening private venture schools—that is, schools
where the teacher had no contractual agreement with a group of
subscribers and hence no salary guarantee before he began teaching,
something that few teachers in rural areas would risk. Outside of
York and Kingston, these private venture schools were probably
rare before the middle twenties; after that they could be found in
increasing numbers throughout urban Upper Canada.

Because of the volume and variety of the sources that have survived, Toronto provides some of the best examples of the number

and longevity of these private venture schools. Between 1815 and 1846 the city newspapers and directories contain notices for fifty-eight of them. From the late twenties, they always outnumbered, by a substantial margin, the grant-aided schools: the *York Commercial Directory* of 1833–34 lists nineteen of them; *Brown's Toronto . . . Directory* of 1846–47 lists twenty-four—in comparison to four and fifteen grant-aided schools respectively. Forty of the private venture schools either did not survive more than a year or so, or left no record of their survival. Eighteen of them can be shown to have existed three years or more—a reasonable test of the efficiency and the economic viability of a non-aided school.

A few of these schools were exclusive. Two or three of them—all female academies—catered to the elite of Toronto and the province at large; board and education at Mrs. Cockburn's school, opened in 1817 and still running in 1846, could cost as much as twenty pounds a quarter year.[29] Other schools served the sons and daughters of the middling ranks of society, charging fees about the same as those of the district grammar schools.[30] But most of the private venture schools were inexpensive. The majority of them, as *The Church* put it in 1841, taught the children of "the humbler classes" and charged fees similar to those charged in the rural common schools.[31] Nearly all of the private venture schools began with the three Rs, and some of them were surprisingly large. Thomas Caldicott's Academy had some eighty students, and the Bay Street Academy usually had a hundred or more.[32]

Toronto, however, was not alone in being well provided with private venture schools. In Kingston, forty-eight can be traced between 1815 and 1846; continuity over three years or more can be demonstrated in eleven cases.[33] A long list could be made of the private venture schools—sometimes with proof of continuity, sometimes not—throughout the thirties and early forties in Brockville, Sandwich, Perth, Cobourg, Niagara, London, Prescott, Cornwall, Grimsby, and other Upper Canadian towns and villages.[34]

There were other kinds of schools in the colony that do not show up in the government statistics. Two joint-stock institutions—the Bath and Grantham academies—offered the elementary subjects at prices comparable to the grant-aided schools, and both had a majority of their pupils in the elementary departments: in 1832, for example, the Grantham Academy had some ninety pupils, only eight of whom were advanced enough to be studying the classics.[35] There was, as well, the Methodist-operated Upper Canada Academy, with a student population in the late thirties of between eighty and a hundred; it, too, took pupils only beginning to learn their letters.[36] And to this list must be added the Upper Canada Central School, an institution that was grant-aided but, because of its separate sources of financing, was never included in the school statistics. The Central School was, in fact, the largest school in the province, with an enrolment that often exceeded three hundred in the thirties and early forties.[37]

Day schools, however, were not the only way children in Upper Canada learned their letters. Some received most of their schooling at home. The English sociologist, Frank Musgrove, has recently pointed out that in Britain in the first third of the nineteenth century, domestic education was still a preferred means of educating children among many middle-class parents.[38] Judging by the number of advertisements for governesses and tutors in Upper Canadian newspapers, it was apparently preferred by many parents in the colonies as well. Sometimes two or three families would hire a teacher to attend a group of children in one of their homes—John Macaulay's daughter began her education this way.[39] Sometimes an educated woman—in many cases a clergyman's wife—would accept a few carefully selected children to educate with her own family.[40] Sometimes a tutor or a governess was hired by a single family.[41] Private tuition of this sort might be expensive or it might not. In 1835, the Solicitor General was prepared to offer what he described as a "liberal salary" to obtain a suitable governess for his two daughters, and Adam Fergusson must have gone to considerable expense to bring a tutor out from Scotland for his sons; [42] but modestly prosperous parents were more likely to be looking for someone "to whom a comfortable *Home* is more an object than mere salary" and they could, apparently, expect to find applicants who would demand less than the cost of sending their children to a boarding school.[43]

With few exceptions, all day schools, aided or non-aided, charged tuition fees, while the cost of domestic education, unless carried out by a child's parents, would equal or exceed the cost of school fees. What happened, then, to the child whose parents could not afford school fees, who lived out of reach of a day school, or who were too uneducated themselves to tutor their own children? Some of these children were assured of the essentials of literacy through the terms of their apprenticeship indentures which, for younger boys, often required their masters to send them to school for a short time.[44] Others could take advantage of the urban evening schools established "for the accommodation of youth, whose other engagements may prevent their attendance during business hours." [45] The evening schools tended to specialize in practical subjects like commercial arithmetic, bookkeeping, and penmanship, but the regular inclusion of the three Rs in their advertisements suggests, as well, that there was a steady demand for even the most elementary training from young people already at work.[46]

For those who could not attend a day school, however, the most accessible means of learning to read, and more rarely to write, was the Sunday school—an institution that appeared in Upper Canada immediately after the War of 1812, and by the thirties was common throughout the colony, urban and rural areas alike.[47] The primary purpose of the Sunday school was religious training. But for Protestants, making a child "wise unto salvation" meant, among other things, enabling him to read his Bible. Thus the Sunday school had, of necessity, to teach children to read if it was not done elsewhere. There was, as well, a more mundane reason for teaching reading: the success of the pedagogical techniques used by the Sunday schools depended on it, as the following comments by George Ryerson demonstrate.

The teacher [Ryerson wrote in 1826] after noting . . . the absentees, etc., proceeds to hear the weekly tasks of scripture, Catechisms, etc., asking questions on them and giving explanations and enters in his book an account of the Chapter, Verses, etc. They then instruct them in some Catechism or other useful subject for some time. . . . The teacher then receives their Tracts and questions them respecting their contents, and gives them a fresh tract. To each child of the reading classes a tract is given, commonly of those published by the London Tract Society; these are selected not only with a view to the instruction of the child but also with a reference to the circumstances, the character or the vices of its parents. . . . The next Sunday the tract is returned . . . and another given. The teacher then gives to each child who is present in proper time, one ticket (pasteboard with a verse of Scripture printed on it) and one ticket for every twenty verses of Scripture, or questions of Catechisms, properly and distinctly recited. To these tickets which are all committed to memory before returned, we attach the nominal value of one-tenth of a penny, and they are redeemed by a present of useful little books of the value of the tickets received.[48]

Thus for both religious and pedagogical reasons, the Sunday schools began their work, when necessary, by teaching the children to read. There must have been many children throughout Upper Canada, who, like the Rev. John Carroll, acquired much of the little formal learning they had at a Sunday school where, as he puts it, "in those days, we did spell as well as read and we learned much relative to the meaning of words . . . ."[49] In Kingston, in 1825, for example, the Sunday school at St. George's Church began with the "elements of education" so that "many children who did not know the alphabet, are spelling and reading with tolerable ease."[50] In Trafalgar township, a school of seventy students included "general reading lessons" and spelling as a regular part of its weekly timetable.[51] A Methodist preacher stationed at Guelph reported in 1842 that his Sunday school had seventy-five pupils, many of whom "have no other opportunity of learning to read, and therefore the institution is of great importance."[52]

There are enough reports of illiteracy in the colony to suggest that at least some children went without any schooling at all. One common reason for this, at a time when the individual parent bore the cost of most forms of schooling, was poverty. The recognition that poverty and illiteracy went hand in hand was, indeed, a spur to the establishment and maintenance of some schools. One of the subsidiary purposes of the Sunday schools was always, as the Toronto Methodists put it, "to impart intellectual instruction . . . to those children whose parents are too poor to afford them the advantages of a week day school. . . ."[53] And the attempt to establish charity or free schools in the larger towns testifies to the existence of parents who could pay school fees. William Macaulay's description of the function of the Central School in Toronto is illuminating on this point: it was, he wrote in 1839, "most useful in educating, in a limited way, great numbers of the poorer class of children in this City, who otherwise would be brought up in the lowest depths of ignorance"; the school should be maintained, he added, "for the instruction of the inferior and indigent part of the population in the first elements of learning."[54] In a similar vein, the editor of the *Kingston Chronicle* urged his fellow citizens to establish an infant school in order to confer "a gratuitous education upon the multitude of friendless, and in some cases fatherless objects, that are to be perpetually met with in our streets." [55]

In rural areas, individual poverty was only one factor that limited access to schooling. In a new or thinly settled township, schooling might be unavailable even to the modestly prosperous. Roads, for example, could be as crucial as money in securing accessibility: "it appears to me," the Rev. John Roaf remarked in the late thirties, "that the prevalence of Education in a neighbourhood depends much more upon the opening of roads . . . than upon any gratuity made directly to its schools." [56] Moreover, even in the midst of educational plenty, an isolated community might still go without. West Gwillimbury, for example, had several schools in 1830; yet a petition signed by twenty-nine residents of the township stated that they were "totally without the means of affording to their children the smallest portion of education, by reason of the want of a schoolmaster within any reasonable distance . . . and are consequently desirous of having a school established in their immediate neighbourhood." [57] Occasionally, there was no school simply because members of a small community disagreed on the religious affiliation of the teacher, on the site of the schoolhouse, or on some other contentious issue. [58]

That some children went without any schooling at all, however, should not be allowed to obscure the fact that schooling in one form or another was widely available. As early as 1817, according to the Gourlay returns, nearly all reporting townships had a school, and where the population was large enough or scattered enough to warrant it, most townships had several. [59] Despite a temporary setback after 1820 when the government grant was sharply reduced, the grant-aided common schools grew steadily from 1816 until, in the late 1830s, there were more than eight hundred of them, scattered over nearly every township in the province. [60] To these means of education must be added the substantial number of non-aided schools in both town and country, and the variety of other ways in which Upper Canadian children learned their letters.

It might be argued, indeed, that we should accept the opinion of the optimists for no other reason than that the pessimists' case is so susceptible to refutation. To acquiesce in E. A. Talbot's verdict is to doubt the authenticity of the school reports of the rearly 1820s, including those for the district in which he lived; it is to assume, moreover, that all the schools reported in the Gourlay returns had either disappeared by 1824 or had never existed in the first place. And ignoring the non-aided schools altogether for the moment, the existence of grant-aided schools in nearly every township of the colony by the late thirties, including many in the newest and most remote, is in itself enough to raise doubts about Lord Durham's knowledge of the subject and Anna Jameson's judgement. Other pessimistic sources are no less suspect. William Lyon Mackenzie, attempting to score political points, charged in 1831 that "in the most populous country townships in the Home District there is not *at this time of year* more than one school of ten scholars, although the number of persons between six and sixteen is over 600! ! !" [61] "This time of year" was, in fact, a time when no rural youngster old enough to help at home would ever be found in school. Or another example: in November 1838, Egerton Ryerson was asserting that because of the "monopolizing" educational policy of the Family Compact, most of the population was "growing up in ignorance." Three months later he flatly rejected the same charge when made by Mrs. Jameson, who, he claimed, was grossly misinformed: "the schoolhouses in every settled township of the Province are so many proofs and monuments of the estimate of education by the inhabitants, and of their desire to confer its advantages upon their children . . . ." [62]

There is, however, a difference between saying that schooling was widely available and that it actually reached most children. The former point has been examined at some length; but can anything be deduced about the latter point? Given the fact that no accurate count of the number of schools is possible, and that there is no systematic way to examine literacy rates through sources drawn directly from the period, it might be best to leave the latter question unanswered, or merely to indicate the number of contemporary observers who believed that literacy was widespread. For those who are prepared to accept the reliability of mid-nineteenth century census data, however, there is one significant piece of quantitative evidence that confirms the optimists' case. The census of 1861 required each householder to indicate the number of persons over twenty years of age within that household who were illiterate. The returns show an astonishingly high literacy rate—

somewhere around ninety per cent—for most areas of Upper Canada. The significant point for the argument here, however, is that the census question dealt only with those *over* twenty years of age. A quick survey of the enumerators returns for sample rural and urban areas shows that literacy was almost universal for those born in Upper Canada; and most of those counted would have received their schooling *before* the 1840s—or at least before the full impact of the Ryersonian school reforms began to be felt.

This general conclusion, that most Upper Canadian children growing up before the 1840s had at least attained literacy, is confirmed by a systematic study of the same census data for one urban community by a member of the O.I.S.E. Canadian History Project. Mr. Harvey Graff has found that in Hamilton, literacy among the native-born was nearly universal, though older people were somewhat less likely to be literate than younger ones.[63] If the census data is even roughly reliable, then it suggests that the opinion of the optimists was fully justified: schooling was widespread and, in one form or another, it reached most Upper Canadian children.

But, the skeptical reader murmurs, the question of quantity is not the most important one; what really perturbed the contemporary critics of Upper Canadian education was its quality. In a memorial to the legislature in 1835, for example, Mahlon Burwell declared that the people of the colony were "at this moment totally uneducated." What he meant, however, was not that there were no schools but that the schools were inferior in character. "The little instruction given to the children," he continued, "has no influence over their morals—does nothing to open or expand their intellectual faculties, much less to direct them in their conduct of life—English reading imperfectly taught, something of writing, and the first five rules of Arithmetic, which the teachers we employ are seldom able to explain, make up the meagre sum total of what the rising generation learn at our Common Schools." [64] His criticism was echoed by a succession of politicians, newspaper editors, clergymen and other observers of the schools.[65] The teachers, they claimed, were inadequate; the pupils attended irregularly; schooling rarely lasted more than three or four years and in many cases only a few months; and children learned little more than the three Rs. As an anonymous writer put it in the *Monthly Review* in 1841, if the defects of the system are so obvious and glaring when tried by ordinary rules, how much more so when judged by the high standards of what education, even in Common Schools, ought to be! On this point public opinion wants raising to a higher standard than generally prevails. To be taught a little reading, writing and arithmetic, is not education in any correct acceptation of the term. This neither develops the faculties of the mind, nor implants a tittle of the means of doing so. It merely enables a man to perform the very lowest part of his duties in business, or as a social being, but the highest parts of those duties are not even noticed. The sentient being is so far from having its faculties cultivated, that it is never even taught their names—it is so far from receiving any intellectual training, that in the vast majority of cases the scholar leaves school without having learned a single fact in relation to his mind and its various powers. Education stops short at the very threshold of the temple that it ought to fill with glory.[66]

"Public opinion wants raising" indeed. This was the voice of the educational reformer speaking—the voice of a growing number of public men in the thirties and early forties who were increasingly convinced that universal schooling, guided by the hand of government, was an essential prerequisite for the political, economic, and social well being of society.[67] It was the voice of Anna Jameson, with the Cousin report on the achievements of Prussian education tucked under her arm, of Egerton Ryerson, stuffed full of the education mania from his reading of the leading English and American journals, of the Rev. William Bell, peddling the notion that the Scottish normal schools held the key to the improvement of teaching in Upper Canada, of a host of others caught up in one of the great panaceas of the age of improvement.[68] But it was not necessarily the voice of the people who built and maintained the schools. And what the critics and reformers called flaws and weaknesses, can, if examined from another perspective, be seen as perfectly comprehensible aspects of a pattern of schooling that fitted naturally into the larger context of family life and work.

Parents, for example, seem to have had a relatively clear idea of what should be taught in school, though it differed sharply from the more grandiose conceptions of the school reformers. Take the following striking statement of purposes drawn up by the subscribers to a school in Norfolk County:

We the undersigned being deeply impressed with the necessity and utility of giving our children an education, by which they will be enabled to read the word of God and transact their own business—And being desir-

ous and anxious of having a school taught for that desirable purpose—
Therefore we mutually agree to engage C. D. Shiemerhorn to teach said
school. . . . Said Shiemerhorn is to teach the different branches of *reading, writing, Arithmetic* and *english Grammar* if all are required. . . .[69]

The ends were clear and the means were limited. Schooling would
enable a child to read his Bible and get on in the world; the three
Rs were sufficient to enable him to do so.

Time and time again—in the school reports, in advertisements
and teachers' contracts, in memoirs—the same purposes are restated.
A teacher's contract from Grantham township requires him to teach
"Spelling, Reading, Writing, Arithmetic, to maintain good order"
and to "suppress all immoral habits and practices among his pupils."[70] A contract from Ameliasburgh binds the master "to teach
Reading, Writing and Arithmetic, if required. . . ."[71] An advertisement for a teacher by a group of school trustees in the Bathurst
District says that "as liberal wages will be given, none need apply
but such as can teach English Grammar well, besides the other
branches usually required in Common Schools."[72] At a time when
local people had unqualified control of what was to be taught,
these contracts and advertisements reflect with rare accuracy the
things they wanted from the school. As Canniff Haight put it, "in
those days most of the country youth . . . were content if they
learned to read and write, and to wade through figures as far as
the Rule of Three. Of course there were exceptions . . . but generally this was the extent of the aspiration of the rising generation,
and it was not necessary for the teacher to be profoundly learned
to lead them as far as they wished to go."[73]

Haight's comment raises a second point. School reformers and
well-educated members of the boards of education might complain
regularly about the quality and the remuneration of teachers, but
the people who ran the schools evidently felt differently. In the
Niagara District, according to the secretary of the board of education, teachers' salaries were "so low as not to induce men of sufficient
qualifications generally to engage in the humble and ill-requited
duties"; yet, he continued, "after the approval and appointment
[of teachers] by the trustees, the board have not rejected teachers
however incompetent from a regard to the wishes of their employers . . . ."[74] Teachers were ill-paid not simply because of the
limited financial means of many rural neighbourhoods, but because

of the limited purposes to be achieved. The school may have been a necessary institution, but it was not, as Haight points out, one that required expensive skills or great learning in the teacher.

Reformers often referred to irregularity of attendance as one of the major defects of the common schools. Seen from the family's point of view, however, it has a different meaning. Irregularity of attendance, wrote one school commissioner in 1842, was due "in some instances . . . to the carelessness, indifference, or possibly poverty of the parents but it is more often caused by their [the children's] services being required at home." [75] Schooling, however valuable it might be deemed by parents, was something to be fitted in with the other needs of the family—the work of the farm, of the workshop, or the home. Being a pupil was a part of growing up, but it was not the child's only, or even primary, role.

The seasonal pattern of school attendance was also determined by the routine of family life. Throughout the rural areas there were two distinct school terms. Children too young to help with the family work and to cope with bad weather and the winter snow were usually sent to school only in the summer months; for older members of the family the pattern was reversed. As a correspondent to the *Kingston Herald* put it, "in almost all the country places in Western Canada, the common schools in the summer season are seldom attended by others, than children *from 3½ years . . . to 12 or 13 years of age.* Few or no adults of either sex can attend. But in the winter season, the reverse takes place, the younger children are withdrawn, and the elder ones *from 16 to nearly 30 years of age attend.*" [76]

Surveying what they took to be the inadequacies of the schools, the educational reformers were often quick to lay the blame for such conditions on the ignorance and indifference of parents and trustees. But it must be remembered that every common school in the colony was the product of voluntary sacrifice. No law required a child to attend school, no schoolhouse had to be built, no teacher had to be paid. The fact that many local people did not see the school in the same light as the educational reformers does not mean they were indifferent to schooling. The majority of the urban private venture schools survived because parents of the "humbler classes," as *The Church* called them, were prepared to pay tuition fees. The same is true of the non-aided schools in the rural parts of the province. And the fact that the government aided some common schools does not lessen significantly the pre-eminent role of local initiative, though it undoubtedly lessened its burdens. In new townships, or in poor or isolated neighbourhoods, government aid was probably decisive in keeping a school open: every grant-aided school in a given district received the same amount of financial aid, and the smaller the number of families involved in supporting a school, the more important the role of the grant would be.[77] But in most cases the government grant was not the main sustaining force. The cost of erecting and maintaining the schoolhouse was borne by the local community or by the parents of the children who attended that school. The grant could be applied only to teachers' salaries, but it was never anticipated that it would cover the whole of that salary, most of which, in fact, was met by tuition fees agreed upon by the teacher and the parents concerned. The common schools of Upper Canada were not "government schools" though the government provided financial aid to some of them; they were the products of local initiative and they reflected local needs.

It must be remembered too that schooling was not cheap. According to the Gourlay report, tuition fees in the rural schools in 1817 averaged ten shillings a quarter year for each pupil. There is no evidence that the cost fell significantly until the Common School Act of 1841 increased the size of the grant, introduced property taxation, and set the maximum fee at one shilling three pence a month.[78] The degree of voluntarism involved in creating the schools and the cost of maintaining them are both proofs against shallow charges of indifference and ignorance.[79]

It was voluntarism, moreover, that accounts for the institutional variety that characterized Upper Canadian educational provision. So long as schooling was primarily the responsibility of the family, parents used whatever means available to attain their ends. Some could afford tutors and governesses. Some used the urban private venture schools. Others had to create a school by co-operative effort. And some had access only to the charity school or the Sunday school. The variety of colonial schooling, however, was not simply an *ad hoc* response to frontier conditions; it was the typical way in which the educational needs of most people were met at the time, not only in Upper Canada but in America and Britain.[80] And educational "improvement" would come, not as some students of the subject would have it, from the natural course of a society maturing from a pioneer to a settled state, but from a new and compelling ideology of schooling that was emerging in the middle decades of the nineteenth century on both sides of the Atlantic. The Upper Canadian educational reformers of the 1830s were among its harbingers in North America.

One final point. Occasionally there are those who point out that no matter how many schools existed, they were still not numerous enough to accommodate all children between the ages of five and sixteen; and thus, in the final analysis, educational provision in Upper Canada was both quantitatively and qualitatively inadequate. The premise is correct but the conclusion is inappropriate. Contemporaries often used the ages between five and sixteen to indicate the years within which schooling should take place, and often enough, advanced educational reformers wanted all children in school long enough to learn more than the three Rs. But no one suggested that all children should attend school between five and sixteen years inclusive; that is an idea that belongs to a later period. And attempts to judge Upper Canadians by a standard of attendance and enrolment which, in fact, was hardly attained in Ontario in the 1930s, let alone a century earlier, is a particularly flagrant form of historical whiggism.

What, then, can be said about the state of schooling in Upper Canada? It was characterized by a variety of institutions, by limited purposes, by voluntarism, and by the high degree of responsibility borne by the family. For children in isolated sections of a settled township, in new townships, or for the urban poor, schooling of any kind might be hard to come by. But for most children the means to attain literacy existed and most children did in fact attain it. Beyond that, the level of schooling became a highly individual matter, for it was parents themselves who decided how long their children would attend school, by whom they would be taught, and in what subjects.

The educational reformers, however, were riding the wave of the future. The Ontario school system that took shape in the middle decades of the nineteenth century first undermined and then destroyed the traditional character of Upper Canadian educational provision. With larger grants and an improved administrative system, the number of non-aided schools that catered to the "humbler classes" declined sharply as these schools transformed themselves into grant-aided institutions.[81] At the same time, "private" schooling began to take on a new meaning—to denote a conscious (and expensive) rejection of the state system. The power given after 1846 to the central educational authority ended effective parental control over the qualifications of teachers and the content of the curriculum. The purposes of schooling became increasingly "public" ones—schools existed to serve the political, economic and social needs of the state and the society. The duty of Government expanded with the expansion of purposes: it was no longer enough to assist local effort—the aim of the Act of 1816; governments would increasingly require local effort, and, in 1871, demand that every child attend school. The new dispensation was introduced, no doubt, with the best of intentions, and justified in the name of progress and humanity. In the process, variety, voluntarism, and the primary responsibility of the family for the education of the child became, in Peter Lazlett's evocative phrase, a part of "the world we have lost."

NOTES

1. Anna Jameson, *Winter Studies and Summer Rambles in Canada* (London, 1838), Vol. I, pp. 34–5.
2. E. A. Talbot, *Five Years' Residence in the Canadas* . . . (London, 1824), Vol. II, p. 116.
3. C. P. Lucas, ed., *Lord Durham's Report* . . . (Oxford, 1912), Vol. II, pp. 184–5.
4. *Journals of the Legislative Assembly of Upper Canada [J.L.A.]*, 1835, Appendix No. 21, 7th Report on Grievances, Appendix to the 7th Report: Examination of Subjects.
5. For example, see the *Brockville Recorder,* 29 Dec. 1836; *Christian Guardian,* 28 Aug. 1839; *Upper Canada Herald,* 10 Dec. 1839.
6. See the *Brockville Recorder,* 14 Oct. 1836, and Public Archives of Canada [P.A.C.], RG5, A1, Vol. 14, J. G. Booth to Harrison, 26 Nov. 1839.
7. *Kingston Gazette,* 30 Oct. 1810.
8. John Howison, *Sketches of Upper Canada* . . . (Edinburgh, 1821), p. 260.
9. Isaac Fidler, *Observations on Professions, Literature, Manners and Emigration* . . . (London, 1833), p. 329.
10. *Kingston Chronicle,* 7 Dec. 1833.

11. Quoted in the *Upper Canada Herald,* 12 Feb. 1839. Similarly see the *Christian Guardian,* 20 Feb. 1839; *Kingston Chronicle,* 13 Apr. 1839.

12. *Brockville Recorder,* 28 Feb. 1839.

13. Compare the complete set of township returns and summary statistics in Robert Gourlay, *Statistical Account of Upper Canada* (London, 1822), Vol. I, and the school returns made by the boards of education in P.A.C., RG5, A1, Vol. 34 (London), Vol. 38 (Gore), Vol. 39 (Niagara), and P.A.C., RG5, B11, Vol. 1–2 (Western).

14. Quoted in J. G. Hodgins, ed., *Documentary History of Education in Upper Canada* (Toronto, 1893–1904) [*D.H.E.*], I, pp. 154–8.

15. P.A.C., RG5, B11, Vol. 3, Report of the General Board of Education, n.d. [1825 or 1826]. Similarly see *J.L.A.,* 1829, Appendix: Report of the President of the General Board of Education.

16. P.A.C., RG5, A1, Vol. 44, Report of the Board of Education, Home District, 13 June 1819. Similarly see ibid., Vol. 38, Report of the Board of Education, Ottawa District, n.d. [1816].

17. *J.L.A.,* 1830, Appendix: Report . . . on the Petition of the Trustees of the District School of the Western District; ibid., Common School Reports, Western District.

18. See *J.L.A.,* 1839, School Reports, 276–9; *The Church,* 7 Aug. 1841.

19. Quoted in F. A. Walker, *Catholic Education and Politics in Upper Canada* (Toronto, 1963), p. 69.

20. *J.L.A.,* 1841, 21 June 1841.

21. *J.L.A.,* 1828, Appendix: Report of a Select Committee on the Petition of Thomas Appleton, Minutes of Evidence. That Stewart, like Appleton, continued to teach in York, see the *Niagara Gleaner,* 23 Jan. 1830.

22. See, for example, P.A.C., RG5, C1, Vol. 21, Papers relating to the Petition of David Walker, 6 Feb. 1840; ibid., Vol. 75, James Walker to Harrison, 8 Dec. 1841; ibid., RG5, B11, Vol. 1–2, Richard Leonard to Hillier, 24 July 1824; ibid., Proudfoot Papers, John Cameron to Rev. William Proudfoot, 16 Jan. 1839; *J.L.A.,* 1839, Appendix: School Reports, London District, 283–92; Public Archives of Ontario [P.A.O.], RG2, C-6-C, Elizabeth Twigg to Murray, 26 Dec. 1843.

23. J. A. Bannister, *Early Educational History of Norfolk County* (Toronto, 1926), pp. 118–22.

24. See, for example, P.A.C., RG5, A1, Vol. 38, Report of the Board of Education, Gore District, 2 Feb. 1818; ibid., RG5, C1, Vol. 65, No. 930, Petition of John Dwyer of Emily . . . , 28 June 1841.

25. See G. W. Spragge, ed., *The John Strachan Letter Book, 1812–34* (Toronto, 1946), pp. 75–9; P.A.C., RG5, A1, Vol. 44, Report of the Board of Education for the Home District, 13 June 1819.

26. See P.A.C., RG5, B11, Vol. 1–2, Report of the Board of Education of the Western District, n.d. [1818]; ibid., RG5, C1, Vol. 72, No. 1760, Papers relating to the Board of Education, Western District, 1841. For an example of the non-aided schools in the Western District, compare P.A.C., Society for the Propagation of the Gospel in Foreign Parts

[S.P.G.], MSS "C," Rev. T. B. Fuller to the Bishop of Montreal, 11 Oct. 1838; and *J.L.A.*, 1839, Appendix: School Reports for 1838, p. 297.

27. See, for example, P.A.C., RG5, B11, Vol. 5, John Talbot to Colborne, 1 Aug. 1834.

28. For a spectacular example of nine years duration see P.A.C., RG5, B11, Vol. 1–2, Richard Leonard to Hillier, 24 July 1824. Similarly see P.A.C., RG5, A1, Vol. 55, I. H. Johnson to Maitland, 1 Jan. 1822; P.A.O., RG2, C-6-C, George Foster to Murray, 1 Mar. 1843.

29. The school was begun in 1817 by Mrs. Goodman (*Upper Canada Gazette,* 4 Sept. 1817), passed on to Mrs. Cockburn in 1821 (*York Weekly Post,* 26 Dec. 1821), and was still running in 1846 (*British Colonist,* 11 Aug. 1846). For a sampling of the expenses of sending a daughter there in the late thirties see the school accounts in P.A.O., Roe Family Papers.

30. For example see the *Patriot,* 10 June 1834, and the *British Colonist,* 18 Aug. 1846 (Misses Winn); *Colonial Advocate,* 14 July 1831, and *British Colonist,* 28 Aug. 1846 (Misses McCord); *Patriot,* 13 Sept. 1839, and *British Colonist,* 13 Nov. 1846 (Mrs. Crombie).

31. *The Church,* 7 Aug. 1841. Fees for individual schools are usually given in their newspaper advertisements.

32. For Caldicott's school see the *Patriot,* 9 Aug. 1833, and *City of Toronto . . . Commercial Directory . . . 1837.* For the Bay Street Academy see the *Patriot,* 5 Jan. 1836, and the *British Colonist,* 11 Sept. 1846.

33. Based on a search of the *Kingston Gazette,* the *Kingston Chronicle,* and the *Upper Canada Herald,* between 1815 and 1846.

34. The relevant newspaper files are most useful but where there is no newspaper other sources are informative. In Cornwall, for example, a girls' school, open for ten years before 1839, turns up in P.A.C., RG5, A1, Vol. 225, Mrs. Blackwood to Arthur, 22 July 1839. Occasionally, where there is only a single source for a school, the proprietor will provide helpful historical information herself, as in the case of Mrs. O'Brian of Prescott, who in an advertisement thanked the public for "their patronage over the last eight years" and hoped it would continue. *Brockville Recorder,* 27 Jan. 1831.

35. On the Bath Academy see *Upper Canada Herald,* 6 Jan. 1830 and P.A.C., RG5, B11, Vol. 5, Petition of the President of the Bath School Society, Nov. 1836. On the Grantham Academy see P.A.C., RG5, B11, Vol. 4, Memorial of the Trustees . . . , Nov. 3, 1832. One other joint-stock academy—the Ancaster Literary Institution—did receive the common school grant and would, therefore, be included in the educational statistics. See P.A.C., RG5, C1, Vol. 98, William Craigie to Bagot, 15 Nov. 1842.

36. See *J.L.A.*, 1836–37, Appendix No. 68: Report of a Select Committee on the Petition of Rev. Mr. Richey; *Christian Guardian,* 1 Feb. 1837.

37. For its history see G. W. Spragge, "The Upper Canada Central School,"

Ontario Historical Sociey Papers and Records, XXXII (1937), 171–91.
38. Frank Musgrove, "Middle-class Families and Schools, 1780–1880," in P. W. Musgrave, ed., *Sociology, History, and Education: A Reader* (London, 1970), pp. 117–25.
39. See P.A.O., Macaulay Papers, John Macaulay to Ann Macaulay, 8 Nov. 1840. Similarly see William Canniff, *The Medical Profession in Upper Canada* (Toronto, 1894), pp. 317–18.
40. See, for example, the *Patriot,* 1 Dec. 1835; *The Church,* 26 Jan. 1839 and 5 Jan. 1844; *British Colonist,* 3 Aug. 1843 and 14 Aug. 1846.
41. See, for example, the *Patriot,* 25 Feb. 1834 and 26 June 1838; *Kingston Chronicle,* 23 Apr. and 5 Oct. 1842; *The Church,* 17 July 1841 and 24 Aug. 1844.
42. See *The Albion* (New York), 6 June 1835; P.A.C., RG5, C1, Vol. 81, No. 2719, Fergusson to Harrison, 13 Jan. 1842.
43. *British Colonist,* 20 Nov. 1839; *The Church,* 4 May 1839. In Britain, at least, governesses' salaries were notoriously low. See M. J. Peterson, "The Victorian Governess," *Victorian Studies,* 14, No. 1 (Sept. 1970): 11–12.
44. For some typical examples see P.A.C., McPherson Papers, Vol. 1, four indentures dated 1840, 1842, 1845 and 1846.
45. *British Colonist,* 5 June 1846.
46. See, for example, *Niagara Gleaner,* 1 Oct. 1825; *Kingston Gazette,* 8 Sept. 1818; *Kingston Chronicle,* 22 Oct. 1826; *Hallowell Free Press,* 8 Nov. 1831.
47. See for example the *Christian Guardian,* 4 Sept. 1830 and 5 July 1843; *The Church,* 1 July, 5 and 19 Aug., and 2 Sept. 1837.
48. P.A.C., RG5, B11, Vol. 3, George Ryerson to Maitland, 9 June 1826.
49. J. W. Grant, ed., *Salvation! O The Joyful Sound* (Toronto, 1967), p. 86.
50. *Kingston Chronicle,* 11 Mar. 1825.
51. *Christian Guardian,* 19 Aug. 1835.
52. P.A.C., Methodist Missionary Society, Synod Minutes, Western District of Canada, Report of Sunday Schools, 1842.
53. *Christian Guardian,* 14 Jan. 1835. Similarly see the *Kingston Gazette,* 29 Mar. 1817; P.A.C., McDonald-Stone Papers, Vol. 4, Ephraim Webster to Mrs. S. Baker, 12 Mar. 1841.
54. P.A.C., RG5, B11, Vol. 5, Documents relating to . . . the Accounts of the Central School: 1. Report of William Macaulay, 8 Aug. 1839.
55. *Kingston Chronicle,* 29 Oct. 1831. Similarly see the *Colonial Advocate,* 12 Nov. 1829, and the *British Colonist,* 18 Sept. 1839.
56. Quoted in *D.H.E.,* III, 269. Similarly see P.A.C., RG5, A1, Vol. 96, Petition of the Township of Nelson . . . 26 Oct. 1829.
57. P.A.C., RG5, B11, Vol. 4, Petition of the Inhabitants of . . . West Gwillimbury, 20 May 1830. Similarly see the *Christian Guardian,* 23 July 1831; J. R. Godley, *Letters from America* (London, 1844), I, p. 210.
58. See, for example, P.A.C., S.P.G., X Series, X7, Mr. Blake's Statement,

No. 1, 28 Oct. 1840, p. 490; ibid., Mr. Morse's Journal, No. 7, 21 Jan. 1841, pp. 513–14; *Bathurst Courier,* 10 July 1835.

59. Since there were no returns from some of the most economically advanced and heavily populated areas—very few replies were received from the Midland and Eastern Districts and none from the Home District—the number of schools reported in Gourlay's volume is probably somewhat less than representative. For the statistics see Gourlay, *Statistical Account,* Vol. 1.

60. School returns were printed annually as appendices to the *J.L.A.* from the late twenties but are rarely complete. Before that, scattered returns can be found in P.A.C., RG5, A1 and B11. A nearly complete set for the Eastern District which indicates the annual growth and the effects of the cutback of 1820 has survived in P.A.C., McGillivray Papers, Vol. 3, School Papers, 1816–31.

61. *Colonial Advocate,* 22 Sept. 1831.

62. *Christian Guardian,* 7 Nov. 1838 and 20 Feb. 1839.

63. Harvey J. Graff, "Towards a Meaning of Literacy: Literacy and Social Structure in Hamilton, Ontario, 1861," *History of Education Quarterly,* 12, No. 3 (Fall 1972): 411–31.

64. *J.L.A.,* 1835, Appendix No. 58, Memorial of M. Burwell on the Subject of Education.

65. See for example the *Gore Gazette,* 24 Mar., 21 Apr., and 26 May 1827; *Upper Canada Herald,* 24 Mar. 1835; *St. Catharines Journal,* 12 Nov. and 10 Dec. 1835; *Brockville Recorder,* 29 Dec. 1836; *Christian Guardian,* 24 Feb. 1836; *Western Herald* (Sandwich), 4 Sept. 1838.

66. Quoted in the *Christian Guardian,* 22 Sept. 1841.

67. Some of the more important aspects of this growing conviction are examined by Susan E. Houston, "Politics, Schools, and Social Change in Upper Canada," *C.H.R.,* 53, No. 3 (Sept. 1972): 249–71, and by R. D. Gidney, "Common School Improvement and Upper Canadian Public Opinion in the 1830s," *Social History,* April 1972.

68. See Anna Jameson, *Winter Studies . . . ,* Vol. 1, pp. 34–5; *Canadian Christian Examiner and Presbyterian Review,* Vol. 2, No. 3 (Mar. 1838). By the early thirties Ryerson was already well aware of the main currents of educational reform: see the *Christian Guardian,* 7 Dec. 1831.

69. Norfolk Historical Society Collection, Contract between Teacher and subscribers dated 2 Oct. 1826, pp. 2761–2.

70. Niagara Historical Society Museum, Second Papers, Articles of agreement between Richard H. Secord and the undersigned subscribers, n.d.

71. "The Bell and Laing School Papers," *Lennox and Addington Historical Society Papers and Records,* 5 (1914): 16–17. Similarly see P.A.O., Education Papers, John Lindsay Contracts; *ibid.,* Miscellaneous File, Agreement between Samuel Dickerson and some inhabitants of Flamboro West, 4 Jan. 1815.

72. *Bathurst Courier,* 12 June 1835.

73. Canniff Haight, *Life in Canada Fifty Years Ago* . . . (Toronto, 1885), p. 157.
74. *J.L.A.*, 1830, Appendix: Report of the Niagara District Board of Education.
75. P.A.O., RG2, F2, Report . . . from No. 1 School Division, Burgess, 1842.
76. *Kingston Herald,* 14 Dec. 1841.
77. See for example P.A.C., RG5, A1, Vol. 51, Report of the Eastern District Board of Education, 7 Feb. 1821.
78. Tuition fees are usually given in the township returns in Gourlay, *Statistical Account,* Vol. 1. Payments in individual cases can be found in the teachers' contracts; see above fns. 69–71. For the law on school finance, see the Acts of 1816 and 1841 printed in *D.H.E.,* I, pp. 102–4, and IV, pp. 48–55.
79. A point rarely acknowledged by any of the observers of Upper Canadian education with the notable exception of John Strachan, who repeatedly pointed out the degree of initiative shown by local people both before 1816 and after; for example, see G. W. Spragge, ed., *The John Strachan Letter Book,* p. 75.
80. For the United States, the classic statement of this argument is Bernard Bailyn, *Education in the Forming of American Society* (New York, 1960). Most recently, see Carl F. Kaestle, "Common Schools Before the 'Common School Revival': New York Schooling in the 1790s," *History of Education Quarterly,* 12, No. 4 (Winter 1972): 465–500. For summaries of the comparable British situation see J. W. Adamson, *English Education, 1789–1902* (Cambridge, 1930), especially Ch. I; E. G. West, *Education and the State* (London, 1965), Ch. 9; L. J. Saunders, *Scottish Democracy, 1815–1840* (Edinburgh, 1950), p. 248ff.
81. I believe, though it does not admit of conclusive proof, that this transformation accounts in large part for the dramatic increase in the number of government-aided schools between 1839 and 1846.

PUBLICATIONS

The following publications are available to members of the Ontario Historical Society . . .

The Town of York, 1815–1834: ed. Firth	$7.50
Muskoka and Haliburton, 1615–1878: Murray	$6.25
The Valley of the Trent: Guillett	$6.25
Ethnic Groups in Upper Canada: Burnet	$2.25

Brant County: C. M. Johnson $4.50

The Defended Border: ed. Zaslow $6.25

Profiles of a Province: ed. Firth $6.25

John Strachan Letter Book: Spragge $5.00

Settlement of the U.E.L. on the Upper St. Lawrence and
    Bay of Quinte in 1784—A Documentary Record $5.75

The Simcoe Papers, 5-vol. set $25.50

Table of Contents, vols. 1–61 of Papers and Records and
    Ontario History $2.00

Back copies of Ontario History, vol. 50 (1958)—present if
    available $1.50

Requests should be sent to:

> Miss Alice Davidson,
> Executive Assistant,
> Ontario Historical Society,
> 40 Eglinton Ave. E.,
> Toronto, Ontario

SUSAN E. HOUSTON

2. POLITICS, SCHOOLS, AND SOCIAL CHANGE IN UPPER CANADA

By the 1830s, the political and religious polarization which had characterized debate on the question of public education in the early colonial period had been muted by the growing political maturity which accompanied the economic and social development of the colony since 1815. Legislative activity in the decade prior to the establishment of an effective, centralized, provincial school system in 1846 reveals the emergence of a shared outlook among propertied elements in both rural and urban communities which would be mobilized by the chief architect of the provincial system, the Rev. Egerton Ryerson (Chief Superintendent, 1844–1876), in a campaign for universal tax-supported common schools.

THE EDUCATIONAL DEBATE in Upper Canada in the 1830s and 1840s mirrored the tensions of two decades of crucial social, economic, and political ferment. Why was the issue of tax-supported, publicly-controlled elementary schooling so contentious at this time? Was it because public schooling was so "in the air" internationally that Upper Canadians could not remain detached? Was this debate merely another chapter in the ongoing church-state issue? [1] Partially; but most importantly the foundation of the provincial school system between 1846 and 1850 was the deliberate creation of Upper Canadians who shared a common outlook and common aspirations. In a society overwhelmingly rural and agricultural, the dominant orientation of this shared outlook was urban. Moderately conservative in social philosophy, the middle classes met the problems of

S. E. Houston is a member of the Department of History, York University, Toronto. This article is reprinted with permission from The Canadian Historical Review, *53, No. 3 (September, 1972).*

rapid social change at mid-century with solutions appropriate to an urban commercial society.

Until very recently, Canadian historians have confined their interest in education almost exclusively to school controversies touching on issues of biculturalism and church-state relations. Commonly their treatment of the development of educational institutions has relied on an analogy to democracy; thus the advance from log school-house to compulsory secondary education for all in Ontario has been enshrined in textbooks and popular literature alongside Canada's march to nationhood. The myth of progress, enlightenment, and humanitarian concern which evolved originally as an account of the history of American education spilled over to fill the vacuum in Canadian educational historiography. In the mythology, the movement for free public education is part of the larger struggle of the lower classes for participation in the democratic process, and the classic alignment of interests shows the "conservatives" in opposition to public school establishment.[2] Accordingly, in Upper Canada John Strachan and his rival Egerton Ryerson, the ascendency of whose influence in educational matters parallels the decline of Strachan's, have traditionally represented the contending forces. Unfortunately, both too much and too little has been made of the North American and international cast of Canadian school provision. The current renaissance in educational history in the United States has so seriously challenged the traditional interpretation that Canadian historians can no longer rely on facile analogies to Jacksonians and Whigs in the school debate. At the same time, faith in the potentiality of education has been associated too narrowly with the United States. As one tenet of Liberalism, the ideology of educational advance was an international phenomenon. "The schoolmaster was abroad": Sir James Kay-Shuttleworth in England, Victor Cousin in France, Thomas Dick in Scotland, Horace Mann and Henry Barnard in the United States, and Egerton Ryerson in Upper Canada. These men, and their counterparts in virtually every European country, formed a community of articulate and self-conscious educational innovators.

The pace and direction of the educational advance in Upper Canada in these two decades was intimately linked to the changes being wrought in virtually every facet of colonial life. As the immigration of the late 1820s and early 1830s filled in empty townships, the primitive spirit-breaking struggle of the pioneer increasingly became a memory. Settlement meant an end to the physical isolation of frontier life and an increasing concentration of population at numerous local centres. While, by 1851, roughly 15 per cent of the population lived in incorporated places,[3] the model of society provided by larger commercial centres such as Toronto and Kingston clearly exercised a commanding influence. The newspaper, with incalculable effect, bridged the distance from farmhouse to county town, to provincial capital, to London and New York.[4] Indeed, Toronto's commercial dominance of her southwestern Ontario hinterland matched a cultural and intellectual influence which contributed significantly to the educational debate.[5]

Growing crime in cities provided early educational critics with a persistent issue. By the 1830s the special problems of urban youth and juvenile criminality became distinguished from the general morass of crime. As one writer observed, "at Toronto great incentives to vice in the very young exist." [6] As early as 1835, legislators saw in the possibility of preventing the children of Toronto's poor from "growing up in idleness and vice, the pupils of old proficients in crime" a telling argument in support of free schooling for poor but promising youngsters.[7] Moreover, there were those who glimpsed a "spirit of insubordination" abroad threatening the honest independence of the working and labouring classes, particularly servants.[8] This fear of violence and civil unrest, and suspicion of the danger of the uneducated mind in the relative freedom of Upper Canadian society were to provide fertile ground for educational promoters. The equation of ignorance and vice, schooling and virtue, would appear in the arguments of spokesmen of various political hues throughout this period, for despite its overwhelmingly rural economy and setting, Upper Canadian society was something of an anomaly. The emotional and intellectual tie of a preponderance of adult settlers with Britain contributed to a sophistication in social attitude which belied the homely setting. It is possible to identify a new state of mind in the colony in the 1830s and 1840s: in socioeconomic terms, this new outlook could be attributed to a "middle class," in towns and cities defined occupationally in the range from artisan to professional, in the countryside more by prosperity.[9] However, occupational categories drawn from the twentieth century may not be particularly relevant to

Upper Canada in the nineteenth century when the distinction between "blue collar" and "white collar," so critical today, was much
less clear.[10] More suggestive, perhaps, are the pervasive images of
commercial prosperity and expansiveness which bound rural and
urban settler alike in a commitment to "improvement." This com-
monality of sentiment, expressive of shared aspirations and anxieties, had its symbolic roots in the city, whose very vitality simultaneously exhilarated and appalled earnest Victorians. As the cause
of a publicly supported, universal system of education gained
momentum in Upper Canada after 1841, this "urban outlook" provided sufficient ground for a consensus favouring common school
promotion to secure bipartisan support for school legislation by
1850.[11]

The problem of government support for common schools had
reached crisis proportions by the mid 1830s mainly because it remained very much as it had in 1820. The inadequacy of the schools
had become a commonplace. The basic administrative structure of
elementary education had been established by the Common School
Act of 1816 (56 George III, c. XXVI) and its amended versions in 1820
(1 George IV, c. VII) and 1824 (4 George IV, c. VIII). While legislative
pressure raised the government grant to £5650 in 1833, there was no
further revision of the school law until 1841. Finance and control
were critical issues which, in the politically self-conscious 1830s,
caused division both amongst and between Reformers and Tories,
Assembly and Council. The financial basis for public education
touched such questions as the possible misapplication by Strachan
of the 1798 School Land Grant and the division of the clergy reserves, and was thus mired deeply in the main political conflict of
the period. With the abolition of Strachan's Board of Education in
1833, control over common school affairs continued to be exercised
informally, but practically, by the Council of King's College.[12]
Again, political lines were drawn as the issue of appointment *v*
election in school affairs provided a test case for the general principle of democratic participation and local responsibility. Thus
throughout the 1830s the reports of the legislative select committees
on education mirrored the dominant political complexion of the
Assembly. The repeated efforts of Tory-weighted committees, ably
chaired by the moderate Mahlon Burwell, to augment government
grants, voluntary subscriptions, and fees by property assessment

were conscientiously resisted by the Reformers, whose wariness of
taxation caused them to press for a grant of 1,000,000 acres from the
Crown Reserves. Such was the strength of Reform hopes that even
farsighted Ryerson, perhaps to his subsequent embarrassment, could
only give a nodding acknowledgment to the equitableness of property taxation before asking whether there might not be a sufficient
quantity of school lands and, if it came to that, might not bank stock
be taxed as well.[13] The goal of Reform administrative proposals was
to place "the direction of education in the hands of those who are
personally interested." [14] Consequently, a proposal such as Burwell's
to give the appointment of a general board and district boards of
education to the governor was "radically objectionable. It makes
the system of education in theory a mere engine of the Executive,
and liable to all the abuse, suspicion, jealousy and opposition of
despotism; and withholds from the system of Common School education in its first and prominent feature that character of common
interest and harmonious cooperation which . . . are essential to
its success, and even to its acceptance with the province." [15] Most
of the annual efforts in aid of education in these years were lost in
Assembly wrangling. However, when in March 1835 a bill to promote education finally passed the Assembly, the Legislative Council rejected its democratic features on the grounds that a town
meeting was not "a proper place to select those who are to preside
over the morals and intellectual improvement of the rising generation; such superintendents ought to be persons of competent education and moral worth, or they cannot discharge the duties of their
office." [16]

As the pressure for a solution to the educational stalemate
mounted, the Reform Assembly in April 1835 authorized three
commissioners to "obtain information respecting the system and
government of schools and colleges." Dr. Charles Duncombe, on
behalf of the commissioners, went to the United States and reported his findings, along with a draft bill for the regulation of
the common schools, in February 1836. As a member of select committees on education, 1831–6, Duncombe was representative of the
men whose interest and concern had led the Assembly efforts in the
cause of education in these years. He has traditionally been portrayed as particularly typical of Reform interest in education, especially in his study of American practices. It is frequently main-

tained that in contrast to Strachan, who knew only too well what he wanted in an educational system, the Reform party was indecisive, united only in opposition and in having an attachment to such American features as elected trustees.[17]

In point of fact Duncombe was not particularly impressed by what he saw on his visit to the United States: in his view the Americans were "equally destitute of a system of National Education." [18] Furthermore, the radicalism of his political views, expressed especially in his support of Mackenzie up to and including the rebellion, has tended to obscure the conservatism inherent in his blueprint for social policy. Indeed, his enthusiasms reveal a model educational promoter. The overriding justification for government support for a common school system, Duncombe argued, lay in the necessity for "ensuring the welfare and safety of the Government": "the great crisis is hastening on when it shall be decided whether disenthralled intellect and liberty shall voluntarily submit to the laws of virtue and of Heaven, or run wild to insubordination, anarchy and crime." Preoccupied with the consequences, for the individual and society, of the new political and economic conditions in Upper Canada and throughout the world, Duncombe saw relief in the disciplining potential of public education: "whatever may have been the state of things heretofore, it is criminal to acquire knowledge merely for the sake of knowledge. The man must be disciplined and furnished according to the duties that lie before him."

Now Charles Duncombe was very likely what Hodgins and history have made him out to be, illustrative of Reform interest in education. However there are two dangers in generalizing about proposals such as he offered in terms of American models. One can be tempted to make an analogy to a dubious interpretation of American educational development in this period in terms of a democratic impulse.[19] Moreover, one can overlook the extent to which Duncombe's commission, his preoccupation and recommendations both continued and extended the argument for public education.

The fact that Duncombe not only reported on schools in the United States separately, but also on lunatic asylums and on prisons and penitentiaries is immensely suggestive, not only of the analogies drawn by legislative minds circa 1835, but of the kinds of concerns which public education might be expected to meet.[20] Ignorance, vice, crime, poverty, drunkenness, and lunacy comprised the staples of nineteenth-century social reform. The possible combinations and progressions of these elements—ignorance and crime; ignorance, vice, lunacy; crime, drunkenness, poverty (but not so commonly, poverty, ignorance, crime)—contributed to a "package" approach to social problems. Thus the century abounded with new theories and practices in penal discipline, more imaginative efforts in the treatment of mental illness, rational schemes for the support of the indigent and dependent population; and plans for public educational systems. Duncombe's three reports together detail the current state of American opinion and practice in crucial areas of reform effort. Further, what their very coexistence suggests, their arguments and recommendations make explicit: Duncombe saw in Upper Canadian society the same social problems which in a more urbanized milieu, such as the Northeastern United States, were critical. The undoubted discrepancy in the stages of development of the two societies lends to Duncombe's reports, in hindsight, the air of a preview, for much of their concern would be repeated over the next half century as Canadian society caught up with where New England and New York had been. But for Duncombe, his recommendations were not a preview: he saw, or thought he saw, the problems already, although they were not the kind which would reach serious proportions in a rural and agricultural society.

Juvenile delinquents, for example: "a class whose increasing numbers and deplorable situation loudly calls for more effective interposition, and the benevolent interference of the legislature." [21] This was not the inevitable lawlessness of a sparsely-settled, highly mobile society. This was a problem endemic to town and city life, the product in large part of the state of landless poverty upon which urban society perched. "Every person that frequents the streets of this city [Toronto] must be forcibly struck with the ragged and uncleanly appearance, the vile language, and the idle and miserable habits of numbers of children, most of whom are of an age suitable for schools, or for some useful employment. The parents of these children are, in all probability, too poor, or too degenerate to provide them with clothing fit for them to be seen in at school; and know not where to place them in order that they may find employment, or be better cared for." The plight of these children undermined popularly held theories of moral culpability. "Accustomed, in many instances, to witness at home nothing in the way of example, but what is degrading; early taught to observe intemperance, and to hear obscene and profane language without disgust; obliged to beg, and even encouraged to acts of dishonesty to satisfy the wants induced by the indolence of their parents—what can be expected, but that such children will in due time, become responsible to the laws for crimes, which have thus, in a manner, been forced upon them?" As convicted offenders, juveniles presented a test case to penal critics, like Duncombe, who would advocate the centrality of reformation in penal discipline. Such children, "pitiable victims of neglect and wretchedness," should be placed under special guardianship, and rescued "from the melancholy fate which almost inevitably results from an apprenticeship in our common prisons." And most importantly, the vicious cycle of ignorance and crime, the awful progression from youthful to adult criminality, provided proof of the urgent need for a common school system.[22] With his statistics from Sing Sing prison, Duncombe started a fashion for quoting jail statistics which would flourish among educational promoters in Upper Canada for generations. This emphasis on the relation of public schooling to crime prevention, so useful in gaining the support of property owners reluctant to bear a tax burden, also communicates a value judgment implicit in the common school movement: the public school as a moral agency. Moreover, one particularly directed toward a class of persons who need the ministering of the school, particularly as compensation for the inadequacies of their "natural" family. Thus, in its beginnings at least, a common school system was an institution established and supported by one group of people, not for their own children, but for the children of others. The Tory image of public schooling as a philanthropy was one which liberally-minded nineteenth-century educational promoters worked hard to dispel by the rhetorical use of "common" school in the sense of "universal." The reasons which they gave for supporting a school system, however, suggest their sensitivity to social distinctions as well as to semantic niceties.

In the light of his conviction of the uses of public education, and his well-informed acquaintance with American practices, Duncombe's particular pedagogical proposals are straightforward. He emphasizes the moral and religious aspects of the curriculum (to the point of preferring sectarian separate schools to the exclusion of religion), the inductive method, and the establishment of normal schools—the whole to be improved by a greater stringency in inspection to bolster the "responsible *profession* of teaching." On the issue of finance, the need was overriding: "our schools want in character, they want respectability, they want permanency in their character and in their support; their funds should be sufficient to interest all classes of the community in endeavouring to avail themselves of them; but whatever the amount should be, it should not be subject to any contingency as an annual vote of the Legislature." [23] By an accompanying bill, Duncombe proposed, by dividing the School Grant, to use it as an incentive to local tax support: one half would be paid to each district in proportion to the number of school age children; the other on the basis of money collected by voluntary assessment, not exceeding one penny in the pound. In the matter of control, the bill's provisions very much expressed the democratic sentiment of Buell's bill of 1831: three commissioners were to be elected at the annual town meeting and would exert effective control over examining and hiring teachers and choosing school sites. In all, as a solution to the educational stalemate, Duncombe proposed to advance Reform efforts to democratize the administration of public affairs at the same time as he breached their resistance to taxation with a compromise of grant and assessment support.

Duncombe's bill passed the Assembly, but was rejected by a select committee of the Legislative Council on the pretext of lateness in the session. In giving a brief statement of their objections, concerned primarily with the "too complicated machinery" for administration, the committee did endorse the principle of an "assessment levied upon each District in support of the schools within the same, equal to the allowance given by the Government." [24] After the summer election of 1836, Mahlon Burwell renewed his proposals for a permanent Common School Fund based on matching grant and assessment revenues. In 1838, very much the same bill passed the Assembly, only to be rejected by the Legislative Council primarily on the point of taxation. This defeat of a principle to which they had lent support previously does not necessarily represent a change of attitude on the part of the Tory councillors.

Quite probably, with economic depression and post Rebellion feelings running high, their point about the burden of education taxes at this particular moment was well taken. In 1839, the first combined assault on the problem of finance saw the Assembly and Council join forces to petition for an appropriation of 1,000,000 acres of waste land for the support of Common schools. The bill passed in the Assembly, but apparently at such a late point that the Council could not act. The Assembly considered a bill authorizing an annual assessment; but perhaps as the land appropriation bill had failed, the matter was not pursued. Thus by 1839 the rigidity of political positions on the common school question appeared to have softened. The rebellion catastrophe and growing disapproval of government reprisals may well have contributed support to efforts to devise an educational system in terms broadly acceptable to an increasingly vocal element urging its provision.

Sir George Arthur's commission of inquiry into the state of affairs in the colony in 1839 included the state of education and its possible improvement. The three education commissioners—the Rev. John McCaul, the Rev. H. J. Grasett, and S. B. Harrison—form a curious trio: the headmaster of Upper Canada College and future president of the University of Toronto; a prominent evangelical cleric and dean of St. James; and an influential moderate reformer and Sydenham's provincial secretary. Two were members of Ryerson's first Board of Education in 1846 and all three members of its successor, the Council of Public Instruction. That they appear to have shared decidedly Tory views on education should caution against a too facile importing of political categories to the educational debate.[25] In many ways the commission's report was out of date before it was tabled in February 1840.[26] Lord Durham had already roundly, if briefly, denounced the educational provisions in Upper Canada. Moreover, Sydenham's style would end the reign of Tory interests which the commission report assumed. Nevertheless, despite its impotence in initiating a policy, the report does illustrate widely-held opinions about a common school system, many of which, slightly modified, would shape the legislation of the 1840s.

Although they deplored the state of education, the commissioners found no fault worthy of mention in the basic design of the school system established in 1816. What was wanting in their view was an efficient application of Strachan's blueprint: a monolithic, government-controlled system which would ensure uniform provision, proper teacher training, and sound financial support. A government-appointed Board of Commissioners for common schools would license teachers, choose textbooks, and generally regulate; the salaried inspector-general would oversee the daily operations of both common and grammar schools. District trustees, nominated by the governor, would coordinate boards of township directors of schools elected by the shareholders of each school who were to have formed a joint stock association to build and maintain the schools. As the Rev. Robert Murray, soon to be the first assistant superintendent of education, Canada West (1842–4), observed to the commission, teachers were to be rescued from the present "system of gross oppression" by uneducated local trustees.

An improvement in the quality and condition of teachers appeared the first step in improving the state of the common schools. It was thought rather unfortunate that the wages of the working classes were so high, for "the income of the schoolmaster should at least be equal to that of a common labourer." However, teachers' wages could be stabilized if a tax of three farthings in the pound complemented the annual parliamentary grant to provide a school fund sufficient to assure a fixed allowance to teachers of £15 per annum. This would then be supplemented by tuition fees. In the debate over finance by endowment or assessment, a third source of revenue—the direct fees of children attending school—appeared insignificant by comparison. Traditionally devoted to teachers' wages, the propriety of tuition fees had never been seriously questioned. Very much in the tradition of the poor laws, the commission would exempt indigent householders and even whole townships from the assessment regulations, and a selected number of pauper children, registered as such, were to be accepted at school free of charge. However, for the rest, the commission was very impressed by the importance of a charge for the education "even of the humblest classes of society"; their suggested fee, however, was "two dollars per quarter." Mahlon Burwell, although no longer representing London in the Assembly, had briefed the commission on his views on tuition fees: "charges of tuition fee . . . are absolutely necessary to arrest and keep enduring the attention of parents to the interests and well working of Common Schools, and should never be dispensed with, but in such cases of indigent parents as the Trustees of Common Schools might, on account of indigence alone, direct that their children should be taught gratuitously." The moderateness of Burwell's conservatism is striking; apparently his support for a common school system of education soundly financed and reasonably controlled (although with a substantial edge in favour of the governor) made him appear to his friends as "too democratic." It is of some interest in a reassessment of Strachan's position that he regarded Burwell's bill to be "on the whole, by far the best measure for the establishment of Common Schools which I have yet seen." [27] That Burwell's attitude on taxation and fees was as moderate as any in the legislature at this time illustrates the distance the debate would travel under Union.

Up to 1841, both the administrative and financial basis for the common school system depended on the increasingly inadequate working of the machinery of local government. The 1841 Common School Act, based largely on Duncombe's Report, applied to the united province. Despite the advantage of the 1841 District Municipal Act, it floundered in Upper Canada partly because the new councils were hampered by existing limitations of an assessment of two pence in the pound. The assessment provisions of the Act were comparable to what had been proposed in the late 1830s; however, the procedure proved to be too complicated. The general inadequacy of the 1841 Act meant a temporary continuation of chaos; but a systemization of education was in the air once the administrative and financial super-structure had been built. Francis Hincks' Act of 1843 (7 Vict., c. xxix) was a major test of the Reform position. While Murray, the incumbent superintendent, deplored his lack of power to effect any measure of uniformity, he quite rightly sensed his position would not be improved by the Reformers, for there existed "in certain quarters a deep-rooted jealousy of such power being committed to one man." [28] Although the 1843 Act substituted assistant superintendents for each section of the province, for the unified superintendency it abolished, it gave the power of supervision to County Superintendents appointed by the court of Wardens for the county. Commenting on his bill, Hincks noted, "in framing this system . . . you will observe that, as in all other instances, the late Ministry have divested the grant of all local patronage. Everything has been left to the people themselves; and I feel perfectly convinced that they will prove themselves capable of managing their own affairs in a more satisfactory manner than any Government Boards of Education or visiting Superintendents could do for them." [29] With the principle of property assessment, Hincks and the reformers were on less sure ground than in their "democratization" of control. Hincks acknowledged that opposition to taxation was widespread and popular: "I know that a prejudice exists against the tax; but it is merely from prejudice and ignorance of its effect. The tax is for the benefit of the resident settlers. The higher the tax, the lower will be the Rate-Bill on the parents. A portion of the tax falls on the non-Residents, on the rich, on those who have no children; therefore, it is for the interest of the people to have the tax as high as the law allows."

The question of the nature of the opposition to property taxation for school support is particularly confused because the contemporary rhetoric of school promotion stereotyped certain sources of opposition and minimized others. Since the issue was not fully resolved until compulsory free elementary schooling was enacted in 1871, debate continued throughout most of Ryerson's superintendency. Unfortunately, the historian's task has not been helped by the assiduous efforts of Hodgins in the *Documentary History* to ensure an interpretation consistent with Ryerson's "achievement." Clearly, opposition to and support for the assessment principle appears sufficiently heterogeneous to preclude simple economic or political polarities, such as Reform *v.* Conservative, rich *v.* poor. As the 1843 Act shows, the Reform leadership had swung firmly behind the taxation clause.[30] Both John Roblin and Baldwin argued on the second reading that the rich man must be made to see that although he was taxed the most, he benefited the most from an "intelligent, orderly population around him." [31] The emphasis placed on the rich man in the stock arguments over taxation suggests that these pleas are intended to persuade the rich to stop objecting—certainly that is Hodgins' gloss. However, Hincks' remarks indicate the opposition was popular: emphasis on the rich bearing the tax burden could as well be interpreted as aimed at placating protesting middle and lower middle income groups with visions of the groaning rich. Certainly it would be illuminating to know just how far down the income scale identification with the expression "rich man" stopped—where the point of perceived benefit met a sense of burden.

What seems clear is that support for taxation was allied with a held conviction of the value of education. The apathy toward schooling characteristic of the back townships had been confirmed by years of nothing but local initiative in school maintenance. But settlement, and fears of republicanism and the undesirable influence American teachers could exercise over the youth of the colony, increased interest in education and provided a common theme to the literature of petitions and local school reports. The urgency with which those concerned with fostering loyalty to Britain, especially after 1837, sought to resolve the problem of alien teachers and American textbooks displays a willingness on the part of the more prosperous element in society, rural and urban, to turn to public education as a means of social control. It is this fear of a motley of Americanism, civil disorder, ignorance, and the lower classes generally in an increasingly socially differentiated society which provided the mainspring of middle class support for education and willingness to assume the burden of taxation for something with which it felt personally unconnected, other people's children. The alternatives were clearly drawn: "unless the provision for the support of education is made certain and permanent, this great country must rapidly sink deeper and deeper in ignorance and vice. No man possessed of property in this Province, who attends for a little to the state of ignorance which pervades the great mass of the many thousands who are annually settled among us, and the ignorance in which our native youth are growing up around us could hesitate for a moment to pay any reasonable tax for the support of education, as he would thereby be increasing the value of his estate, and securing himself and his posterity in the possession of it." [32] In values and attitudes, prosperity brought a common conservatism to those Upper Canadians who benefited from it; and a common fear of the undisciplined and uneducated mind. Egerton Ryerson, as a member of that group and spokesman for its attitudes, argued for a common school system in precisely the terms which would ensure its general acceptance.

Ryerson's various roles as Methodist, educator, and polemicist bear the stamp of his essentially conservative social and political philosophy.[33] Moreover, as he made disarmingly clear to Sydenham, he very much regarded his own opinions, "superficial or well-

considered" to be "such as any common sense practical man, whose
connections and associations and feelings are involved in the
happiness and well being of the middle classes of society, might be
expected to entertain." [34] An early and strong commitment to
"Canadianism" was one of Ryerson's most remarkable traits, with
significance for both church and educational history. His preoccupation with adapting educational practices to the "civil and
social institutions, and society, and essential interests" of Upper
Canada counterpoints struggles within Methodism.[35] Hodgins
described the chief outlines of the school system to an American
audience in 1855 as "identical with those of other countries, but
in its adaptation to the wants of the country and the genius of the
people, it is essentially Canadian." [36] The undue emphasis since
placed on the identity of common features has somewhat obscured
the seriousness of Ryerson's intention. Certainly the search for
American models for the origins of aspects of Canadian education
has been encouraged by the widespread tendency of nineteenth-
century Canadian writers to build their case on quotations. Ryerson
was no exception; his annual reports as chief superintendent are
larded with excerpts from American and European educators and
detailed explanations of their practices. Horace Mann, secretary of
the Massachusetts Board of Education, 1837–48, was a favourite to
whom he acknowledged, "you will perceive from my Report how
largely I have availed myself of your observations on European
schools, and how fully I concur with you in opinions as to the
merits of the Government authorized methods of teaching." [37] As
he admits, in regard to teacher training as with so much of his
educational thinking, Ryerson shows a striking similarity to Mann.
The Journal of Education, tours of school conventions, and the
very rhetoric of his argument seem to reveal his debt. However,
much of the quotation at least was calculated effect. As Ryerson
confided to Draper, "in pointing out *defects* in systems of instruction
and modes of teaching I have almost invariably quoted *American*
authors—and have thus *incidentally* exposed the defects of almost
every part of the American system, and have *practically* shown that
every redeeming feature of the American School System has been,
or is being borrowed from European Governments. I have also
quoted the same authorities on almost every point most likely to
be objected to by radical writers or partisans." [38] The broad

similarity in tactic and argument derives from a similarity in roles: Ryerson, Mann, Henry Barnard of Connecticut—all were self-conscious educational promoters. They agreed on many features of a public school system because they shared much the same social philosophy and, as a consequence, a similar belief that for a school system to be effective as an instrument of social policy, a concept of public education must be woven into the fabric of a society.

To see in the common school system an instrument for forging a national identity was almost commonplace in the nineteenth century. Ryerson's "Canadianism" was a qualified one, however; he saw the school system rendering "this Country British in domestic feeling, as I think it now is intentionally at least in loyalty." [39] His role in defence of Metcalfe in 1844 accentuated his sense of mission. As he reminded Higginson from France in 1845, his "leading idea" was "not only to impart to the public mind the greatest amount of useful knowledge based upon, and inter-woven throughout, with sound Christian principle, but to render the Educational System, in its various ramifications and applications, the indirect, but powerful instrument of British Constitutional Government." [40] This enthusiasm, fed by the events of the inter-vening decades, had carried Ryerson far from his youthful suspicion of the dangers involved in a "system of education in theory a mere engine of the Executive." [41] Now he saw "much of importance in respect to Canada" in how Louis Philippe solved the problem "of governing a restless people upon ever popular principles and yet strengthening the Throne." His interest in the French system was absorbed by "the peculiar connection of the whole system with, and its influence upon, the thinkings and feelings of the public mind, and the other various parts of its Governmental machinery, com-bining to produce the general results, and the connection of these with other branches of public policy." [42] Ryerson's professed "lead-ing idea" explains the particular vigour with which he assailed American textbooks in the first months of his appointment. "Anti-British in every sense of the word," such books were "one element of powerful influence against the established Government of the Country." [43] Because he believed there to be a correlation, geograph-ically, between the heavy use of American textbooks and support for the 1837 rebellion, their sinister influence, "silent and imper-ceptible in its operations," was to be countered by the immediate and widespread adoption of Irish National textbooks.[44] American teachers were not as dangerous, although they had been proscribed by the alien clauses of the 1843 and 1846 Acts.[45] Sensing public opinion against repeal, Ryerson waited until 1848 to drop the restriction on alien teachers.[46]

Non-denominational Protestantism could provide a common faith on which to rest the shared loyalty basic to a national consciousness.[47] Certainly Ryerson's commitment to a belief in the non-sectarian character of Christianity in the common schools was both consistent and firm: "Christianity—the Christianity of the Bible—regardless of the peculiarities of Sects, or Parties is to be the basis of our System of Public Instruction, as it is of our Civil Constitution." [48] Ironically, Ryerson's innumerable public hassles with various political and religious critics complemented an attempt to isolate the school and the very subject of education from religious sectarianism and political debate. The key word was *harmony*. In the field, district wardens were to be alert to the possibility that controversy might "disturb the harmony, or weaken the energy of united action in the work of educational instruction." [49] Centrally, the Education Office would operate "in such a way as will contribute most to the harmony and wishes of the community." [50] Thus, not only would neighbours find common cause in local school affairs, but, hopefully, a shared recognition of the value of the school system as a whole would span the gulfs of nationality, religion, location, occupation—and class—which divided Upper Canadians.[51] Finally, the school experience itself would contribute by its "commonness"— that elusive ideal of universality to which educational promoters clung while never dreaming of sending their own children to the public school. Something of this lies behind Ryerson's growing disapproval of the separate school idea.[52] He sincerely believed that "all that is essential to the moral interests of youth may be taught in what are termed Mixed Schools." [53] As the issue of Roman Catholic schools blossomed from a protection for minority rights to a full-scale challenge to the public system, Ryerson feared the consequences of the social isolation of Irish Catholic urban poor who by and large comprised the separate school population. The inferiority of their schools could well perpetuate their position of social inferiority: "it is to be feared that many children set off and assigned to the separate school suffer serious disadvantages in com-

parison with other children residing in the same neighbourhoods;—
apart from the disadvantage of their isolation, the salutary influence
of the emulation and energy which arises from pursuing the same
studies in connection with the youths of other classes in the
community, and with whom they are to act and associate in future
life." [54] Similarly, with "the masses" generally. The main system
once established, Ryerson directed his campaigns against parental
apathy and neglect of children's schooling at points progressively
lower on the social scale. His comprehensive view of public education provided the mainspring: "not the mere acquisition of certain
arts or of certain branches of knowledge, but that instruction and
discipline which qualify and dispose the subjects of it for their
appropriate duties and employments of life, as Christians, as persons
for business and also as members of the civil community in which
they live." Such a view offered no contradiction to an implicit
acceptance of a hierarchically ordered society. Education, like the
Bible, should be universal property; but although he would extend
its reach, even by compulsion, to the lowest levels of society,
Ryerson very much regarded the organization of the school system
as adapting to "the wants of the several classes of the community
. . . their respective employments or professions." [55]

The common school system was clearly for the poorer classes who
"need the assistance of the Government, and . . . are the proper
subjects of their special solicitude and care"; the rich, with grammar
schools and more, "can take care of themselves." [56] It seemed not
to matter to men such as Ryerson that the story they repeated of
the sons of the manufacturer and the door keeper sitting side by
side was apocryphal, for neither they nor their friends sent their
boys to the common school.[57] The idea of harmony between social
classes, not of an end to social classes, provided the story's appeal.
Thus, with a mid-Victorian's strong sense of property, Ryerson
promoted public education to accomplish the tasks for which the
social conservative would instinctively use it: to prevent pauperism,
crime, vice, ignorance, and contribute to the increased productivity
of the labour force.[58] The fear and concern of the middle class for
the consequences of the transformation which the colony was
experiencing were to be answered by an educational system which
would neutralize its potential for social disruption. The heavy influx
of famine Irish in 1847 merely made the position of the common

school system unassailable. Estimating an addition, in one year, of destitute immigrants equal to nearly one-sixth of the total resident population, Ryerson could warn Upper Canadians that "the physical disease and death which have accompanied their influx among us may be the precursor of the worse pestilence of social insubordination and disorder." Congregations of ignorant, poverty-stricken immigrants in towns and cities animated the pictures of slums and pauperism which educational promoters had been painting; it appeared obvious that, without schools, Irish children would perpetuate racial behaviour patterns and grow up "in the idleness and pauperism, not say mendicity and vices of their forefathers." [59]

There seemed no doubt in 1846 that a province-wide common school system would have to be imposed on Upper Canada. Certainly Ryerson was resigned to spending much of the next two or three years promoting it in the districts, "in many cases again and again." [60] However, his basic conviction "that a system of public instruction should be in harmony with the views and feelings of the great body of the people, especially of the better educated classes," [61] elicited increasing response from the urban and rural middle classes. The debate on the proper financial support for the common school system is indicative of this growing support. That the debate had advanced significantly in the five years since the Union is clear when one contrasts the Hincks' Bill (7 Vict., c. XXIX, 1843) with that which Draper introduced three years later. The 1843 Act provided for the government grant to be at least matched, but not more than doubled, by district, city, and town councils authorizing an assessment on all ratable property; the balance of the teachers' salaries to be supplied by an additional rate bill imposed on all parents of school children by the local school trustees. The Act made optional provision for "free" schools in cities or towns only. Ryerson suggested the rate bill be abolished entirely. In the draft of the 1846 Common School bill presented to the Assembly, the obligations of district councils to levy an assessment to equal the government grant were similar to those of 1843. In addition, however, local school trustees had the duty of levying rates on the property of all inhabitants equal to the aggregate sum received from the legislative grant and the district levy, in the place of the rate bill against the parents.[62] In Ryerson's opinion these provisions were crucial. The rate bill was a form of discrimination; it meant

that poor parents withdrew their children from the school so as not
to be billed for its support. He felt the case was incontestable:
"Education is a public good; ignorance is a public evil. What affects
the public ought to be binding upon each individual composing it.
In every good government, and in every good system, the interests
of the whole society are obligatory upon each member of it." [63]
At the same time, however, he forecast the opposition of "the rich,
and the childless, and the selfish." Draper stoutly defended the
proposed section in committee on the principle that "all should
possess every facility of education, and that those who possess
property should assist and pay for the education of the children of
their poorer neighbours; and thus raise the lower classes in the scale
of moral and intellectual beings." [64] But despite the frankness of
his appeal, he "was well beaten"; the rate bill was reintroduced.[65]

Ryerson thought he saw the villain. Writing to urge Draper not
to give up the assessment clause, "above all others . . . the *poor
man's* clause, and at the very foundation of a system of public
education," Ryerson complained of objections

by precisely the class of persons—or rather by the individuals that I expected. I have heard one rich *man* objecting to it—a Methodist—a magistrate—a man who educates his own children at College and in Ladies'
Seminaries—but who looks not beyond his own family. He says, I am told,
"he does not wish to be compelled to educate *all the brats* in the neighbourhood." Now to educate "all the brats" in every neighbourhood is the very
object of this clause of the bill; and in order to do so, it is proposed to
compel selfish rich men to do what they ought to do, but what they will
not do voluntarily.[66]

By November he was more specific "Mr. Robert Baldwin and his
friends, and some Members on the opposite side of the House of
Assembly, united to oppose this clause of the Bill, and it was lost." [67]

In trying to assess the significance of Baldwin's opposition to the
extension of the very principle which he had supported since 1841,
one is involved in the question of the degree to which antipathy to
Ryerson personally influenced the educational debate. Political feeling ran high in the debate on the school bill. Price challenged
Draper as to whether Ryerson, rumoured to be attempting to
introduce the "Prussian system of education" into Canada, had
really drafted the bill.[68] Ryerson's salary and his close working
relationship with Draper provided Reform spokesmen with easy

targets.[69] But even Ryerson felt he "could not have imagined that so much party feeling would be brought to the consideration of such a subject." [70] Significantly, Baldwin justified his opposition to the free school idea on the grounds that "it was better to make the parents pay something for the benefit they receive, and then they would be more interested in the school." [71] The class implications of the "incentive" argument appealed particularly to those well established in prosperity who, convinced of their social responsibilities, nevertheless distrusted the intelligence and morality of their charges. Baldwin's personal reservations on this point may well have been such as to combine easily with the general Reform politicking over the bill. Behind the formal legislative opposition of such Reform leaders as Baldwin and J. H. Price, Ryerson perceived real resistance: "it is from the class of the community which they represent, or are identified with, that the only difficulties in carrying into effect an efficient system emanate." [72] The anticipated objections of the "independent yeomanry of the country" suggest part of this opposition. Many individuals desire to give their children a better education than can be obtained in common schools, who can ill afford it." [73] To those straining for a foot in the door of a grammar or private school, a common school tax added to such school fees would be "very oppressive." Here was Ryerson's mission field: some could be placated by a common school sufficiently improved by trained teachers and "systematization" to which they could send their own children free; "the more affluent," "the intelligent portion of the people," could be convinced of the wisdom of educating other people's children.[74]

The Reformers diligently stirred up opposition to Ryerson, the school system, and free schools when the 1847 school bill made free schooling compulsory in cities and towns. Obviously urban mechanics and artisans were thought to be sympathetic to arguments about the infringement by compulsory taxation of their parental right to pay for their own children's schooling. Editorials goaded the parents of common school youngsters with taunts of "pauper education" now that they no longer paid for themselves.[75] But the opposition was short lived. In 1849 Malcolm Cameron's attempt to reverse the trend of systematization succeeded with a curiously garbled common school bill which actually received royal assent. However, at Ryerson's urging, Baldwin suspended the offending legislation before it could take effect, thus clearing the way for the major school legislation of 1850. As a gesture to the opposition of various district councils and the city of Toronto especially, where the schools were closed for the year 1848–9, Ryerson compromised on the parental rate bill. But while free schools remained optional until 1871, the cities and towns quickly capitulated, led by Toronto in 1851. Suspicion lingered, apparently, among the mechanics of Yorkville in 1852; but by then the Rev. John Roaf, whose extreme voluntaryism would keep resistance alive, was a minor voice.[76] Most of the Reformers—especially the Toronto leaders—had become free school supporters and educational promoters in their own right.[77]

There is no doubt that Ryerson was committed to the end of the rate bill for humanitarian as well as strategic reasons; he was conscious of the desire for schooling as well as of the need. However, his public arguments suggest something less than his full interest in the principle. He saw abolishing the rate bill as a step toward the goal of greater systematization. A trustee's rate bill, or assessment, upon all the inhabitants of a school section would be "a second edition of the school tax imposed by the District Council." "After a year or two," the whole school tax would be consolidated into a "District Fund to pay teach [sic] quarterly, the same as all public officers. You can then have a District Board—a gradation of teachers salaries—independence of teachers of local trustees, their appointment by and accountability to a more efficient tribunal—the whole receiving a common direction and a common stamp from the Government." [78] The draft bill which Draper introduced was designed to ensure the "common stamp" much as the McCaul Commission had envisaged. Ryerson was critical of the 1843 Act, and the fragmenting of authority among local superintendents so jealously urged by Reformers, on the grounds it contravened the principle of responsible government: one responsibility, one authority.[79] His design balanced local and central control. District superintendents had considerable power to raise money and manage local operations; but the superintendent, advised by an appointed Board of Education, controlled the distribution of government grants, authorized textbooks, established the much sought-after normal school for training teachers, and devised regulations on general matters of school policy. The appointment of district superintendents by the Crown would ensure the vital link in communication. On this, however, Ryerson was defeated, and the existing provisions for appointment by distinct municipal councils remained in effect. That Ryerson did "not attach much importance to the clause," is indicative of the extent to which he had sufficient forces on his side.[80] Pressures for centralization came from within the common school system: already the cities were moving to consolidate; to grade the schools, and within the schools the classes.[81] Such hurrying toward the future aroused considerable opposition, among Reform sympathizers especially. Their instincts for localism and voluntaryism were offended by visions of "Prussian despotism." [82] Readers of the *Mirror* were warned to beware "the destructive snare of the Prussian saddlebag centralizer" and his "educational police system" whose local school inspectors were "detectives." [83] The Gore District Council memorialized the Legislature in November 1847 to have the School Act repealed as being without a redeeming feature: the system was unwieldy, the normal school unnecessary, the paying of superintendents extravagant. A realistic assessment of Upper Canadian society indicated that the schools must remain very much the way they are, for teachers were either immigrants on their way to better things, or "those whose Physical Disabilities from age, render this mode of obtaining a livelihood the one suited to their Decaying Energies." [84]

But visions of the future were at the centre of the appeal which the common school system had for its supporters. Ryerson and the other "common sense practical" men concerned with the "well being of the middle classes of society" did not focus on the present for it was changing too quickly. The last twenty years had transformed Upper Canadian society and the experience of this, combined with a Victorian's belief in progress, fostered impatience for tomorrow. No one could stand still. "How is the uneducated and unskillful man to succeed in these times of sharp and skilful competition and sleepless activity? And these times are but the commencement of a spirit of competition and enterprise in the country. The rising generation should, therefore, be educated not for Canada as it has been, or even now is, but for Canada as it is likely to be half a generation hence." [85] The United States tantalized with an image of what was to come: the people, the railways, the factories, and cities both exhilarated and appalled. If "the youth of the rural districts . . . are much behind the age," with education the rising generation might "be prepared, at least, to make some near approach to that place in the social scale, which their more intelligent, because better educated, neighbours, now threaten to monopolize." [86] Public apathy was the obstacle, "the deadliest enemy to improvement." But in responding to the educational needs of a growing community, a provincial system of common schools had time on its side. The attractions of localism and voluntaryism proved fragile barriers against the inroads of efficiency. Those who, with Ryerson, saw the common school as a force for social cohesion, a unifying tendency with which to counter the pluralism implicit in the increasing complexity of Upper Canadian society, swelled the ranks of educational promoters.

An educational system is not like a school, a bank, or an industry, any one of which might be described in terms of one man's "achievement." Thus an overemphasis on Egerton Ryerson's long career as chief superintendent has distorted the extent to which the educational debate encompassed fundamental issues of social organization. Social, economic, and demographic circumstances had contrived by the 1840s to involve the aspirations of many Upper Canadians with the issue of public education. Thus the establishment of a common school system in 1846 bears witness to the pervasive influence of attitudes susceptible to the promises of an educational solution to social problems. From then on, the development and internal elaboration of the public school system would provide the middle class with their main strategy for meeting the problems of their changing society.

NOTES

1. See J. S. Moir, *Church and State in Canada West* (Toronto 1959).
2. Ellwood P. Cubberly, *Public Education in the United States* (Boston, rev. ed. 1934), and Charles E. Phillips, *The Development of Education in Canada* (Toronto 1957), provide classic statements of the progressive view. For an overview of recent European work in this field, see Gillian Sutherland, "The Study of the History of Education," *History,* 54 (1969): 49–59.
3. See Leroy O. Stone, *Urban Development in Canada* (Ottawa 1967) and Jacob Spelt, *The Urban Development in South-central Ontario* (Assen 1955).

4. J. M. S. Careless, "Mid-Victorian Liberalism in Central Canadian Newspapers, 1850–67," *Canadian Historical Review*, 31, 3 (Sept. 1950): 221–36.

5. F. H. Armstrong, "Toronto in Transition, 1828–1838" (unpublished PH.D. thesis, University of Toronto, 1965); J. M. S. Careless, "Frontierism, Metropolitanism, and Canadian History," *Canadian Historical Review*, 35, 1 (March 1954): 1–21.

6. R. H. Bonnycastle, *Canada and the Canadians* (2 vols., London 1849), I, 195.

7. Mr. Speaker Bidwell in debate on the school bill, 30 March 1835, *Christian Guardian*, 8 April 1835.

8. Bonnycastle, *Canada and the Canadians*, p. 196.

9. J. S. Hogan, *Canada: An Essay* (Montreal 1855), p. 27. Commenting on rural Upper Canadian fashions, Hogan observed that "the coats of the men are indistinguishable from those worn by professional men and merchants in town."

10. See M. B. Katz, *The Hamilton Project: Interim Reports* I & II (Toronto 1969, 1970); also, Peter Goheen, *Victorian Toronto, 1850–1900* (Chicago 1970).

11. Support for common or elementary schooling, of course, carries no implications for support of educational facilities at other levels; see Lawrence Stone, "Literacy and Education in England, 1640–1900," *Past and Present*, 41 (Feb. 1969): 69–139.

12. J. George Hodgins, *Documentary History of Education in Upper Canada* [DHE] (2 vols., Toronto 1897), II, 15. Strachan was also president of the Council, and much of the membership was overlapping.

13. *Christian Guardian*, 15 Jan. 1834.

14. Ibid., 7 Dec. 1831.

15. Ibid., 15 Jan. 1834.

16. DHE, II, 198–9.

17. G. M. Craig, *Upper Canada, the Formative Years, 1784–1841* (Toronto 1963), pp. 198–9; Judson Purdy, "John Strachan and Education in Canada, 1800–1851" (unpublished PH.D. thesis, University of Toronto, 1962), pp. 108, 130–1. In a letter to Draper, 22 April 1846, Ryerson suggested that although Reform educational policy was deliberately modelled on American practices, the inevitable time lag rendered it always slightly passé. J. George Hodgins, ed., *Ryerson Memorial Volume* (Toronto 1889), pp. 77–8.

18. *Journals of the House of Assembly of Upper Canada*, 1836, App. 35, p 64.

19. M. B. Katz, *The Irony of Early School Reform* (Cambridge, Mass. 1968).

20. *Journals of the House of Assembly of Upper Canada*, 1836, App. 30, p. 71.

21. Ibid., App. 71, p. 4.

22. Ibid., App. 35, pp. 57-60.

23. Ibid., p. 11.
24. DHE, II, 339.
25. Ryerson to Draper, 14 May 1846, Hodgins Papers, Public Archives of Ontario (PAO) provides insight into the problems Ryerson perceived in securing membership on the Board of Education which reflected the various religious denominations and at the same time preserved the necessary aura of social respectability.
26. *Report of the Committee on Education: Appendix B to the Fifth Report of the General Board (3 Vic. 1840). Also in* DHE, III, 243–83.
27. Strachan's reply to the Commission's circular of inquiry, 12 Dec. 1839, DHE, III, 267.
28. Murray to P. Thornton, 28 March 1843. Education Office, Canada West: Letter Book A, pp. 239–40, PAO.
29. Francis Hincks, *Reminiscences of His Public Life,* pp. 175–7, quoted in DHE, IV, 242.
30. Apparently Baldwin's commitment to the taxation principle was strong as early as 1841; see Egerton Ryerson, *Introductory Sketch of the System of Public Elementary Instruction in Upper Canada* (Toronto 1851), pp. 4–5.
31. Report of the educational proceedings of the Legislature, 1843, DHE, IV, 240.
32. Murray to Alex McMillan, 12 April 1843. Education Office, Canada West: Letter Book A, pp. 251–2.
33. Historians at least are virtually unanimous in their assessment of Ryerson as a "conservative"; see Goldwin French, *Parsons and Politics* (Toronto 1962), p. 103; Clara Thomas, *Ryerson of Upper Canada* (Toronto 1969), p. 52; C. B. Sissons, *Egerton Ryerson: His Life and Letters* (2 vols., Toronto 1937), I, 3.
34. Ryerson to Sydenham, 5 Oct. 1840, cited in Sissons, Ryerson, I, 562.
35. "Observations made by the Rev. Egerton Ryerson at the commencement of the session, 1841, Victoria College," *Christian Guardian,* 3 Nov. 1841. Both Goldwin French, *Parsons and Politics,* and G. W. Brown, *Canada in the Making* (Toronto 1953) document the Canadian theme in the history of Methodism in Upper Canada in the first half of the nineteenth century.
36. J. G. Hodgins, "History and Systems of Education in Upper Canada, 1855," a paper read before the American Association for the Advancement of Education, New York, 1855.
37. Ryerson to Horace Mann, 23 Dec. 1846, DHE, VI, 213.
38. Ryerson to W. H. Draper, 30 March 1846, Hodgins Papers.
39. Ryerson to Higginson, 8 March 1845, DHE, V, 108.
40. Ryerson to Higginson, 30 April 1845, DHE, V, 240.
41. *Christian Guardian,* 15 Jan. 1834.
42. Ryerson to Higginson, 30 April 1845, DHE, V, 239.
43. Egerton Ryerson, *Special Report on the Measures which have been Adopted for the Establishment of a Normal School and for Carrying*

into Effect Generally the Common School Act (Montreal 1847), pp. 14–15.

44. "Special report on the operation of the Common School Act of 1846," DHE, VII, 110–11.

45. The elimination of alien teachers prescribed by the 1843 Act was to take effect 1 Jan. 1846. In the debate on the 1846 bill, Baldwin and Price tried to secure an extension of the right of aliens to teach until such time as the normal school was functioning. They lost.

46. Chief Superintendent to Hon. James Leslie, 14 Oct. 1848, *Copies of Correspondence Between Members of the Government and the Chief Superintendent of Schools on the Subject of the School Law for Upper Canada and Education Generally* (Toronto 1850).

47. *Annual Report of the Normal, Model, Grammar and Common School for 1851,* pp. 19–21; see also, Timothy Smith, "Protestant Schooling and American Nationality, 1800–1850," *Journal of American History,* 53 (1967): 679–95.

48. Ryerson to Hon. D. Daly, 3 March 1846, *Copies of Correspondence;* also DHE, VI, 72.

49. "Circular no. 3, Wardens of the District Municipal Councils, Oct. 1, 1846."

50. Ryerson to Rev. A. MacNab, 26 Oct. 1844, Sissons, *Ryerson,* II, 77.

51. Harmony provided Ryerson with an enduring cause; for example, "The tendencies of the age and all the institutions and enterprises of our country, are to co-operation and union among all classes of citizens, rather than to isolation and estrangement from each other," *Dr. Ryerson's Letters in Reply to the Attacks of the Hon. George Brown* (Toronto 1859), p. 22.

52. Ryerson publicly regretted separate schools "on this account and almost on this account alone": the isolation of Catholic children "from intellectual competitions and friendships with the other children of the land," *Annual Report,* 1857, p. 24.

53. "Report on a System of Public Elementary Instruction for Upper Canada, 1846," DHE, VI, 158.

54. *Annual Report,* 1855, p. 13.

55. "Report on a System of Public Elementary Instruction," DHE, VI, 142.

56. Ibid., 146. At a public meeting, 10 Jan. 1852, the chairman of the Toronto Board of Trustees testified that his inspection of the common schools had revealed that the majority of the students were "those called poor classes . . . the respectable mechanics, small traders, the honest labourers of the city," Toronto Public School Board, *Report of the Past History and Present Condition of the Common or Public Schools of the City of Toronto* (Toronto 1859), p. 35.

57. Ryerson's speech, 10 Jan. 1852, ibid., p. 36. In a letter to his daughter Sophie, 2–5 Jan. 1862, Ryerson asks for help in persuading Charley to go to an English public school, in the footsteps of Judge Hagarty's boy; Sophie is to point out to her brother "how pleasant and useful

it would be to him all his life." "Letters to Sophie," United Church Archives.

58. "Report on a System of Public Elementary Instruction," DHE, VI, 143–5.
59. Egerton Ryerson, "The Importance of Education to a Manufacturing and a Free People" (a speech given on tour, fall 1847), *Journal of Education of Upper Canada,* Oct. 1848, p. 300.
60. Ryerson to the Rev. A. MacNab, 31 March 1845, Sissons, *Ryerson,* II, 87–8.
61. *Annual Report,* 1851, p. 21.
62. "Draft of a Bill for the Better Establishment and Maintenance of Common Schools in Upper Canada (now slightly changed), 9 Vic., c. xx. Education Office West, March 1846," Hodgins Papers, p. 25, sect. xxvi, sub-sects. 5 & 6.
63. Ryerson to Hon. D. Daly, 3 March 1846, *Copies of Correspondence,* p. 23.
64. House of Assembly, 16 April 1846, *Mirror of Parliament of the Province of Canada March 20–June 9, 1846* (Montreal 1846), p. 73.
65. Draper to Ryerson 22 April 1846, Hodgins Papers. There is some disagreement as to how badly Draper was beaten as the vote has not been recorded. Ryerson used the phrase "by a small majority" which Hodgins interpreted as "a majority of four or five," "Remarks and Suggestions on the Common School Act, 7 Vic., c. xxix, Accompanying a Draft of a Bill (now), 9 Vic. c. xx, Education Office (West), March 3, 1846," Hodgins Papers.
66. Ryerson to Draper, 20 April 1846, Sissons, *Ryerson,* II, 101.
67. Ryerson to James Wallace, 9 Nov. 1846, DHE, VI, 291.
68. *Mirror of Parliament,* p. 69. Oddly, Draper insisted that it was his bill, despite Ryerson having submitted a draft, 3 March 1846. That the measure was given first reading as an *amending* bill suggests that Ryerson might not have had such a *carte blanche* with educational legislation as commentators have assumed.
69. George Metcalfe, "Draper Conservatism and Responsible Government in the Canadas, 1836–1847," *Canadian Historical Review,* 42, 4 (Dec. 1961): 300–24.
70. Ryerson to Draper, 30 April 1846, Hodgins Papers.
71. *Mirror of Parliament,* p. 73.
72. Ryerson to Draper, 14 May 1846, Hodgins Papers.
73. *Mirror of Parliament,* p. 73.
74. See Hammett Pinney, warden of the Dalhousie District, to Ryerson, 7 Feb. 1847, DHE, VII, 128–9.
75. *Dundas Warder,* 12 May 1846. Robert Spence, editor, attacked Ryerson throughout 1847–8. Also *Examiner,* 10 May 1848.
76. *Globe,* 31 Jan., 5, 17 Feb. 1852.
77. For a discussion of the reversal of Reform policy on free schools in Toronto, see Peter N. Ross, "Free Schools in Toronto, 1848–52" (unpublished MS, OISE, 1968).

78. Ryerson to Draper, 30 March 1846, Hodgins Papers.
79. Ryerson to Daly, 3 March 1846, DHE, VI, 72.
80. Ryerson to Draper, 30 April 1846, Hodgins Papers.
81. Chief Superintendent to Hon. D. Daly, 27 March 1847, *Copies of Correspondence,* pp. 25–9. Also *Annual Report,* 1850, sect. 15.
82. For a report of *Banner and British Colonist* charges, see DHE, VI, 214–15; also *Globe,* 6 Jan. 1847 and *Examiner,* 29 April, 22 July, 12 Nov., and 9 Dec. 1846.
83. *Mirror,* 12 May 1848.
84. Memorial of the Gore District Council, 10 Nov. 1847, DHE, VII, 114–16.
85. Ryerson, "The Importance of Education," p. 300.
86. Report of the Colborne District on the Gore Memorial, DHE, VII, 116–18.

PETER N. ROSS

3. THE FREE SCHOOL CONTROVERSY IN TORONTO, 1848-1852

In 1871 the Ontario Legislature passed an education act that required school boards to provide schooling through local taxation. Its first attempt in 1847 at such legislation, aimed at cities and towns only, had failed to win public support, and almost resulted in the dismissal of Egerton Ryerson, Superintendent of Schools. The political crisis was generated primarily in Toronto. In 1848 the City Council, after a five-month long public controversy, refused to levy sufficient taxes for the schools, thus forcing the Common School Board to close the schools for a year. In 1851, when the Board declared the schools free, the resulting controversy was relatively uneventful. An examination of this period in a total context reveals how vulnerable the schools are when caught in the cross-currents of powerful social and political issues for which schools and education are of peripheral concern.

DURING THE MID-NINETEENTH CENTURY the interplay of social problems that derived from the contemporary Irish immigration and older religious and political animosities sharply divided the people of Canada West. The notoriety of the Irish for poverty, ignorance and delinquency magnified racial and class divisions. Moreover, the growth of both Roman Catholic and Orange factions reinforced bitter religious differences. Added to this imported religious problem was the continuing struggle to lessen Anglican ascendancy by asserting voluntaryism. Another substantive issue centred on the

P. N. Ross is a member of the faculty of Lakeshore Teachers College, York University, Toronto.

reshaping of municipal government to assure greater local autonomy. The election of the Reform Party in 1848 focussed attention
on many long-standing inequities in the province: a catalyst, this
victory heightened the expectations of Reform supporters for far-
reaching change. Toronto, large and expanding, was exposed more
than most communities to the cross-currents of controversy. The
implications of the foregoing issues for the provision and organization of education became apparent when the Toronto Common
School Board attempted to introduce free schools. In 1848 a
sustained campaign against tax-supported schools resulted in the
closing of the common schools for a full year, until July 1849; yet,
two years later, when many measures enacted by the Reform
Government had taken effect, the schools were declared free without
arousing widespread opposition. An examination of this controversy
reveals the extent to which social and political influences affected
school organization in mid-century Canada West.

Although several writers have touched on this struggle in their
examination of education in Toronto or Ontario, none has paused
to consider two intriguing and related questions. Why was it possible
to close the schools for a full year over the issues of free schools?
Why was it possible, only two years later, to establish a system of
tax-supported schools? At the time, Egerton Ryerson, Chief Superintendent of Schools for Canada West, blamed "wealthy selfishness
and hatred of the education of the poor and labouring classes" for
the closing of the schools. (1) Later educational writers (2) have
accepted Ryerson's explanation without examining the decision in
the context of 1848; consequently, the impression has been created
that a group of wealthy Torontonians mounted a concerted campaign against free schools. Toronto has thus been stigmatized as
a "stronghold against free schools." (3) A closer examination of
the event indicates that other, more significant influences intervened
to check the introduction of tax-supported schools. In January 1852,
after the Toronto Common School Board had decided to support
the schools through property assessment, a protest meeting was held
in the St. Lawrence Hall. Some later writers, again relying on
interpretations from the past, have viewed this meeting as an
example of the heated attacks directed at promoters of free
schools. (4) In actual fact, the meeting was an unexciting, one-sided
debacle for the opponents of the Board.

The origin of this controversy was the passing in 1847 of an act concerning the administration of common schools in cities and towns of Canada West. (5) The act introduced three changes: consolidation of all school sections within an urban municipality under a single board of trustees, appointment of school trustees by the municipal council, and financial support of schools by a combination of legislative grants and municipal taxes. The act affected very few communities, but some it affected profoundly, and none more than Toronto. Prior to the act Toronto was divided into fifteen school sections, each managed by an elected board of three trustees. Approximately one-half of the budget for schools was raised by fees. The implementation of the act had a visible effect. It dissolved the neighbourhood boards and replaced them with a single six-trustee board appointed by the Toronto City Council. Moreover, it removed the board's prerogative of raising funds by fees.

In November the recently appointed Toronto Common School Board studied a detailed memorandum drafted by the Superintendent, G. A. Barber. (6) Underscoring the extensive powers of the Board to co-ordinate the system of common schools, he recommended a number of improvements possible under the new organization. The Board could close the single rooms that served as schools in the different sections of the city and replace them with permanent school buildings each containing three classrooms. Such buildings would permit the teachers to group the youngsters into three divisions. Barber predicted that Toronto would eventually need eight schools of this type. In the memorandum he also dealt with the overall cost of schooling in the city. In 1846 the fifteen boards had spent £1750. of which provincial grants and municipal taxes had provided £950. and fees from parents £800. For 1848 Barber proposed a budget of £2000; however, he assumed that one-half of the money would be collected in fees. He plainly misconstrued the intention of the act in regard to financing schools.

The trustees, who shared Barber's confusion on this question, had accepted the ideas put forth in his memorandum. (7) In January Ryerson distributed a circular on the provisions of the act that referred to property assessment as the single means of raising local funds. (8) Charging that the act was unclear on this point, the Board asked for an interpretation from J. H. Cameron, Solicitor-

General in the Tory administration responsible for the act. (9) He
stated that the Board should transmit its estimates to the City
Council, which would have to levy a sufficient amount through
taxes. (10) On February 28, 1848, the Board met with two standing
committees of Council, Education and Finance. At this meeting the
legality of supporting schools entirely from public funds dominated.
Dissatisfied with Cameron's answer, the Board appealed to Robert
Baldwin, Attorney-General in the newly-formed Reform ministry,
to whom they explained that the Education Committee of the
Council could not accept the proposed system of financing. (11)
He concurred with Cameron's interpretation. (12) In its first report
to Council the Education Committee rejected the opinions of the
two legislators and emphasized the prerogatives of an elected city
council. (13) The Assembly could not require a council to levy an
estimate prepared by a subordinate, and appointed, board. In the
course of the controversy no one challenged this statement.

In its first report the Committee also included the Board's request
for £2009. 17s. 7d., which would have required a rate of 4½d. on
the assessed pound. In the previous year the City had raised its
share of the education budget by levying taxes of 1d. on the
assessed pound. The Committee recommended that the Council
refuse to accept this estimate for 1848 and, on May 15, this body
did reject the estimate by a vote of 13 to 2. (14) One month later,
on June 14, the Committee, without the benefit of a statement
from the Board, suggested that the Council levy a tax of 1¼d. on
the assessed pound. (15) This scheme would have permitted the
Board to pay expenses incurred during the first six months of the
year; however, for the remainder of 1848 the schools would have
to be closed. The Council deferred a decision on the proposal to
permit time for a reaction by the trustees.

Finally, on Saturday, June 24, two days before the next regular
council meeting and only six days in advance of the deadline for
closing the schools, the Board turned in a greatly reduced estimate,
which required a tax of 1¾d. on the assessed pound. (16) On June
26, the Committee tabled its final report recommending a levy of
1½d. on the assessed pound "to meet the expenses for Common
School purposes for the whole of the current year." (17) This was
merely a gesture since the Committee had earlier acknowledged
the need for a rate of 1¼d. on the assessed pound for the first half

year. The schools could not have operated during the second half
year on an additional £112. After prolonged discussion the Council
voted nine to eight to levy 1¼d. on the assessed pound; therefore
on July 1 the common schools were closed. (18)

The majority of the six councillors who were absent from the
meeting on June 26 must have supported the decision; for, despite
the closeness of the vote, the Council did not revoke its stand, when
the members reconsidered the question in July. (19) At this meeting
an unidentified alderman remarked that he refused to consider free
common schools for the immigrant Irish children. Undoubtedly,
there were reasons, other than financial, for resistance to tax-supported schools. On July 1, 1849, when the Board received the
annual grant from the Legislature and a matching grant from the
Council, the schools were re-opened.

During the common school controversy the newspapers, which
reported the Council meetings in some detail, roundly condemned
one side or the other in articles and editorials. Favouring free
schools were the Methodist and pro-Ryerson *Christian Guardian*
and the Conservative *British Colonist,* owned by Hugh Scobie, a
member of the province's General Board of Education. Arrayed
against free schools were the *Church,* the official organ of the Anglican Church and the three Reform newspapers: George Brown's
Globe, James Lesslie's *Examiner,* and Charles Donlevy's Catholic
Mirror. Although the school question produced a heated controversy, the press consistently disregarded the Board.

The trustees, early placed in a disadvantageous position, were a
hidden factor in the development of the issue. Their request for a
budget of £2000. precipitated the crisis; yet no member of the
Board championed the necessity for free schools. Nor did any trustee
respond to stinging remarks, such as that of Donlevy:

If they are not actuated by the most hostile feelings to the true interests
of education, they must be six of the most profound blockheads in
Toronto: for to tell the inhabitants of this city that they must be taxed
four pence in the pound, for school purposes, is just equivalent to declaring that there shall be no schools at all. (20)

The Board, which comprised F. W. Barron, Principal of Upper
Canada College, John Elmsley, John McMurrich, Mayor George
Gurnett, J. Cameron, and William Cawthra, "was apparently under

strong Conservative control;" (21) consequently Donlevy's remarks may have been regarded as partisan sniping. The trustees had discussed the possibility of having free schools the previous November, but they deferred to the Council's judgment when the budget became a political issue. In one communication to this body they observed:

Your Committee do not feel prepared to subscribe wholly to the views of the Chief Superintendent upon so important a matter unless the opinion of Council thereon should corroborate his position. (22)

They accepted that Council exercised the final political and financial powers; thus, having made a sincere effort to comply with the new act, they let the initiative pass to the Council. Out of six board meetings called between March 28 and May 23, five were cancelled because a quorum was lacking. (23) Whatever the original motives that caused the trustees to support free schools, in the midst of the controversy it was apathy, not hostility nor stupidity, that must have characterized their feelings.

In May Ryerson censured the Council for its refusal to raise the Board's estimates (24) although this body was never unanimous in its attitude to the idea of free schools. An analysis of the councillors in terms of political persuasion, wealth and occupation is helpful in understanding their position.

In response to the first report of the Standing Committee, only two councillors—George Duggan and G. P. Ridout—supported by Mayor G. Gurnett, favoured a levy of 4½d. on the assessed pound. All three were Tories whose occupations were barrister, hardware merchant, and justice of the peace. Members of prestigious occupations, they also included two of the five richest men on Council, according to property assessment. (25)

Table 1 shows that, in the division of June 26, the supporters of keeping the schools open tended to belong to more prestigious occupations and to possess more wealth than their opponents. In terms of assessed property, the former possessed considerably more than the latter; consequently, despite Ryerson's accusation, one might argue that at least some of the wealthy community leaders concurred with him in his view of free schooling as a force for social harmony, especially in a period of mass immigration from Ireland. (26)

TABLE 1

Analysis of Members of City Council:
Voting to Close Schools, June 26, 1848

Data on Councillors	Opposed to Free Schools	Favoured Free Schools
Trustees in One of the Toronto School Sections in 1847 [a]	3	1
Occupations [a] and the *Average* Assessed Value of Property [b]		
Professional	1	5
	£59.10s.	£201.3s.
Merchant	2	2
	£197.10s.	£316.15s.
Innkeeper	1	
	£140.	
Manufacturer	2	1
	£206.10s.	£90.
Artisan	3	
	£79.10s.	
Total Value of Property	£1246.	£1729.5s.
Average Value of Property [c]	£138.9s.	£216.3s.
Political Persuasion [d]		
Orangeman	4	
Tory	2	3
Reformer	3	
Unknown		5

[a] George Brown, *Director of the City of Toronto and the County of York, 1847.*
[b] City of Toronto, Assessment Rolls, 1847.
[c] The average assessed value for all property in the city was £18.8s.
[d] *Examiner*, July 5, 1848.

It is impossible to determine with any certainty the political allegiance of each councillor, and in the case of the school supporters no one raised the question. In the *British Colonist,* (27) however, Scobie accused Reform councillors of conspiring to close the schools, a charge that was repeated in the *Christian Guardian.* (28) Angered by this accusation, Lesslie of the *Examiner,* in order to demonstrate that others also objected to financing the schools wholly by public funds, identified the political persuasion of the opponents as follows: four Orangemen, two Tories, and three Reformers. (29) Both Tories had served as elected trustees in 1847, a fact that possibly accounted for their attitude. The unlikely alliance

of Reformers and Orangemen deserves closer attention as part of
the larger context of potent socio-economic and political forces that
affected educational decisions.

Public discussions of the issue settled mainly on the impropriety
of imposing heavy taxes on Toronto property, and with good reason.
On the one hand, a large proportion of the people did not regard
universal education highly. On the other, reference to the financial
burden was a shrewd argument designed to arouse opposition in
a city undergoing a severe depression—a depression that lingered
from 1847 to 1849. At a time when the Board's estimate was common knowledge the *Christian Guardian* published a gloomy article
on the effects of the financial difficulty in Toronto:

The state of affairs throughout the Province in monetary or commercial
matters, is truly disheartening. Business is now in a state of stagnation;
money it is almost impossible to collect; and failure after failure of many
parties, whose solvency none seriously doubted, has rendered merchants
unwilling to dispose of their goods except for immediate payment. (30)

Evidently, 1848 was an inopportune time to attempt a costly innovation.

In the 1840's Toronto attracted large numbers of Irish immigrants. Regarded as a vicious element in a city that was predominantly Anglo-Saxon and militantly protestant, they appeared to be
evenly divided between Orangemen and Roman Catholics. (31)
The newspapers displayed an open resentment of the newcomers
on several grounds: their large numbers, their poverty, the cholera
epidemic. (32) In addition, the Irish were stereotyped as criminals.
Colourful reports of the discontent and rebellion smouldering in
Ireland reflected Tory Canadian disgust. In Toronto, although they
constituted only one-third of the population, the Irish committed
two-thirds of the crimes. (33) Of course, the Orangemen viewed
catholicism as the crux of the Irish problem. At the roots of Canadian attitudes to the Irish lay a complex of conscious and subcon-
scious fears.

It is understandable that city councillors would be affected by
these fears. The anti-Irish feeling displayed by an alderman in July,
when the Council reconsidered its decision reinforces Lesslie's claim
that the Orangemen were implicated in the refusal to support free
schools. The *Christian Guardian* reported:

He [an alderman] maintained that in consequence of the unprecedented emigration of last year, nearly one thousand pauper children from Ireland were introduced into the City; and then with a heartlessness truly astonishing, repudiated the idea of the ratepayers of the city required to afford the advantages of education to these helpless orphaned ones. (34)

The alderman's sentiments appear to have been fairly representative of feeling in Toronto.

The viewpoint of many in the Anglican Church, which most Orangemen would support, complicated the religious aspect of the free school principle. Many Anglicans, still preferring a sectarian school system, rejected Ryerson's concept of a generally acceptable Christianity for the common schools. One writer to the *Church* addressed Ryerson and his supporters on the merits of sectarian schools:

We shall bestow a greater boon upon the community by establishing a good system of church education than by helping you in a system of no-church education. (35)

The *Church* concurred with the *Globe* in its stand against quadrupled taxes for schools, arguing that many citizens were already paying dearly for education in private schools. (36) Although the Anglicans would finally lose the struggle for sectarian education, they did, in the meantime, assist others in the obstruction of common schools.

The most important element of resistance, however, was that instigated by the Reformers. The local Reform newspapers pilloried the notion of free schools and its principal advocate—Egerton Ryerson. Only three of the opposing councillors were Reformers, but, in view of the intemperate attacks in the Reform press, it is clear why Scobie attributed the Council's actions to the members of this Party. (37)

Since the Act of 1847 was identified as a Tory measure despite Ryerson's assertion that it was passed unanimously, (38) party rivalry played a large part in the schools question. The Reformers claimed that the imposition of taxation for the support of education in cities and towns was despotic legislation. Lesslie accused Ryerson of wanting "property to pay indiscriminately for the support of education" and of abrogating the "chartered privileges" of the City. (39) Underlying the accusations was the belief in local autonomy and, therefore, in the right of a municipality to select its own method of raising money for education. Similarly, the creation of appointed boards conflicted with Reform convictions about elective institutions. Lesslie, a local trustee himself in 1847, wondered, "When did the Solicitor-General discover the incompetency of the people to elect school trustees?" (40) Brown, sensitive to a conspiracy, feared Anglican control of the schools since, in his view of Toronto, a "High Church Tory corporation" appointed the board and since the law permitted boards to decide upon the provision of sectarian education. (41) Control of education, even if indirectly, by a central authority was anathema to the Reformers. On this theme Donlevy warned his readers to beware "the destructive snare of the Prussian saddle-bag centralizer" and his "educational police system." (42)

The controversy provided an outlet for the settlement of old political scores, especially against the Superintendent of Education. (43) Although Reformers objected on principle to any measure that removed control from the local community, embarrassing Ryerson delighted them since, as they saw it, his involvement in the Metcalfe affair * had gained him the superintendency. When the Reform Party won the election of 1848 Lesslie, joined later by Brown and Donlevy, immediately pressed for Ryerson's dismissal. (44) Baldwin refused to comply with this demand. The Reform newspapers then proceeded to attach the Superintendent's name to the question of free schools in Toronto. Their reports of Council meetings served as a thinly disguised means of impugning Ryerson's policies and character. (45) The worst slight was attributing the closing of the schools directly to Ryerson. (46)

---

* In 1843 Sir Charles Metcalfe arrived in Canada to replace Sir Charles Bagot as Governor-General. He was instructed to check the practice of responsible government that had been developing under his predecessor; consequently, he did not consult the Reform administration led by Baldwin and Lafontaine about appointments. Forming a Tory administration, he went to the electorate in 1844 and sought a Tory majority in the Legislative Assembly. Ryerson, at this time an influential Methodist clergyman and Principal of Victoria College, involved himself in the controversial election writing nine public letters in support of Metcalfe and the Tories. When the Tories won the election and Metcalfe appointed Ryerson Superintendent of Education, the Reform press denounced him. At different times, his independence in politics had led him to espouse William Lyon Mackenzie, Governor Bond Head, Robert Baldwin, and Governor Metcalfe: he had vacillated between Reformer and Tory.

The decision on free schools was considered, and concluded, at a time when the commingling of a variety of factors worked in favour of resistance to the innovation. The two significant elements— Orange bigotry and Reform partisanship—for example, produced an alliance which was only possible in the climate exacerbated by the novelty of the Act, the increased municipal cost of operating common schools, the social problems related to the influx of the Irish, and the depression. "Wealthy selfishness" appears to be an irrelevant factor.

By 1851 the situation had changed considerably. Laws passed in 1848 and 1849 in the Assembly were designed to control immigration and thus to prevent the squalid conditions resulting from an uncontrolled influx of immigrants. The depression had cleared and Canada, which had strengthened its commercial ties with the United States, was clearly undergoing an economic recovery. In the newspapers Toronto was being discussed as a future railway centre. At the same time the Reform Party had implemented much of its program, although it now faced dissension as a radical wing demanded more extensive reforms. (47)

Even the situation as far as Ryerson was concerned had changed by 1851. Throughout 1848–49 the Toronto Reformers anticipated his removal from office. (48) The bitterest attacks had no apparent effect on Baldwin, although Lord Elgin stated that he had to use his influence in 1848 to prevent the ministers from cashiering the Superintendent. (49) In 1849 Malcolm Cameron, a radical Reform minister, attempted to undermine Ryerson's position by having passed a common schools act that reversed many of his previous policies. (50) Ryerson successfully appealed to Baldwin for the disallowance of the act. As the latter had decided to judge him on the basis of official actions, not on past political indiscretions, he found no justification for dismissing him. (51) For most Reformers the disallowance of the act ended any hope of removing Ryerson. By 1850 Brown and Lesslie simply maintained silence on the matter, while Donlevy declared himself willing to do likewise:

Now that our Responsible rulers have decided upon overlooking the treason, we are content to acquiesce in the amnesty, and to permit the malefactor to evince his penitence by a strict adherence to the paths of official duty. (52)

The passage in 1850 of a common schools act prepared by Ryerson to remedy the defects of the contentious acts of 1847 and 1849 disarmed Reform resistance even more. It restored elected school boards and permitted them to gather fees to supplement the taxes levied for schools. (53) In effect, although Ryerson remained as Superintendent, the Reformers had won the two significant points for which they had campaigned in 1848.

The Toronto schools had remained closed in the second half of 1848 and the first half of 1849; however, on receipt of the legislative grant in July the trustees re-opened the schools. In 1850, with Ryerson's concurrence, (54) they collected fees and operated the schools for the full year. On September 3, 1850, an election was held in accordance with the remedial legislation. At the first meeting of the Board, in October, the trustees selected Dr. Joseph Workman as Chairman over George P. Ridout. (55) Both men had served on the Council's Standing Committee on Education in 1848. Workman, a Reformer, had opposed free schools whereas Ridout, a Tory, had supported them. In 1851 they were once again in opposition over free schools, the former advocating non-sectarian free education and the latter holding out for sectarian provisions in the scheme. In the election of 1851 the sectarian issue in the form of a campaign for more separate schools for Roman Catholics resulted in a spirited fight in two wards—St. James and St. Patricks. Promoters of non-sectarian education, one of whom was Lesslie of the *Examiner,* carried both wards. (56) In 1851 the Board was primarily concerned about resolving the free schools question; however, the trustees were also forced to consider the two subsidiary issues raised by this question, the support of sectarian education and the provision of permanent school buildings.

At the Board's first meeting in January 1851, Workman, whom the trustees again appointed Chairman, suggested the construction of six schools in as many years. Two trustees, D. Paterson and A. A. Riddell then moved:

Whereas the present system of taxing the people for school purposes, and then compelling them to pay a heavy school rate is unwise and detrimental to the cause of education: Be it therefore resolved—That with a view of encouraging general education, the Common Schools of this city be free to the scholars during the year 1851. (57)

An amendment referred this motion and the Chairman's suggestion about buildings to a Committee on Free Schools, consisting of Lesslie (Chairman), Workman, Ridout, Paterson and Riddell. (58) On February 26 Lesslie tabled the Report, (59) which outlined four proposals: development of tax-supported common schools, construction of school houses, provision of school libraries, and the exclusion of "everything of a sectarian character from the instruction given."

In vindicating its proposals the Committee enunciated two guiding assumptions. First, "the education of the young is intimately and inseparably connected with the welfare of the State." The Committee had discovered that, according to the educational statistics, 3400 of 6150 youngsters in Toronto did not enrol in any school. The reasons reported were poverty, parental indifference, sectarianism and inadequate accommodations. The examination of sectarianism, occupying one-quarter of the report, was certain to anger supporters of sectarian schools because adopting a voluntaryist stance, it assumed that such schools were injurious to the "welfare of the State." The Committee wrote, "The state may impose a tax for general education, but it has no right to impose a tax to support any form of religious faith or worship." It admitted the right of a religious group to teach its dogma, if the particular faith raised its funds from its adherents. Sectarian privileges, it asserted, were demanded "not as much by the people as their religious teachers." This barbed statement would offend Bishops Strachan and de Charbonnel.*

The second assumption which derived from the first was "The doctrine has been established beyond all doubt that the want of early culture is the fruitful cause of all crime." If, the Committee contended, youth did not receive instruction, "the broad avenue of vice would be supplied with its victims, and our Courts and Prisons be supplied with their youthful criminals." (60) The argu-

---

* John Strachan, Anglican Bishop of Toronto, 1839–1867, was the leading spokesman for Anglican supremacy in Upper Canada (Canada West). As the province moved towards universal schooling supported by public funds, he pressed for separate schools for Anglicans. Similarly, Armand Francois Marie de Charbonnel, a French nobleman, who in 1850 succeeded Michael Power as Roman Catholic Bishop of Toronto, campaigned vigorously for legislation to establish separate schools for Roman Catholics.

ment was borrowed from American reports and substantiated by statistics from New York State. The Committee admitted:

There are no criminal statistics in Canada to which reference can be made in proof of this doctrine, but from the testimony of those familiar with our Penitentiary and Prisons the fact is undoubted.

Considering the lack of Canadian statistics and the lack of public alarm in the newspapers about local crime, the argument appears artificial; however, it did echo Ryerson's warnings about the Irish in 1848. (61) Its only basis was that Toronto would emerge as an industrial centre similar to cities in the United States and Britain. Certainly members of the Committee anticipated the advent of industrialization and they expected a corresponding increase in crime and social problems; yet they possessed serene confidence that a proper environment would effectively mould the behavior of growing young people. (62) In this way they could avoid the excesses characteristic of the growth of industry.

One of the striking features of the Report was its dependence on American sources, including Horace Mann, the Report of the Superintendent of the Common Schools of New York (quoted three times), and criminal statistics for New York State. Of course, the non-sectarian schools of the United States were particularly attractive to the Committee. For the attendance figures in Toronto schools it referred to Ryerson's annual report; otherwise, it ignored the Superintendent. Since Lesslie was Chairman of the Committee it is not surprising that Ryerson was ignored.

The vote to adopt the Report divided the trustees seven to four in its favour, the only point of discussion being the section on sectarian education; (63) thus on April 1, 1851, the common schools became fully tax-supported. The only concerted resistance to this plan came from Roman Catholics and High Church Anglicans on the issue of denominational education. This may well explain the opposition by the four trustees, one of whom, W. Gooderham, was certainly an Anglican. *Table 2* is a comparison of the opposing trustees' occupation and wealth. In rank order of assessed wealth the two richest and the two poorest trustees supported free schools; thus wealth appears an irrelevant consideration. Additional evidence that religion was an important factor in the Board's decision lies in the alignment of newspapers in the issue. The *Christian*

TABLE 2

Analysis of Members of Common School Board:
Vote to Adopt Report on Free Schools, March 1851

Data on Trustees [a]	Opposed to Report	Favoured Report
Occupation [b] and *Average* Assessed Value of Property [c]		
Professional		1
		£733
Merchant	2	4
	£629.	£628.18s.
Distiller	1	
	£342.	
Artisan		2
		£79.2s.
Assessed Value of All Property	£1600.	£3406.16s.
Average Assessed Value	£533.7s.	£486.14s.
Rank Order of Wealth Based on Assessment	3, 5, 8	1, 2, 4, 6, 7, 9, 10

[a] Two men, one from each voting group, could not be traced because more than one Torontonian had the same name.
[b] H. Rowsell, *City of Toronto and County of York Directory for 1850–51.*
[c] City of Toronto, Assessment Rolls, 1851.

Guardian, British Colonist, Globe, North American, and *Examiner* supported the Board and, likewise, held a voluntary position in matters of state and religion. On the opposing side, the Reform but Catholic *Mirror,* the Orange *Patriot,* and the *Church* decried secular schools.

The religious issue was raised early in 1851, when the Roman Catholics, who had three separate schools, applied for four additional schools. The Board refused to support the request. The Catholics forwarded two candidates for the January election, but they were defeated by voluntaryists. In the course of the dispute about the separate schools, the trustees advanced a number of justifications for their stand. They objected to Bishop de Charbonnel's interference in school affairs especially since they favoured a system which excluded "everything of a sectarian character." Preferring to consolidate their resources, they despaired of dividing the school fund effectively among four more schools. They also argued that, since they provided three separate schools in Toronto, they were discharging their responsibility beyond the requirements of the act of 1850, which obliged a school board to provide "one or more" separate schools in its section. (64) Toronto reported sixteen school sections, but the act regarded it as a single section; hence the situation was sufficiently ambiguous to create and sustain disagreement, as even Attorney-General Baldwin agreed. The Catholics challenged the legality of the Board's decision in court. The judge ruled:

We are disposed to think the limits of separate schools are in the discretion of the Board of Trustees. . . . The Board, and not the applicants, is to prescribe the limits of separate schools. (65)

Donlevy accused the trustees of exhibiting "bad faith" with their legalistic wrangling, and complained "The Catholic citizens are taxed to support Protestant schools." (66) The Catholic community turned to charity schools managed by the Christian Brothers to supplement the separate schools. (67)

Support for the Catholics came from an unexpected quarter. Thompson's Orange *Patriot,* which carefully reported both the court case and Board meetings, concurred with the Catholic aim:

We hold the Romanists to be doing their duty, in seeking separate schools, though we hold them to be in an erroneous belief—and we hold the refusal to admit the members of the Anglican Church, or any other "Sect" to a similar privilege, to be unwise, unjust, and unconstitutional in the highest degree. (68)

Thompson was joined in his campaign against the Board by the High Church Anglicans. Bishop Strachan publicly denounced "the torrent of socialism and infidelity" which, as a result of secular schools, threatened "total anarchy." (69) The *Church* printed a series of abusive articles on the socialism inherent in free, nonsectarian schools and the effect of these schools on the religious faith of the common people. (70) In its outbursts this newspaper revealed a reactionary apprehension of the common school's power to level out social classes. Like the Catholics, the Anglicans finally established a charity school—St. James Parochial School—"particularly for the poorer members of [their] communion" and there educated the youngsters according to sectarian principles. (71)

Neither Catholics nor Anglicans objected to the idea of schools being free. Both were willing to conduct charity schools in which religion featured strongly in the curriculum, as a moulder of their future communicants' behaviour. Moreover, what they feared most about common schools, the mixing of social classes, could be avoided if the poor attended charity schools, and the rich private schools.

Just prior to the school elections of 1852 resistance to free schools climaxed in a petition that, while complaining of "the present heavy Tax" and "the prospect of a permanent and increasing City Debt for the purchase of land and the erection of School Houses," called for a public meeting to protest the Board's decision to build schools. (72) The petition was in response to arrangements to purchase three sites at a total cost of £1256. and to begin construction in 1852 at an estimated cost of £800. for each building. (73) Significantly, only Thompson's *Patriot* published the petition; it also carried Mayor Bowes' announcement of a meeting to be held in the St. Lawrence Hall at 7:00 P.M. on January 9. (74)

As is so often the case with petitions, it would be signed for a variety of reasons by the ninety-six men whose names were listed in the *Patriot*. Some, opposing the Board's policy regarding non-sectarian education, would view the petition as a means of thwarting the extension of common schools. Some would be supporters of private schools. Likely, most did fear increased taxes for school construction. Angus Dallas, the only person to present a case for the petition at the meeting, had recently rented accommodation to the Board for £20. per annum for five years. (75) A building program represented a loss of income for him. Moreover, he probably resented the grossly insulting remarks that trustees directed at conditions in the rented accommodation in their attempts to justify the construction of buildings.

An examination of Table 3 reveals several characteristics of the petitioners. Twenty-four artisans and forty-seven merchants dominated the group, with the latter comprising seventeen storekeepers, five importers and twenty-five wholesale merchants. In comparison to the trustees, classified in Table 2, the petitioners were poorer in each occupation except that of artisan. Similarly, on the average they were considerably poorer than trustees: they possessed property assessed at an average of £278. 1s. 4d. whereas the two groups of trustees owned property assessed at an average of £533. 7s. and £486. 14s. Only nine petitioners had property assessed in excess of £500. Again, the opposition to free schools can be attributed neither to the very poor nor to the wealthy.

TABLE 3

Analysis of Petitioners Protesting the School Board's Policy
of Constructing School Buildings, January 1852

Occupations	Number on Petition [a]	Number Located on Assessment Rolls [b]	Average Assessed Value of Property
Professional or Public Employee	6	5	£142.12s.
Merchant	47	40	392.5s.
Manufacturer	2	1	179.
Gentleman	1	0	—
Distiller	1	1	85.1s.
Innkeeper	1	1	311.
Artisan	24	17	144.5s.
Employee	4	3	62.5s.
Unknown	10	1	78.
Total Value of All Property			£19,186.13s.
Average of All Property			278.1s.4d.

[a] H. Rowsell, *City of Toronto and County of York Directory for 1850–51.*
[b] City of Toronto, Assessment Rolls, 1851.

The reports of the six newspapers that published accounts of the meeting highlighted the hollowness of resistance to free schools. (76) Dallas opened the meeting and addressed the standing audience of three to five hundred people. In a rambling and inaccurate speech he deplored the failure of free schools in Massachusetts, where money was "squandered" on the system. He asserted that the trustees in Toronto believed their own system was defective. He then charged that the Toronto Normal School was ineffective. (77) Finally, he read out a resolution censuring the School Board. No one in the audience supported his accusations. Alderman S. Thompson seconded the motion of condemnation, but carefully dissociated himself from Dallas' statements, explaining that he was acting on behalf of a group of his constituents. H. J. Boulton, whom Dallas understood would support his motion, declared that he could not, in conscience, endorse it.

Ryerson, Brown and three trustees—Workman, Lesslie and Riddell—all promoters of free schools dominated the remainder of the meeting. They ridiculed Dallas' charges and corrected his erroneous statements. After replying to some of the charges, Ryerson stated that "he had no hesitation on one point—that the Metropolitan City of Canada West should have at least one decent School-house." (78) According to all the newspaper reports, however, it was Workman, who presented a masterly reply to the motion of censure. When he explained the building program, he scoffed, "Why it would appear as if they [the trustees] were going to take up every vacant lot in this city." (79) He stressed the inadequacy of the accommodations and the adverse effects of this situation on the morals and health of the pupils; for example, "sometimes as much as 30 per cent of the scholars were absent from contagious disease." (80) As a consequence, he did not permit his youngsters to attend a common school. He attacked two of the petitioners present at the meeting for their selfishness. Both Dixon and Urquhart sent sons to Upper Canada College and the University of Toronto, which were assisted by public funds. In view of this illiberality, he objected to accusations of pauperism against "the respectable tradesmen and mechanics and operators" because their children attended common schools. (81) When the vote was finally called for, five hours after the meeting had begun, the overwhelming majority supported the Board. The issue which had been discussed was not free schools, but school accommodation. Doubtless the implementation of tax-supported education underlay the attack on the building program, since the former would likely create an urgent need for more classrooms.

The next week, on January 14, the election of school trustees confirmed the victory for the Board and for voluntaryism. The *Christian Guardian* noted that a "combination of certain parties" was determined to "control" education and to "impart such instruction as suits their own peculiar views." (82) Brown reported more pointedly, "The Roman Catholics and High Churchmen made an unholy alliance to carry in persons in the elections in favour of sectarian schools." (83) He accused the Orangemen of assisting Dr. King, a Catholic candidate, in his campaign in St. James Ward. The "unholy alliance," like the combination of Reformer and Orangeman in 1848, was an unlikely union possible only for a short time and around a specific issue.

Considering the resistance to free schools in 1848 it is striking how impotent the opposition was in 1851. The schools act of 1850 had restored local autonomy, as the Reformers viewed it, in two important matters—election of trustees and financing education.

Within the context of other, larger changes, such as Canadian control of immigration and improved economic conditions, a modified stand on the education issue was warranted. In 1851 objections to free schools centred on Anglican and Roman Catholic desires for sectarian education; however, the Toronto electorate decidedly opted for voluntaryism. The Board was supported in its intention to use the schools to promote social harmony. Ironically, Ryerson's view prevailed. In the beginning of the controversy the Reformers had determined to destroy the Superintendent; in the end they endorsed a position similar to his, that free schools would prevent crime and contribute to social harmony.

NOTES

1. *Toronto Herald,* May 18, 1848.
2. J. G. Hodgins (ed.), *Documentary History of Education in Upper Canada,* Vol. 8. Hodgins used Ryerson's letter to the *Toronto Herald* as the basis for his explanation of the closing of the schools. The explanation is repeated in several modern books: H. M. Cochrane (ed.), *The Centennial Story: The Board of Education for the City of Toronto, 1850–1950* (Toronto, 1950); E. C. Guillett, *In the Cause of Education* (Toronto, 1960); C. E. Phillips, *The Development of Education in Canada* (Toronto, 1957); C. B. Sissons, *Egerton Ryerson: His Life and Letters,* Vol. 2 (Toronto, 1947).
3. Clara Thomas, *Ryerson of Upper Canada* (Toronto, 1969), p. 113.
4. The meeting was treated in this fashion by Hodgins, Cochrane, Guillett and Sissons.
5. 10 and 11 Vic., c. 19, Statutes of Canada.
6. Minutes of the Common School Board, Toronto, November 23, 1847. Library, Toronto Board of Education.
7. Ibid., November 29, December 6, and December 13.
8. "Circular no. 3, heads of Cities and Town Corporations in Upper Canada, explanatory of the new system of Schools for Cities and Incorporated Towns, January 15, 1848."
9. Ryerson to Cameron, February 1, 1848. Education Office, Canada West: Letter Book D, p. 262, Public Archives of Ontario (P.A.O.)
10. Ibid., Ryerson to Barber, February 7, 1848, p. 273.
11. Ibid., Ryerson to Baldwin, March 23, 1848, p. 333.
12. Ibid., Ryerson to Barber, April 15, 1848, p. 364.
13. "Report of the Standing Committee on Education," May 1, 1848. Toronto City Council Papers, P.A.O.
14. Minutes of the Council of the City of Toronto, May 15, 1848.

15. Ibid., June 14, 1848.
16. Hon. J. Elmsley, trustee, and Barber to C. Daly, City Clerk, June 24, 1848. Toronto City Council Papers, P.A.O.
17. Ibid., "Report of Standing Committee on Education," June 26, 1848.
18. Minutes of the Council of the City of Toronto, June 26, 1848; *Christian Guardian,* July 12, 1848. One interesting reaction to the closing of the common schools was the building of a charity school. (See John Pope, "The Enoch Turner School 1848," *York Pioneer* (1971), pp. 19–26.) In 1842 a group of Irish protestants had organized a subscription for the building of a church and a school. Little Trinity Church was built in 1844, but on its completion no funds remained for a school. In response to the Council's decision in June, Enoch Turner contributed the money for building a school, completed in November. When the Toronto Common School Board adopted a free school policy, his building, now the city's oldest standing public school, was turned over to the Board.
19. *Christian Guardian,* July 26, 1848.
20. *Mirror,* March 24, 1848.
21. D. C. Masters, *The Rise of Toronto, 1850–1890* (Toronto, 1947), p. 43.
22. Barber to Daly, March 10, 1848. Toronto City Council Papers, P.A.O.
23. Minutes of the Common School Board, Toronto.
24. *Toronto Herald,* May 18, 1848.
25. Assessment Rolls, City of Toronto, 1848, P.A.O. Despite obvious deficiencies, these rolls give a sound indication of relative wealth.
26. An examination of the monthly copies for 1848 of the *Journal of Education for Upper Canada* (edited by Ryerson and his assistant, J. G. Hodgins) reveals that Ryerson was forcefully promoting the relationship between free schools and social order. A particularly useful example is the article by Ryerson, "The Importance of Education to a Manufacturing and a Free People," October 1848, pp. 289–301.
27. July 4, 1848.
28. July 5, 1848.
29. July 5, 1848.
30. April 19, 1848.
31. Masters, *The Rise of Toronto, 1850–1890,* pp. 21–31. By 1851, 11,305 of the City's 30,775 people were listed as Irish in the Census.
32. The newspapers reported extensively on the situation in Ireland and the repercussions in Britain and the United States. They also published detailed reports and commentary on the growing problems associated with the arrival of the Irish in Toronto. In particular, see *Examiner,* October 27, 1847, *Patriot,* May 9, 1848, and June 2, 1848, and *Globe,* July 1, 1848. This issue of the *Globe* featured a committee investigation into local immigrant conditions and its revelations of wretchedness. See also Lieut.-Col. G. C. Page, Royal Engineers, to Mayor of Toronto, May 12, 1848, Toronto City Council Papers, P.A.O. That prevailing attitudes to the Irish were hostile is evidenced by the

defensive tone of the *Mirror:* August 13, 1847; October 1, 1847; April 21, 1848; June 30, 1848.

33. Examiner, March 3, 1848. Of the 1466 persons (1087 male and 379 female) apprehended for a variety of crimes in 1847, 980 (675 male and 305 female) were Irish.

34. *Christian Guardian,* July 26, 1848.

35. *Church,* July 2, 1847.

36. Ibid., May 19, 1848.

37. *British Colonist,* July 4, 1848.

38. Ryerson to *Globe,* May 1848. Education Office, Canada West: Letter Book D, p. 395, P.A.O.

39. *Examiner,* May 10, 1848.

40. Ibid., April 4, 1848.

41. *Globe,* May 10, 1848.

42. *Mirror,* May 12, 1848.

43. Concentrating their attention on Ryerson, the Reform editors recalled the Metcalfe incident of 1844. They also vituperated the Superintendent of Toronto Schools, G. A. Barber, who owned the Conservative *Toronto Herald.* At the Council meeting of June 26 the Reform members directed a particularly partisan attack on both men. See *Christian Guardian,* July 5 and 12, 1848, and *Examiner,* July 5, 1848.

44. *Examiner,* January 26, 1848.

45. During April and May Reform editors published articles demanding Ryerson's dismissal. The headlines were often suggestive: "Working of the Ryersonian School Bill," "Egerton Ryerson's School Bill in Toronto—How It Works—A Tax of Fourpence Halfpenny in the Pound Required to Carry Out Its Provisions," "Dr. Ryerson and the City School Bill."

46. *Examiner,* July 5, 1848.

47. *The North American,* founded as a radical Reform, or Clear Grit, newspaper, and the *Examiner* demanded more far-reaching reforms. The Clear Grits established an eleven-point program and pressed Baldwin, who was cautious, on these points.

48. Lesslie worked persistently for Ryerson's removal. See *Examiner,* January 24 and October 10, 1849.

49. Sissons, *Ryerson,* p. 160.

50. 12 Vic., c. 83, Statutes of Canada, especially sections 2, 10, 12, and 30 altered the direction of Ryerson's policies. It reduced the Superintendent's power, abolished uniform textbooks, restored the use of fees in cities and towns, and granted wider powers to school boards. Since it was believed to have been drafted by Ryerson, the bill passed in the Assembly after a perfunctory reading.

51. George E. Wilson, *The Life of Robert Baldwin* (Toronto, 1933), p. 258.

52. *Mirror,* August 10, 1849.

53. 13 and 14 Vic., c. 48, Statutes of Canada.
54. In strict accordance with the Act of 1849 this measure was legal. The Act had passed third reading in the Assembly, but Baldwin disallowed it until remedial legislation could be enacted. As a result, the Act of 1847 applied to the situation. In a draft of a bill he was preparing for 1850 Ryerson intended to offer urban municipalities a choice between supporting schools through fees and taxes, or taxes only; therefore, he distributed a circular in which he outlined this choice. See "Circular to the Chairmen of Boards of Trustees for Cities and Incorporated Towns in Upper Canada, December 19, 1849," enclosed in correspondence, Barber to Daly, January 2, 1850. Toronto City Council Papers, P.A.O.
55. Minutes of the Common School Board, Toronto, October 23, 1850. At this meeting the Board decided to open its meetings to the public. Several newspapers responded to this decision by regularly reporting the proceedings of the Board.
56. *Examiner,* January 15, 1851.
57. Minutes of the Common School Board, Toronto, January 15, 1851.
58. Ibid., All members of the Committee supported the principle of free schools, although Ridout differed from the others on the question of non-sectarian schools.
59. Ibid., February 26, 1851. See also: James Leslie, "Report on Free Schools," *Report of the past History, and Present Condition of the Common or Public Schools of the City of Toronto* (Toronto, 1859).
60. In 1848 Ryerson had employed this same appeal. He had warned: "The physical disease and death which have accompanied this influx [the Irish immigration] among us may be the precursor of the worse pestilence of social insubordination and disorder." ("The Importance of Education to a Manufacturing, and a Free People," *Journal of Education for Upper Canada,* October 1848, p. 300.) By 1851, although unacknowledged, Ryerson's warning was being heeded. Toronto, undergoing economic growth, faced further change in the direction of industrialization as had been experienced in Britain and the U.S.A. There was an unusual preoccupation with criminal statistics from both countries. On March 27, 1851, a letter in the *Globe* expressed sentiments which must have had wide currency at this time:

> Increasing as these Provinces are, in population and wealth—*in anticipation of possible agitations* political and social, let us lay the foundations of order deep in the affections of a free, instructed, and virtuous people—reason, justice, policy, and Christian philanthropy alike urge us to promote, by every means, the moral and religious education of the masses. (Italics mine)

The stress on crime indicates an ambivalence—jubilation compounded with fear—to the future progress of Toronto.

61. The Reformers had appointed a commission, of which George Brown was a member, to investigate prison conditions; thus there was some awareness of the local situation.

62. Examples of the notions entertained by laymen about education can be found in M. B. Katz, *The Irony of Early School Reform: Educational Innovation in Mid-Nineteenth Century Massachusetts* (Cambridge, Mass., 1968). During the early 1850's a group of American manufacturers in Lawrence, Massachusetts, looked to education to create a suitable environment for the shaping of morals and intellect and thus to prevent the degradation characteristic of industrialized Europe. These men anticipated clear-cut gains from education.

63. Minutes of the Common School Board, Toronto, March 5, 1851.

64. 13 and 14 Vic., c. 48, sec. 19, Statutes of Canada.

65. *British Colonist,* February 18, 1851.

66. Between January and March 1851 Donlevy protested the Board's decision. He had plainly parted ways with the editors of the other Reform newspapers on the issue of education. These editors and the trustees maintained that the schools were common and non-sectarian, not Protestant.

67. *Mirror,* January 9, 1852.

68. *Patriot,* March 8, 1851.

69. *Christian Guardian,* January 14, 1852.

70. From January to March 1852, the *Church* printed a series of articles opposing the Board's policy of non-sectarian education: "The Tares Springing Up," "The Free School Mania"; and several others under the headline, "Socialism and Free Schools."

71. *Church,* January 1, 1852.

72. *Patriot,* January 9, 1852.

73. Ibid., November 28, 1851.

74. Ibid., January 9, 1852.

75. Ibid., February 25, 1851.

76. Although the meeting was ignored by the *Church* and the *Mirror,* the two newspapers whose readers were most interested in its outcome, it was reported in the *Globe, North American, Examiner, British Colonist, Christian Guardian,* and *Patriot.*

77. *North American,* January 22, 1852.

78. Ibid.

79. *Examiner,* January 14, 1852.

80. Ibid.

81. *North American,* January 22, 1852.

82. January 14, 1852.

83. *Globe,* January 15, 1852.

Part II

The Child, the Family and the State

SUSAN E. HOUSTON

4. VICTORIAN ORIGINS OF JUVENILE DELINQUENCY: A CANADIAN EXPERIENCE

Large scale immigration and rapid social development had brought both prosperity and drastic social inequalities to the commercial cities of Upper Canada by the middle decades of the nineteenth century. Much of the anxiety fostered among the propertied classes by the spectacle of urban poverty focused on the popular image of the Street Arab. Key institutional innovations of the period—the common school, the juvenile reformatory and the industrial school— were shaped by the classic effort of mid-Victorian Canadians to comprehend the dimensions of change in their social environment and in the life experience of youth.

THE VICTORIAN SOCIAL CONSCIENCE was troubled on many accounts, and perhaps no more so than by the plight of delinquent youngsters. Few causes cut so deeply into the delicate weave of moralism and economy out of which much nineteenth-century social policy was fashioned.

The demographic and economic revolutions that transformed western European societies in the late eighteenth and early nineteenth centuries had combined to encourage a radical redefinition and revaluation of childhood and youth. (1) Within middle-class families children assumed a more conspicuous and integrated role. Moreover, the family provided many Victorians with an archetype —emotional, organizational, and ideological—with which to interpret their experience of social change. Their anxiety about that

S. Houston is a member of Department of History, York University. This article is reprinted from The History of Education Quarterly *with permission.*

change is well revealed by the energy and dismay with which many reformers responded to the spectacle of an unprecedented number of other people's children surviving—and thriving—unrestrained in society at large. Not surprisingly, the solution they devised was the creation of surrogate institutions for the lower classes appropriately analogous to middle-class family life.

The Province of Canada in the middle of the nineteenth century comprised (in abbreviated form) the present day provinces of Ontario and Quebec. With the notable exceptions of a handful of relatively sophisticated urban centres such as Toronto and Kingston, much of the English-speaking settlement of Canada West had only recently emerged from the pioneer era. The decade of the 1840s had witnessed the transformation of a straggly, fledgling community into a bustling provincial society impatient to participate in the promise of mid century in a half-empty continent. These English Canadians were confident in their expectation of progress and in their provincial enthusiasm were untroubled by the discrepancy between their modest state and the societies of New York or London. (2) Indeed, their familiarity with metropolitan events and fashions was a matter of considerable pride. They were self-conscious mid-Victorians. (3) Thus as Torontonians hurried from installing gas lighting to constructing railroads, they diligently unearthed the social problems that they knew, from the experience of Manchester, Boston, and elsewhere, must be there. In a city of just over 30,000 they were not disappointed. Irish famine victims, coming at the end of a decade of relatively substantial immigration, had provided the province with a class of landless urban poor on a scale not known before. (4)

To some citizens the increasingly familiar figure of the street urchin—ill clad, undisciplined, and, most importantly, unschooled— assumed sinister significance. Destitution and dependency had too often provided an accompaniment to pioneer settlement; and after more than half a century a patchwork of philanthropic societies and meagre public facilities, originally the offspring of some crisis, constituted a real, if feeble, support for both the needy and their propertied neighbours. (5) Urban poverty, inflated with immigrant misfortune, seemed more desperate but rarely intractable. (6) The self-reliance and confidence engendered by the visible triumph of rural settlement encouraged resort to the simple and congenial strategy of relocating the poor "elsewhere," in the countryside. (7) Thus the prize-winning essay on Canada at the Paris Exhibition of 1855 could boast, "it would, therefore, appear that though Canada cannot boast of the extreme wealth of older nations, she is wholly free from the other extreme of pauperism and its painful and debasing concomitants, ignorance, want, disease and crime." (8) Others, however, were less optimistic. The experience of the summer of 1847 in port and transit cities, swollen with destitute Irish, eroded confidence in traditional resources and gave new urgency to proposals for reform that had previously seemed unnecessarily grandiose. (9) The strain that the famine victims and their children placed on the medical, welfare, and educational institutions of the burgeoning society hastened the task of social definition for which many energetic colonists yearned impatiently. The threat was clear, as Egerton Ryerson, Chief Superintendent of Education and model school promoter, warned: "The physical disease and death which has accompanied their influx among us may be the precursor of the worse pestilence of social insubordination and disorder. It is therefore of the last importance that every possible effort should be employed to bring the facilities of education within the reach of the families of these unfortunate people, that they may grow up in the industry and intelligence of the country, and not in the idleness and pauperism, not to say mendicity and vice, of their forefathers." (10)

Whereas previously, care of orphan and destitute children had been channelled through quasi-public Houses of Industry or local municipal authorities, (11) the problem no longer seemed so self-evidently solvable. Not only were there many more children in need, they were no longer so clearly orphaned: the semiorphanage of the child with one or two living but utterly dissolute parents posed questions that the legal enactments did not cover. (12) The structure of the recently established provincial common school system (although only optionally free) now provided a definition of "neglect" and "vagrant"—as "not being in school"—that enlarged and clarified the impression of a critical social problem. Not insignificantly, the Catholicism of the Irish immigrants shattered the virtual Protestant consensus in Canada West at a time when, for political reasons, the Protestantism of English-speaking Canadians was pitted against the Catholic, French-speaking community of

Canada East in an increasingly embittered provincial legislature. In terms of social policy, the Catholic factor soon resulted in the duplication of philanthropic activity. (13) The separate Roman Catholic school system, the inception of which predated the famine immigration, owed most to the critical balance of culture interests in Canada; however its operation, and aspirations, grew dramatically in response to the urban Irish communities. (14)

Curiously, the problem of the street arabs appeared superficially immune to the anti-Catholic sentiment that festered in ultra-Protestant circles. Catholics and Protestants alike saw their presence as a symptom of more basic and ominous flaws in their new society. "The idleness and dissipation of a large number of children, who now loiter about the public streets or frequent the haunts of vice" were, in the opinion of one prominent Catholic philanthropist, "creating the most painful emotions in every well regulated mind; and in some degree involving the imputation, that the social condition of the body corporate of which they form a part, cannot be of the highest order." (15) Although the poverty of the children was tacitly acknowledged, in that their begging was a persistent cause for concern, (16) it was their habits rather than their condition that roused the ire of reformers. It seemed common knowledge that "ignorance and idleness are in truth the grand causes of crime." (17) While benevolent ladies seeking support for a new charity for Protestant orphans and destitute females felt "there is little doubt, that poverty and destitution are the precursors of immortality and crime," they feared the spiritual rather than the physical consequences of being "driven from the path of uprightness and purity into the vortex of iniquity and irrecoverable degradation in consequence of being unable to procur *immediate* employment either as seamstresses or servants." (18) In 1851 liberally minded school trustees capitulated to the idea of free schools, conscious of the responsibility imposed by the doctrine "established beyond all doubt that the want of early moral culture is the fruitful cause of almost all crime." (19)

Crime was not, in itself, a novel preoccupation of Canadian reformers. Nearly twenty years before, as cholera shadowed the arrival of a bumper crop of immigrants, alarmists had urged the necessity of more stringent immigration restrictions and better law enforcement. (20) The provincial penitentiary, started in 1833 after the plan of the New York State Prison at Auburn, was witness to the enthusiasm of this earlier generation for penal reform. Reformers at midcentury were quite as susceptible to the consolation provided by prison structures and police, but they perceived their problem as less tangible and therefore more alarming. Chronically inadequate jail provision and an increase in felonies were now only part of the story, the tip of an iceberg. What was glimpsed were the consequences of a way of life, of a commitment to certain values and goals exemplified by the city, railroads, mechanics, Progress, Democracy, and Steam. Both despite and because of their anomalous position on the fringe of what they regarded as the epitome of nineteenth-century social development, English Canadians tried anxiously to keep pace, intellectually, with the lead of New York and London. Thus, although circumstances in the 1850s hardly warranted it, they were stirred by the modish ideological argument about the virtues and vices of urbanization and the temptation to identify with the country or the city as the custodian of the virtuous life. Not unexpectedly in a population overwhelmingly composed of independent rural landowners on the crest of prosperity there was a vital sentiment idealizing yeoman virtues, pioneer struggles, and the superiority of life on the land. (21) But nonetheless, by mid century the counter theme had gained able publicists. Egerton Ryerson, lecturing on the "Social Advancement of Canada" in 1849 characterized the present time as "pre-eminently with us an ocean of change, the waves of which are obliterating so many ancient landmarks." (22) The vision of Canada's destiny, he proclaimed, clearly hinged on "simple manufactories growing into prosperous towns, and towns swelling into cities—canals and railroads intersecting the various districts, and commerce covering rivers and lakes."

The issue went beyond that of material progress, although the way to that seemed clear enough, "as no country ever yet has become great and prosperous without manufactures." (23) At root, the cause was civilization. Steam technology seemed to its disciples to presage a new age of moral as well as material achievement. As T. C. Keefer, Canadian engineer and arch railway promoter, explained in 1850:

The civilizing tendency of the locomotive is one of the modern anomalies which, however inexplicable it may appear to some, is yet so fortunately patent to all, that it is admitted as readily as the action of steam, though the substance be invisible and its secret ways unknown to man. Poverty, indifference, the bigotry or jealousy of religious denominations, local dissensions or political demagogism, may stifle or neutralize the influence of the best intended efforts of an educational system; but that invisible power which has waged successful war with the material elements, will assuredly overcome the prejudices of mental weakness or the designs of mental tyrants. It calls for no co-operation, it waits for no convenient season, but with a restless, rushing, roaring assiduity, it keeps up a constant and unavoidable spirit of enquiry or comparison; and while ministering to the material wants, and appealing to the covetousness of the multitude, it unconsciously, irresistibly, impels them to a more intimate union with their fellow men. (24)

But if civilization was generally accepted as the cause, the course to victory seemed less self-evident to many. An emotional and ideological investment in a future symbolized by urban and manufacturing concerns was accompanied by a poorly disguised anxiety about the increasing evidence of corporate and personal demoralization. The Romanticism that tinged the mid-Victorian Canadian's acceptance of the dark side of city life also contributed a cynicism and world-weariness to his analysis of existing social ills. Crime was the hub of the problem. Crime represented "an evil under which all cities, however prosperous they may be (those of this continent especially) suffer from." (25) Moreover, the problem was quite specific; Toronto in the 1850s seemed in danger from "crime which appears to have come in like a flood into our usually quiet and well-ordered community." (26) The "crimes" that swelled the goal statistics—vagrancy, disorderly conduct, and intoxication—were precisely those to which juveniles were most susceptible, while being "some of the elements that demoralize society, that supply the place as the ranks of detected criminals are thinned, and that must be reformed, if any important progress is made by man in the course of virtue and civilization." (27) A touchstone to Victorian morality was provided by the equation of conduct and character. An emphasis on character provided the thread that linked shades and waves of reform opinion through much of the nineteenth century. It also lent essential plausibility to the strategy of reformation that provided the chief rhetorical justification for experiments in social engineering. All of this was buttressed by the religious emphasis of the Victorian years that functioned in Canadian society as a particularly pervasive social norm. (28) Thus the campaign against ignorance (and the mandate of the school system) encompassed more than reading; illiteracy was deplored, but more as the visible sign of that other ignorance that was the root of personal and social deviance. In this ideological context, the necessity to provide for neglected children could appear a crusade "to civilize the street-arab and convert the vagrant from the alarming vice of idleness to habits of honesty and industry." (29)

The obvious existing institution that might transform the street arab was the common school. Few school supporters needed the urging of the Chief Superintendent to link the promotion of education with "administration of justice, organized systems for the repression or prevention of crime, and other important subjects. (30) The existence and promised redemption of ignorant, ill-mannered street children proved to be a stock argument of free school promoters. It effectively dramatised the ingredients of character formation and social mobility that contributed much to the appeal of the common school idea. As the *Globe,* chief publicist for colonial liberal opinion, predicted: "Educate the people and your gaols will be abandoned and your police may be disbanded; all the offences which man commits against his neighbour and against his own peace will be comparatively unknown. . . . If we make our people intelligent, they cannot fail to be prosperous; intelligence makes morality, morality industry, industry prosperity as certainly as the sun shines." (31) Not only schools, but teachers also claimed recognition for the fight against crime and social demoralization. Common school teachers felt they were entitled "to higher consideration than has hitherto been awarded them" on the grounds that they contributed "so largely to the diffusion of intelligence, to the development of mind, to the promotion of virtue, and to the prevention of crime." (32) To make their case, Canadian school promoters, like their American counterparts, relied on the seemingly incontrovertible logic revealed by the association of crime and school statistics to the point where it was generally conceded that "the results of these prison statistics and of our school system cannot be separated." (33)

However, there are pitfalls in a casual dependence on statistics and extravagant claims to reform. Critics of the centralised, non-sectarian, publicly tax-supported provincial school system fought back with statistics of their own designed to show that if merely secular education did not cause crime, it did not stop it either. (34) The world of public debate in Canada in the 1850s was sufficiently intimate that critics mined each other's works for examples or conclusions that could be quoted and exploited with cheerful disregard of their original ideological intent. For example, one of the senior judges adopted the unschooled vagrant children as a personal crusade. Not only was Mr. Justice Hagarty much quoted by others, he had a public forum in addresses to grand juries and in the press. His stature was such that no one could seriously impugn his motives; and his conclusions, based on the incidence of juvenile crime and nonattendance at school, seemed harder still to contradict. (35) While other jurists earnestly criticized existing provisions for coping with street arabs, (36) Judge Hagarty was the most articulate: "an ulcer is eating into the vitals of our social system in the shape of crowds of people growing up in neglect and ignorance, rapidly ripening into crime, too many of them destined to form the chief population hereafter of our goals and Penitentiaries." (37)

Thus, despite what seemed its obvious centrality in the debate over the vagrant children, the issue of schooling played an equivocal role. On the one hand, as the extension and elaboration of urban school systems in the next decade contrived to ensure that more children stayed in school longer, vagrancy or "not attending school" quickly passed from being evidence of misfortune to being an offence. At the same time, doubt mounted as to the capacity of the common school to encompass the vagrant children in their poverty, unruliness, and lack of parental care. (38) The presence of the street arabs, with their potential for demoralization and redemption, seemed to mock the facile rhetoric of reformers. Their capacity for exaggeration, fed by a romantic optimism and longing to share the trials as well as triumphs of the age of improvement, tempted social critics to extravagant estimates of the problem. Special school census returns temporarily at least allayed the worst fears of mass numbers of unschooled and unoccupied youngsters. (39) But so long as school promoters, and their critics, clung to the ideal of the common school—that all children of school age, not regularly employed, ought to be in school and until such time constitute "a public blot, disgrace and danger" (40)—the question of the vagrant children simmered below the surface of municipal affairs.

While philanthropists and school promoters cherished their emotional and ideological investment in the equation of ignorance and crime, jurors, judges, and prison inspectors publicized the grim reality that faced juveniles once embroiled with the law. Diatribes on the necessity for classification of prisoners and proposals for the more humane treatment of juveniles had become commonplace by midcentury. (41) However, the 1850s brought a new shrillness to the debate. Despite the odd suspicion that "the march of refined benevolence has converted our prisons into palaces," (42) a chronic lack of funds had combined with population pressures to reduce conditions in many local jails to visible chaos. (43) The irregularities and brutality in the provincial penitentiary reached sufficiently scandalous proportions to require a public inquiry. (44) The commissioners appointed in 1849 in effect provided an administrative blueprint and rationale for the Canadian penal system. The presence of a leading politician and journalist—George Brown, publisher of the Toronto *Globe*—as secretary to the commission, and its driving force, helped transform the intimate debate of the necessarily few informed and concerned penal reformers into a subject of public discussion. Prison discipline became fashionable. Thus much of the enthusiasm and impatience of midcentury Canadian social critics focused on adapting ideas current among British and American prison reformers to what were increasingly seen to be intolerable abuses.

The place of reformation in the hierarchy of prison objectives lingered as an issue among English Canadian social critics into the 1860s. Rooted in assumptions about human nature, both psychological and theological, mingled with ideals of social organization, attitudes on prison reform revealed ideological affinities that blurred more conventional political and social categories. The *Globe,* in its impatience, struck the dominant chord, feeling it "not necessary in these days to discuss what should be the ends of prison discipline. . . . All civilized governments . . . now avow . . . the one great end of all secondary punishments should be the reformation of the criminal, and that this can only be effected by implanting habits of industry and religious and moral principles." (45) George Brown's dual role as political and prison reformer assured that this essentially liberal view carried strong political overtones. (46) However, support could come from unlikely quarters. The die-hard Tory Anglican Church, in its official paper, endorsed liberal prison reform while carefully pointing out that this did not entail sympathy with the corresponding political sentiments. (47) On the other hand, the Methodist *Christian Guardian* revealed the tendency of a theological pessimism as well as a keen appreciation of property in its repudiation of "the view of those who say that the principal end of punishment is the *reformation* of the criminal. We believe the principal end of punishment is to *punish* the offender as a warning to others, and a means of maintaining the authority of the law." (48)

"The youthful delinquent" provided Canadian reformers with a popular enthusiasm but one that, despite its acknowledged priority, proved a contentious issue. Much of the theoretical discussion of juvenile reform with which Canadians were familiar was premised on a distinction between neglected and destitute children and criminal children. Both classes needed care; but the reforming enterprise was seen to hinge on separate institutional arrangements appropriate to each. Unfortunately, while the progressivism of the reformers' analysis rested on precisely this refinement in classification, the perspective of penal reform itself provoked a confusion between the two. Perhaps because they read about crime, rather than lived amongst it, the problem assumed specially harrowing proportions in the imaginations of Canadians inflamed by the modest evidence of their own cities, slums, and dangerous classes. This did not seem the moment to define too narrowly the interests of penal reform. Thus the Penitentiary Commissioners in 1849 recommended a House of Refuge for the Reformation of Juvenile Delinquents to consist of two, strictly separate departments with a similar discipline combining education, labour, and healthful exercise: one for children convicted of crime; the other "for children whose parents or guardians, by vagrancy or vicious conduct, are unwilling or incapable of exercising proper care and discipline over them; and for children whose parents and guardians make complaint to the proper authority, that from the incorrigible conduct of such children they are unable to control them." (49) These latter children, who could be committed by any two justices of the peace or city magistrates "on a case being shown," would be under the supervision of the managers of the institution until their majority, eligible to be apprenticed "to learn such trades or other employments as in their [the managers'] estimation will be most conducive to their reformation and amendment."

It was a fine line that would separate those two departments, and the urgency for reformation appropriate to the class of criminal children cast a harsh light on those whose bleak prospects constituted their major offence. The distinction in states between *neglected* and *criminal* in effect translated as *potentially* vs. *actually* criminal. From the reformers' point of view, the neglect and destitution from which these children suffered stemmed not so much from a want of material resources as of the exercise of proper parental authority and the virtues of order, diligence, and obedience on which the social fabric depended. They were destitute, as they were ignorant, of that experience of restraint so necessary to the development of moral character and without which a man's social and personal life would remain mired in an anarchy of indulgence. Sensuality, which the undisciplined irregular habits of the street arabs so disturbingly exemplified, represented in the lexicon of middle-class morality "the grave of all social progress. A sensual man is a mere animal. Sensuality is the greatest enemy to social progress." (50) Thus reformers could believe simultaneously in the inevitable degradation of the neglected children and in their redemption and a new moral order in society. "If the class of neglected children who, left to the natural course of things, will grow up lawless and depraved, and ripe for the commission of every crime, could only be taken care of and placed under influences favourable to their becoming reputable and useful members of society, it stands to reason that, the source from which our criminal population is constantly recruited being dried up, there would be vastly fewer criminals, and a great diminution of crime and of the trouble, anxiety, and expense, of which it is the fruitful cause." (51)

Moreover, the extent to which even those juveniles charged and convicted of identifiable "crimes" were *criminals* seemed troublesomely unclear. Jurors especially nibbled at the edge of questioning the concept of criminality as applied to juveniles, particularly "the unthinking boy and the young girl, untainted by the germ of immorality, incarcerated for the first time and perhaps for some reckless freak or trifling technical offence." (52) Stealing goods valued at sixpence, (53) or finding money in the street and keeping some—such "pilfering" could seem not inappropriate to childhood and quite unrelated to the adult offence denoted by the legal charge of larceny. (54) Undoubtedly the central place given to the reformation and regeneration of criminals in new theories of penal discipline inspired midcentury social reformers to invest financially and emotionally in the elaboration of prison systems. At the same time, however, the very centrality of reformation, once glibly adopted, forced reformers to clarify what, in fact, the offence was: to probe into the nature of criminal behaviour beyond its technical labelling.

In the context of juvenile reform, issues of culpability, punishment, and regeneration were both blurred and sharpened as the sentimentalism endemic to the Victorian era muddied the analytically critical distinction between the unfortunate and the criminal. The shallow complacency and emotional self-indulgence that could mirror optimism and self-confidence in the Victorian mentality provide the stuff of nineteenth-century popular culture including reform tracts. Stock figures of little match girls and chimney sweeps mark a particular strain in the popular imagination of the period; at first dependent on English and American reprints, Canadians in time created their own versions. (55) Orphans and waifs were irresistible subjects for the adjectives "poor," "little," "unfortunate," and "blameless." Their innocence was clearly emotionally as well as theologically satisfying. "The child who has never learnt the meaning of sin; the thoughtless youth who has strayed for the first time from the paths of honesty; the frail girl who has been taught to pilfer from her earliest years—perhaps by her mother" (56)—such images punctuate the discussion of juvenile reform. (57) And although much of this sentimentality served as mere sugar-coating, the very pervasiveness of the pathetic image tempted reformers to cast both their arguments and analyses in terms that blunted— and in some instances confused—their purpose. In effect, prison reformers created for themselves a complex and ambiguous figure of a blameless child who is nevertheless guilty. (58)

Moreover, the figure of the hapless child was intimately linked to that of the family. A belief in the capacity as well as the necessity for education and training sustained the reform impulse. The family and the home—in the sense that they represented the primary socializing experience—were central to this process. The sentimentalizing of neglected children and their absent or inadequate home life masked a profound optimism about the possibilities for reforming children by altering their environment. While these mid-Victorian reformers did indeed anchor their analysis of social problems firmly in personal character, nevertheless, character before adulthood was pliable. Reformer's logic made the solution seem self-evident. "The radical source of juvenile depravity is the want of healthful home influences. To many of the vagrant children . . . the idea of parental authority, or domestic restraint, is associated with drunkenness, brutal violence, or profanity. Fear has been developed in the place of the natural affections of childhood; and the most potent element for their reclamation is to be looked for in such kindly influences as are calculated to awaken the dormant affections natural to youth." (59)

Arrangements to mobilize "kindly influences" were themselves dominated by the home/family image. Nineteenth-century reformers created social institutions as compensatory agencies. They devised a gradation of institutions from schools to prisons to complement, supplement, and, *in extremis,* to substitute for, the family/home experience they regarded as seminal. As reformers debated the issue of juvenile delinquency, differences of opinion between the promoters of the reformatory and its critics were rooted in alternative and shifting ideas of the nature of family relationships and their appropriate institutional analogue. Thus two questions underlie much of reform discussion in this period. First: When is a family not a family? If "the evil influence of wicked parents" is viewed as "the greatest evil to which these poor children are exposed," (60) when can one justifiably remove children from their natural parents? (61) Secondly: When is a nonfamily a family? What are its minimal requirements, emotional, physical, and educational; and do these change with the age and stage of the child?

One of the strengths and weaknesses of the family metaphor by midcentury stemmed from a superficial simplicity of roles: a family seemed to comprise parents and children. Thus, whatever agency assumed the parental role—the school, the prison, the state—the prerogatives of authority and responsibility were axiomatic. Similarly with the dependent. When the idea of special institutional arrangements for juveniles was first bruited, existing legal definitions suggested that all under 21 years were nonadult, therefore "youthful

offenders" and, in the paradigm of the family, children. (62)
Experience of the reformatory prompted criticism of its operation,
support for alternative arrangements, and finally its reform. But
this debate merely confirmed the original premise: it was universally
hoped that, so altered, these new institutions would constitute the
home experience so essential to reformation. Experience of the
reformatory did, however, force a more incisive definition of the
clientele and their appropriate environment.

In the boom years of the 1850s the campaign for juvenile reform
was led by the two Inspectors of the Provincial Penitentiary. Osten-
sibly sharing similar liberal political sympathies, they nevertheless
articulated widely divergent views of the scale and nature of the
problem and its remedy. Following the initiative of the 1849
proposals, an obvious course was the establishment of a juvenile
reformatory. Andrew Dickson so effectively identified himself with
this proposal he was appointed warden of the first juvenile prison
in 1858. (63) Dickson built his argument for the reformatory on
the rhetoric of political economy and a thorough familiarity with
the work in American houses of refuge. (64) Since, along with
cities and social advancement generally, Britain and the United
States had experienced large-scale juvenile crime, Canada's future
seemed clear: if the problem did not seem critical now, it would
soon become so. At the moment, however, criminals were clearly
less prevalent than the poorer classes; hence Dickson's appeal was
essentially philanthropic. He envisaged an omnibus institution:
"To the unprotected and homeless, it would be a place of shelter;
to the tempted and friendless, a refuge; to the orphan and wander-
ing, a home; to the idler and vagrant, a Work-house; to the erring,
a House of Correction; to the innocent and indigent, protection;
to the vagrant and ignorant, a School; to the unregenerate, a
Temple; to the miserable, an Asylum; to the guilty and criminal,
a reformation; and to all, a place of industrial and agricultural
improvement." More specifically, the new institution was to be
defined by the needs of its clientele: Youth. "The period bordering
on adolescence shows most evidently a greater tendency to crime
than any other. This obviously arises from the power and energy
of the passions, and as yet the defective cultivation of the mind
and training of the morals." His blueprint for discipline envisaged
four hours of school work, under conditions of "strict silence,"

behind an essential detention wall, since "there can be no probability that persons who have been free from restraint during their whole life, idle, ignorant, vicious and even criminal, will quietly remain and industriously toil on, with the hope it will do them good in the end." Ideally the educative and penal aspects of reformation could be balanced under the rubric of a *home:* a place "to which in after life they will look back as to a home, with many happy and grateful feelings, and from which they may be sent forth as useful apprentices to the trades, or as reformed members to their friends and society."

While Andrew Dickson's promotion of the reformatory grew out of his endorsement of the values and problems of an essentially urban milieu, Wolfred Nelson argued in an intellectual tradition rooted in a stratified, hierarchical society. Nelson, exiled as a *Patriot* leader after the Lower Canadian Rebellion of 1837, shared with the Roman Catholic chaplain of the penitentiary a deep suspicion of any institutionalization of reformation. (65) Although passionately concerned to improve the conditions of the poor and unfortunate classes (model houses for the labouring classes were his hobby-horse), Nelson denied the necessity of a reformatory. The few genuinely criminal children, he thought, could be housed in separate cells in existing penal institutions. Vagrant children should be in the country on model farms operated by committed, Christian philanthropists, not put in public institutions that were inherently nonreforming and taught trades that would lure them to the city "where lies the cause of perdition of the best educated youths." Distinctions that Dickson would muddy, Nelson would preserve; not only between classes of problem youths, but between institutional arrangements as well. In Nelson's view, a prison was to punish. A nonpenal, publically supported penal institution, such as a house of refuge, might well "hold out inducement to the poor, idle and immoral, to cast their ill-bred offspring on the State for support and sustenance." Moreover, it would be precisely the home-like qualities of a juvenile prison that would be self-defeating: it would encourage recidivism. In Nelson's vision, the youthful offender "becomes attached to it as a home; the plasticity of his young mind leads him readily to assimilate his ideas with all that surrounds him, the very restraint he is placed under loses its irksomeness, and becomes congenial with his feelings, and thus ultimately and insensibly, he cherishes his abode. . . . Under

such influences is it at all marvellous that he should ere long entertain a desire to return to a place in which he has passed his happiest
years."

The liberal climate of the 1850s in English Canada proved intol-
erant of the conservatism that animated Nelson's critique of reform
institutions. Thus his distinctions between criminal and punishment
vs. vagrant and reform were lost in the genuine enthusiasm that
greeted the establishment of two reformatory prisons, one on a
marshy island in French Canada, the other isolated on Georgian Bay
in military barracks remaining from the defence of the upper Great
Lakes in the War of 1812. Despite the unprepossessing locations,
reformatory boasters could herald the openings as "a new era in the
history of Canadian penal institutions; a new triumph of intelligence and Christianity over the wickedness and barbarism of the
world." (66) The reformatory's promoters had shown an uncertain,
but nevertheless real appreciation of the "peculiarities of youth,"
an awareness of youth or adolescence (a term they used occasionally
but inconsistently) as a stage in development especially susceptible
to both distracting and reforming influences. (67) This insight was
countered from the beginning by the judicial practise of sending
offenders up to 21 years of age to the reformatories. The need to
classify, which had initiated the movement for a juvenile prison,
was thus made more acute by its founding, for in the more intimate
world of the reformatory the distance between 10 and 21 could be
as great as that between 15 and 40. In addition, although the
government had indicated its intention to introduce a bill enabling
municipalities to establish reformatory schools—in response to the
vagrant children—no provision was forthcoming. (68) Thus the new
institutions inherited the confusion between the criminal and
vagrant classes that ambitious and well-intentioned reformers found
so tempting.

The dangers of such confusions, compounded by unrealistic expectations, were made painfully obvious in the first year at Isle-aux-
Noix Reformatory. Warden Dickson was relieved of his duties under
scandalous circumstances following mass escapes of older prisoners
and charges of immoral conduct (owing to the presence of both
male and female prisoners), and excessive brutality. Ironically
Dr. Wolfred Nelson assumed control of the institution, temporarily,

before returning to his post as chairman of the newly appointed Board of Inspectors of Asylums, Prisons and Public Charities.

For the next decade, the inspectors wrestled to refine the role of the reformatories. Having once been established, these institutions could not be abandoned because so much more than money was invested in their capacity to reform not only their inmates but society at large. (69)

The isolation of youth as a particular stage of development was intimately linked to the modifications in traditional penal discipline around which reformatory prisons were designed. However, the presence of youth of all ages and conditions aggravated the tension between the inescapable reality of the reformatory as a prison, (70) and the reformers' eagerness to continue to respond to the inmates in the child role associated with the family/home image that they cherished. One tactic was to arbitrarily redefine the reformatory as a "place of refuge and of education." (71) By contrast to the pathetic condition of neglected children still at large and of the youngsters who were sent to local jails, the circumstances in the reformatories could still seem "a blessed provision . . . which thus rescues the hapless street arabs from certain ruin." (72)

More effective, however, was the move to again try to distinguish between neglected and potentially criminal children, for whom some less costly and less harsh regime would suffice, and the criminals who needed the rigour of penal discipline. To economy-minded citizens in the straitened circumstances of the early 1860s, one of the reformatory's chief liabilities was its cost. (73) It was increasingly the view of the prison inspectors that the street arabs for whom "admirable and costly common Schools are perfectly useless," needed to be in "Homes" or "Ragged schools." These were to be run by voluntary agencies "for the benefit of destitute and neglected pauper children" who might be, variously, vicious and incorrigible, vagrant, without parents or protectors, "or children whose parents or natural protectors, from poverty or other causes, are unable or unwilling to afford them that education which they require and to which they are entitled." (74) Owing in large part to the publicity given by the prison inspectors, the ideas of "Homes" for nonorphaned, non-criminal children received immediate and substantial support. The publicists for Boys and Girls' Homes (in the *Globe's* opinion, such

an attractive name, suggesting the family principle) (75) appro-
priated much of the sentimental rhetoric that, a decade earlier, had
been used to promote the reformatory. (76) However, the scope
of these philanthropies was dependent not only on voluntary contributions but on the voluntary attendance of the children. The
prison inspectors had visualized a more permanent enterprise. The
authority of judges and city recorders to commit destitute and
neglected children for certain limited periods seemed essential. In
their view, "Homes" were to fill a crucial intermediate link "between
our Common Schools and our juvenile reformatories. While they
partake, to some extent, of the character of both, they are entirely
distinct, and properly distinct from both, and form in fact their
natural and necessary supplement." (77)

Under the guise of the industrial school movement, city school
trustees, philanthropists, and municipal politicians campaigned to
secure for the magistrates the power to sentence neglected and
vagrant children. Pressure particularly from the school authorities—
increasingly recognizing the impossibility of their being included
in the common school—helped clarify the justification for forcibly
detaining the street arabs who were not yet "criminals": the law
should "deal with their ignorant and disordered condition as itself
a species of crime." (78) The advent of compulsory school attendance
in 1871 and the Industrial School Act in 1874 temporarily halted the
debate; but since neither was acted on, they did not substantially
alter its dimensions. The problem of a class of children, plainly too
poor and too undisciplined to be in school, remained.

The relative failure of the "homes" movement to achieve the
status of an alternative institutional solution to the problem of
juvenile delinquency left the reformatory with its heterogeneous
population. Narrowing the age range seemed to provide an answer.
When exactly was the period of youth, the inspectors wondered.
Some inmates were clearly too young, were indeed "children" (and
conveniently also the same ones most likely to be delinquents
through poverty, not having had time to become more vicious);
others were clearly too old for the reformatory's primarily educative
approach. (79) The older prisoners were easier to define. The
inspectors and wardens repeatedly urged stiffer regulations for the
reformatory, after the fiasco in Lower Canada in 1860: no one was
to be sentenced over the age of 16 years for by 21 he was a "full-

grown man." (80) Moreover, the older prisoners were always the
ones who tried to escape, who exerted unfavourable influences on
the younger ones, and brought the reformatory into disrepute. (81)

Defining the earliest age was more difficult. Here the absence of
alternative provisions kept alive reformers' dreams of justifying the
reformatory as a "home." The warden and chaplains repeatedly complained about the provision of the Act Respecting Young Offenders
(1875) which provided the option of a two-year sentence on summary
conviction for anyone under 16 years. (82) The average age of those
sentenced under these provisions was 13, "nearly all drawn from
haunts of vice, many of them orphans or half-orphans." (83) Urging mandatory indefinite sentences, reformers drew an analogy to
their own circumstances: children need time to grow up—a longer
period of dependency—the poor outcast just as well as the judge's
son who is kept "at school and college until he is twenty, nor does
he permit him, in all that time, to be from under his own careful
eye." (84) One need not be too precise about the year. The *Globe*
thought 17 was the age at which parents stop exercising control over
their children. (85) The Protestant chaplain thought 16 the earliest
time by which a youth might have gained some steadiness of character. (86) However, the strategy was clear. The reformatory would
be justified by what had come to seem a natural period of dependency between the state of childhood (under 12 years) and adulthood
(over 18 or 20).

When, with Confederation in 1867, the Province of Ontario
assumed the direction of the reformatory prison, the new inspector
responded to the youthfulness of the reformatory population by
declaring it to be "a Reform and Industrial School rather than a
place of compulsory detention for criminals." (87) In the early
1870s, it seemed only commonplace to distinguish between youthful
criminals and "the army of children known as 'Homeless and
Destitute,' 'Neglected and Abandoned,' 'Orphans and Vagrants,' "—
they, along with anyone under 12 years of age, belonged in municipal industrial schools. Moreover, criminality could be defined more
narrowly still: "unless a lad has committed some grave offence
against the law," he should not be sent to the reformatory. (88)
Such a rational apportioning of social classes and age groups was,
however, premature. The onset of an economic recession and a
general hardening of attitudes amongst now complacent reformers

contributed to the failure of cities to establish the industrial schools. Moreover, with a rising crime rate among under 16 year olds (now its natural point of comparison), the effectiveness of the reformatory was in doubt. (89) Operating dramatically below capacity owing to a lack of confidence on the part of the judges in its operation, the reformatory could be rejuvenated by empowering police magistrates to sentence youngsters to the reformatory if no other agency was able to respond to their delinquent condition. Formal cause would have to be shown, but once again "the gravity of the offence committed" was not to be the issue. "Some crime that brings him within the reach of the law" would suffice to send a boy to the reformatory "if his parents have lost all restraining influence over him, or perhaps exercise their influence to his moral injury, and if the boy's habits and associates are likely to lead him on to the commission of more serious crime." (90)

The intimacy that bound a life style of poverty to the conception of juvenile delinquency could, it was felt, be best appreciated by the magistrates who "must acquire a more perfect knowledge of young offenders in cities and towns, and their surrounding influences, than it is possible for any other judge to obtain. For it is only by careful enquiry and examination into the circumstances connected with the commission of crime by juvenile offenders, the knowledge of the temptations to which they are exposed, the influence of their homes, and character of their parents and associates, that an intelligent conclusion can be arrived at, or a just sentence passed upon them. The condonation of some petty misdemeanor particularly in the case of the very young offender, may prove to be fatal, where the lad is allowed to go back to vicious haunts and depraved company, undeterred from further crime by experience of its punishment." (91)

By 1875, with the magistrates' help, the reformatory was again the focus of reform enthusiasm. Its population exploded. Seventy-one youngsters were admitted in the year 1874–1875, boosting the total number from 139 to 173. Despite official reservations about very young inmates, the trend to ensuring the care of young delinquents for the whole of their formative period of growth was clear. Sixty-one, or 35 percent, of the 173 inmates in 1875 were 12 years of age or younger when admitted, a jump from the 29 percent of the previous year. A new institution, the central prison, had opened to deal with incorrigibles and those unsusceptible to reformatory influences. The reformatory itself was to be transformed: what had been for too long offensively a prison for youth would be made "attractive and, in the true sense of the word home-like." (92)

As modern commentators on juvenile delinquency have observed, the distinction between a "neglected" and a "delinquent" child is a difficult and often arbitrary one. (93) The confusion between morals, welfare, and the enforcement of each that coloured mid-Victorian reformers' perception of the problem of youth persisted, to be codified by the next generation in the "progressive" but ambiguous legislation associated with the juvenile court. But the experience of the mid-century years had been crucial in formulating the concept of juvenile delinquency. (94) At first with impatience, later with determination, Canadian reformers responded to the disordered conditions of urban life as roadblocks and unwanted side-effects to the social advancement to which they aspired. They devised institutional substitutes for a version of family life that they considered indispensable to moral and social development. In so doing, Victorian Canadians acknowledged a degree of public responsibility for two classes of dependents: the lowest, vagrant class in society that would be systematically stifled by eliminating its future, and young people who, lacking the degree of care and restraint that reformers out of their own experience had come to regard as normal, would be maintained in a stage of dependency at public expense. By 1875 the reformatory was, in effect, the high school for the lowest classes.

NOTES

1. See F. Musgrove, *Youth and the Social Order* (Bloomington, 1963), chaps. 3 and 4. Much of the recent work on adolescence by American historians has tended to emphasize its peculiar appropriateness to nineteenth-century American social experience: see John and Virginia Demos, "Adolescence in Historical Perspective," *Journal of Marriage and the Family* (November 1969): 632–38; Joseph F. Kett, "Adolescence and Youth in Nineteenth Century America," *Journal of Interdisciplinary History* 2 (1971): 283-98; David Bakan, "Adolescence in America, from idea to social fact," *Daedalus* (Fall 1971): 979–95.

2. For an anthology of articles on the intellectual climate of mid-nineteenth-century Canada, see W. L. Morton, ed., *Shield of Achilles* (To-

ronto, 1970); also J. M. S. Careless, *The Union of the Canadas: The Growth of Canadian Institutions, 1841–57* (Toronto, 1967).

3. J. M. S. Careless, "Mid-Victorian Liberalism in Central Canadian Newspapers, 1850–1867," *Canadian Historical Review* 31 (1950): 221–36; *Brown of the Globe,* 2 vols. (Toronto, 1959–1963); Robert Kelley, *Transatlantic Persuasion: The Liberal-Democratic Mind in the Age of Gladstone* (New York, 1969).

4. For the impact of the Irish famine immigration generally, see G. Tucker, *Canadian Commercial Revolution* (Toronto, 1961); Kenneth Duncan, "Irish Famine Immigration and the Social Structure of Canada West," *Canadian Review of Sociology & Anthropology* (February 1965), pp. 19–40. For Toronto specifically, see Peter Goheen, *Victorian Toronto* (Chicago, 1970).

5. Richard B. Splane, *Social Welfare in Canada, 1791–1893* (Toronto, 1965).

6. For an illuminating collection of documents on early welfare activity, see Edith Firth, *The Town of York,* 2 vols. (Toronto, 1962–1967).

7. *Globe,* June 21, 1848; also ibid., 2.

8. J. Sheridan Hogan, *Canada, an essay* (Toronto, 1855), p. 63.

9. "Report of the Commissioners on the Subject of Prisons, Penitentiaries, etc.," *Journal of the House of Assembly of Upper Canada,* 1836, app. 71. The report's author, Dr. Charles Duncombe, was an American-born reformer who after the abortive rebellion of 1837 returned to the United States.

10. Egerton Ryerson, "The Importance of education to a manufacturing and a free people," *Journal of Education of Upper Canada* 1 (October 1848): 300.

11. For a general review, see Splane, *Social Welfare;* the essential provisions are to be found in 39 George III c. 3 (1799); 9 Vic. c. 70 (1846); 14 & 15 Vic. c. 11 (1851).

12. A twenty-year campaign by the officers of the Protestant Orphans Home and other charitable institutions to prevent parents from removing children from their custody succeeded in 1873 with "An Act to amend the Act respecting Apprentices and Minors," *Statutes of Ontario,* 35 Vic. c. 17.

13. *Report of the Trustees of the House of Industry for 1852* (Toronto, 1853). At the annual meeting, January 19, 1853, the managers were exonerated by an investigation into charges by Roman Catholic board members of discrimination against Catholic families. The Roman Catholic authorities subsequently developed a complex of orphanage, poor house, and hospital around the House of Providence.

14. Ryerson maintained that "separate schools were designed for . . . places where the then strong (more so than now) and often exaggerated, feelings between the Irish Protestants and Roman Catholics did not permit them to unite in the school education of their children" (*Special Report on the Separate School Provisions of the School Law*

of Upper Canada . . . [Toronto, 1858], p. 14). The political ramifications of the separate school issue have been thoroughly canvassed
in J. S. Moir, *Church and State in Canada West: Three Studies in the
Relation of Denominationalism and Nationalism, 1841–1867* (Toronto,
1959) and Franklin A. Walker, *Catholic Education and Politics in
Upper Canada* (Toronto, 1957).

15. Hon. John Elmsley, Toronto Board of School Trustees, "Minutes,"
    December 6, 1847.

16. Report of the Annual Meeting, Toronto House of Industry, *British
    Colonist,* February 4, 1851; "First Annual Report of the Board of
    Inspectors of Asylums, Prisons and Public Charities," Canada, *Sessional
    Paper* [hereafter cited as *S.P.*], no. 24 (1861).

17. *Globe,* July 20, 1850.

18. "Draft Circular for the preliminary meeting advertising Orphans Home
    and Female Aid Society, Toronto, 9 June, 1851," Toronto Public
    Library.

19. Draft report on Free Schools, Board of Common School Trustees,
    Globe, March 8, 1851.

20. J. Jerald Bellomo, "Upper Canadian Attitudes Towards Crime and
    Punishment (1832–1851)," *Ontario History* 64 (1972): 10–26.

21. See especially the poetry of Alexander McLachlan (1818–1896) "the
    Burns of Canada": *Poems* (Toronto, 1856); *Lyrics* (1858); *The Emi-
    grant and other poems* (1861). For a general discussion of the juxta-
    position of the agrarian myth and the commercial frontier, see Michael
    Cross "Dark Druidical Groves" (Ph.D. diss., University of Toronto,
    1968).

22. Egerton Ryerson, "A Lecture on the Social Advancement of Canada,"
    Journal of Education 2 (December 1849): 184.

23. Memorial to the Legislature, Municipal Council of the United Coun-
    ties of York and Peel, *Journal of the Board of Arts and Manufactures*
    5 (1865): 59.

24. T. C. Keefer, *Philosophy of Railroads* (Montreal, 1850), pp. 8–9.

25. *Brown's Toronto General Directory* (Toronto, 1856), p. xxi. The
    religious press was fond of bemoaning the vice and moral depravity
    of commercial towns; see especially the Anglican *Church,* April 14,
    April 21, May 12, 1853.

26. *Globe,* January 5, 1855.

27. Special Report of Andrew Dickson, March 10, 1853, "Annual Report
    of the Inspectors of the Provincial Penitentiary," *Journal of the Legis-
    lative Assembly,* 1852–1853, app. I.I.I.

28. In its report on the *Prisons and Reformatories of the United States
    and Canada* (Albany, 1867), the Prison Association of New York com-
    mented on the exhausting round of religious observance and promo-
    tion that contributed to the pervasive religious influence which char-
    acterized the Provincial Penitentiary at Kingston (p. 195). By contrast,
    the report was severely critical of the degrading physical punishment

that, it felt, counteracted the operation of moral and religious agencies (p. 166); the incredibly cramped cell accommodation, which was the smallest encountered in the survey (pp. 102–4); and the severity of the silent discipline (p. 175).

29. Separate Report of T. J. O'Neill, "Annual Report of the Board of Inspectors of Asylums, Prisons and Public Charities," *S.P.*, no. 14 (1865).

30. Egerton Ryerson, "The Spirit in which the present educational movement should be directed" (1852) in *Historical and Other Educational Papers and Documents,* ed. J. George Hodgins, 3:27.

31. *Globe,* December 11, 1851.

32. Advertisement of the Toronto Teachers' Association, *Globe,* October 1, 1850.

33. Reply of the Grand Jury to Mr. Justice Hagarty in *Documentary History of Education in Ontario,* ed. J. George Hodgins, 20:73–74.

34. Rev. J. M. Bruyere to Ryerson, January 27, *Dr. Ryerson's Letters in reply to the Attacks of Foreign Ecclesiastics* (Toronto, 1857), p. 81; A Protestant, *Statistics of the Common Schools . . . in a series of Seven Letters to Hon. John A. Macdonald* (Toronto, 1857), p. 25; Adam Townley, *Seven Letters on the non-religious Common School System of Canada and the U.S.* (Toronto, 1853), pp. 12–13.

35. For characteristic charges to the Grand Jury by Hagarty, see *Globe,* January 9, 1857; October 12, 1858. For the *Globe's* rebuttal, October 14, 1858; January 4, 1866; February 27, 1868.

36. Hon. Chief Justice W. H. Draper, *Globe,* November 13, 1858; October 12, 1859; "Copies of Reports of the Judges of the Superior Courts for Upper Canada and Presentments of Grand Juries and other papers on the Subject of Gaol," *Journal of the Legislative Assembly,* 1856, app. 34.

37. *Globe,* January 9, 1857.

38. Compare Thomas Henning, "The Applicability of our Educational System to the Social Condition of Large Cities," *Canadian Journal,* 2d ser. 3 (September 1858): 422–37, and *Globe,* August 8, 1861, favouring the inclusion of vagrant children in the common school, with the negative argument, *Globe,* October 14, 1858, August 6, 1863, December 27, 1865, February 27, 1868; and *Leader,* July 22, 1862.

39. *Annual Report of the Local Superintendent of the Public Schools of the City of Toronto* for 1862, 1863.

40. *Annual Report of the Normal, Model, Grammar and Common Schools,* 1863, p. 6.

41. *Journal of the House of Assembly of Upper Canada,* 1836, app. 71; "Second Report of the Commissioners appointed to inquire into the Provincial Penitentiary . . . ," *Journal of the Legislative Assembly,* 1849, app. B.B.B.B.B.

42. *British Colonist,* January 9, 1849.

43. *Journal of the Legislative Assembly,* 1856, app. 34. For the Toronto-York county problem especially, see presentments of the Grand Juries, *Globe,* January 19, 1850, November 6, 1854; editorials, October 12, 1854, July 14, 1855.
44. "First Report of the Commissioners appointed to inquire . . . ," *Journal of the Legislative Assembly,* 1849, app. B.B.B.B.B.
45. *Globe,* July 20, 1850.
46. Brown's role on the Commission contributed substantially to the bitter enmity between himself and John A. Macdonald, political leader of the opposing Liberal-Conservative forces. See J. M. S. Careless, *Brown of the Globe* 1 (Toronto, 1960).
47. *Church,* September 1, 1853.
48. *Christian Guardian,* December 26, 1860.
49. "Second Report of the Commissioners . . . ," *Journal of the Legislative Assembly,* 1849, app. B.B.B.B.B. In 1850 and 1851, bills were introduced to provide for two Houses of Correction for Juvenile Offenders: in both years they were dropped.
50. Egerton Ryerson, "Elements of Social Progress; a speech reported by the London *Prototype*," *Journal of Education* 13 (1860): 51.
51. *Globe,* July 11, 1863.
52. Ibid., January 19, 1850.
53. Ibid., April 13, 1850.
54. Ibid., July 5, 1853. See also the separate reports of J. M. Ferres, "Annual Report of the Board of Inspectors of Prisons, Asylums, etc. for 1861, 1862," *S.P.,* no. 19 (1862), *S.P.,* no. 66 (1863).
55. *Globe,* December 27, 1868, January 26, 1869.
56. "Address on the subject of Prison Discipline," by George Brown, *Globe,* April 30, 1850.
57. See especially the "Annual Report of the Board of Inspectors of Asylums, Prisons, etc. for 1862," separate report by J. M. Ferres, *S.P.,* no. 66 (1863).
58. In their preliminary report for 1860, the newly appointed Board of Inspectors characterized the reformatory population as "these poor children, orphans for the most part, whose greatest crime is, not unfrequently, that of an unfortunate parentage" (*S.P.,* no. 32 [1860]). See also separate report of E. A. Meredith, *S.P.,* no. 19 (1862); and general report for 1865, *S.P.,* no. 6 (1866).
59. "Report of a meeting interested in the formation of an Industrial School, May 20, 1868," *Journal of Education* 21 (May 1868).
60. Mr. J. W. Gwynne, Charge to the Grand Jury, *Globe,* April 9, 1868.
61. By the mid-1860s, the frustration that moved the *Globe* (January 4, 1866) to contemplate extending the magistrates' powers prompted T. J. O'Neill in his separate report as prison inspector to argue, "It is clearly the duty of society to call on the State to supply, by legislation, to the truant vagrant child, that place which there is either no natural

parent to fill, or which the parent, by reason of his immorality or negligence, is incompetent to fill" (*S.P.,* no. 14 [1865]).

62. The years 7, 14, and 21 were defining ages under common law. Children under 7 years were deemed absolutely incapable of crime; a child under 14 years was unlikely to be convicted on his own confession unless there was strong evidence "that he was perfectly conscious of the nature and malignity of the crime" (William Conway Keele, *The Provincial Justice or Magistrate's Manual,* 2d ed. [Toronto, 1843], pp. 129–30). Also Israel Lewis, *A Class Book for the Use of Common Schools and Families In the United Canadas, entitled Youth's Guard against Crime* (Kingston, 1844), pp. 20–21.

63. Established under "An Act for Establishing Prisons for Young Offenders," 20 Vic. c. 28 (1857).

64. Special report of Andrew Dickson, March 10, 1853, "Report of Inspectors of the Provincial Penitentiary," *Journal of the Legislative Assembly,* 1852–1853, app. I.I.I.

65. A general review of prison economics: an essay appendix to "Report on District and Other Prisons in Canada East," *Journal of the Legislative Assembly,* 1852–1853, app. H.H.; see also the report of the Roman Catholic Chaplain, "Report of the Inspectors of the Provincial Penitentiary," *Journal of the Legislative Assembly,* 1852–1853, app. I.I.I.

66. *Journal of the Legislative Assembly,* 1859, app. 29.

67. See Protestant Chaplain's report, *Journal of the Legislative Assembly,* 1854–1855, app. D.D.

68. Legislative Assembly, May 5, 1857, *Globe,* May 6, 1857.

69. Separate report of E. A. Meredith, *S.P.,* no. 19 (1862).

70. The incidence of punishment rose dramatically in the Penetanguishene Reformatory. In 1860, with a total population of 70 inmates, 55 under punishment consumed 271 meals of bread and water, and 7 inmates received a total of 60 lashes. In 1865, with a total population of 134, 89 under punishment had 1,643 meals of bread and water, and 35 inmates received 546 lashes.

71. Separate report of J. M. Ferres, *S.P.,* no. 19 (1862).

72. Separate report of T. J. O'Neill, *S.P.,* no. 14 (1865).

73. *Globe,* July 11, July 15, 1863.

74. Separate report of E. A. Meredith, *S.P.,* no. 19 (1862).

75. *Globe,* September 19, 1859.

76. See the Boys Home, *Annual Report* (Toronto, 1861ff); The Girls' Home and Public Nursery, *Annual Report* (Toronto, 1860ff).

77. Meredith, *S.P.,* no. 19 (1862); also General Report of the Board, *S.P.,* no. 6 (1866).

78. Rev. James Porter, "Child Neglect," 7th Annual Convention, Teachers' Association, 1867, *Journal of Education* 20 (October 1867); 165. Also the legislative petition of the Public School Board of the City of To-

ronto for an Industrial School Act, *14th Annual Report of the Local Superintendent of Schools . . . 1872*, pp. 120–21.

79. Report of the Warden, Penetanguishene Reformatory, *S.P.*, no. 66 (1863), and *Ontario S.P.*, no. 4 (1871–1872).

80. Ibid., *S.P.*, no. 39 (1864); General Report of the Board, *S.P.*, no. 14 (1865).

81. *Ontario S.P.*, no. 4 (1871–1872), reports by the warden and the inspector.

82. Report of the Warden, *S.P.*, no. 40 (1867–1868); *Ontario S.P.*, no. 13 (1868–1869).

83. *Ontario S.P.*, no. 6 (1870–1871).

84. Separate report of J. M. Ferres, *S.P.*, no. 66 (1863).

85. *Globe*, March 3, 1868.

86. *Ontario S.P.*, no. 2 (1872–1873).

87. *Ontario S.P.*, no. 6 (1870–1871).

88. *Ontario S.P.*, no. 2 (1872–1873).

89. *Ontario S.P.*, no. 4 (1871–1872), no. 2 (1874). The reformatory in 1872–1873 absorbed less than ten percent of the juvenile population committed to the common jails.

90. *Ontario S.P.*, no. 4 (1875).

91. *Ontario S.P.*, no. 2 (1874).

92. Ibid.

93. *Juvenile Delinquency in Canada:* The Report of the Department of Justice Committee on Juvenile Delinquency (Queen's Printer, 1967), §96, 109.

94. Ibid., §68–70, 138–40. Ontario legislation, The Children's Protection Act (1893) exemplified the interest of Canadian "progressives." See also, W. T. McGrath, ed., *Crime and Its Treatment in Canada* (Toronto, 1965) and Anthony M. Platt, *The Child Savers: The Invention of Delinquency* (Chicago, 1969).

5. EDUCATION AND THE METAPHOR OF THE FAMILY: THE UPPER CANADIAN EXAMPLE

In the middle of the nineteenth century, many promoters of education in Upper Canada also became advocates of an idealized concept of family life. Proponents of different concepts became involved in the question of how best to provide the advantages of family life for students who had to live away from home, and their debate centered on the nature of boarding halls. The question of how best to replace the family for adolescents away from home—and therefore of what the ideal family really was—are shown as central to the debate. The nature of the family, its duties and its relationship to other educational institutions, had become and would remain, basic components of Canadian educational ideology.

THE CONDITION of the family was a subject that much preoccupied school promoters in Upper Canada. Like educators in other times and places they blamed the weaknesses of the family for many social ills; at the same time they put forth an idealized portrait of domestic relations as a major hope for social progress. Besides the usual vague complaints and exaggerated hopes, they also had some very specific anxieties about the family, among them two that were clearly associated with the spread of formal schooling and that occurred in many parts of the United States as well as in Canada. The first was the recurring suspicion that some kinds of schools, especially those controlled increasingly by the state, were gradually undermining family authority. (1) The second, which is the subject

Alison Prentice is an assistant professor in the Department of History, Atkinson College, York University. This essay first appeared in The History of Education Quarterly *(Fall 1972).*

of this essay, was intimately related to the first and concerned the education of children and adolescents away from home. How could schools and colleges replace the authority, affection, and advice normally provided by families, for these absentees from the domestic fireside?

The need to send some children to school away from home posed an increasingly serious problem. The obvious answer to some educators was that despite their size, schools ought to imitate families. Indeed it is fairly clear that without the ability to see the schools and colleges that they founded as substitute families or households, many of the early school promoters would have thought their own creations dangerous both to the youth attending them and to society at large. It was the metaphor of the family (2) that made possible for such people the transition from the instruction of children at home, or in small household-like settings, to their schooling in institutions outside and often far away from relatives and friends.

Not all Upper Canadian educators thought that schools could successfully replace the family however. Mid-century discussions of the subject reveal the existence in fact of doubt and finally serious disagreement among school promoters whose basic attitudes were otherwise often very similar. What accounts for the differences of opinion and for the depth of feeling sometimes associated with them? The argument that I wish to develop here is that these debates were fundamentally related to changing conceptions of the ideal family. (3) As the ideal of the large patriarchal household, with its many public functions, gave way to that of the relatively small, democratic, and private family, educators saw schools and colleges in new ways. Or conversely, as they perceived or promoted what they believed to be essential changes in education, they were forced also to look at the family in a new light. It is impossible to say which was cause and which effect; changes in the conceptions of the ideal family and ideal education were interrelated and occurred over a long period of time, as different individuals and groups were gradually won over to new attitudes. (4) Both of course were tied to the disappearance of pre-industrial economic ways, to rapid population growth and urbanization; but then these in turn must have depended in part on shifts in ideas about family life and education that predisposed people to seek and accept a new social order.

I

To what extent did the traditional ideal of the family still persist
in early Upper Canada and what was this ideal? It is worthwhile
noting, first of all, that traditional attitudes and practices could
easily have survived in Upper Canada longer than in many parts
of the United States or Western Europe. The colony was first settled
by conservative fugitives from the American Revolution. It was
also tied by legislative union for twenty-seven crucial years in the
middle of the century to the conservative and Roman Catholic
province of Lower Canada (Quebec). Add to this the isolation from
change caused by pioneer conditions, the probable conservatism of
immigrants attracted to the colony, and the relative slowness of
economic development compared to that of many of the neighbouring states, and it is entirely plausible that in Upper Canada one
would find many vestiges of pre-industrial society.

For a definition of the traditional family, one must go to diaries
and letters. These suggest that many early nineteenth-century Upper
Canadians did not yet define the family as exclusively composed of
biologically related people. Peter Laslett has pointed out that in
pre-industrial Britain the word "family" was often used where most
twentieth-century speakers would use "household," that is, to denote
occupants of the same dwelling, (5) and it is not surprising that in
British colonies this use should have continued. Certainly households enlarged by the occupancy of people unrelated to the biological family occurred frequently, if only among those who could
afford to perpetuate such arrangements. Schoolmasters often lived
in the homes of their employers, as did apprentices, friends, and
servants of one type or another. Frequently also the living quarters
shared, as in one-room log houses, were extremely cramped. But to
what extent was the distinction between household and family, as
they are generally understood nowadays, still blurred?

Evidence that there was no absolute distinction even as late as
1846 may be found in a discussion of voter qualifications that took
place in that year? When asked if boarders were "householders"
under the school law, and thus qualified to participate in the election of school trustees, Upper Canada's Superintendent of Schools,
Egerton Ryerson, replied that they were not. "It appears to me

that a man is a householder within the meaning of the Act who rents any sort of house; but a boarder in a family forms part of that family, and cannot, I imagine, be a householder, merely because he has the exclusive occupation of a room." (6)

Further clues may be found in the use of the word "friends" during the period as an all-encompassing term to designate parents, guardians, and relatives, as well as dependent members of households. It was the students' friends who came to the annual exhibitions at John Strachan's grammar school in the 1820s. (7) Upper Canada College in the 1830s expected the friends of scholars to let the headmaster know when they planned to withdraw their charges from the school. (8) It was once again the friends of students who would be kept informed of breaches of discipline that occurred at the Upper Canada Academy in 1841. (9) Certainly some children were sponsored at school by people other than their parents, but it is also apparent that there was no absolute or final distinction between friends and family in Upper Canada during the first half of the century.

Many people expected that their way in the world would be made easier by friends and felt the lack when this was not the case. They also admitted that friends would occasionally be a burden. As one young teacher confided to Egerton Ryerson in 1849, there was little hope of getting a school in the city if one had "neither friends nor interest" there. (10) Another petitioner requested Ryerson's assistance in gaining admission to the newly formed provincial Normal School in 1850. Death had taken his friends, he apologised, hence the necessity of appealing to a stranger. Attendance at Normal School was going to be difficult for this teacher because he had to support an aged father and "a friend"; there were many others like him, he said, who "with want staring them in the face as well as their little families," could ill afford to take time out for special training. (11)

For a long time, the blurred line between family and friends, and the political and economic power of a network of certain notorious friends in the province, was a basic Upper Canadian political issue. The "Family Compact," an ill-defined but functioning elite that monopolized or attempted to monopolize property and power in the colony during the first part of the century, became the focus of most political and social criticism. It was this elite in fact that was almost the creation and certainly a major vehicle of one of the province's most famous educators, John Strachan. Lured to Upper Canada from Scotland in 1799 by the promise of a university to be founded, Strachan had stayed to become a popular grammar school master. It was through a prosperous marriage to the young widow of a member of the wealthy McGill family, but above all through his students and friends (the friends who were ultimately stereotyped as the Family Compact), that he gradually climbed to a position of eminence in the colony, reaching the pinnacle of power as the first Anglican Bishop of Toronto. (12)

Only the privileged few could belong to the Family Compact; most were destined merely to wish that they had useful and influential friends. More, perhaps, could claim membership in a traditional household. But nearly everyone who had anything to do with children could share in the normal processes of education, which took place for most people at home, since the family's formal educational role was still extensive. Bishop Jacob Mountain made much of contemporary neglect of duty in this respect in 1822. "How many complaints of rebellious children, how many exclamations of astonishment at the perverseness and ingratitude of dependents," the Bishop complained to his Quebec parishioners, "might justly be charged back upon the heads of the Parent and Master!" The moral was obvious.

To Servants, then, to Apprentices, to Labourers retained in our employment, to all our dependents, to all who feel our influence, (especially if they are young, and wholly withdrawn from the charge and inspection of their own friends,) but far above to our own children, we owe it as a sacred duty to think of the furtherance of their salvation. (13)

As might be anticipated, spiritual education was not the only obligation of household heads; contracts frequently stipulated that apprentices receive some elementary literary instruction, (14) and parents as well as masters and guardians expected or were expected to teach their charges the three "R's." John Strachan noted with a certain amount of professional alarm in fact that many parents actually considered themselves as knowledgeable as schoolmasters in the art of instruction, claiming that the only reason they sent children to school was the "want of time" to teach them at home. (15) A private school which appeared very early in Upper Canada's history invited parents to send "their" pupils to be taught; clearly teachers were not the only ones to have pupils at the turn of the century. (16) Instruction at home was to most people, and for some time after 1800, still the norm, and probably in many rural areas the most practical solution. Household heads, parents, guardians, and friends all shared the responsibility of teaching the young, along with the occasional schoolmaster.

Coexistent with these traditional views of the ideal family's educational duties were certain ideas about the structure of the family, which was still perceived to be patriarchal. To King's College divinity professor James Beaven in 1846, the family was to be compared to a limited monarchy; one of the greater faults of American republicanism was the related or consequent weakness of parental authority in the United States. (17) A decade before, another writer had rejected "monarchy" in favour of the term "patriarchy" itself, in a comparison of school and family government: "Like a household, a literary institution should have but one head, and that head should have the ability to govern or he is unfit for his office." (18)

The traditional ideal family may thus be characterized as follows. It was enlarged by the inclusion of friends or dependents over and above those members who were biologically related. It had formal educational obligations beyond the early nurture of its own children. Finally, it was governed by a male parental figure. But it could not be said, even in the early part of the century, that this ideal held absolute sway over every mind; and as time wore on, there was evidence that new ideas were being given increasing publicity in Upper Canada. First of all, there was the tendency to see the family more and more as an entity composed strictly of people who were biologically related. Secondly, the whole idea of the Family Compact, of getting ahead through the efforts of well-placed friends and relatives was gradually discredited. In addition, notions about the purposes and structure of the family were visibly changing as the institution came to be seen more and more as a private retreat from the world and one that for large portions of the week was almost entirely governed by women. Finally, new and contradictory educational roles were perceived for the family, which was urged both to protect its children from the viciousness of the larger society and at the same time prepare them to enter it. The function of formal literary instruction and of much moral education as well was increasingly transferred to schools and colleges, to which parents were asked and ultimately compelled to commit their children for longer and longer periods of time.

There was very little, of course, that was novel in what I am calling the new family ideal, as it was eventually adopted by many people in Upper Canada. Philosophers and educators as different in their views as the New England Puritans (19) and Jean Jacques Rousseau (20) had preached or practiced one or another of the tendencies described above. All that can be said is that a subtle shift occurred in Upper Canada, as in other places before and since, as more and more people saw that the traditional ideals of the household-family or of elite networks like the Family Compact could no longer be effectively sustained in what was rapidly becoming a mass society.

Two of the earliest exponents of the new ideal in Upper Canada were men who were concerned also with the expansion of formal educational institutions. One was a little-known promoter of mechanics' institutes called Walter Eales. The other was Egerton Ryerson, Chief Superintendent of Schools in the province from 1844 to 1876 and, from that high eminence, in a good position to popularize his opinions.

The ideal family described by Eales in 1851 already suggests the direction of change. The centre of it was no longer the patriarch, but the highly idealized wife, queen of a realm of peace who kept the house all week in anticipation of her husband's return on the sabbath.

It is . . . cheering for the matronly wife, to be privileged, for one day in seven, to entertain her lord in the peaceful realms wherein she lives and reigns. Exiled to a great extent from his presence in the week, she ardently longs for the day, when her husband shall fill the vacant chair beside the hearth, irradiate the cottage with his smiles, and delight her ear with that voice, whose tones of tenderness whispered away her heart in the romantic days of her early youth. (21)

The mother was the first book read by her children, according to *The Canadian Gem and Family Visitor,* one of the first Canadian periodicals directed to women. Woman was the centre of the domestic circle; she should "diffuse sunshine and warmth through the whole atmosphere of the home." (22) But it was Eales who explained why. Families, in his view, constituted havens from the rest of society. They were the "arks" that sheltered mankind "from the raging tumults and storms of life" and especially from the world of work where the mechanic spent most of his time and where he was surrounded by "comparative strangers." For the returning husband the wife made the home into a much needed oasis of calm; for the children starting out, it was a happy memory—strong fortification against the coming encounter with "the wild waters of a turbulent world." (23)

But perhaps the best promoter of the new outlook was Chief Superintendent of Schools, Egerton Ryerson, who is interesting not only because of his apparent commitment to the new ideal but because his life and writings are themselves illustrations of the change. One of the numerous children of a loyalist landowning family, he had been an adolescent convert to Methodism and, during the late 1820s and 1830s, one of the most vociferous critics of John Strachan and the Family Compact. His campaign against the Compact idea found its major expression in the statist and bureaucratic ideology of the provincial school system, and ultimately Ryerson, as superintendent, became a promoter of the new family ideal. But he had also been a founder of the Methodist Upper Canada Academy and his letters and autobiographical writings frequently suggest that he clung to the patriarchal concept of family government (perhaps the last vestige of the traditional family idea to go in any society). He appears to have maintained in Toronto, in spite of continuing financial difficulties, a traditional household with its usual complement of servants and nonfamily members—the latter often young Europeans who were temporary protégés of his. (24)

Some of Ryerson's official correspondence during the early years of his superintendency also suggests loyalty to the older family ideal, especially the statement (quoted above) that boarders constituted family members for purposes of the 1846 School Act. When queried about the responsibilities of guardians to pay rate-bills for the schooling of dependent children in 1850, he replied that their duties were no different from those of parents in this regard. (25) But by the 1860s and 1870s, materials coming out of the Education Office suggest a growing commitment to the ideal of the small, self-contained biological family, unencumbered by boarders or unrelated dependents on the one hand, or guardians on the other. It is true that much of this propaganda was directed to members of the growing urban middle classes of society, or constituted unfavorable commentary on working-class people whose aspirations and attitudes were insufficiently middle class for Ryerson and his fellow propagandists to suffer gladly. Indeed its class orientation was one of the significant things about the new family ideal. Increasing loyalty to it was clearly a reflection of a gradually changing social order in which the formally schooled, with small families and universalist values, were slated, in theory at least, to become the new establishment. The new ideal was also closer to what most people could afford to achieve, given the economic realities of Canadian or perhaps of any society.

For Ryerson, economic self-sufficiency was a major family goal and common school textbooks that he published in the 1870s made much of this theme. Parents are exhorted to maintain their children, and reminded of the guilt of those who would, through drunkenness or other vices, expose their offspring to hunger or nakedness and "throw them as paupers upon others to support." But they are also advised to refrain from seeking wealth as such; a respectable standard of living, in accordance with the family's "position and circumstances," is held to be enough. (26)

What Ryerson and many of his contemporaries worried about increasingly was the tendency of families to put material goals ahead of the schooling of their children. As the *Journal of Education for Upper Canada* complained in 1854, there were selfish parents who kept their children away from school "on the slightest pretext of pressure of business," and would "starve their intellects in order to enrich their own pockets." (27) A respectable standard of living was not to be bought apparently at the expense of formal education. In fact by 1864, Ryerson was able to state explicitly that the obligation to educate children was more imperative than the duty to clothe and feed them. (28) In addition, the duty to educate was for him as for others increasingly equated with sending children to school. Instruction at home seemed less and less acceptable and local superintendents of common schools were obliged to give specific reasons for poor average attendance, where this existed, in their annual reports to the chief superintendent. A compulsory attendance law was finally passed in 1871.

Ryerson was among those who saw the protection of children from the larger society as an important function of the family. He compared the selection of library books to the care that parents took, or ought to take, in the selection of their children's companions. Any "intelligent and discreet" parent, furthermore, would prefer the high-priced land of an industrious and moral community for raising his family to a "neighbourhood of drunkenness, lawlessness and vice." Although the intention was to show that widespread schooling would increase property values, the underlying assumption was that all right-minded and virtuous people would and should attempt to isolate their families from the evils of society, presumably by moving their homes away from those districts inhabited by its worst elements. (29)

Children had to be protected, but the home did not on that account have to become a prison. The secret, according to Ryerson, was to make the domestic household more attractive than the world outside. "If parents would protect their children from the snares and dangers of seeking social enjoyment abroad, they must make the home the seat of such enjoyments." (30) Somehow the family (always complemented by the school) was to become the focus of children's lives. It had to be an environment, however, in which there was some room for differences of opinion, especially in spiritual matters. In 1854, Ryerson took a stand against the expulsion of baptized children from the Methodist Church for nonattendance at class meetings. He argued essentially for the right of the unconverted to remain within the church of their parents, thus helping, as C. B. Sissons has pointed out, to push Methodism in the direction of becoming a family church. (31) The implication, as with the tribalism attributed by Edmund Morgan to the New England Puritans, (32) was that the strength of the family was now more important than the purity of the church, and that adolescents needed a measure of freedom within the confines of both. Traumatic departures from the parental home would be avoided by seeking, in theory at least, a slightly more democratic model for the family.

Thus Upper Canada's chief superintendent of schools gradually advocated new functions and a new structure for the family: a nuclear household of parents and children, an inward-looking institution that was to concentrate on the nurture of its own offspring at home and in schools. But the contradictions inherent in this idea —of children separated from society on the one hand but committed to society's schools on the other—led to anxiety, which was expressed particularly clearly in discussions about the pros and cons of boarding halls.

II

To John Strachan and many other supporters of denominational colleges in Upper Canada, boarding schools and colleges were viable substitutes for the Christian family. It was this, perhaps, more than any other fact, that accounted for the depth of their concern when they believed that these institutions were being attacked, and, in Strachan's case, for the urgency with which he set about the work of founding Trinity College. His ambition to establish a university in Upper Canada had been thwarted until 1843, when King's College finally opened its doors; but the secularization of King's by the University Act of 1849 once more left Strachan without an institution of higher learning that he could conscientiously support. His response to these events was Trinity, which was established in 1852 as a Church of England institution and the embodiment of Strachan's views on the relationship between education and the family. "It will constitute a great Christian household," he promised, "the domestic home of all who resort to it for instruction, framing them in the Christian graces, in all sound learning, and sanctifying their knowledge, abilities and attainments to the service of God and the welfare of their fellow men." (33)

It was to be a rule of Trinity that all students should be resident in the college, except those given special permission to live with their parents in or near Toronto. (34) In his 1852 inaugural address, Strachan explained why. He admitted that no system of education could really replace "the domestic fireside," but argued that because so many young men would come from a distance, it was essential to provide that which came nearest it. It would gladden the hearts of parents to know that, though their children were no longer immediately under their eye, everything would be done "to supply the place of paternal counsel and maternal tenderness." (35)

Now one of our principal objects in this Institution will be to bring back to the hearts and affections of our youth the fresh and innocent impressions of early infancy . . . the holy truths . . . which a pious and tender mother whispered into their ears, invoking the protection of their God and Saviour before she kissed them and consigned them to their night's repose. . . . Our desire is to build upon this holy foundation, to form ourselves into a large Household, and to keep as near as may be practicable to the order and economy of a well-regulated family. (36)

Strachan expressed the conviction that there would grow among the young men "an affectionate brotherhood," and that such intimacy could only be provided by residential college life. This and all other advantages would be lost if the students were "scattered about and living here and there in lodgings" in the city. (37)

There were two further reasons for preferring the family boarding hall to lodgings. One was the age of the scholars, who Strachan estimated would be between 18 and 22 and therefore in his view at the most critical period of their lives. The other was the dangerous environment created by the city. In vague but alarmist terms Strachan stressed the dangers awaiting young men cast loose in a large city like Toronto, without friends or counsellors. To leave them to choose their lodgings, hours, and companions, and to govern their own religious lives, was to court, he thought, their almost certain destruction. (38)

Not all college or boarding school authorities went to such lengths to defend or promote the residence of their scholars. There had always been purely practical reasons for most such arrangements. It had long been a common practice for grammar school masters, among others, to take in boarders in order to make their schools available to those who lived too far away to be day pupils. This usage continued at least into the 1860s. In the early days, these small schools probably functioned much like other families enlarged by the inclusion of apprentices or servants. But they were not advertised as such. Most notices simply stated that the master would concern himself with the manners and morals as well as the literary attainments of his charges. (39) Nor were the benefits of family life apparently connected with the boarding hall planned for Upper Canada College in 1831; it was designed, according to the Board of Education minutes at least, to reduce expenses for youth coming from distant places. (40) It was therefore a major change of emphasis when, by the middle of the century, the supporters of denominational colleges everywhere began, like Strachan, to relate the need for boarding halls to the necessity of providing the warmth and restraint associated with the household or family.

Egerton Ryerson was an interesting exception to this trend. Before he became superintendent of schools, he had been one of the major promoters of the Methodist Upper Canada Academy, and from 1842 to 1844 had been principal of its successor, Victoria College. His early vision of the academy had placed it in the small community of Cobourg, at a remove from the "polluted waters of corrupt example," in a district of "moral and intelligent people." (41) Even with these precautions, the rules of the institution were very strict; the students lived in boarding halls and were prevented as much as possible from contact with the townspeople. (42) But Ryerson's experience as principal of the college must have altered his opinions, (43) for by 1847, although he remained a strong supporter of Victoria and of denominational colleges generally, he was steadfastly opposed to the idea of boarding halls. They were specifically rejected for the provincial Normal School that Ryerson founded in Toronto during that year, in spite of the fact that faculty-supervised residences were considered an essential part of Dublin Normal, the institution on which the Upper Canadian training school was modelled, (44) and despite the fact that students were to come to it from all over the province.

Ryerson's counter proposal and the one decided on was to arrange for nonresident pupils to board in the city with local families. The houses were approved and licensed by the Council of Public Instruction, which also saw to it that the headmaster inspected them regularly and that the strict rules governing the extracurricular lives of students were carefully enforced. (45) There was certainly little free choice of lodgings or companions, no freedom in the matters of hours of attendance at public worship, in fact none of the options that Strachan later insisted were the necessary alternatives to properly supervised boarding halls. Certainly many Normal students were well over the 22 years of the oldest Trinity College scholars, and a large number, old and young, had been teachers before coming to the school. But there were also many young women, most students of both sexes were under 22, and the minimum age was only 16. (46) What then accounts for Ryerson's insistence on city lodging arrangements for the Normal School?

In his history of the American boarding school, James McLachlan makes the point that similar family boarding arrangements in early nineteenth-century academy towns reflected a conception of the community as an important extension of the school. It, too, transmitted values and knowledge to the learners. He also argues convincingly that such close integration of school and community presupposed "a relatively stable, homogeneous society." (47) Parents and teachers alike would have had considerable confidence in the townspeople whose households the students shared, because it was expected that similar values were shared as well.

Several explanations for Ryerson's choice seem plausible at this point then. One could argue that he was simply less pessimistic than Strachan about the dangers of the Toronto environment to which the students would be exposed. But this seems quite inconsistent with his early arrangements for the Upper Canada Academy, and with later complaints of the moral ruin that had befallen unsupervised youths in the wicked metropolis. (48) Toronto was smaller and less evil perhaps than some of the big American or European cities; it certainly had its fair share of informers who let the authorities know what Normal School students were up to—especially if their activities had moral or political implications. Reports came into the Education Office naming students who had been seen at the theatre, in the company of the opposite sex, or in taverns; students were even turned in for attending a meeting for former rebel William Lyon Mackenzie. (49) But although it may have been a factor, it is doubtful that the predictable or relatively homogeneous nature of the Toronto community was the only or even the major reason for Ryerson's preference for family boarding arrangements for the Normal School.

A more likely explanation is to be found in the character and background of the students who came to the school from out of town. It is probable, to begin with, that they were not as wealthy as the grammar school graduates who would attend Trinity, and most did not expect to stay for more than one year. Many students came for a summer or winter session only and even then at considerable financial sacrifice. It is possible that Ryerson may have considered living in urban families as a way of transmitting new and different values to the predominantly rural youth who came to the city and that he considered the exchange of rustic ways for a degree of urban sophistication part of the preparation of a teacher.

But certainly this was not all, as Ryerson made clear in statements about boarding halls made at a later date. For Ryerson was opposed to such halls not only for the Normal School and for the short-lived Model Grammar School associated with it, (50) but for almost any school or college, regardless of the character of the students or the community in which it was situated. In an 1850 letter to a trustee of the classical grammar school at Kingston he explained why.

> As to connecting a Boarding Hall and Master's Residence with your School Houses, I would advise you to have nothing to do with the one or the other, but reserve all your resources for your School House and School. . . . In regard to a Boarding Hall in connection with any Academy, Grammar School or College, experience has led to its abandonment, almost universally in the United States, on both economical and moral grounds. The Boarding Hall of Upper Canada College, which has not been used as such for several months, has been nearly the financial ruin of that Institution, and a great injury to the morals of numbers of pupils. . . . (51)

It is unclear whether Ryerson was right or wrong about the decline of boarding halls in the United States. In some circles educators and parents were increasingly turning to them as they became disillusioned with the urban environment and caught up, like Strachan, with a vision of boarding schools modelled on the Christian family. (52) In others, however, parents and educational reformers promoted the establishment of public high schools in part, quite explicitly, to enable them to both educate and keep at home their adolescent children. But Ryerson was definitely right about Upper Canada College. The boarding halls connected with that school had had a long history of trouble, and in March and once again in June of 1849, the master in charge had begged to be relieved of responsibility for them. (53) Later in 1856, a Mr. J. W. Stephens declined the headmastership because he did not wish to become involved in overseeing the boarding houses, (54) and discipline problems and scandals involving masters as well as students seemed to take up an inordinate amount of the University of Toronto Senate, the governing body of the school.

Ryerson elaborated very little on the moral dangers associated with boarding halls, but one of his basic points is crucial to an understanding of the institutions he created and his conception of the ideal family. This was that such halls weakened rather than strengthened the domestic feelings, exciting, as he put it, "a disrelish for the quiet and retirement of the domestic circle, and a fondness for the extravagance and bustle of public places." The social tastes and feelings learned at school were as important as the intellectual knowledge acquired, and therefore the nearer the living arrangements approached "those at home, or a private family," the better. Students who came from a distance should be boarded privately in the homes of the masters or with other families in Kingston. (55) The essential point was that no boarding hall could really duplicate what Ryerson conceived to be the important characteristics of family life.

The practical financial considerations were also a factor. Buildings cost money both to construct and maintain, as Ryerson was fully aware from his connections both with Victoria College and the Normal School. Trustees and governments rarely found sufficient funds, nor did the chief superintendent wish additional costs to be born by the students, as the weekly cost of living subsidy paid to first year Normal students proves. One might attempt to save money by building dormitories instead of separate bedrooms for the pupils, but then they were dangerous to the morals, especially of young boys, as Ryerson pointed out in the Kingston letter. (56)

It is probably true that many institutions, especially those paid for by the government, simply could not afford boarding halls of the type idealized by Strachan. When schools and colleges reached a certain size, the former convenient arrangement of master and pupils living together was no longer easily financed. It would take the strong convictions of a Strachan and the metaphor of the Christian family to foster financial and moral support for the larger boarding schools and colleges of the mid century. But if cost was one factor, another was one's view of the ideal family. Ryerson disliked boarding halls because they were too "public"; privacy, tranquility, and retirement were for him the dominant virtues of family life, and he opted for rather old-fashioned family boarding arrangements to promote his modern view of proper domestic relations. Strachan's version of the Christian household at Trinity, on the other hand, represented an innovation of sorts, but one clearly designed to perpetuate the traditional or older view of the family: its virtues were community of fellowship, worship, and concern, as well as the advice and assistance provided by patriarchal authority. Although he shared with Ryerson the value of privacy, and once advised a friend not to take in boarders out of respect for the "peaceful tranquility" of his amiable family, (57) this did not affect Strachan's view of the new, larger educational institutions. That students should live the public lives deplored by Ryerson seemed to him entirely natural.

Despite this basic difference of emphasis, both solutions to the problem of nonresident students focussed on reproducing the advantages of family life as Strachan and Ryerson perceived them. And several times during his long career, Ryerson implied that his position was not very far at all from Strachan's. In 1847, he expressed the view that boarding schools were even the best answer for some— in this case for Indian children, for whom he recommended agricultural labour schools in which farmer, schoolmaster, and "parent" were one person. But these would probably have been, if developed, small institutions that really could have functioned like traditional pupil-master households. The interesting thing about them was Ryerson's own feeling that his proposal was impractical; he thought it the ideal solution, but doubted in fact that one man could any longer be found who could, or would wish to, perform the three functions of father, farmer, and teacher at once, a possibility that several decades before surely would have struck no one as remote. (58)

But then by mid century day schools were seen by Ryerson and most of his contemporaries as the usual institutional substitutes for family education, possibly because it was thought increasingly important by middle-class parents and educators that children live at home with their natural families. But lest parents should become alarmed about what went on in day schools, here too the family metaphor was used. The authority of the teacher had to be great, as the superintendent of schools wrote to a somewhat beleaguered grammar school master in 1859; he needed considerable power to exercise discipline in his "large family." (59)

A measure of Ryerson's ability to accommodate several viewpoints almost at once, and of the closeness of his views to those of Strachan in some essential ways, is the fact that if there was no alternative, he was able to accept Strachan's version of the family boarding college in its entirety. Thus an 1854 report on King's College, New Brunswick, which was largely his work, recommended the accommodation of students with private families, but qualified the advice with the aside that, if a boarding hall was found to be a necessity, provision should be made therein for "the observance of all the duties of a Christian family." (60) When students had to live away from home, residential colleges were certainly preferable to institutions that did not concern themselves at all with the moral or religious lives of their pupils.

The long battle between the denominational colleges and the nonsectarian University of Toronto, as King's College was renamed, over provincial funds for higher education, found Ryerson on the side of the denominational colleges for this reason, in spite of the fact that he was for some years a member of the university's governing senate. The university adopted the boarding hall concept for its undergraduate college and claimed to take an interest in the extracurricular lives of its scholars. For Ryerson, however, as for Strachan, proper family guidance and restraint were inseparable from religion, and if he had doubts about the wisdom of boarding halls in general, he was at one with other critics of the university in being virtually certain that the ideal of the Christian family could never be approached in a large nondenominational institution. (61)

The fact that neither the Toronto Normal or Model Grammar Schools, nor probably the grammar school at Kingston, could very well have been under denominational control may have been an important additional reason for Ryerson's preference for boarding students with local families. It would seem entirely possible that he rejected Strachan's version of the "public" boarding hall for the institutions that he was concerned with partly because the public that would attend or control them was far too diverse. Strachan's community was limited by the shared values of a common religion, insofar as the faculty and most of the students at Trinity would be members of the Church of England, and of a common grammar school background. In the Normal School, this was not the case; all the major denominations were represented among the students, and educational backgrounds varied. (62) Strachan was still able to visualize an educational institution that served a recognizable and easily defined community and when it came to Victoria College, Ryerson could do the same. But institutions like the normal and grammar schools of the province were characterized by the diversity and transience of their student bodies, and this was a fact that could not be ignored. It was this fact, indeed, that made the very distinction between public and private education seem increasingly necessary.

This distinction did not take root easily in Canada, however. Ryerson joined with Strachan and the other promoters of denominational colleges in demanding for them a share of provincial educational funds, a share that they ultimately received with university federation in the latter part of the century. And in the meantime, publicly financed religious institutions, in the form of Roman Catholic separate schools, defended their existence successfully in Upper Canada as in other British North American colonies. But they were not without opponents. On their side, supporters of nonsectarian institutions like the University of Toronto seem to have doubted the wisdom of either close denominational supervision or the protective family ideal, at least as applied to college-age students. Was it really a good idea to protect youth from the mixed society that in the end they would have to enter and confront?

I am by no means sure that a youth, who has soon to go out into the world without any control, is not the better for a preparatory training amongst those of his own age, with such supervision as can always be exercised in College; and that a higher tone of morality may not be cultivated under the influence of the public opinion of a large body, than by mixing only with a limited society. (63)

What can one conclude about the nature of Upper Canadian society or the social attitudes of educators from these discussions? To begin with, no matter what point of view was taken, they clearly expressed a deep anxiety about the relationship of the child, especially the adolescent, to the larger society. The complexity of Egerton Ryerson's approach to the subject may have been extreme, but it was not untypical. Toronto at mid century was perhaps small enough that Normal School students could occasionally be recognized, but it was big enough for Walter Eales to complain that a man's workmates might often be "relative strangers" and for Ryerson and other school and college authorities to insist on extremely restrictive rules governing student life, no matter what the age and previous experience of the scholars. Upper Canada does not seem to have undergone the strong rejection of cities that occurred in the United States and resulted there in the founding of large numbers of boarding schools and colleges in remote rural areas, but it cannot be said that the use of private family boarding arrangement presupposed great confidence in the stability or homogeneity of the community either.

Ryerson's commitment to the new family ideal and to the idea that students should live in the relative seclusion that he associated with private family life seems to have been a response rather to the feeling that both the society and the new educational institutions that he was building were too large and complex to be familial as he understood the term. Unlike Trinity, the Normal School could never be a family; real families and the inward-turning family ideal seemed more appropriate answers to the heterogeneous realities of the emerging mass society, as Ryerson saw it.

And too, there was the fact of class. Few Upper Canadians could afford the luxury of maintaining either the traditional household or expensive residential colleges. Perhaps this was why people like Egerton Ryerson continued, without any great feeling of contradicting themselves, to seek state financial aid for the latter. Elites would always be necessary and for them the old ideology of the family as household was not inappropriate. The new ideology of the family on the other hand, like the common school system itself, was designed to serve different people, in particular the urban middle class of an emerging mass society. (64)

NOTES

1. The theme of the family and the state and others referred to briefly in this essay are discussed in my thesis, "The School Promoters: Education and Social Class in Mid-Nineteenth Century Upper Canada (Ph.D. diss., University of Toronto, 1974).
2. James McLachlan, *American Boarding Schools: A Historical Study* (New York, 1970). For McLachlan, it was "one of the major controlling metaphors in American social thought and popular culture" in the antebellum period (p. 115).
3. A helpful discussion of ideal as opposed to actual family patterns may be found in Marion J. Levy, Jr., "Aspects of the Analysis of Family Structure," in Ansley J. Coale et al., *Aspects of the Analysis of Family Structure* (Princeton, N.J., 1965).
4. Philippe Ariès, *Centuries of Childhood: A Social History of Family Life* (New York, 1962). The gradual acceptance of new ideas by different social classes is one of Ariès major themes.

5. Peter Laslett, "Size and Structure of the Household in England Over Three Centuries," *Population Studies* 23, no. 2 (July 1969): 202. See also, *The World We Have Lost* (Cambridge, 1965).

6. Egerton Ryerson to Arch. Fletcher, January 15, 1846, Ontario Archives Education Papers: RG 2, C 1, Letterbook C, p. 17 [the Education Papers of the Ontario Archives are hereafter re-referred to under Code and Series numbers as listed in the archives, RG 2, etc.].

7. John Strachan, *A Letter to the Rev. A. N. Bethune, on the Management of Grammar Schools* (York, Upper Canada, 1829), p. 43.

8. "Minutes of the Board of Education for Upper Canada, 1823–1833," February 23, 1831, RG 2, A, p. 152.

9. *Circular of the Upper Canada Academy* (Cobourg, Upper Canada, 1841), p. 15.

10. Edward Dewar to Egerton Ryerson, November 13, 1849, RG 2, C-6-C.

11. Joseph H. King to Egerton Ryerson, July 12, 1850, RG 2, C-6-C.

12. For details of Strachan's early views and the Family Compact, see my article, "John Strachan and Early Upper Canada, 1799–1814," *Ontario History* 52 (1960):3, and R. E. Saunders, "What Was the Family Compact?" *Ontario History* 49 (1957):4.

13. Rev. G. J. Mountain, *A Sermon on the Education of the Poor, the Duty Of Diffusing the Gospel, and, more particularly, on the Importance of Family Religion* (Quebec, 1822), pp. 16–18.

14. For an example, see C. E. Phillips, *The Development of Education in Canada* (Toronto, 1957), p. 111.

15. Strachan, *On the Management of Grammar Schools,* p. 36.

16. J. C. Hodgins, ed., *Documentary History of Education in Upper Canada* (Toronto, 1894), 1:32.

17. John A. Irving, "The Development of Philosophy in Central Canada from 1850 to 1900," *Canadian Historical Review* 31, no. 3 (1950): 257–59.

18. *Doctor Charles Duncombe's Report upon the Subject of Education* (Toronto, 1836), pp. 30–31.

19. Edmund Morgan, *The Puritan Family* (Boston, 1956).

20. Eva Figes, *Patriarchal Attitudes* (New York, 1970).

21. Walter Eales, *Lecture on the Benefits to be derived from Mechanics' Institutes* (Toronto, 1851), p. 11.

22. *The Canadian Gem and Family Visitor* 2, no. 2 (February 1849):35–36.

23. Eales, *Mechanics' Institutes,* p. 12.

24. C. B. Sissons, ed., *Egerton Ryerson: His Life and Letters,* 2 vols. (Toronto, 1937–1947), and *My Dearest Sophie: Letters from Egerton Ryerson to His Daughter* (Toronto, 1955).

25. Egerton Ryerson to John Russell, March 23, 1850, RG 2, C 1, Letterbook E, pp. 156–57.

26. *First Lessons in Christian Morals for Canadian Families and Schools* (Toronto, 1871), p. 21; *First Lessons in Agriculture; for Canadian Farmers and their Families* (Toronto, 1871), pp. 171–72; and *Elements*

of *Political Economy; or How individuals and a country become rich* (Toronto, 1877), especially p. 9.

27. *Journal of Education for Upper Canada* 7, no. 9 (September 1854): 148.
28. *Annual Report by the Chief Superintendent of Schools for Upper Canada* (1864), pt. 1, p. 26.
29. *Elements of Political Economy,* p. 140.
30. *First Lessons in Christian Morals,* p. 26.
31. Sissons, ed., *Egerton Ryerson,* 2:268.
32. Morgan, *The Puritan Family,* chapt. 7.
33. Hodgins, ed., *Documentary History,* 10:59.
34. Ibid., 9:114.
35. Ibid., 10:64.
36. Ibid.
37. Ibid., pp. 64–65.
38. Ibid.
39. Ibid., 8:302; see also Headmaster of the Cobourg Grammar School to J. G. Hodgins, February–March 1859, and Master of the Barrie Grammar School to Ryerson, May 15, 1865, RG 2, C-6-C.
40. *Minutes of the Board of Education,* RG 2, A, p. 155.
41. Hodgins, ed., *Documentary History,* 2:4.
42. *Circular of the Upper Canada Academy,* pp. 16–17.
43. A memorial from the students to Ryerson on his retirement as principal suggests that his residence among them was "anything but agreeable," and at least one letter to him implies that he had complained at some length about the difficulties of his position. Memorial from Students of Victoria College, 1844, and James Spencer to Egerton Ryerson, January 9, 1843, *Ryerson Correspondence,* United Church Archives, Toronto.
44. T. C. Young to J. G. Hodgins, June 3, 1847, RG 2, C-6-C; and Hodgins, ed., *Documentary History,* 7:99.
45. *Council of Public Instruction Records,* RG 2, B (3 vols.), contains many references to student discipline and staff inspection of boarding houses.
46. *Toronto Normal School Register of Students, 1847–1873,* RG 2, H.
47. McLachlan, *American Boarding Schools,* p. 47.
48. Hodgins, ed., *Documentary History,* 16:288; and ibid., 17:178.
49. See for example Anonymous to Ryerson, February 21, 1849, and Robert Yathy to Ryerson, March 26, 1849, RG 2, C-6-C.
50. Hodgins, ed., *Documentary History,* 13:65.
51. Ibid., 9:206.
52. McLachlan, *American Boarding Schools;* and M. B. Katz, *The Irony of Early School Reform* (Cambridge, Mass., 1968), pp. 51–52.
53. Hodgins, ed., *Documentary History,* 8:192.
54. Ibid., 12:224 and 267.
55. Ibid., 9:206.

56. Ibid.
57. Strachan to Dr. Brown, December 1, 1818, in *The John Strachan Letterbook: 1812–1834,* ed. G. W. Spragge (Toronto, 1946), p. 184.
58. Ryerson to Varden, May 20, 1847, RG 2, C 1, Letterbook C, p. 380.
59. Ryerson to Muir, September 6, 1859, RG 2, C-6-C.
60. Hodgins, ed., *Documentary History,* 16:5.
61. "The University Question in a Series of Letters," *Documentary History,* ed. J. G. Hodgins, 16:261–300, contains Ryerson's defense of denominational colleges.
62. The diversity of religious backgrounds was apparent from the beginning. Of 108 students who attended during the fairly typical 3d session (1848–1849) there were 6 Roman Catholics, 21 members of the Church of England, 42 Methodists, 20 Presbyterians, 6 Baptists, 2 Congregationalists, and 13 whose denominations were other or not given. *Annual Report of the Chief Superintendent of Schools* (1859), table M.
63. Hodgins, ed., *Documentary History,* 15:194.
64. The relationship of educational innovation to perceptions of social class in the mid-nineteenth century I have explored elsewhere. *See* note 1.

6. "TO CREATE A STRONG AND HEALTHY RACE": SCHOOL CHILDREN IN THE PUBLIC HEALTH MOVEMENT, 1880–1914 *

Between the 1880s and 1920s a growing band of English Canadians worked to change the nature and improve the quality of family life, to establish new systems of child and family welfare, to transform Canadian education, and to organize child and family health care. Of these reform efforts the public health movement had the most immediate, the least ambiguous, and the most accurately measurable positive effects on the lives of Canadian children. This essay, examining the public health movement, analyses the manner in which concern for the health of children, interacting with scientific discoveries and the development of professions, contributed to the assumption of new responsibilities by the state.

BETWEEN THE 1880s and the 1920s a growing band of English Canadians created and began to test a new consensus on the situation of the child in their society. In the four major dimensions of their enterprise they worked to change the nature and improve the quality

---

* In an address to the Canadian Public Health Association meeting in Montreal in December 1911, James Roberts, who was the Medical Health Officer for Hamilton, Ontario, argued: "Our chiefest concern is with the children, the rising generation. We should aim first of all to create a strong and healthy race" (James Roberts, "Insanitary Areas," *Public Health Journal* [hereafter cited as *P.H.J.*] 3 [April 1912]: 182). I gratefully acknowledge the help of my colleague, Professor John Calam, in the preparation of this paper.

Mr. Sutherland is a member of the Faculty of Education, University of British Columbia. This essay first appeared in The History of Education Quarterly (*Fall 1972*).

of family life, to establish new systems of child and family welfare, to transform Canadian education, and to organize child and family health care. (1) Of these reform efforts the public health movement had the most immediate, the least ambiguous, and the most accurately measurable positive effects on the lives of Canadian children.

Canadians got down to public health work at a particularly auspicious time. "I recall," wrote the first secretary of the Ontario Board of Health, Peter H. Bryce, in 1910, that "three wholly remarkable events" took place in 1882: Louis Pasteur dramatically proved the effectiveness of immunization for anthrax in sheep, Robert Koch discovered the tuberculosis germ, and the provincial government established the Ontario Board of Health. (2) That Bryce joined these three events so closely together sharply illuminates the fact that Ontario established its Board, the first such permanent body in Canada, at the beginning of the bacteriological era in public health. First the Ontario and then the other provincial boards of health were able to begin their work by using the knowledge that the earlier sanitary phase of the public health movement had already produced. However, because they were new institutions, not tightly tied by tradition to any particular procedures and staffed by the extremely enthusiastic workers that characterize the first generation of reform enterprises, they were also able to incorporate easily into their practices many of the dramatic and effective bacteriological discoveries of the last two decades of the nineteenth century. In fact, children and then infants became the prime beneficiaries of many of the medical discoveries made in the battle against communicable diseases. In the combination, then, of sanitation and bacteriology, public health workers gradually developed potent machinery for improving the health of children.

Canadians built what they came to call their public health movement around a professional core of public health physicians, sanitary inspectors, and public health nurses. Municipal and provisional boards of health and, to a lesser extent, school boards and provincial departments of education employed these health workers. When Ontario established its Provincial Board of Health under the provision of the Board of Health Act of 1882, Canada achieved its first permanent public health organization. Prior to this time, the provinces had set up public health boards only on a temporary basis in response to the threat of particular emergency situations. Two

years later, the legislature passed a new Public Health Act, based on
the English Consolidated Public Health Act of 1875, which greatly
strengthened the powers of the Ontario Board. The other provinces
gradually followed Ontario's lead and, as Bryce explained, the 1884
Act became "practically the Public Health Act of seven other
provinces." (3) Quebec and New Brunswick set up permanent
provincial health boards in 1887, as did Nova Scotia, Manitoba,
and British Columbia in 1893, Alberta in 1907, Prince Edward
Island in 1908, and Saskatchewan in 1909. (4) These Boards, their
municipal counterparts, and the other public agencies that gradually
got involved in public health gave their professional employees
financial and other support that ranged from grudging to enthusiastic. In their efforts to add to the range of public health services,
many community, provincial, and national organizations both
prodded and supported this official apparatus. In turn, the professionals and their amateur supporters gradually formed a number
of specialized health groups and societies such as the Canadian
St. John's Ambulance. the Canadian Red Cross Society, the National
Sanitarium Association, the Canadian Association for the Prevention of Tuberculosis, the Public Health Committee of the National
Council of Women, and the Canadian Public Health Association.

As their numbers grew and their public support increased, and
they both generated their own knowledge and put to use that which
was discovered elsewhere, those in the Canadian public health
movement sharpened mightily the focus of their work. From their
initial preoccupation with sanitation as a means of protecting and
improving the health of Canadians as a whole, they turned to
sorting out the distinct groups in the population for which they
could expect more specialized public health measures to yield worthwhile results. As part of this process they gradually centred in on
three aspects of child health. In the first phase of this work, which
is the subject of this paper, they strove to protect and then to
improve the health of school children. Next they began the difficult
task of reducing mortality among infants and young children.
Finally they tried very hard to come to grips with what those
involved described as the "problem" of feeblemindedness. In these
three endeavours, those in the public health movement failed only
in the case of the feebleminded; otherwise they achieved a quite
remarkable degree of success. Not only did they bring about an

undoubted improvement in the health of school-aged children but, by the end of the era, they were beginning to bite into the much more complex problems of infant mortality.

In Canada as it had elsewhere, the public health movement lighted on school children as its first clearly perceived client group among the young. In the first phase of this effort, from the 1880s to the early years of the twentieth century, health workers made sanitation the school's first line of defence against disease. In its second annual report, in 1883, the Ontario Board of Health explained that it had "good reason to believe" that many schoolrooms were "in a very unsanitary condition" and that "neglect of precautions to prevent the spread of contagious and infectious diseases, overcrowding and many other causes of diseases" were common. (5) It was, however, one thing for a board of health to set minimum sanitary standards for schools and another thing altogether to persuade local school boards to apply them. In 1891, the secretary recorded in the minutes of a local school meeting in the London area that it had been "Moved and seconded, that a vote be taken of those present how they feel on ventilating the schoolhouse. Twenty-eight against it and one for it." (6) Even urban school systems only very slowly implemented the new sanitary standards. In 1897, teachers, parents, and pupils directed many complaints to the local trustees about the unsanitary conditions in Victoria schools. (7) The state of Toronto schools at the turn of the century also provoked sharp debate in that city. (8) In rural areas the battle against filth continued to be an unremitting one. As late as 1920, a rural medical health officer in Nova Scotia explained that of 30 schoolhouses he had recently visited, only one had satisfactory toilets and in no less than 28 of them "urine and feces were over the seats and floors." (9)

If infectious diseases breached these modest and ineffectively enforced sanitary barriers, then regulations that excluded infected children from school supposedly formed the next line of defence for both school pupils and the wider community. After suffering through a particularly widespread diphtheria epidemic in 1886, for example, Ontario decided to compel parents, teachers, and health officials to report "the existence in any house of smallpox, cholera, scarlatina, diphtheria, whooping cough, measles, mumps, glanders or other contagious diseases." These regulations forbad both children with these diseases and their families to associate with other children and excluded them from school. (10) Since the medical profession still had not agreed on whether tuberculosis was infectious or how to treat it this disease was not on the list. When they faced substantial outbreaks of infectious diseases, local school and health officials characteristically responded by closing schools entirely until the incidence of infection declined. In March 1885, for example, the New Westminster, B.C., school board decided "to close the public schools during the prevalence of scarlet fever." (11)

In their efforts to limit the spread and effect of contagious disease, however, public health workers initially faced even greater public apathy, reluctance, and opposition than they did in their work in improving sanitation. Over the century since Jenner's work of 1796–1800, medical workers demonstrated time and again the efficacy of vaccination against smallpox. As recently as the epidemic of 1855, Canadians saw how, by means of a well-organized and vigorously pursued effort of vaccination and quarantine, Ontario kept its deaths from smallpox to 84 while over the same time 3,175 people died of the disease in Montreal alone. (12) In most provinces school trustees had the power to exclude unvaccinated children from school. (13) Except when they were faced by an actual outbreak of smallpox, however, such as the one in British Columbia in 1892, trustees were extremely reluctant to enforce vaccination regulations. (14) In 1910, for example, a public health officer reported that "thanks to the 'Conscientious Scruples' as by rule permitted," 1,500 public school pupils in Halifax were not vaccinated. (15) In 1911 the Toronto School Board refused to enforce compulsory vaccination laws and the Ottawa Board of Health took the same stand in 1912. (16) As late as 1920, Saskatchewan health officials found that "very few children of school age" had been vaccinated. (17)

To back up their two main lines of defence, and to assist them in their work in other areas, public health officials also made modest forays into the field of school curriculum. They tried diligently to interest practising teachers in public health and to ensure that new teachers had proper grounding in physiology, hygiene, and public health. (18) In addition, they worked to have hygiene, physiology, and, later, physical culture included among the compulsory subjects in elementary schooling. (19) Their reason for taking this position was a simple one: the "susceptible minds of the young," argued a committee of the Ontario Board of Health, were "particularly adapted to receive and retain such instruction, which will afterwards be spread broadcast among the masses, thus preparing the way for the enforcement of sanitary laws." (20)

By the turn of the century, then, Canadian public health officials had established two sets of controls, which were by no means universally enforced, with which they tried to protect the health of children while they were at school. First, they set minimum standards of sanitation for school premises and, second, they excluded from school those children who were obviously suffering from a stated list (which omitted tuberculosis) of infectious diseases. Health workers hoped, as well, that teachers would give their pupils some instruction in hygiene and perhaps some physical training as well. So far as such youngsters were protected at all, the general provisions made for the public health of the community sheltered the health of infants and other children not attending school.

Over the next two decades a whole cluster of developments made very radical changes in preventative health work for children in Canada. Undoubtedly the most important cause of these changes was the astonishing growth in medical science, especially in bacteriology. (21) Turning laboratory discoveries into effective weapons of public health, however, was a complex matter taking place over a considerable number of years. Consider, for instance, diphtheria. Diphtheria found its main victims among school-aged children and since the public health movement campaigned against the disease with increasing vigour over these years, the fight against it provides an excellent example of the intimate connection between bacteriology and the health of the young. In 1891 and 1892, for example, the Ontario Board of Health reported that not only was diphtheria "a disease peculiarly liable to attack with malignity children under ten years," but also that there was "no single cause" that contributed "so largely to the dissemination and continuance of this pest as the introduction of its contagion in the schoolroom." (22) Since diphtheria germs lost virulence "by free exposure to sunlight, moisture and fresh air," the Board explained that the main preventative was proper ventilation of schoolrooms. (23) The work against diphtheria proceeded, almost simultaneously, on a number of different fronts. While scientists and physicians explored and developed as rapidly as possible the practical potentialities of a series of laboratory discoveries, public health officials were hard at work explaining to colleagues, to physicians in private practice, and to the general public precisely what they had learned and persuading, cajoling, and occasionally coercing them to use the product of this new knowledge.

Between 1884 and 1894, French, German, and American bacteriologists—particularly Friedrich Loeffler, Emile Roux, Alexandre Yersin, Karl Fraenkel, Emil von Behring, and W. H. Park—made the central core of discoveries that gradually led to the control of diphtheria. They proved, to summarize their work very briefly, that a powerful, soluble toxin produced by the Klebs-Loeffler bacillis caused the general symptoms of diphtheria; that, in addition to the obviously ill, convalescents and even well persons could infect others with the disease; that laboratories could use the blood of animals (especially horses) to produce a powerful antitoxin; that this antitoxin was an effective agent against cases of diphtheria; and that it prevented diphtheria from developing in persons who had been exposed to the disease. (24) Three practical results flowed almost immediately from these discoveries. First, with the discovery that diphtheria was a true zymotic disease, public health officials brought it under their control. In 1891, for example, Ontario passed an Order-in-Council that directed health authorities to handle diphtheria as they did smallpox. (25) Second, physicians began to use laboratory tests both to diagnose accurately cases of diphtheria and to govern the quarantine period of diagnosed cases and those relatives who had unfortunately been incarcerated with them. Other places quickly copied this work that began in North America in 1893 under the leadership of the indefatigable Dr. Hermann L. Biggs of the New York City Public Health Department. Since the Ontario Board of Health had established a laboratory in 1890, it was able to conduct tests for diphtheria almost as soon as that in New York. (26) Third, doctors began to use antitoxin to treat both diagnosed cases of diphtheria and those who had been exposed to the disease. While a Berlin doctor first used antitoxin on a human patient in 1891, Roux himself made the treatment widely known through his classic paper to the Eighth International Congress of Hygiene and Demography in Budapest in September 1894. (27) Again Dr. Biggs's New York Public Health Department, which began producing antitoxin in the autumn of 1894, took the North American lead in this work. (28)

Canadian public health authorities quickly followed suit and by 1899 their use of antitoxin had produced a notable decline in diphtheria deaths. (29) By 1905, the decline was clearly worldwide. (30)

As health workers and some of the general public came to realize that society had at last some means for exerting much tighter control over diphtheria, they embarked on the first arduous phase of the public health movement's efforts against the disease. Although Hamilton's medical health officer, Dr. W. F. Langrill, argued optimistically that if public health workers had "the same support in control of diphtheria as smallpox, it would be no longer prevalent," he also demonstrated that his fellow physicians were clearly one very important part of the problem. (31) "Just recently," he reported in 1901, "a child died from what the attending physician called laryngitis. . . ." Suspicious of this diagnosis, Langrill interviewed the doctor who "claimed the disease was not diphtheria, but admitted that two children in the same family had just previously had a 'sore throat with some traces of membrane. . . .' " Meanwhile the child's family conducted a public funeral for their son with "small boys acting as pallbearers." The result of this negligence, Langrill concluded, was that "five neighbouring children were infected with diphtheria . . . all in a severe form." (32)

Families of infected children also stood in the way of effective control of diphtheria. Where isolation hospitals existed, as they did in most sizable centres in Ontario by 1903, medical health officers had the power to place diphtheria cases in them. (33) Families that placed their afflicted children (usually accompanied by their mothers) in such hospitals not only reduced the likelihood that the disease would spread in their households and neighborhoods, but they also increased the chances that the children would survive the attack of the disease. (34) While some families welcomed such an opportunity to improve the odds for their children and to avoid the often severe hardships of family quarantines, when others objected, health officers were often very reluctant to use their powers. Other families avoided both quarantines and the isolation hospital by concealing cases of the disease.

Recalcitrant parents and physicians, however, were not the only problem; public health workers themselves had to learn through long experience that only if they distributed it free would physicians and families use antitoxin as early, as frequently, and as widely as was necessary to exploit its full potentiality as a means for controlling the disease. In 1914 Ontario began, for instance, to distribute biological products, such as diphtheria antitoxin, from its own laboratories at prices much below commercial ones. Eventually, in 1916 the Ontario government made these products free to everyone. (35) The Saskatchewan Bureau of Public Heath made similar arrangements. Even so, the death rate from the disease remained at about eight percent of cases because, as the Bureau lamented, "the people of our country fail to recognize cases in the early stage when if antitoxin were freely used the death rate would be negligible." (36) School trustees had much to learn as well. As part of his work in dealing with a diphtheria epidemic in Oshawa in October 1920, the District Medical Health Officer "called a meeting of the School Board and the Board of Health" but "only after much discussion" did they eventually agree that "all school children should have an immunizing dose of Anti-toxin." (37)

While the public health movement gradually implemented the results of the first round of discoveries, medical researchers continued to work on diphtheria, thereby opening up the second phase of the campaign against the disease. By using the Schick test, devised in 1913, physicians could sort out in older children those susceptible to diphtheria from those who had developed an immunity to the disease. To the former, they could then give toxin-antitoxin to build up their immunity. (38) By the early 1920s Canadian public health authorities and physicians were beginning to use both procedures fairly regularly. (39) Both phases of this campaign against diphtheria had positive, measurable effects on the disease. For the first, Ontario reported that between 1903 and 1918 the death rate for diphtheria in that province fell from 31 to 12 for every 100,000 population. (40) For the second, as toxin-antitoxin gradually provided children with permanent immunity, the incidence of diphtheria in the Canadian population went from 76.7 per 100,000 of population in 1926 to 57.1 in 1931 to 18.6 in 1936 to 24.9 in 1941 to 20.7 in 1946 to 1.8 in 1951, to .3 in 1972. (41)

In addition to providing new knowledge and new techniques, this great research effort on diphtheria and other diseases had other positive effects on the health of children. Since it contrasted so sharply with the plodding progression characteristic of improvements in sanitation, the very momentum with which one bacteriological discovery followed on another, and the speedy and dramatic way in which many of them displayed their effects, became in themselves important parts of the improvement process. The rapid series of discoveries seem, indeed, to have been at the root of the characteristically missionary zeal and the sometimes almost millennial expectations of many health workers. Their enthusiasm was highly infectious and quickly spilled over into the general public as well. In the early years of the century, Canadians began to raise the level of their expectations in the area of public and especially of child health.

As they had been 20 years before in the earlier emphasis on sanitation, school pupils were the first group of children to reap some benefits from this new bacteriological era in public health. In the light of the growing fund of new knowledge, public health workers and the general public began at the turn of the century to focus their attention more sharply on the health of school children. When they did so they saw two very obvious weaknesses in existing arrangements. First, while either a physician or sanitary inspector decided whether or not a particular school met minimum sanitary standards, generally the teacher had the far more difficult task of diagnosing that a pupil had an infectious disease and excluding him from school. By the time such diseases as diphtheria, or even tuberculosis, reached the point in their cycle where a teacher saw that a child was sick enough to be excluded from school, the ailment had often reached an advanced stage and may already have spread to other pupils in the schoolroom. It was obviously no longer sufficient to rely on teachers or private physicians to locate and quarantine infected children. If they were to utilize fully the improved diagnostic tests and more effective methods of treatment public health workers decided that they must screen every child for infectious diseases. But even when the teacher or family physician properly and accurately diagnosed infectious disease and kept the child out of school, there was very little assurance that his family would provide him with the necessary treatment, that they would protect themselves from the infection, or that the child would not, outside of school hours, pass the disease on to his friends and acquaintances.

To solve these problems, some people concluded, clearly public health workers should inspect and visit pupils as well as schools. In 1901, for example, the Windsor, Ontario, School Board required children who had been away for over a week be examined by their family physicians or the medical health officer before they could return to school. (42) But this step, worthwhile as it probably was (for one thing it brought a dramatic improvement in school attendance) focused on the wrong end of the problem; doctors examined children only after a disease had run, or almost run, its course. As the Ontario Board of Health stated in its report both in 1899 and 1901, in its opinion the next stage in the control of infectious diseases in children was, at least during emergencies, to have "physicians visit the schools to examine for suspects . . . and to follow up the absentees to their homes. . . ." (43)

As Canadian health authorities and others interested in this work began to press seriously for such procedures, they examined carefully what was going on elsewhere. While medical inspection of school children had been discussed in France as early as the end of the eighteenth century, it was not until the last three decades of the nineteenth century that the nation made any substantial efforts to implement such ideas. And, although regular medical inspection of pupils began in Brussels as early as 1874, throughout Sweden in 1878, and in Paris in 1879, the early efforts made in Britain and the United States were the major influences on Canadian developments. (44) The latter, particularly, provided the models that Canadian centres usually followed. In contrast, too, to the sanitary phase of the public health movement, when provincial, state, or national authorities generally took the initiative, in all three countries municipal authorities in urban centres took the lead in introducing school inspection work.

In 1890 the London School Board appointed the first school medical officer in Britain. In 1893 the Bradford Board copied this action and other boards gradually followed suit. (45) This early work stimulated considerable discussion and enquiry in Britain that eventually produced national legislation. In 1907 the British Parliament passed the Education (Administrative Provisions) Act that set up a School Medical Department under the Board of Education that was to encourage local school authorities to undertake regular medical inspection of school children as rapidly as possible. (46)

In the face of an epidemic of diphtheria in 1894, Boston established North America's first school medical inspection system. Philadelphia and Chicago followed suit the next year. (47) Despite these pioneering ventures, however, the New York Department of Public Health created the scheme that became the most influential model for Canadian practice. In 1897 the Department appointed 150 physicians as part-time school medical inspectors. As Dr. Hermann Biggs explained to a meeting of the British Medical Association in Montreal later the same year, he directed the doctors to inspect, each day, the children that teachers excluded from class and to send home every pupil "found to be suffering from any form of general contagious disease or any contagious disease of the eye or parisitic disease of the skin. . . ." (48) In 1902 Biggs added two new steps to the procedures. First, he required school physicians to make, every seven to ten days, a routine examination of all pupils for contagious disease and minor infections of eyes or skin. (49) Second, and following the suggestion of Lillian D. Wald of the Henry Street Settlement, he appointed a corps of school nurses to follow up the work of the doctors. (50) In 1905, Biggs further broadened the scope of the school medical system when he instructed the doctors to begin examining children for noncontagious physical defects. (51) If a physician found any such problem, he notified the parent of it by post card. The department soon discovered, however, that the parents corrected only a very small proportion (it estimated six percent) of the defects reported to them. To deal with this situation and other problems of child health, the New York Board of Health established a separate Division of Child Hygiene, under Dr. S. Josephine Baker, and immediately increased its staff of school nurses to 141. In September 1908, the nurses began to visit the homes of all children discovered to be suffering from physical defects in order to persuade the parents to provide the necessary treatment. (52) One year later, the Department claimed that already the nurses' visits had raised the level of treatment from 6 to 83 percent. (53) By 1911 some 443 American cities had duplicated such systems. (54)

To get first-hand information about the situation in Europe and Britain, Canadians attended both the second and third medical congresses on school hygiene. (55) Canadian organizations also brought out English officials to explain their work. In April 1911, for example, Dr. George Auden, Chief Medical Superintendent of the Birmingham Schools, spoke on medical inspection to a meeting of the Ontario Education Association and other Canadian organizations. (56) More often, however, Canadians evaluated their initial efforts against those systems set up in the United States. In 1909 in her report on medical inspection in Canadian schools to the International Congress of Women, Mrs. J. N. Smillie listed Canadian efforts in terms of their being attempts "to follow in the footsteps of New York and other large American cities." (57) Addressing the first meeting of the Commission of Conservation, in 1910, Dr. Peter H. Bryce argued that in establishing and operating a school medical inspection, Canadians should copy the example of New York. (58) In outlining the aims for medical inspection in public schools in Canada, an editorial in the *Public Health Journal* used only American experience as its evidence. (59)

In the 1890s, Dr. J. G. Adams, a Toronto dentist, made the first major effort to have health professionals examine the physical condition of Canadian school children. After conducting an extensive survey of the condition of children's teeth both in Canada and elsewhere, Adams concluded that children's teeth decayed "at a much earlier period than they did formerly" and that the teeth and mouths of "a large percentage" of children were "in a very unhealthy and often disgusting condition." (60) In 1896, Adams aroused the interest of the Toronto Trades and Labor Council, the Hamilton Local Council of Women, and the Toronto Dental Society in the matter, and stirred some public discussion through newspaper reports of his conclusions. (61) In response to a number of requests, the Ontario Board of Health appointed a committee to look into the situation. In its report, the committee agreed with Adams' conclusions, and, referring to similar efforts in Germany and Britain, strongly recommended that local boards of health and school trustees appoint dental inspectors to examine the teeth of school pupils. (62) It did not, however, suggest that such inspections be made mandatory.

At this point the whole matter foundered. The Toronto School Board refused to add "three or four thousand dollars on to our already over-burdened taxpayers." (63) The provincial Department of Education completely ignored the suggestions of its sister agency. Except for the Hamilton Local Council of Women and the Toronto Trades and Labor Council, the public demonstrated at best only lukewarm support for the scheme. Some local councils of women could not agree that dental inspection was a matter of first priority, arguing instead that perhaps the state of pupils' eyes was a more serious problem. Other critics explained that the out-patients departments of some hospitals gave free care to the teeth and eyes of poor children. (64) No organizations made really vigorous efforts to persuade health or school boards to overcome their natural reluctance to venture into a new area of service. From this short-lived campaign, however, some laymen learned that sometimes one had "to step outside the ordinary routine of practice" in order to implement new standards of preventive health care and, further, that because it was "easy to investigate them with regularity and without risk of repetition," school children made excellent experimental subjects. (65)

After Adams' efforts failed, Canadians waited some years before trying again in any substantial way to introduce preventive medicine into their schools. Like Adams' plan, they directed their first efforts at only one dimension of the whole problem. In 1903 the Vancouver School Board decided that, because of the "prevalence of defective vision" amongst its charges, it should provide instruction for city teachers in the mechanics of eye testing. The Board therefore arranged for two nurses from the City Hospital to give instruction to the teachers. (66) During the same year some Ontario communities began to deal with local epidemics of children's diseases by employing physicians on a temporary basis to examine school children and to visit those who were absent.

In 1906, under the aegis of the municipal Board of Health, Montreal began the first regular and systematic medical inspection of school pupils in Canada. (67) The following year the Sydney, N.S., medical health officers began to inspect school pupils on an annual basis. In the same year, the Vancouver School Board appointed a physician as full-time medical inspector of school children and the Hamilton Board appointed Canada's first school nurse. In 1907, as well, Ontario passed legislation that permitted school boards, if they wanted to, to undertake school medical inspections. By the end of 1910, in addition to the four communities already noted, Halifax, Lachine, Toronto, Brantford, Winnipeg, Edmonton, and Nelson, B.C., made some form of medical inspection of their school pupils. In 1914 the *Public Health Journal* made a national survey of the work. (68) By this time, in the three maritime provinces, only four Nova Scotia communities—Amherst, Halifax, Truro, and Sydney—

reported that they conducted any form of school medical inspection. In the province of Quebec, the cities of Montreal, Westmount, and Lachine inspected their pupils. In Ontario, fourteen communities— Toronto, Ottawa, Kingston, London, Brantford, Niagara Falls, Brockville, Saulte Ste. Marie, Steelton, North Middlesex, Hamilton, Peterborough, Stratford, and Fort William—made school medical inspections. (69) In the prairie provinces, the cities of Winnipeg, Regina, Saskatoon, Prince Albert, Calgary, and Edmonton inspected their school children. Under the terms of British Columbia's legislation, passed in 1910, which called for an annual inspection of all school pupils, teachers, and school janitors in the province, medical inspectors worked in Victoria, Vancouver, Nelson, New Westminster, and South Vancouver. (70) Other communities across Canada reported that they were seriously considering instituting school medical inspection.

Once it entered the work, the Toronto School Board rapidly surpassed the others and erected one of the most comprehensive and widely reported school medical systems in the world. As such, it quickly became the model for many other Canadian communities. Starting about 1906, the Toronto Local Council of Women and other groups tried to persuade local health and school officials to introduce medical inspection into the city schools. (71) In this endeavour they met the very firm opposition of Dr. Charles Sheard, Toronto's Chief Medical Officer. In response to the agitation by the Council and some of its affiliated groups Sheard sampled the health of Toronto school children but "decided against appointing scores of doctors and nurses" because "there was not sufficient data to warrant it." (72) In Sheard's opinion school medical inspection was "a pure fad, instituted principally by women," who were "apt to give way to sentiment" and listened "to the talk of agitators" who wanted "easy billets for their friends, with good pay and little work." (73)

At this point, the publisher of the Toronto *Telegram,* John Ross Robertson, entered the affair. For a long time, Robertson had been extremely active in the improvement of the health of children and had been substantially responsible for the growth and development of Toronto's superb Hospital for Sick Children. (74) When, in the early part of 1910, Robertson became interested in the Council of Women's campaign for school medical inspection he entered into it with his usual journalistic flair. He investigated how New York and other places managed school nursing and medical inspection and himself wrote a series of reports on the subject for his newspaper. In addition, he offered $2,500 to the Toronto School Board to pay the costs of a school nursing experiment in the Toronto schools for a year. By deciding early in 1910 to conduct a medical survey to discover the number of mentally defective children in the schools of Toronto, the School Board had already demonstrated its own growing interest in health matters. (75) Robertson's intervention in the affair apparently convinced the Board that it would also have to begin medical inspections. Accordingly it turned down Robertson's offer but on February 25, 1910, bypassing the municipal Board of Health, it put $2,500 in the year's estimates for medical inspection. Very soon thereafter it hired Miss Lina Rogers as its first school nurse and soon-to-be director of school nursing. (76)

Once underway, the Toronto School Board rapidly expanded its school medical system. In 1913, the Chief Inspector of Schools, James L. Hughes, stated with pride that Toronto was spending in that year almost as much for medical care as the whole educational system had cost only ten years earlier. (77) By 1914 the School Health Department took care of the health of the 45,000 Toronto school pupils with a staff of one chief medical officer, 21 physicians who worked as part-time medical inspectors, one dental inspector and four dental surgeons who worked part-time, one superintendent of nurses, and 37 full-time school nurses.

In 1914, when the *Public Health Journal* made its survey of medical and dental inspection in Canada, school and public health authorities could put their responses into the context of twenty years of North American and about eight years of Canadian practice in this matter. Partly because they had been able to build effectively and with little modification on American efforts, Canadian workers had accumulated a surprisingly wide range of practical experience in school inspection over a short time. One may, therefore, ask of the 1914 reports and other contemporary Canadian material three important questions: what were school and health workers trying to accomplish with school medical inspection, what means did they use to accomplish their task, and how effective were they in reaching their goals?

At first, Canadians who favoured the medical inspection of school children saw their purpose in essentially negative terms; they wanted to reduce or to eliminate the evil of disease from their communities. As they actually got into the work, however, Canadian school medical workers and their supporters, in common with their British and American counterparts, gradually shifted their goal to the much more positive one of creating a nation whose children were all in rude good health. By 1914, moreover, many urban centres in Canada had shifted the focus of their public health work in schools from premises to pupils. To control communicable disease, health professionals regularly inspected school buildings and examined pupils, teachers, and janitors. Instead of the teachers having to do so, physicians or nurses now excluded the sick pupils and readmitted those who had recovered. In Ottawa, for example, the school physician examined the children for "scarlet fever, diphtheria, tonsilitis, measles, German measles, mumps, smallpox, chicken pox, whooping cough, ring worms, contagious skin diseases and pediculosis." (78) In some places, such as Vancouver, Edmonton, Calgary, Winnipeg, Toronto, Montreal, and Halifax, physicians inspected the pupils. In others, such as Regina, Prince Albert, Kingston, and Niagara Falls, school nurses made the initial inspections. (79) Although medical inspectors in British Columbia were supposed to examine teachers and janitors for infectious diseases once a year, there and elsewhere they seem to have made such inspections only on initial appointment. In 1914, for example, the Halifax medical officer reported only that he had examined eight new teachers "with the result that four were passed as 'satisfactory,' the balance being given either 'modified' or 'unsatisfactory' certificates." (80)

Since these were the years, too, when the great crusade against tuberculosis was growing "in equipment and strength," all inspectors showed particular interest in this disease. (81) In 1910 the Hamilton School Board assigned one nurse to full-time detection of tuberculosis among school pupils. (82) In that year alone she detected 20 cases, which were sent to sanitoriums. Toronto placed one assistant medical officer in charge of tuberculosis inspection and, in 1913, the city opened up a "forest" school for pretubercular and other sickly children. (83) Other centres, such as Hamilton and Vancouver, instituted "open air" classrooms for the same group. (84) In all areas, school nurses gave particular attention to locating tubercular children and those who were "contacts." (85)

In addition to searching out communicable diseases, most inspectors also looked for chronic defects. As the examiner in North Middlesex put it, "the body of the school child was considered a machine in order to answer the question, 'It is in good running order?' " (86) In Regina, the school nurse examined "particularly for defective eyesight, defective hearing, enlarged tonsils and adenoids, carious teeth, pediculosis, for symptoms of tuberculosis, lateral curvature, goitre, and chorea." (87) Generally, as the Nelson, B.C., medical inspector explained, her duty in such cases began and ended "with recommendation for treatment" and she customarily notified parents "requesting them to take the child to the family physician." (88) No authority reported that it invited parents to be present at the inspection of their children. Indeed, in at least some places, physicians conducted their examinations *en masse*. The South Vancouver medical inspector reported that pupils were "brought into the teacher's room apart from the class-rooms in groups of ten, boys and girls separate." Despite this rather wholesale procedure, the same inspector explained it was "the rarest exception to have objections made by either parent or pupil." (89)

The incidence of inspection varied greatly from place to place. Probably the most thoroughly inspected pupils were those of Toronto. Almost as well served were the 550 pupils in Steelton, Ontario. Other centres, such as Regina, Edmonton, Winnipeg, Lachine, Sydney, N.S., and certain British Columbia areas, established less frequent but systematic examination. Often the main work of the doctor was to inspect or examine those pupils referred to him by the school nurse or teacher. In Montreal, for example, physicians visited large schools every day and small schools at least twice a week to examine referrals. In Kingston, a school nurse visited each school twice each week and inspected all the pupils in their classrooms every two weeks.

Such a bewildering array of practices reflected local differences in what the school or health board knew about child health and preventive medicine, how much interest they had in the matter, and how much in the way of services they felt the local taxpayer would support. It also clearly demonstrated that the public health movement had not yet developed an optimum pattern of inspection and referral, or divided the task between physician and nurse in such a way that the skills and time of both were used effectively and efficiently. Nevertheless, by 1914 the school nurse was clearly moving into the central position in school medical programmes. As she moved between school and home she found of necessity that she had to add preventive medicine, teaching, and even social welfare to her primary task of preventing the spread of communicable diseases. In the school, she did some or all of the routine inspections, examinations, readmissions, and often minor first aid work as well. She kept up the medical records of the pupils, taught health to teachers and pupils through such means as lectures, demonstrations, and "nose blowing" and "tooth brushing" drills, and ran school health clubs like the Little Nurses League in Winnipeg, or the Little Mothers Classes in Regina, Vancouver, Victoria, and Stratford. In most places, however, her main task was to visit the home of the infected pupil who had been excluded from school and of the child who had an untreated chronic condition. Often, these early home visits opened the school nurse's eyes as to just how much there was to do. (90) Especially in poor homes, nurses kept a sharp eye out for cases of infectious diseases, including previously concealed cases. In Lachine, for example, the medical inspector (in this instance a physician) discovered contagious diseases in 17 percent of the 751 homes he visited over one school year. (91) When they saw how fruitful such work could be, school boards and health boards directed the nurse to exploit to the full the wider opportunities opened up by home visits.

When her powers of persuasion proved to be insufficient, the school nurse in Toronto and other cities was able to coerce the parents. If they refused to do anything for a child who was "really suffering from want of medical or surgical attention," the nurse referred the case to the Juvenile Court which took "prompt action." (92) In Toronto, the Court fined some poor parents for refusing to carry out school medical officers' orders for operations "on children suffering from adenoids and enlarged tonsils." In commenting on this matter, the editor of the *Public Health Journal* argued that "parents must not be allowed to stand in the way of their children's complete recovery. . . ." To do so would "render negatory the very useful system of inspection that has been adopted in the schools." (93)

As physicians and nurses sorted out their separate roles in school health services, Canadian dentists began to argue that they too had an important place in any comprehensive programme. On November 22, 1910, as the last of a series of public meetings in Ontario, Dr. John W. Dowd, formerly of Toronto and more recently inspector of schools in Toledo, Ohio, addressed a dinner held in his honour by the Toronto Dental Society. An honoured guest of the evening was the pioneer of dental inspection of school children, Dr. J. G. Adams. (94) This impressive occasion culminated a campaign by the Toronto Dental Society "to have a dental inspector appointed . . . to instruct teachers and pupils how to take care of their teeth and mouths to the end that length of life and happiness may be increased." (95) There was about this particular campaign and other efforts to promote dental hygiene a certain flamboyance, an excess in claims and rhetoric that sometimes brought them close to being a caricature of the whole children's health movement. In his address, for example, Dr. Dowd ingeniously argued that if one assumed that "the dental surface in the ordinary mouth is from 22 to 24 square inches" and only 8 percent of this area was properly cared for, then there was left "5 square feet of uncleaned surface in every schoolroom." If this area were visible to the naked eye, Dowd went on, "there would be a panic" but because it was not, the pupils involved were "breathing everywhere, coughing everywhere, expectorating nearly everywhere" with the result that disease "developed among the men and women in the world." (96) In 1911 an editorial in the *Public Health Journal* claimed that "fully 99 percent" of children were "in need of dental treatment." (97)

The activities of the Toronto Society were the most active Canadian manifestation of what its promoters called the "oral hygiene crusade." (98) This movement, which began in Germany in the closing decades of the nineteenth century, arrived in North America early in the twentieth. It produced a great flurry of activity on this continent in the years between 1908 and World War I. This campaign had a variety of roots in contemporary dentistry. First, a new generation of better-trained dentists displayed a growing concern for preventive work. As well, some of the excitement and sense of imminent accomplishment that the bacteriological discoveries gave to medicine in these years spilled over into dentistry. Finally, dentists were anxious to demonstrate that their craft was on the rise and that in fact it was well on the way to becoming one of the important professions of the modern community.

These factors alone, however, could not account for the successes achieved by the dental movement. On one hand, behind all the exaggeration and the self-seeking quality of the campaign, there was a serious situation. As Dr. Adams had been some years earlier, the pioneers of medical inspection were appalled at the dreadful state of the teeth of the children they examined. (99) In his annual report for 1911, the Montreal health officer, Dr. J. E. Laberge, explained that 19,843 of the 59,685 children his department had examined over the year suffered from decayed teeth. While this did not necessarily mean that these children were suffering from "any serious physical disability," Laberge argued that "it was necessary to take cognizance of such matters, as defective teeth often meant that there was some deeper-seated malady, such as tuberculosis, bad digestion and so forth." (100) On the other hand, public support for the school to inspect and even to treat children's teeth, which revealed itself in the Toronto dinner, was another example in the sharp rise in the standards that Canadians were applying to the health of children. Dentists in the crusade offered no really convincing evidence that the teeth of Canadian children were then any worse than they had ever been. In contrast, however, to their response to Dr. Adams' alarms in 1896, by 1910 some Canadians were clearly willing to do something about the situation.

When the real state of their pupils' teeth was reported to them, most school or health boards decided to have medical inspectors include defective teeth among the chronic conditions they reported to parents. Despite the enthusiasm of some parts of the dental profession for a separate school dental service, and the model for one that Toronto and later Vancouver provided, however, it was the school nurse who eventually undertook most of the work for preventive dentistry in the school. She examined teeth, persuaded parents to have caries treated, demonstrated the proper use of the tooth brush, conducted tooth-brushing drills, sometimes provided children with free tooth brushes, and often arranged for free treatment for poor and indigent children. (101)

Public health workers, school officials, and school and health board members often expressed their pleasure with the early results of the medical inspection of Canadian school children. While one may ask whether the actual effects of what they did supported these generally subjective feelings on the matter, two difficulties stand in the way of a really precise and accurate answer to this question. First, as the example of diphtheria clearly showed, the vigorous pursuit of this disease by medical inspectors was perhaps only the most important of a number of factors that initiated its decline. Second, Canadian school medical workers neither subjected their early work to vigorous scientific analysis nor did they keep the kinds of records that would have permitted others to do so. In their speeches, articles, and official reports on the topic, Canadian workers generally took as given the fact that foreign and Canadian centres already inspecting their pupils had fully proved the worth of the practice. Such statements of worth as they did offer were general ones like that of British Columbia's Board of Health, which explained that there could be "no doubt of the progress . . . being made" by means of medical inspection. (102) Public health workers clearly saw their tasks as extending the practice to areas where it did not yet exist and expanding the scope of the service where it did. When health officers included statistics in their annual reports, they recorded without analysis such items as the number of classrooms and pupils that they had inspected over the year and the number and types of defects they had discovered in them. In 1918, the Calgary School Board reported, its medical inspector conducted 950 physical examinations, and its school nurses made 3,862 inspections and visited 969 classes and 219 homes. In addition, the Board's eye, ear, nose, and throat clinic tested 4,981 pupils and treated 392 eye cases, 72 ear cases, and 52 nose and throat cases and its dental clinic treated 522 children, performing 1,041 dental operations on them. (103)

Nevertheless, public health workers, school boards, and boards of health offered a great deal of not very precise though definite evidence that medical inspection was an effective device for the improvement of public health generally and the health of children in particular. Montreal, with the longest experience in the work, made consistent though low-keyed claims as to the worth of what it did. In 1909, three years after the city began such work, Mrs. Smillie reported to the International Congress of Women that medical inspection had sharply decreased the incidence of contagious diseases in the schools. She noted particularly that "no serious epidemic of measles, scarlet fever or diphtheria" had occurred "since the installation of regular inspection. . . ." (104) In 1911 the city's health officer disclosed that although his inspectors had concluded

that 27,348 of the 59,685 children examined in the year "were not
in a satisfactory state of health," when he compared this situation
to their findings of preceding years, he saw nonetheless "a great
improvement." (105) In 1914 the Montreal Board of Health concluded that by the means of school medical inspection, "pediculosis
and scabies have almost disappeared from the schools" and there
had been "a great diminution of contagious diseases in the city."
The Board was so pleased with these and other results of its work
that, in 1918, it organized a separate division of child hygiene for
Montreal schools. (106)

Elsewhere, medical inspectors also reported many positive results
of their work. In an entirely typical statement, the school medical
inspector for Saint John, N.B., reported, four years after beginning
the work in that city, that there had been "a great lessening of
the number of more serious conditions found in the school." The
effect of this change, he went on, was to make his work increasingly
"preventive as well as curative." Of the physical defects calling
for reports to parents he found that, in 70 percent of cases, they
were "promptly attended to" and even in poorer districts he
obtained this percentage of treatment "eventually by following up
and rectifying the cases." (107) In 1919 the Vancouver school
medical officer explained that in the previous year alone his department increased by 125 percent the number of treatments that it had
"secured for children suffering from various physical defects." (108)
In 1921 the Hamilton medical health officer boasted of the "vast
improvement" that two years of dental inspection and treatment
had made on the teeth of school children in Hamilton. Over this
time his department's surveys and clinics had reduced from 90 percent to 70 percent the number of children whose teeth needed
treatment. (109) While "parents, teachers, and medical men,"
testified as to the worth of medical inspection, noted the British
Columbia Board of Health in the same year, they also strongly
brought home to the Board the need for "follow-up work." (110) By
the early 1920s most health officials would probably have concurred
with the conclusion on school medical inspection reached by the
Chief Medical Officer for New Brunswick, Dr. George G. Melvin.
Although no public health activity in his province presented such
difficulties and involved "so great a direct expenditure," Melvin
wrote, yet in view of what was "possible to accomplish, and the

outstanding importance of that accomplishment," the province just had to overcome the difficulties. (111)

By the time the nation went to war in 1914, public health workers and their supporters had persuaded urban Canadians of the undoubted merits of maintaining sanitary schools and of medically inspecting school children. While such reformers had taken a long time to implement sanitary standards, in only fifteen years they had popularized the idea of inspection to the extent that most urban school systems in Canada either inspected their pupils or were on the verge of doing so. In their school medical services members of the public health movement firmly believed that they had developed and demonstrated the worth of a practical and effective way of making Canada a healthier and happier nation. By this time, too, many workers were eager to take what they saw as the next obvious step in their efforts, that of extending their service to all the children in small towns and country districts. When Alan Brown observed, however, that Canadian child care materials gave him "the impression that they were not intended for use outside the city limits" he put his finger on the major flaw in the whole public health apparatus as it affected rural children. (112) As they began to tackle rural work systematically, public health workers first discovered that they had to shift their principal sphere of activity from the municipal to the provincial level of government. Next, and far more important, they found that they had to subsume the school medical inspection campaign under the until then distinctly separate crusade to protect and improve the health of infants and young children. At this point, the effort to improve the health of school children ceased to be a separate entity in the public health movement and became but one part of a much wider campaign to improve the health of all Canadian children. (113)

NOTES

1. I examine this reform movement as a whole in my forthcoming Ph.D. dissertation, *Children in English-Canadian Society* (Toronto, 1975). See also my article "The Urban Child," *History of Education Quarterly*, 9 (Fall 1969): 305–11.
2. Peter H. Bryce, "History of Public Health in Canada," *Canadian Therapeutist and Sanitary Engineer* 1 (June 1910): 278–91.

3. Ibid., p. 290; see also Peter H. Bryce, "The Story of Public Health in Canada" in *A Half Century of Public Health: Jubilee Historical Volume of the American Public Health Association,* ed. Mazÿck P. Ravenel (New York, 1921), pp. 56–66.

4. R. D. Defries, ed., *The Development of Public Health in Canada: A Review of the History and Organization of the Public Health in the Provinces of Canada, with an Outline of the Present Organization of the National Health Section of the Department of National Pensions and National Health, Canada* (Toronto, 1940), pp. 15, 35, 49, 56, 67, 90, 101, 115, 131. For the background to the Ontario legislation, see Bryce, "History of Public Health," pp. 287–90, and R. D. Splane, *Social Welfare in Ontario, 1791–1893: A Study of Public Welfare Administration* (Toronto, 1965), p. 199. For an account of the English Public Health Act of 1875, see W. M. Frazer, *A History of English Public Health, 1834–1939* (London, 1950), pp. 114–25.

5. Ontario Board of Health, *Report,* 1883, p. xlvi.

6. Ibid., 1891, p. 38.

7. See, for example, *Victoria Colonist,* April 13, 1897, p. 8, and May 14, 1897, p. 8.

8. Ontario Board of Health, *Report,* 1898, pp. 68–75; Toronto *Globe,* May 2, 1900, p. 7, and May 4, 1900, p. 12.

9. A. C. Jost, "The Conservation of Child Life," *P.H.J.,* 11 (November 1920): 503–12.

10. Ontario Board of Health, *Report,* 1887, pp. iii–v.

11. New Westminster *British Columbian,* March 14, 1885. See also *Victoria Colonist,* October 17, 1891, p. 1, *British Columbian* May 11, 1894, p. 3, *Colonist,* January 8, 1900, p. 4, and Toronto *Globe,* June 19, 1900, p. 12.

12. Ontario, Board of Health, *Report,* 1885, pp. 29–34.

13. Ibid., 1887, p. v; ibid., 1888, pp. iv–vi.

14. *British Columbian,* June 3, 1892, p. 4.

15. *P.H.J.,* 2 (April 1911): 184.

16. Ibid., 2 (May 1911): 221; ibid., 3 (May 1912): 249–55.

17. Saskatchewan Bureau of Public Health, *Report,* 1919–1920, p. 8. For an account of the legal status of compulsory vaccination, see Peter Frank Bargen, *The Legal Status of the Canadian Public School Pupil* (Toronto, 1961), p. 79.

18. See, for example, Ontario Board of Health, *Report,* 1882, pp. 168–76; ibid., 1883, pp. xlv, 400–8.

19. See, for example, ibid., 1883, pp. xlvi, 242–43; ibid., 1890, pp. xiii–xvi, lxxxix–xcvii; *British Columbian,* April 9, 1892, p. 4.

20. Ontario Board of Health, *Report,* 1883, pp. 242–43.

21. George Rosen, *A History of Public Health* (New York, 1958), pp. 344–403.

22. Ontario Board of Health, *Report,* 1892, p. 19; ibid., 1891, p. 1.

23. Ibid., 1892, p. 19.

24. Privy Council, Medical Research Council, *Diphtheria: Its Bacteriology, Pathology and Immunology* (London, 1923), pp. 44–63, 126–29, 232–35; C.-E. Winslow, *The Life of Hermann M. Biggs: Physician and Statesman of the Public Health* (Philadelphia, 1929), pp. 102–30; Rosen, *History of Public Health,* pp. 319–20, 333–36; and Ontario Board of Health, *Report,* 1890, pp. lvii–lxii.

25. Ontario Board of Health, *Report,* 1901, p. 8.

26. Ibid., 1890, p. lxxviii; Defries, *Development of Public Health in Canada,* pp. 77–88.

27. Medical Research Council, *Diphtheria,* pp. 61–62.

28. Hermann Biggs, "The Development of Research Laboratories," New York Department of Health, *Monthly Bulletin* 1 (March 1911): 54–56.

29. See, for example, Ontario Board of Health, *Report,* 1899, p. 12.

30. R. H. Mullin, "Recent Advances in the Control of Diphtheria," *Canadian Medical Association Journal* 14 (May 1924): 398–406.

31. Ontario Board of Health, *Report,* 1903, p. 46.

32. Ibid., 1901, p. 93.

33. Ibid., 1903, p. 48.

34. In a crude comparison of home versus hospital treatment Bryce demonstrated this fact as early as 1903. Ibid., 1903, p. 52. See also the much more accurate confirmation of the efficacy of hospital treatment in Toronto between 1912 and 1919 in Mullin, "Recent Advances."

35. Ontario Board of Health, *Report,* 1920, pp. 37–38; Defries, *Development of Public Health in Canada,* pp. 77–88.

36. Saskatchewan Bureau of Public Health, *Report,* 1917–1918, p. 17.

37. Ontario Board of Health, *Report,* 1920, p. 167.

38. Medical Research Council, *Diphtheria,* pp. 349–61.

39. See, for example, Ontario Board of Health, *Report,* 1921, p. 204.

40. Ibid., 1920, p. 37.

41. M. C. Urquhart and K. A. H. Buckley, eds., *Historical Statistics of Canada* (Toronto, 1965), p. 45.

42. Ontario Board of Health, *Report,* 1901, pp. 110–11.

43. Ibid., p. 6; see also ibid., 1899, pp. 72–74.

44. Rosen, *History of Public Health,* p. 365.

45. Frazer, *English Public Health,* p. 257.

46. Ibid., pp. 256–58, 323–24.

47. Rosen, *History of Public Health,* p. 366.

48. Winslow, *Biggs,* p. 157.

49. Ibid., p. 186.

50. Lina Rogers Struthers, *The School Nurse: A Survey of the Duties and Responsibilities of the Nurse in the Maintenance of Health and Physical Perfection and the Prevention of Disease Among School Children* (New York, 1917), pp. 17–18.

51. Winslow, *Biggs,* p. 193.

52. Ibid., pp. 214–15.

53. Ibid., p. 215; for a more detailed account of the work of the Division of Child Hygiene, see "Division of Child Hygiene," New York Department of Health *Monthly Bulletin* 1 (January 1911): 14–16, and Ernst J. Lederle, "The Needs of the Department of Health," ibid., 1 (October 1911): 236–37.

54. Russell Sage Foundation, *What American Cities are Doing for the Health of School Children: Report Covering Conditions in 1038 Cities* (New York, 1911). The report was summarized for Canadians in *P.H.J.*, 2 (September 1911): 433.

55. Ontario, *Sessional Papers*, 1907, no. 62, pp. 23–26; James Kerr and E. W. Wallis, eds., *Transactions of the Second International Congress on School Hygiene, London, 1907*, 3 vols. (London, 1908); A Maloine, ed., *Ille Congrès International D'Hygiène Scolaire, Paris, 2–7 Aout, 1910*, 3 (Paris, 1911), p. 9.

56. George A. Auden, "School Inspection and the Public Health Service," *P.H.J.*, 2 (May 1911): 207–10. See also L. Haden Guest, "Poverty and School Clinics," ibid., 2 (July 1911): 317–19; L. Haden Guest, "School Clinics," ibid., 4 (May 1913): 272–77.

57. International Congress of Women, *Report of the International Congress of Women, held in Toronto, Canada, June 24–30, 1909*, 2 vols. (Toronto, 1910), 2:57.

58. Commission of Conservation, *Report*, 1910, p. 132.

59. *P.H.J.*, 2 (June 1911): 276.

60. J. G. Adams to P. H. Bryce, February 10, 1896, quoted in National Council of Women [hereafter cited as N.C.W.], *Yearbook*, 1896, p. 463; A. E. Webster, "Status of Dentistry," *Dominion Dental Journal* [hereafter cited as *D.D.J.*] 22 (December 1910): 571–607.

61. N.C.W., *Yearbook*, 1896, pp. 35, 41–42, 457–70; Ontario Board of Health, *Report*, 1896, pp. 76–82; *Colonist*, July 25, 1896, p. 8.

62. Ontario Board of Health, *Report*, 1896, pp. 80–82.

63. N.C.W., *Yearbook*, 1896, p. 459.

64. Ibid., pp. 49–50, 457–60, 469–70.

65. Ibid., p. 467.

66. Vancouver School Board, *Report*, 1903, p. 17.

67. J. Edouard Laberge, "Inspection médicale des maisons d'éducation," *Bulletin Sanitaire* 9 (1909): 117–24.

68. *P.H.J.*, 5 (February and March 1914): 91–98, 150–60.

69. While the *P.H.J.* did not list Fort William, the National Council of Women's Public Health Committee in 1911 noted it as one of a number of communities where medical inspection was under way (N.C.W., *Yearbook*, 1911, pp. 43–47).

70. See also Alice Ravenhill, "The Health of Public School Children in British Columbia," *The Child* 4 (June 1914): 697–99.

71. N.C.W., *Yearbook*, 1910, pp. i–ii.

72. Edward Miller Steven, *Medical Supervision in Schools: Being An Account of the Systems at Work in Great Britain, Canada, the United States, Germany, and Switzerland* (London, 1910), pp. 182–83.

73. Ibid.

74. Alfred Wood, "The Largest Sick Children's Hospital in the World," *Canadian Magazine* 12 (February 1899): 314–18; Toronto *Evening Telegram,* December 20, 1909, p. 18; Toronto *Globe,* June 1, 1918, pp. 5, 7; "John Ross Robertson," in J. E. Middleton, *The Municipality of Toronto: A History* (Toronto and New York, 1923), pp. 57–58.

75. *Evening Telegram,* January 14, 1910, p. 18; *Globe,* January 28, 1910, p. 14.

76. *Globe,* February 25, 1910, p. 16; *Evening Telegram,* February 25, 1910, p. 10.

77. Bruce N. Carter, "James L. Hughes and the Gospel of Education: A Study of the Work and Thought of a Nineteenth-Century Canadian Educator" (Ed.D. diss., University of Toronto, 1966), p. 360.

78. *P.H.J.,* 2 (December 1911): 588–89.

79. Jean Browne, "School Nursing in Regina," *P.H.J.,* 5 (February 1914): 91–92; "Medical Inspection of Schools in the Middle West," ibid., pp. 94–95; "Medical Inspection of Schools in Ontario," ibid., 5 (March 1914): 159–60.

80. "Medical Inspection of Schools in Nova Scotia," *P.H.J.,* 5 (February 1914): 98.

81. N.C.W., *Yearbook,* 1912, p. 102; John J. Heagerty, *Four Centuries of Medical History* (Toronto, 1928), pp. 226–45.

82. Ontario Board of Health, *Report,* 1910, pp. 148–50.

83. Struthers, *The School Nurse,* pp. 132–43; see also Leonard P. Ayres, *Open Air Schools* (New York, n.d.).

84. Daniel Hockin, "The Rotary Clinic," *Twenty-fifth Anniversary of Rotary Club of Vancouver, Canada: 1913–1938* (Vancouver, 1938), pp. 14–15.

85. See, for example, Canada, Department of Health, *Handbook of Child Welfare Work in Canada for the Year, March 31, 1922* [hereafter cited as *Handbook*], ed. Helen MacMurchy (Ottawa, 1923), p. 56.

86. *P.H.J.,* 5 (March 1914): 160.

87. Browne, "School Nursing in Regina," pp. 91–93.

88. "Medical Inspection of Schools in British Columbia," ibid., 5 (March 1914): 150.

89. Ibid., p. 153.

90. Struthers, *The School Nurse,* pp. 1–4.

91. "Medical Inspection in Quebec," *P.H.J.,* 5 (March 1914): 156.

92. Struthers, *The School Nurse,* p. 40.

93. *P.H.J.,* 4 (February 1913): 94.

94. "Complimentary dinner to John W. Dowd, by the Toronto Dental Society, Nov. 22, 1910," *D.D.J.,* 22 (December 1910): 570–600.

95. "Editorial Notes," *D.D.J.*, 22 (October 1910): 511–12.
96. John W. Dowd, "The Mouth and the Teeth as Factors in Public Health," *D.D.J.*, 22 (December 1910): 573.
97. *P.H.J.*, 2 (May 1911): 221.
98. For the origin and development of the oral hygiene crusade, see E. B. Hicks, "Free Examination of School Children's Teeth: What Oral Hygiene Means to Them," *D.D.J.*, 22 (October 1910): 460–66; Arthur Day, "What is Being Done Outside of the Dental Office for the Improvement of the Human Mouth," *P.H.J.*, 3 (May 1912): 235–39; Professor Dr. Dieck, "The Care of the Teeth of School Children in Germany," ibid., 4 (June 1913): 366–69, and Robert M. McCluggage, *A History of the American Dental Association: A Century of Health Service* (Chicago, 1959), pp. 248–53. For what dentists saw as the social implications of their work see the talk by Dr. A. W. Thornton, Toronto, to the Canadian Public Health Association's 1912 meeting entitled "The Dentist as Social Worker," *P.H.J.*, 3 (September 1912): 524; and W. D. Cowan, "Dental Caries in School Children and Dental Inspection," ibid., 4 (November 1913): 602–5.
99. See, for example, James Stuart, "Public School Medical Inspection," *Canadian Therapeutist* 1 (August 1910): 379–81.
100. *P.H.J.*, 3 (April 1912): 222; see also, C. P. Kennedy, "Report on the Mouths and Teeth of the Children in Two Public Schools of Toronto," *D.D.J.*, 22 (December 1910): 571–72, and A. E. Webster, "Dental Inspection of Two Schools in Toronto," ibid., pp. 600–4.
101. See, for example, Struthers, *The School Nurse*, pp. 141–42, 205–25, and Browne, "School Nursing in Regina," p. 93.
102. British Columbia Board of Health, *Report*, 1920, p. 15.
103. Canada, Dominion Bureau of Statistics, *Historical Statistical Survey of Education in Canada* (Ottawa, 1921), p. 110.
104. International Congress of Women, *Report . . . 1909*, 2:58.
105. *P.H.J.*, 3 (April 1912): 222.
106. *Handbook*, p. 153.
107. Ibid., pp. 82–83.
108. Vancouver School Board, *Report*, 1919, p. 39.
109. Ontario Board of Health, *Report*, 1921, p. 317.
110. *Handbook*, p. 40.
111. Ibid., p. 78.
112. Alan Brown, "Problems of the Rural Mother in the Feeding of Her Children," *P.H.J.*, 9 (July 1918): 297.
113. See *Children in English-Canadian Society*, pt. 2.

Fig. 1. Hamilton Central School, 1853 (courtesy of the Metropolitan Toronto Library Board)

Fig. 2. The house that supposedly was built in Niagara before 1812 and used by Mrs. Young as a private school (with a log lining) (courtesy of the Metropolitan Toronto Library Board)

Fig. 3. Public health conditions in the schools in the early 1900s (courtesy of Ontario Archives, Toronto)

Fig. 4. John Rudolphus Booth and his family, taken in September 1871 (courtesy of the Public Archives of Canada)

Fig. 5. "Uncared For" (courtesy of the Metropolitan Toronto Library Board)

Fig. 6. A neglected child, photographed in Manitoba (courtesy of
the Public Archives of Canada)

Fig. 7. A model school in Ottawa, taken in June 1899 (courtesy of
the Public Archives of Canada)

Fig. 8. A photograph showing the inadequate lighting conditions that prevailed in schools in the early 1900s (courtesy of the Ontario Archives)

Part III

Science, Professionalism, and the Higher Learning

DOUGLAS LAWR

7. AGRICULTURAL EDUCATION IN NINETEENTH-CENTURY ONTARIO: AN IDEA IN SEARCH OF AN INSTITUTION

Despite a consensus about the need for public agricultural education in nineteenth-century Ontario, several attempts to create a new institution modeled on British or American examples failed. These early attempts encountered a number of problems: the conflict of purposes between the improvers and the local farm people, the paucity of agricultural science, and the total lack of experience in organizing instructional programs for large numbers of the adult population. Not until the early twentieth century was the long-standing goal institutionalized in the Ontario Agricultural College. In the end problems of institutional role definition had combined with the development of agricultural science to create both a new profession and a highly successful way of assisting farmers.

IN 1870 JOHN CARLING, Ontario's Commissioner of Public Works and Agriculture, repeated one of the most persistent ideas of the nineteenth century: what this country needed, he said, was some kind of agricultural education in "the science of farming." (1)

There were several reasons for Carling's concern for systematic agricultural education. One of the most significant was the rising prestige of science. Even clergymen were asserting that the nineteenth century was "eminently the age of science," (2) and there

Mr. Lawr is an Assistant Professor in the History of Education Department, Althouse College, the University of Western Ontario. This essay first appeared in The History of Education Quarterly *(Fall 1972).*

was ample evidence to support such a claim. An obvious illustration was the number of institutes and societies formed to celebrate the scientific spirit. One of the oldest of these, the Canadian Institute, was established in 1848 to provide a forum for the discussion of all branches of the natural sciences, and before many years had passed societies dedicated to the study of virtually every aspect of natural history and the natural sciences sprang up in all the provinces. (3) At this time also the practical and natural sciences were entering the country's universities. But science was not to be contained by the walls of erudite institutes nor her application reserved for the study of natural phenomena; her spirit imbued many of the intellectual disciplines with her characteristics, real or imagined. The scientific method was infused into literature to produce the literary genres of realism and naturalism, and a science-inspired theory of causation, applied to history and political philosophy, nourished the growth of nineteenth-century determinism, both economic and social. In such an intellectual environment, it is not surprising that the spirit of science was often invoked in behalf of the farmer from the lecturn and the press, or that "scientific agriculture" and "the science of farming" were two phrases much in vogue. That "the minds of the agriculturals should be irradiated with the beams of science" was a typical expression of time. (4)

Another reason for Carling's concern arose from the view, widely held in some quarters, that many farming practices in Ontario were backward and much in need of improvement. While there were many excellent farms in Ontario, there were also many regions barely emerged from the pioneer period. Farming practice on these lands tended to be primitive and exploitive, and agriculture under these conditions scarcely developed beyond the subsistence level. At a time when it was claimed that agriculture was the mother of industry and the source of prosperity, such haphazard farming methods threatened the economic development of the whole country. (5) Bringing scientific methods of production to the farmers through agricultural education seemed a good way to strengthen the province's basic industry.

There was more to "scientific agriculture," however, than a knowledge of good farming techniques; also implied in the term was a disposition of mind conducive to experiment, to observation, and, what was more important, to change. This was "scientific" used in the sense of "progressive" farming. It was the spirit of science (or the scientific method) influencing the farmer, rather than the results of science applied to the farm. Used in this way, the term "scientific agriculture" was meant to act as an antidote to the mind-set of pioneer farmers who started with little and achieved a modest success by virtue of the virgin fertility of the soil, the cash crop, and their personal habits of hard work and frugality. These were the farmers who "set it down as a self-evident truth that the only requisites for success in farming were physical strength, industry, prudence, and economy." (6) The intent of many persons concerned with agricultural improvement was to augment the effectiveness of these moral principles of hard work and strict economy with objective attitudes more conducive to experimentation, innovation, and change. "We must get farmers interested in scientific agriculture," claimed one friend of agricultural education, because farmers must be made aware "that progress and improvement are possible." (7) Thus, proper attitudes as well as required skills were subsumed in the term "scientific agriculture."

Small wonder, then, that Carling should call for some form of agricultural education in the science of farming, or that it should be a recurring demand throughout the nineteenth century. But what form should it take? What kind of "school" could do the job? How could the idea of education in the science of agriculture be institutionalized? As it turned out, these proved to be difficult and complex questions, and three attempts were required before the issue was successfully resolved.

The first attempt to institutionalize agricultural education began with the establishment of the Chair of Agriculture in King's College, Toronto. Like many other Upper Canadian institutions, the model was imported from abroad. There were precedents for it on both sides of the Atlantic; Chairs of Agriculture were established in Edinburgh and Oxford in the 1790s, and in 1804 a Professorship of Natural History was established at Harvard. (8) But the immediate reasons for establishing a Chair of Agriculture for Upper Canada arose out of an attempt to settle the indigenous "University Question" that agitated the colonies in the 1830s and 1840s by widening the purview of the institutions of higher education. The Chair first appeared in Robert Baldwin's University Bill of 1843, which set out the educational purposes he sought to achieve (9):

the state must control educational resources (the property endowments); the state had a responsibility to distribute the advantages
of these resources throughout the various levels of society; and if
public education was to serve a larger proportion of the population,
the state university would have to expand its curriculum to include
"the various branches of useful knowledge." (10) State support,
secularism, and a desire to share the benefits of science with the
industrial and agricultural classes of the province—these were the
main principles supporting Baldwin's conception of a University.
In short, the constitution of a state university must be so constructed that "all sections of the community may enjoy its advantages and share in its arrangements." (11) And a Chair of Agriculture, it was assumed, would allow the agricultural class to participate in the advantages of a state-supported university.

Baldwin's University Bill did not pass the Legislature, but the
next year, probably in an attempt to preempt Baldwin's ground,
Anglican-controlled King's College established ten new professor-
ships, including a Chair of Agriculture, in the "various branches of
useful knowledge." (12) Although no professor was appointed to
the Chair, it was carried over into the new provincial University of
Toronto in 1850, and next year George Buckland was brought from
England to become its first incumbent. In 1852 the new Board of
Agriculture acquired a plot of land in the vicinity of what is now
Varsity Stadium "to afford the Professor of Agriculture a ready
means of giving practical illustration and effect to his class lectures
and to facilitate testing of imported seeds, plants, and imple-
ments." (13) In 1856 an academic Department of Agriculture was
set up in the University with its own admission standards and its
own two-year diploma course. (14) Although Agriculture was not
included in the subjects prescribed for the Bachelor of Arts degree,
scholarships of £30, or approximately $150, were available to stu-
dents intending to pursue agriculture as an occupation. The first
year of the course was in academic work in Agricultural Chemistry,
Comparative Physiology, Mineralogy, Geography, Surveying, Bot-
any, Management of Property, and Farm Finance. The second year
was given over entirely to "practical agriculture." (15) Theoretically, at least, instruction in scientific agriculture was well under
way in the University of Toronto.

But by 1860 it was evident that agricultural education at the University was a failing cause. Although there was a professor, an experimental plot, a course, a scholarship, and a diploma, there were only a few students. When the Commissioners Appointed to Enquire into the Expenditure of Funds at the University of Toronto reported in 1862, they could find only six students taking Agriculture, and only "one or two" in the Diploma Course. They properly concluded that "few young men desire to attend University to study Agriculture." (16) The Chair of Agriculture, the educational innovation of the 1840s designed to bring the benefits of the University to the rural community, was declared a failure on all sides.

Interest in the idea of educating farmers' sons in the science of agriculture flagged with the creation and the failure of the Chair of Agriculture. The Education Department's *Journal of Education,* which monitored educational opinion expressed in the province's main newspapers and journals, found little to report on the subject. The silence was broken only by the reports of the annual meetings of the Provincial Agricultural Association when speakers invariably decried the sorry state of agricultural education. (17) The Chair of Agriculture was the tag end of a larger educational movement of the 1830s and 1840s, which created, among other things, the administrative basis of the public school system. By the late fifties much of the energy of this educational movement was successfully expended, and the relatively small matter of a Chair of Agriculture was of concern to only a few of the leaders in the agricultural societies. Inserted in the school system to round out an educational ideology, with little thought given to its application or its function in the farming community, the Chair was severely handicapped from its very inception.

After 1868 a variety of new schools and institutions were created or aided by the state so that particular occupational groups might avail themselves of the benefits of a practical education, thereby improving their own lot through self-help, as well as raising the value of their contribution to society. In 1868 Commissioner Carling resumed the government grant to the Mechanics Institutes, so they might fulfill their role as "Peoples' Colleges" by providing the "industrial classes" with a scientific and practical education through evening sessions. (18) Two years later the same government (Sandfield Macdonald's) proposed to establish a College of Technology to train the "artisan classes" or the skilled technicians. The eventual results of this proposal was the School of Practical Science and, finally, the Faculty of Applied Science in the University of Toronto. (19) In 1871 the Public School Act made elementary education free by abolishing the rate bills, and also set up a new institution, the high school, designed specifically to provide an "English and scientific education," presumably of wider application than the classical content of the former grammar schools. Thus, in the years immediately following Confederation, there were renewed efforts on several fronts to bring science to the producing classes. And since farmers were the foremost producers, the period also saw the initiation of the second venture in agricultural education.

Once again foreign precedents provided the prototype institution, only this time the American example predominated. After the early 1850s agricultural and manual-labor schools were established in the eastern and midwestern United States, and when public aid was made available, state agricultural colleges appeared in New York, Michigan, Pennsylvania, Maryland, Iowa, and Minnesota. When the Morrill Land Grant Act provided a federal endowment for them in 1862, the agricultural colleges appeared as a real possibility for higher education in the science of farming. As a result, Carling delegated the Reverend William Clarke, editor of the *Ontario Farmer*, to visit these American institutions "to ascertain the establishment, cost and mode of sustaining such colleges" in Canada. Clarke was favourably impressed with the American agricultural colleges in general and the one in Michigan in particular, and his report was influential in determining the kind of institution eventually established at Guelph. (20)

But it would be a mistake to assume that the Ontario School of Agriculture was planned as a carbon copy of the American colleges; the British influence was also at work here. From the beginning the OSA was connected to an experimental farm, and at that time no American college was provided with an agricultural experimental station; not until 1875 was the first of these established in Connecticut. The experimental farm was brought to Ontario from Britain, where it had evolved from the earlier model farm. Agricultural schools with small model farms were an integral part of the Irish educational system, (21) and various schemes to create similar schools in Ontario had been proposed since the 1840s. When the scientific method was applied to the model farm, it became an experimental farm. In 1843 the world's first agricultural experimental station began at the Rothamsted model farm, England, under the direction of J. B. Lawes and the soil chemist, J. H. Gilbert. (22) This new development was not long crossing the Atlantic; within a few years the Board of Agriculture for Canada West established an experimental farm in connection with the Chair of Agriculture in the University of Toronto. Little wonder, then, that the first distinctly agricultural school in Ontario should have its own experimental farm.

As in the case of the Chair of Agriculture, there were also local circumstances and influences at work in shaping this second attempt at institutionalizing agricultural education. Some of these became obvious in the controversy over the location of the new agricultural school.

In November 1871 the Sandfield Macdonald government bought 600 acres in Mimico at a cost of $46,000 for the purpose of establishing a provincial agricultural school and model farm. (23) This site had a number of points in its favour. It had a variety of soils, it was on the Great Western line, and it was situated only seven miles from Toronto. But in the following month, Edward Blake's Reformers replaced the Macdonald government and Archibald McKellar, the new Commissioner of Agriculture, appointed the Council of the Agricultural and Arts Association to report on the Mimico site, since "wide differences of opinion prevail[ed] as to the eligibility of the site purchased by the late Government." (24) After a thorough tour of inspection the Council condemned it, unanimously. The commissioner then sent them to investigate an alternative site north of Guelph, near Elora, but while in Guelph on this mission the Council found a 550 acre farm to the south of town that they liked better and that they recommended be purchased. In December 1873 the government closed the deal for the Guelph site. (25)

The change of site threw the agricultural school into the political cauldron. In the months before a new location was found, many members of the Legislative Assembly proposed to situate the school in their home ridings. The Liberal-Conservative opposition, who had their own expert report in support of their choice of the original Mimico site in 1871, never forgave the Reformers for abandoning it at an additional cost of $30,000. Although there is no evidence to suggest that the relocation of the site was motivated by purely political considerations, suspicion and bad feeling clouded the young institution's prospects for a generation or more. (26)

But the relocation was important for more than political reasons; it also had a bearing on the kind of institution to be established. The move from Mimico meant that the new agricultural school was to be removed entirely from the ambit of the University. No one, of course, proposed another Chair of Agriculture, but Professor Buckland spoke in favour of an arrangement that would have placed the school close enough to the city to enable it to benefit from the presence of University men. Buckland had no illusions about the type of work to be done at an agricultural school; his plan was "simply to give the young farmers reliable information on the actual results at which scientific men have already arrived which have a bearing on agricultural practice." (27) Yet in the view represented by Professor Buckland, the "scientific men" should be drawn from the University, even though the place where the "youth intended for farming" came to hear them would be outside it. In this scheme, agriculture could benefit from the learning of the University, yet remain independent of it. But the move to Guelph indicated that even a tenuous connection was not considered necessary, and that the "scientific men" at the agricultural school should have nothing to do with the University. The observation expressed by the Provincial Agricultural Association president that "we failed in our attempt to combine literary and agricultural courses . . . [because] the general overpower the special" summed up the prevailing view. (28) The failure of the Chair of Agriculture convinced its advocates that agricultural education was a delicate creature in need of special care and protection.

The move to Guelph also meant that the agricultural school should avoid as far as possible the influence of the city. Reverend Clarke's admonition that "there must be no connection with the University of Toronto or any other existing institution of learning," and that the school must not be located "in Toronto or any other leading city of the province," was an example of this "no contamination" viewpoint. (29) Clarke was even more apprehensive of urban influences than he was of the University's. An agricultural college in or near a city would have been highly inappropriate, because of another purpose assigned to the new institution. It was hoped that through training in the "science of farming" rural youth would "learn to appreciate their calling as an intellectual and dignified pursuit," and thus help to mitigate, at least, a serious and increasing evil of the day—the strong inclination of so many young men in the country "to abandon the hearths and vocations of their fathers to swell the already overcrowded walks of commerce and the professions in our towns and cities." (30) The new school should not only teach good farming, it should also spearhead the effort to "urge the importance of a higher standard of mental culture and a general uplifting of that noblest and yet most despised of human pursuits, Life on a Farm." (31)

In the spring of 1874 the Ontario School of Agriculture opened for business with a principal, a rector, 550 acres, and 28 students. Although Commissioner Carling had originally spoken of providing a "higher institution" offering instruction in the science of farming, the new institution at Guelph was really a type of secondary school. Admission requirements were fulfilled by the successful completion of the High School entrance examinations. Course work was rudimentary and practical. An 1877 agricultural examination paper asked for the points of a good Ayrshire cow, the requisites of a good building, the source of hydrogen in plants, and the parts of an insect. (32) To encourage farm youth to attend, board and tuition were free, and each successful student was to receive a $50 bonus at end of term. As an added inducement, the new school advertised that the moral and religious character of the pupils would receive "watchful attention amid the temptations incident in town life—to which young men from the country are peculiarly liable." (33)

And so agricultural education had found a new home. But it was not to be a happy one, for the history of the OSA for the next few years was one of increasing tribulation and opposition. In the very first weeks the newly appointed principal, Professor H. McCandless of Cornell, resigned after a dispute with the rector, the Reverend William Clarke. The rector's resignation followed shortly. Arrangements were made to have Charles Roberts of the Royal Agricultural College, England, assume the principalship, but he declined the post at the last minute. In the meantime, William Johnson of Toronto was named principal, then president of the School, a post he held until he was succeeded by James Mills. (34) Later, the minister of agriculture had to mediate several disputes between

President Mills and his farm managers. Most of these internal disorders arose over the question of the proper purposes of an agricultural school, which were far from clear at this point.

A barrage of criticism began with the opening of the OSA in 1874 and continued for a decade and more. The nature of this criticism indicates that there was widespread opposition to this new agricultural education institution. It manifested itself in many forms. Because of the political controversy that attended the change of site, many staunch Liberal-Conservatives were content to dismiss the whole business as a particularly blatant example of Grit chicanery, and refused to have anything to do with it. As for the Grits, any enthusiasm they might have harboured for the school was carefully concealed, especially in the provincial budget debates. In a period when economy was next to godliness, retrenchment was always more popular among the voters and their representatives than a flourishing agricultural school. Throughout most of the nineteenth century the school's budget was always well scrutinized by both the government and the opposition, (35) and, except for the minister of agriculture, it had few friends at court. Perhaps the real estimation of the agricultural school was reflected in the fact that for years the maximum salary paid to a professor of agriculture was exactly one half the maximum rate paid to a professor in the School of Practical Science. (36)

Much of the early criticism revolved around the type of students the agricultural school attracted. In 1877 the Leader of the Opposition pointed out indignantly that each pupil in the School was costing the province $800, and that these students so costly to the public purse "were all gentlemen's sons." (37) By "gentlemen's sons" he was probably referring to the growing number of nonresident students attending the agricultural school, although at that time only ten percent of the student body was so classified. Most of these nonresidents were the sons of English gentlemen, who thought it prudent to send their inexperienced boys to an agricultural school in preparation for taking up land and a new home in western Canada. (38) Not all the "gentlemen's sons," however, were nonresidents. Because the native well-to-do were generally quicker and more able than their less affluent neighbours to take advantage of any educational opportunity, the agricultural school was also indicted for "only educating rich men's sons at the expense of the poor." (39) Neither charge, of course, helped raise the School's value in the public estimation.

The most impassioned opposition to the agricultural school emanated from the pages of the most widely circulated agricultural journal, the *Farmers' Advocate*. During the seventies and eighties the *Advocate's* testy founder and editor, William Weld, gave widespread coverage to the notion that the agricultural school and its experimental farm were political hoaxes and expensive frauds perpetrated on the taxpayers by conniving politicians. Weld's criticisms stemmed from a number of factors. Chief among these was his fear that government activity in disseminating agricultural information challenged his own publishing business. After all, the *Advocate* ran regular columns identical to the various departments in the college—Dairy, Apiary, Entomology, Poultry, Livestock, Veterinary—and Weld tended to view the college as his rival. But there was also a matter of principle involved here: Weld was representative of that side of agrarian ideology that distrusted all government activity. All politicians were "intriguers and speculators," and all state intervention was an imposition. The agricultural school was a government outfit controlled by politicians for their own advantage, and was therefore at best useless and at worst harmful to the farming interests. (40) The instruction was too bookish, the so-called "model" farm operated at a loss (what else could be expected of a state-supported operation!), and the information issued by this political institution "no farmer should read, except probably those involved in agricultural booms." (41) Weld's criticisms were typical of those who believed that the government had no business in anything that could be done at all by private enterprise. To him it was axiomatic that what was left for the government to do was done badly.

But the School was created to bring scientific agriculture to the farmers, and if they accepted it, patronized it, and benefited from it, then the institution's purpose was achieved. What was the reaction of the agricultural classes?

The only independent farm organization in Ontario in the 1870s, the Patrons of Husbandry, better known as the Grange, was officially on record in favour of an agricultural school and experimental farm. (42) This was a view shared by practically all farmers who rose to positions of leadership in agricultural organizations. Indeed, these were the men who had pressed for its creation. As a Farmers' Institute poster proclaimed, "Farmers who know most of their profession are usually the most anxious to learn more." There was also some evidence in the early years to suggest that younger farmers were more amenable to the idea of an agricultural school than their elders. For example, David Wilson of Kent County testified to a Royal Commission that he did not send his sons to the College (as it was then known), because he had seen men working there with gloves on in the summer. Later, his nephew testified that he thought well of the institution, planned to send his sons there, and he did not think dirty hands a necessary virtue in a farmer. (43)

But for the great majority of farmers, indifference was the most common reaction. (44) For a generation after its opening the agricultural school could not attract more than a few score of students from Ontario farms, and most of these only stayed for one or two terms. Farmers, of course, were influenced by the kinds of criticism already mentioned. But there were also specific reasons why so many farmers did not consider it necessary to patronize the School. It was generally conceded that it was not necessary, or even desirable, to provide an agricultural education for boys who stayed home on the farm, because, as one observer noted in 1895, many farmers claimed they did not need a "college education" to perform their work. Moreover, education tended to take the boy away from the farm, or, at least, make him dissatisfied with rural life. And finally, any extra money in the family was likely to be used to send one or two sons through the regular schools for a professional education, leaving little for the boy who stayed home on the farm. (45) Even the argument that the School was the special institution of the "agricultural classes," created to help preserve their way of life and increase their profits, won little support for it in rural Ontario. When farmers thought about agricultural education at all, they thought about it in connection with the rural public schools. The local common school was the school of the agricultural classes. (46)

Clearly, the OSA aroused more than its share of criticism and opposition. Who was to blame? Was it shortsighted politicians unable to see past the next election, carping agricultural editors, and complacent and anti-intellectual farmers?

Only partly; the fact that representatives of so many groups did not consider the OSA an essential institution was symptomatic, not a cause of, the School's fundamental problem—the failure to find a vital function to perform in society. A specialized school like the OSA could only achieve the acceptance that comes with indispensability if it had a corner on a clear-cut expertise that was demonstrably valuable to the section of society it was supposed to serve. This is precisely what the OSA lacked, and it was this absence of explicit purpose that was the source of much of the school's problems. Underlying much of the criticism of the OSA was the gnawing suspicion that the institution had nothing to offer.

The institution's definitional problem as manifested in its failure to find an acceptable educational function was not entirely of its own making but arose in part out of the inherent ambiguities in the idea of agricultural education itself. For example, the lack of a distinct and unequivocal expertise reflected the limitations inherent in the concept of the "science of agriculture" throughout most of the nineteenth century. Scientific agriculture was not based on a body of systematically organized knowledge derived from fundamental research into the nature of things, for the underlying sciences that dealt with plant and animal culture were not yet developed. There was little known about the principles of animal and plant nutrition because the biochemical sciences were in their infancy. Nor was there a scientific basis for animal breeding developed before the twentieth century; indeed, the term "genetics" had yet to be coined. Further research in animal biology had to wait on the invention of the binocular microscope in the next century. (47)

Because agricultural science was relatively undeveloped, its role was still primarily descriptive rather than prescriptive. It provided little new knowledge to help the farmer in his struggle against the elements. Entomology offers a good illustration. In the 1860s and 1870s Canadian entomologists began publishing an impressive selection of articles describing the habits and appearance of injurious insects. They were encouraged and patronized in their efforts by governments eager to reduce the devastation caused by insects. (48) Yet, valuable as this preliminary work was, these scientists were not able to prescribe effective control measures, and the destruction in the fields continued. In 1875, when crop losses to insects were estimated at $20 million a year, (49) the best remedies a professor of agriculture could suggest were the traditional ones of salt, soot, ashes, soap lye, tobacco wash, coal tar, and paris green. (50) The Ontario School of Agriculture found itself charged with the responsibility of imparting to farmers a scientific agriculture when, in fact, no such science existed. An analogous situation confronted the land-grant agricultural colleges in the United States, and little headway was made there until 1887, when federal money was made available to finance the necessary basic research. In Canada, the Dominion Experimental Farm system set up in 1886 served a similar function. In the meantime some farmers could, and in fact did, claim that current agricultural methods were in advance of scientific theory. (51)

Another inherent weakness in agricultural education in mid century was that it taught a type of farming not entirely relevant to Ontario conditions. Many of the advocates of agricultural improvement spoke from their knowledge of and experience in the best traditions of advanced agriculture as practiced in Britain—intensive cultivation, mixed farming, and the improvement of livestock. It was these characteristics of improved British farming that formed the subject matter of much of the agricultural education in early Ontario. (52) When the OSA opened in 1874 all it could offer in the way of scientific agriculture were lectures on the advantages of intensive cultivation, manuring, the use of improved seed, livestock breeding, and crop rotation (plus, as one student put it, training in hard work and long hours). (53) Although such methods were praiseworthy, they were not economically attractive to Ontario farmers until well into the second half of the nineteenth century. The limited availability of capital resources, transportation facilities, and market opportunities characteristic of pioneer agriculture necessitated an extensive type of farming that relied heavily on cash-cropping. Not until the grain staple moved west, and eastern agriculture turned to the export of dairy products and the supply of a growing home market did the methods of the British improvers become realistic. It is difficult, of course, to determine an arbitrary date for this transition, but the greatest changes in the direction of mixed farming took place after 1880. (54) In the meantime, much of the subject matter of agricultural education was not entirely pertinent to the Ontario situation.

These were the circumstances facing James J. Mills when he assumed the presidency of the OSA in 1879. Judging by his actions,

Mills was determined that his school would find salvation in good works, that it would become an indispensable institution providing valuable educational services to the community. In this he was assisted, at it happened, by three developments of the late nineteenth century—advances in the agriculturally related sciences, the changing economic conditions of Ontario agriculture, and the increasing role of the state. Indeed, so pronounced were the changes made after 1880 that this date serves as a convenient point to mark the beginning of the third attempt to institutionalize agricultural education.

The new institution to emerge was the Ontario Agricultural College. Basically, it was formed by Mills out of the old OSA in an attempt to clarify and extend the latter's educational purview. The OSA was never sure whether it was a college or a high school; it had many of the accoutrements of a college, but the programs and the limitations of a secondary school. In 1880 Mills arranged to have the name changed officially to the Ontario Agricultural College and Experimental Farm, and substantial change in structure followed in 1888 when the OAC affiliated with the University of Toronto. (55) These developments enabled the agricultural college to launch its three-pronged program, each part of which was designed to serve a particular need in agricultural education. There was the original two-year course that had minimum entrance requirements and did not lead to a degree but to an "Associate of the College" Diploma. This was the program designed for boys returning to the farm, and it gave the College the flexibility it needed to mount courses designed to meet specific demands of the farming industry. The second program led to the new Bachelor of Science in Agriculture degree. This program under the jurisdiction of the Senate of the University showed that the OAC was not content to remain in the educational backwaters but would attempt to take its place as a respectable scientific institution. Taken together, the two programs allowed the College to reconcile its own ambitions as an institute of higher education with its original commitment to practical agriculture.

Mill's third thrust into agricultural education was his highly successful extension program. One phase of this program, the Short Course, soon became the most popular offering on campus; by 1900 over 60 percent of the total enrollment were registered in Short

Courses in livestock and grain judging, poultry raising, dairying, etc. (56) These courses owed their wide acceptance to the fact that they dealt directly with the specific needs of the agricultural industry as they emerged in the late nineteenth century. They were strictly a service function; no fees were charged nor examinations written. Another method of agricultural extension—one which capitalized on the popularity of the Short Courses—was the June Excursion, which became almost an institution in its own right in Ontario. Begun in the 1890s, these Excursions were actually one-day courses designed to show the farmer what was going on at the College and what it had to offer him. Informality prevailed and every attempt was made to make the farmers and their families feel that this, indeed, was their institution. Arriving by train in the morning, the visitors were welcomed by President Mills, treated to a picnic lunch and lemonade, and shown around the grounds where demonstrations were arranged by every department. These June Excursions generally brought about 35,000 to 40,000 people annually to the OAC. (57)

But Mills was not content with an extension program that brought farmers to the College; the College would also have to go to the farmers. Consequently, in the mid-1880s Mills and the Commissioner of Agriculture, S. C. Woods, organized Farmers' Institutes throughout the province. Wood had legislation passed to provide a $25 grant to any group of farmers who would set up an Institute in their county, and Mills abolished the Easter vacation at the OAC so that the Christmas holiday could be extended to give the professors three full weeks to address the Institute meetings. Later, as the organization developed, much of the speaking was done by former students or graduates of the College, so that it is not stretching a point to refer to the Farmers' Institutes as a kind of extension department of the OAC. By 1902 these Institutes claimed a membership of nearly 24,000, and it was estimated by the Department of Agriculture that over 125,000 rural people had attended the meetings that year. (58)

Another successful example of the College's thrust into extension work was the Travelling Dairies, sponsored jointly by the Department of Agriculture and the OAC. Begun in 1891, these Travelling Dairies consisted simply of a number of wagons outfitted with butter-making equipment, a demonstrator, and a lecturer, usually someone connected with the Agricultural College. For the next six years these wagons toured the province demonstrating to small groups of interested farmers the requirements necessary to produce good butter, proper milk handling techniques, the use of cream separators, the value of good stock, etc. Thousands of farmers saw the demonstrations, and according to President Mills, the "marked improvement" in the quantity and quality of the province's export butter was a direct result of the Travelling Dairies. (59) If it was true, it was certainly a credit to the College.

Meanwhile, new developments in the agriculturally related sciences provided the College with an expertise that was not available to even the best of farmers. Of course, the great advances in these sciences came after World War I, but the accomplishments of the period 1880–1910 were not insignificant. In the 1880s, microbiologists isolated the anthrax, rabies, and cholera bacilli, and, what was more important to the farmer, prepared vaccinations to control these diseases so fatal to man and animal. By 1900 plant physiologists understood the principles of nitrogen fixation, and by the end of the next decade ten of the twelve known mineral nutrients required for plant growth were established. As a result, "the old static view of the soil was replaced by a dynamic and biological view," (60) and the OAC began a soil-testing program to determine for farmers the exact type of fertilization their land required. At the same time, the refinement of various insecticides, particularly the arsenates and sulphates, allowed the OAC botanist and entomologist to lead in the battle against destructive insects— most notably in the fight for survival the orchard men were waging against the coddling moth. (61) Gradually, the advance of agricultural science would make the College indispensable to the well-being of Ontario farmers.

Advances made on the Experimental Farm also helped to raise the OAC in the public's estimation. For years the Farm had been a source of embarrassment—its perennial crop of Canada thistle being its main distinction. During the nineteenth century some experimental work was done at the College and carried on by the Associates and other graduates through the Ontario Agricultural and Experimental Union formed for that purpose in 1879. (62) But experimental agriculture is slow, painstaking work, and the Farm did not really begin to show results until the early twentieth century. By then, under the capable direction of Professor Zavitz, the Farm was able to develop two exceptionally successful strains of feed grain—OAC 21 Barley and OAC 72 Oats. It was claimed that in a few years this OAC strain of barley increased the crop's yield per acre by 17 percent. (63) Tangible results like this demonstrated to all that the OAC was building up an expertise that was valuable to the agricultural industry. Agricultural science was beginning to show dividends.

It is significant that the first breakthrough on the Experimental Farm should occur in two feed grains, oats and barley, as opposed to the cash-crop varieties, for it demonstrates the leadership role the OAC was assuming in the transition of Ontario agriculture from staple crop to mixed farming. The change-over from cash crops to animal products demanded the use of new techniques and new technology, and these were demands the OAC could fulfill. Of all the new areas into which agriculture was moving, dairying was the most exacting, and it was here that the OAC was able to perform its greatest service. By the end of the century the Dairy Department under Professor H. H. Dean was running a series of Short Courses and other educational programs that played a significant part in the advancement of the cheese and butter industries in Ontario. Developing methods to analyse milk, preserve cream, and manufacture "soft" cheese were only a few of the College's contributions to these new agricultural industries. (64) Thus did changing economic conditions give the OAC a demonstrably valuable expertise.

The Dairy School work, the Farmers' Institutes, the Excursions, the specialized Short Courses, were all undertaken in cooperation with the Department of Agriculture or its predecessor. Throughout most of the century, agricultural improvement programs were the responsibility of private or semiprivate organizations like the Agricultural Societies, the Provincial Agricultural Association, and the Council of Agriculture and Arts. But after 1880 most of these efforts were either taken over or replaced by government-sponsored programs designed to bring scientific agriculture to the farmer and assist him in the transition to mixed farming. This growing role of the state in agricultural education required the services of new personnel with new skills and this, of course, was exactly what the OAC could supply; by the end of the century the OAC was virtually a branch of the Department of Agriculture. As the incidence of state intervention increased, so did the functional utility of the College.

One of the most significant results of the union of state and college was the birth of a new professional group—the agriculturalists. These were the professionals who were organizing and manning the new government bureaucracies set up to administer the recently acquired responsibilities in agricultural improvement. Without this new class of white-collar farmers, state involvement in the agricultural industry would have been severely limited, if not impossible, and without these new government jobs the B.S.A. degree courses at Guelph would have had little vocational value. Until the 1880s Ontario had traditionally imported its agricultural experts from New York (Cornell) and Britain. At that time the demand was small, and Canadian openings were quickly filled. As a result, many OAC graduates had to find employment in the United States. Then, as government activity increased around the end of the century, agricultural experts were more in demand, and the flow to the U.S. was reversed. Former OAC graduates returned to Canada to work in Ontario or Ottawa. One of these, George C. Creelman, class of 1888, returned from the University of Missouri to become the second superintendent of Farmers' Institutes in 1899, and later served as president of his alma mater.

By the first decade of the twentieth century OAC graduates were well established in the provincial Department of Agriculture. In 1906 the Ontario Minister, Nelson Monteith, held a B.S.A., and his deputy was a former professor at the Agricultural College. Among the chief officers, the superintendent of Farmers' Institutes was an OAC graduate, while the director of the Livestock Branch and the accountant were both associates of the College. These men, along with the Factory Inspection Branch, the director of Colonization and Forestry, and the superintendent of Agricultural Societies, made up the Department of Agriculture. It was a young, college-trained department. The minister was 43 years old and the average age of his officers was 33 years. (65)

The agricultural education program that proved the most enduring and best illustrates the liaison between state and college was the provincially sponsored district representative system, begun in 1907. The purpose of this program, according to its originator, Deputy Minister C. C. James, was "to establish branch offices of our department and move the Agricultural College closer to the Farmer's home." (66) In the first year of operation, OAC graduates established offices in six Ontario counties. As district representatives of the Department of Agriculture, the men were responsible for conducting Short Courses in the townships during the winter, arranging stock-judging demonstrations and seed grain competitions, supervising orchard and crop demonstrations plots, and generally giving the kind of assistance and direction that could come from personal contact. (67) By 1920 there was an OAC graduate functioning as a district representative in every Ontario county and district but one, and a special branch was created in the Department of Agriculture to administer the work.

The new "agriculturalist" was also well represented in the dominion Department of Agriculture, for here, too, the state was becoming increasingly involved in attempts to upgrade and increase farm production. The extent of this involvement was reflected in the growth of the federal department's staff. In 1887 there were 27 people in Agriculture; twenty years later the number had risen to 1,000, which meant, in effect, that the staff had doubled every four years. (68) Many of these new jobs materialized under the authority of the original Commissioner of Dairying, J. W. Robertson. About four out of five of the men appointed to the senior positions by Robertson (a former professor in the OAC) were graduates of the College. In 1904 a Live Stock and a Seed Branch were established in the federal department, and the different backgrounds of the two men assigned to the new posts illustrate the contrasts in the old and the new type of agricultural expert. The Live Stock Commissioner, F. W. Hodson, was one of the "old" type of agriculturalist. He received his training through his practical experiences as a farmer, through participation in various agricultural organizations, and finally as an editor of an agricultural journal. The Seed Branch Commissioner, George H. Clark, did not have such a record of practical experience. Instead, he was a graduate of the Agricultural College.

OAC men were not only in demand in Ottawa and Ontario, but throughout Canada and beyond. (69) The dairy work done by James W. Robertson, H. H. Dean, J. A. Ruddick, and others gave them an international reputation. New Zealand, for example, imported three Canadian experts to organize her dairy industry, and others found employment in other parts of the Empire, as well as the United States. The college-trained agricultural expert was becoming a worldwide phenomenon, and training them became one of the most important functions of the OAC.

Before the outbreak of World War I, then, the OAC had weathered the worst of the storm. The establishment of a highly competent Dairy Department put the College in possession of an expertise and a technology not available to the average farmer. The profusion and the popularity of the Short Courses in dairying and other areas demonstrated that the College did, indeed, have something to teach that could not be readily learned on the farm. By the end of the century the "model" farm was brought under control, and the experiments undertaken began to show results. As the years wore on and economic conditions improved after 1896, many of the indispositions of the seventies and eighties were swept aside by the onrush of prosperity. With the return of good times the College received larger grants, and its budgets were not subjected to so close a scrutiny as they once occasioned. But one event more than any other exemplified the OAC's victory over her critics and the new role she was to play in the twentieth century. In 1905 one of her graduates, R. J. Deachman, B.S.A., was appointed editor of the *Farmers' Advocate* and the influential journal changed from a hostile critic into one of the College's most loyal supporters. There was a good deal of accuracy in the *Advocate's* assessment in 1908 that "these be truly halcyon days for the OAC." (70)

Agricultural education had found its home at last.

NOTES

1. Commissioner of Agriculture and Arts, *Report,* 1870, p. xi [hereafter cited as *Agriculture and Arts*].
2. Rev. [E. Hartley] Dewart, Toronto, "Characteristics and Tendencies of the Time," Ontario Teachers' Association, *Minutes,* 1871, p. 31.
3. Henry J. Morgan, ed., *The Dominion Annual Register and Review 1886* (Montreal, 1887), pp. 231–34.
4. *British American Cultivator* (Toronto), June 1845, p. 176.
5. *Agriculture and Arts,* 1868, p. 8.
6. President James Mills, Ontario Agricultural College and Experimental Farm, *Report,* 1885, p. 3 [hereafter cited as OAC *Report*].

7. John Bryant, publ., "Agricultural Education," Ontario Teachers' Association, *Minutes*, 1890, p. 25.

8. Alfred Charles True, *A History of Agricultural Education in the United States*, USDA Publication no. 36 (Washington, D.C., 1929), p. 12.

9. John G. Hodgins, *Documentary History of Education in Upper Canada* 5 (Toronto, 1912): 187, 190 [hereafter cited as *DHE*]; ibid., 6:63.

10. Expressions of these three principles can be found in the various Petitions printed in *DHE*, and in an excellent editorial review in the *St. Catharines Journal*, May 15, 1845.

11. Quoted in N. Burwash "Origins and Development of the University of Toronto," in *The University of Toronto and its Colleges, 1827–1906*, ed. Maurice Hutton (Toronto, 1906), p. 30.

12. *DHE*, 5:145.

13. *Journal and Transactions of the Board of Agriculture of Upper Canada*, 1856, 1:246.

14. *DHE*, 12:275.

15. *Journal of Education* (Toronto), June 1857, pp. 87–88.

16. *DHE*, 17:67.

17. *Journal of Education*, February 1866, p. 22.

18. *Agriculture and Arts*, 1868, p. 4.

19. W. H. Ellis, "Faculty of Applied Science," in *University of Toronto*, ed. Hutton, pp. 180–3.

20. Ontario, *Sessional Papers*, 1873, no. 32, p. 2.

21. Donald H. Akenson, *The Irish Education Experiment* (London, 1970), p. 149.

22. Sir John Russell, "Rothhamsted Experimental Station," *Encyclopaedia Britannica* (1959), 19:571–2.

23. Ontario, *Sessional Papers*, 1873, no. 32, p. 16.

24. Ibid., 1871–1872, no. 5, p. 19.

25. Ontario, Legislative Assembly, *Journals*, 1873, pp. 220–1.

26. Ibid., p. 224. An eye-witness account of the opposition to the Guelph site is presented in Charles Clarke, *Sixty Years in Upper Canada* (Toronto, 1908), pp. 194–96; see also R. L. Jones, *A History of Agriculture in Ontario 1613–1880* (Toronto, 1946), p. 335.

27. Ontario, *Sessional Papers*, 1871–1872, no. 55, pp. 14–15.

28. *Journal of Education*, December 1873, p. 181.

29. Ontario, *Sessional Papers*, 1871–1872, no. 55, p. 18.

30. Ibid., p. 15.

31. Ibid., p. 13.

32. Ontario School of Agriculture and Experimental Farm, *Report*, 1877, pp. 32–39.

33. *Journal of Education*, May 1874, p. 74.

34. *Agriculture and Arts*, 1874, pp. xi–xii; 1875, p. xiii.

35. *Farmers' Advocate* (London, Ont.), March 1882, p. 83.

36. Ibid., February 17, 1910, p. 263.

37. Ibid., February 1877, p. 29.
38. Most of the nonresidents were from England. For an account of one such student, see Lillian Rea Benson, "An OAC Student in the 1880s," *Ontario History,* 42, no. 2 (April 1950): 67–80.
39. *DHE,* 15:188.
40. *Farmers' Advocate,* May 1879, p. 98.
41. Ibid., June 1887, p. 162; February 1886, p. 39.
42. J. E. Middleton and Fred Landon, *The Province of Ontario, A History* 1 (Toronto, 1927): 474; Canada, Select Committee of the House of Commons on the Agricultural Industry, *Report,* 1884, p. 174.
43. Canada, Royal Commission on the Relations of Capital and Labor in Canada, *Report,* vol. 2, "Evidence–Ontario" (Ottawa, 1889), pp. 446–48.
44. "Letter to the Editor," *Farmers' Advocate,* March 1882, p. 83.
45. T. F. Patterson, in Ontario, Farmers' Institutes, *Report,* 1895, p. 43.
46. There are many references in support of this assessment. One of the most forceful is a letter in the *Farmers' Advocate,* September 26, 1912, pp. 1678–79. The same preference was common among American farmers. See, for example, the *Proceedings of the 18th Session of the National Grange of the Patrons of Industry,* 1884, p. 82.
47. There is a brief account of the development of agricultural science in Stephen F. Mason, *A History of the Sciences* (New York, 1962), pp. 517–20; see also, Duncan McLarty, "A Century of Development of Agricultural Science in Western Ontario," *Western Ontario Historical Notes* 5, no. 2 (June 1947): 49; W. Kaye Lamb and Thomas W. M. Cameron, "Biologists and Biological Research Since 1864," in *Pioneers of Canadian Science,* ed. G. F. G. Stanley (Toronto, 1966), pp. 36–43.
48. Robert Glen, "Entomology," *Encyclopedia Canadiana* 4 (1970): 19–20.
49. Canada, Select Committee of the House of Commons on the Agricultural Industry, *Report,* 1884, p. 152.
50. *Agriculture and Arts,* 1875, p. 263.
51. J. Thomas, New York State Agricultural Society, in *British American Cultivator,* February 1847, pp. 51–58. Indeed, until the end of the century, some progressive innovations were introduced to Ontario farms in spite of the agricultural scientists. One example was the practice of dehorning cattle. A full account is given in Canada, *Sessional Papers,* 1893, no. 2.
52. See Kenneth Kelly, "The Transfer of British Ideas on Improved Farming to Ontario During the First Half of the Nineteenth Century," *Ontario History,* 43, no. 2 (June 1971): 103–11.
53. "President's Address," in *Agriculture and Arts,* 1878, p. 195; Benson, "OAC Student," p. 71.
54. For the changes in Ontario farming in this period see "The Development of the Agricultural Industry, 1870–1910," in Douglas A. Lawr, "The Development of Agricultural Education in Ontario, 1870–1910" (Ph.D. diss., University of Toronto, 1972), pp. 1–29.

55. An interesting development in view of the founders' antipathy toward University association.
56. OAC *Report,* 1901, p. 220.
57. Ibid., 1902, p. xiii; 1903, p. xvi.
58. Ontario, Superintendent of Farmers' Institutes, *Report,* 1902–1903, p. 5.
59. OAC *Report,* 1903, p. ix.
60. René Taton, ed., *Science in the Nineteenth Century* (London, 1961), p. 407.
61. OAC *Report,* 1909, pp. 24–36, 85–86.
62. Ontario Experimental Union, *Report,* 1889, p. 5.
63. *Farmers' Advocate,* July 24, 1913, p. 1294.
64. OAC *Report,* 1909, pp. 97–98.
65. *Farmers' Advocate,* March 29, 1906, pp. 494–95.
66. C. C. James, "History of Farming in Canada," in *Canada and its Provinces,* ed. Adam Shortt and Arthur G. Doughty, 18, no. 2 (Toronto, 1914):582.
67. Ontario Department of Agriculture, *Report of the Oxford County Agricultural Representative,* 1913, p. 10 (typescript in ODA Office, Woodstock).
68. Canada, Department of Agriculture, *Canada Agriculture, The First Hundred Years* (Ottawa, 1967), p. 5.
69. J. A. Ruddick, *An Historical and Descriptive Account of the Dairying Industry in Canada,* Department of Agriculture Bulletin no. 28 (Ottawa, 1911), p. 56.
70. *Farmers' Advocate,* June 15, 1905, p. 882; ibid., February 27, 1908, p. 357.

PETER N. ROSS

8. THE ESTABLISHMENT OF THE PH.D. AT TORONTO: A CASE OF AMERICAN INFLUENCE *

This essay explores the formidable influence of American universities on the decision to offer a doctorate at Toronto. It traces how the idea of research and graduate study was brought to Canada from Germany and the United States during the last quarter of the nineteenth century and how by the end of the century the acceptance of the doctorate and the graduate school in the United States influenced the decision-makers at the University of Toronto. Although very little has been written on the history of graduate education in Canada, the problem of American influence is a recurring and dominant theme in our social and economic history.

IN 1902 THE UNIVERSITY of Toronto joined American universities in celebrating the twenty-fifth anniversary of Johns Hopkins University. For the occasion, A. Bruce Macallum, (1) Professor of Physiology and holder of the Johns Hopkins' Ph.D. (1888), wrote a short essay in commemoration of the American institution. (2) He acknowledged the contemporary debt owed to Johns Hopkins and, by inference, the obligation of Toronto to its example:

But what the Johns Hopkins University lacked in age it made up in service to American scholarship and higher education. In those few years it completely reformed American university ideals, and it developed the

---

* I am grateful to Lois Adair and Michael Katz for reading and criticizing an earlier version of this article. Of course, errors and omissions remain my responsibility.

Mr. Ross is a member of the faculty of Lakeshore Teachers College, York University, Toronto, Canada. This essay first appeared in The History of Education Quarterly *(Fall 1972).*

higher university work on this continent to a degree that no other university succeeded in doing. (3)

In the same year Macallum and James Loudon, (4) President of Toronto (1892–1906), represented their University at the celebrations in Baltimore. (5) During the proceedings, Loudon and Principal William Peterson of McGill University received the LL.D. In conferring the degree Daniel C. Gilman, President of Johns Hopkins, remarked:

We welcome them in the brotherhood of scholarship which knows of no political bounds, appreciating what they have done to uphold the highest standards of education in two great universities, with which we are closely affiliated. (6)

Peterson brought greetings from Canada. He alluded to "the great hospitality which the Johns Hopkins University has ever extended to our graduate students." (7) Moreover, he underscored the inspiration given to North American intellectual life by the University's attention to thorough training for investigators.

Toronto reciprocated the warmth demonstrated by the Baltimore institution. In 1902 it conferred its honorary degree on Ira Remsen, the newly installed President of Johns Hopkins. The next year it further admitted its obligation when it awarded the LL.D. to Gilman, whom Loudon introduced as "the apostle of the research movement in America." (8)

At Toronto interest was not confined to the work of Johns Hopkins. Proponents of reform attended to other aspects of American higher education. In 1894 the University adopted the degree of Doctor of Paedagogy, just four years after its creation at New York University. (9) After 1896 the struggle for a sound system of financing at state universities received increasing attention. Toronto supporters pressed the Legislature of Ontario for annual grants, but George W. Ross, (10) Minister of Education, rejected the idea of direct public support for the provincial university. (11) Reformers were fascinated by the research movement that had resulted in the emergence of a new kind of university in the United States—a university that featured a graduate school and a commitment to the research function. In 1897 Loudon attempted to have the Senate at Toronto establish a graduate school; however, he had to be content with the introduction of the Ph.D. (12)

Canadians have been ambivalent in their attitude to the United States. On the one hand, they have regarded American innovation as worthy of imitation. In 1902 Loudon observed:

Besides, such is the geographical position of Canada with regard to the United States, and such the commodity of social and intellectual life, that the universities of these two countries must inevitably develop along parallel lines. (13)

Recently, Claude Bissell, past-President of Toronto, commented, "there is no greater inducement to growth and development among Canadian universities than their proximity to the American scene." (14) On the other hand, the anticipated effects of American vigor have caused grave concern. In 1915 Macallum, reacting to the powerful attraction of American graduate schools for Canadians, warned:

It would be disastrous ultimately to Canadian unity if the Faculties of the younger Universities of this Dominion, and especially of those of Western Canada, were, either wholly or in greater part, recruited from graduates of the American Universities. (15)

The current controversy over the proportion of American professors in Canadian universities is evidence of the continuation of this longstanding anxiety. (16) Canadians have viewed their enterprising neighbor's influence with admiration mingled with apprehension.

In the matter of the Ph.D., Canadian consternation was related to American success. Between 1865 and 1900 reformers were attempting to fashion a distinctly new American university. (17) The peak of this activity was reached in the 1890s; its object was the transformation of the institution. At first, Americans turned to the example of the Germans with their rigorous training in research for a professional career, but what they created was not strictly a German style university. In his inaugural address as President of California, in 1872, Gilman described the eventual American university:

The university is the most comprehensive term that can be employed to indicate a foundation for the promotion and diffusion of knowledge—a group of agencies organized to advance the arts and sciences of every sort, and train young men as scholars for all the intellectual callings of life." (18)

As each large institution took on the general characteristics of a "university" as defined by Gilman, the introduction of the Ph.D. marked a significant stage.

The Ph.D. degree reached its pre-eminent position in America after a period of only thirty years. In 1860 Yale announced its regulations for the degree and awarded it the following year. (19) In the 1870s Pennsylvania, Cornell, Harvard, and Columbia followed this lead. In this early period the doctorate was evidently an accretion, tacked on to the program of the college and under its governance. No distinct status attached to its loose organization. In 1875 Gilman, who was a Yale graduate and a faculty member when it introduced the Ph.D., was appointed president of Johns Hopkins. The founding of this university represented a new departure for American higher education. The University offered the doctorate. Moreover, it advertised fellowships for students interested in graduate work. Significantly, these awards were intended to attract students from other universities, and this they did most effectively. Another innovation at Johns Hopkins was the creation of a graduate school. This organization ensured a distinct status for advanced study; therefore, for imitators a second pattern had emerged. (20) From their beginnings, in 1889 and 1892 respectively, Clark and Chicago copied this arrangement. The latter, by its very size and success, quickly gained recognition as the epitome of the American university. Harvard and a number of the larger state universities— Michigan (1892), Nebraska (1896), Kansas (1896), and Massachusetts (1897)—also imitated Johns Hopkins.

The nineties was a pivotal decade in American higher education. An increasing number of institutions improved their research facilities and introduced the Ph.D. Presidents of the innovative universities were often scientists and always expansionists. (21) The rising rate of production of Ph.D.'s, with superior training and facility in research, stimulated a demand for professors holding the degree, and this was exacerbated by expansionist policies. The degree represented "the label of academic respectability, the mark of professional competence, the assurance of a certain standard sameness of training, experience and exposure to the ideals, the rules, the habits of scientific German scholarship." (22) In 1902 Remsen noted the value of the degree in certifying a graduate's training and the attitude of many colleges "that none but Ph.D.'s need apply." (23)

Acute competition characterized this period; yet it led to sterile imitation of what was successful. "As American universities became more intensely competitive—in the nineties and after—they became more standardized, less original, less fluid." (24) They felt compelled to follow the example of the prestigious and experimental leaders. (25)

Supporters of the state universities were growing apprehensive of increased competition from the large private eastern universities. According to Nevins, "the principal inferiority of the state universities lay in graduate work." (26) In 1896 President Angell of Michigan warned his regents that the University lagged badly in this area and that, if this were not corrected, they would "have their development arrested at their present stage, and so [would] fall behind the universities which depend for their support on private endowments." (27) Likewise, Illinois determined to forward its position in relation to the other universities. (28) At Wisconsin there existed a genuine fear of losing brilliant students to powerful eastern states. (29) In this decade these public institutions perceived themselves operating at the periphery of innovative activity and confronted by a cruel choice between competing or becoming second-rate. They had no real option, however, since to survive as credible agencies of higher education they had to compete.

While American universities were being transformed, a similar development was underway at Toronto. As in the United States, the process, visibly at work in the 1870s, reached a peak in the 1890s.

During the 1870s Canadians who were concerned about improving higher education looked to Europe for inspiration. They referred to German universities in hyperbolic terms. They could exclaim, "Germany, foremost in the higher education of men . . ." or "Germany, that centre of modern intellectual life. . . ." A laudatory article in an early issue of the *Varsity*, the student newspaper, claimed:

Everyone . . . studying the physical sciences must acknowledge that, both in the quantity and quality of her original scientific work, Germany has far outstripped any other nation. (30)

In an address to the Canadian Institute, a society for the promotion of research, Loudon, who was its president in 1877, displayed considerable knowledge of the situation in Europe. (31) He discussed the research movement in some detail, with particular reference to Germany and France. In regard to the former, he commented on the advantages of cultivating research. Discounting Germany's spectacular military prowess, he declared:

It is, in fact, to the intellectual pre-eminence of the Germans and their devotion to science that the recent extension of their boundaries and their political unification are largely due.

The government supported scientists by supplying well-equipped laboratories and honors; therefore the teacher could devote his life to the comprehension of a special subject. Wistfully, Loudon compared Canadian and German universities. "In this new world the University Professor is obliged to profess and teach a range of subjects which in a German University engage the attention of half a dozen professors." In Ontario at this time there were several competing denominational colleges and the nondenominational provincial university, Toronto. Effort was too thinly diffused to assure excellence. Yet, despite the handicaps, a group of alumni at Toronto had tried to have the University introduce the Doctor of Science degree in 1874. (32)

In 1880 Canadians demonstrated an interest in the growth of graduate studies in the United States. In January a graduate who was exhorting the Senate at Toronto to initiate a stronger program in science outlined the growth of the research movement in America. (33) He described the founding of Johns Hopkins and the "pride of nationality" that forced Americans to offer graduate studies rather than see their students seek higher learning in Germany. The new institution intended "to bring together students who are qualifying to prosecute original research in literature or science." (34) Later in the same year the Chancellor of the University of Toronto, Edward Blake, (35) discussed a series of changes he hoped to see introduced. (36) If the University did not reform its program, he observed, students would simply migrate to foreign centers for advanced work. Once they had left Canada and were aware of the opportunities open to them elsewhere, "the chances were against their ever returning." (37) Two years later, another Toronto graduate who had enrolled at Johns Hopkins described its program. (38) With four other Canadians, three of them alumni of Toronto, he had been welcomed there. Moreover, in the second year of his stay, fellowships had been awarded to three Canadians. (39)

In 1882 a Senate report on income and expenditures tackled the question of Toronto's limited objectives as an arts college. (40) It raised the possibility of broadening the curriculum to include law and graduate studies. While it emphasized the importance of advancing Toronto as an intellectual center, it recognized the practical limitations imposed by inadequate funding. The Ontario government chose to ignore the recommendations for direct provincial support. As a consequence, the only tangible gain was the establishment of nine fellowships. (41) This move was of symbolic as well as practical importance since it represented the first official undertaking in research activities by the University. The appointees were to possess outstanding academic merit and teaching ability. They were expected to "furnish most valuable assistance in the work of tuition" and, at the same time, be "engaged in pursuing some special lines of study." Since it involved both teaching and research, the plan resembled the scheme for *privat-docents* in Germany. At Johns Hopkins Gilman had deliberately avoided having fellows teach and had emphasized the necessity of prosecuting research. (42) Toronto fellows received $500 for their services, the amount paid at Johns Hopkins. To prevent the fellows becoming junior lecturers, Toronto restricted tenure to three years. When called on to defend the fellowship plan, President Daniel Wilson of Toronto (1880–1892) (43) invoked a nativist argument as the best means of justifying it.

But I entertain no doubt of the fellowships proving most beneficial in promoting post-graduate study; and, as I should trust, in due time training from among our own men some who will prove worthy and able to fill professorial chairs as they may become vacant. (44)

The idea that Toronto would produce its own teachers was well accepted. The critics were persuaded to acknowledge the advantages of the scheme for potential Canadian professors. (45)

In 1883 Loudon pressed the Senate to introduce the Ph.D. as a natural goal for the fellows to pursue. (46) The recommendation won some support from students, who thought it would have the beneficial effect of providing a challenging stimulus to graduates. (47) The Senate vacillated on the proposal before it finally adopted it in principle. A committee was appointed to arrange for the implementation of the degree, but it never reported. (48)

In the meantime, the fellowship scheme proved successful. It attracted candidates and initiated them into a career in scholarship. One unanticipated consequence was that it encouraged many to leave Canada for advanced studies in the United States. By 1897, fifty-three fellows had held the award. It was possible to trace forty-five of these men in their subsequent careers. (49) Seventeen of them eventually earned the Ph.D.: twelve earned it in the United States, three in Germany, and two at Toronto. Moreover, including the recipients of the doctorate, eighteen had studied in the United States and six in Germany. Twenty-five entered university teaching, twelve in Toronto, twelve in the United States, and one at Queen's in Kingston, Ontario. Two others pursued careers in research with the Canadian government while the others entered the professions of law, medicine, and teaching. One-third of the fellows received the Ph.D. despite the handicap of having to migrate to a foreign country. In 1915 Macallum, one of the fellows who went to the United States, rued the lack of opportunity at the University of Toronto in the 1880s. He asserted that had the Ph.D. been introduced in 1883 it would have advanced the University's standing considerably and would have proven a useful and a valuable goal for the fellows. (50)

During the last twenty years of the century, Canadians paid increasing attention to American universities and correspondingly less to German ones. Local periodicals carried articles about the former, often comparing them to the University of Toronto. The *Canada Educational Monthly,* for example, published papers by Canadian students and American scholars. (51) Successful Toronto alumni in the United States wrote observations for the *Varsity* comparing the situations in both countries. (52) These contributions concentrated on the shortcomings of the University and eulogized the substantial changes being made in American universities of comparable size. In addition, the library received American publications, including calendars, copies of dissertations, and journals such as *Science.*

More important than published information were personal contacts. Torontonians kept in touch with scholars in Germany and France, as well as in the United States. In 1890 a benefactor underwrote the cost of sending a scientist to Germany to examine the results of Koch's experiments on tuberculosis. (53) Loudon maintained a friendship with Rudolf Koenig in Paris from 1876 until the latter's death. (54) They exchanged visits, and Koenig kept Loudon informed of his experiments on acoustics. Toronto graduates studied under renowned professors such as Wilhelm Ostwald at Leipzig, Basil L. Gildersleeve at Johns Hopkins, G. Stanley Hall at Clark, and William James at Harvard. Their correspondence served to keep professors in Toronto informed about scholarly work elsewhere. Many graduates—among them Macallum and W. J. Alexander from Johns Hopkins, F. Tracy from Clark, J. G. Hume from Harvard and Freiburg, and W. L. Miller and S. M. Wickett from Leipzig—returned to the University of Toronto imbued with the research spirit and resolved to attempt reforms at home.

Moreover, Toronto attracted foreign instructors who introduced novel ideas. An Englishman, W. J. Ashley, was appointed Professor of Political Economy in 1888. For fourth year students he initiated a seminar that focused on historical and contemporary economic issues. In 1889 he persuaded the minister of education to provide funds for a series of studies similar to those printed at Johns Hopkins and European universities. (55) In 1892, he resigned to accept a position at Harvard, where he was assured the opportunity of devoting his time to his specialty, economic history. (56) In 1889 W. J. Baldwin of Princeton accepted the Professorship of Philosophy at the University of Toronto. Like Ashley, he managed to obtain financial support for his research. The government provided a grant of $1,100 to equip a laboratory in experimental psychology for demonstrations and advanced research. In 1893, Baldwin was attracted to Johns Hopkins to fill the chair vacated in 1889 by G. Stanley Hall. (57) Before Baldwin left he was instrumental in having the University of Toronto appoint A. Kirschman, an assistant in W. Wundt's laboratory of experimental psychology. Kirschman undertook the management of the laboratory at Toronto, where he experimented with perception and color aesthetics. (58)

Although some staff members moved to positions in American universities, this was never a serious problem. It was more often the students who found these institutions attractive. In 1895 Loudon complained to Ross about the loss of young men. (59) He listed the names of forty Toronto graduates who held posts in American colleges and universities. They were scattered across the country, many in the larger institutions. In 1897 he published a list of some eighty graduates "who within the previous three years had obtained fellowships, scholarships, or teaching positions in universities of the United States." (60) The calendars of the various institutions testify to the popularity of their graduate schools for Canadians. Since Loudon had easy access to this source, he was well aware of the magnitude of the problem.

Why were such large numbers of Canadians drawn to American graduate schools at this time? The *Canada Educational Monthly,* a supporter of innovation at Toronto, touched on the obvious answer. No opportunities existed in this country for advanced studies, while seemingly unlimited opportunity characterized the situation south of the border. (61) The schools were world-renowned and alive to the possibilities of research. Many of the scholars had international reputations. Besides these powerful psychological reasons for attending American universities, there were compelling practical considerations. The Ph.D. was tangible evidence of its holder's achievement of professional status in a discipline. Once having attained unofficial recognition as a certificate, it had become a requirement for a professorship. William James observed:

America is thus as a nation rapidly drifting toward a state of things in which no man of science or letters will be accounted respectable unless some kind of badge or diploma is stamped upon him. (62)

A. T. DeLury, who debated studying for the doctorate at Chicago, inquired about its usefulness in acquiring a position. In reply, Professor Oska Bolza wrote, "As to your chances of securing a university position after taking a degree from our University, they would, I am convinced, be very good." (63) The University of Toronto did not require the degree, but it was known that the president approved of it. This would enhance its value in the eyes of young scholars. Another benefit derived from the magnanimity of American universities. A great many Canadians, including A. T. Chamberlain at Clark, Pelham Edgar, G. W. Johnston, and A. W. Stratton at Johns Hopkins, and G. F. Hull, F. R. Lillie, and S. J. MacLean at Chicago, received financial assistance through fellowships.

Finally, as mentioned earlier, proximity was a significant consideration for students; none of the prestigious eastern universities was more than two days by rail from Toronto. In 1894 John Squair, (64) Associate Professor of French at Toronto, argued that the university would have to give the Ph.D. on the American, rather than the German, plan:

And another reason in its favour is our proximity to the United States, whose systems we may be forced to imitate because we most certainly shall be forced to compete with them more and more as time goes on. (65)

The contiguity of the United States, and the vigor of her universities, did lead to competition that in turn created a need for imitation.

By the mid-1890s, conditions at the University of Toronto, including an acute awareness of American rivalry, supported a transformation. This was a period of innovation in scientific education. (66) Increasingly, the relationship between science and economic progress was expounded in Canada. The development of the country's natural resources depended on the production of specialists; therefore, strengthening the University would stimulate national growth. (67) At the opening of the Biological Building in 1889 one speaker noted, "Every important scientific discovery in the past has sooner or later found its practical application, and always to the benefit of man." (68) Discoveries could also prove profitable. On a variety of occasions speakers referred to the example of the German chemical industries. In 1897 an article in the *Canada Educational Monthly* stated, "The progress of the province is very largely dependent upon the efficiency and completeness of the University." (69) Boundless optimism concerning the future was reflected in the attitudes expressed in the City of Toronto, which had expanded rapidly during the preceding quarter century and was now one of the twenty largest cities in North America. (70)

In 1887 the Legislative Assembly passed the Federation Act, which encouraged the consolidation of the denominational colleges within the University of Toronto; it also permitted the organization of a medical faculty. (71) As a result of this Act, the staff of the Toronto School of Medicine was appointed to the University's Faculty of Medicine in 1887, and Toronto grew rapidly in enrollment, and a building program was necessary to keep pace with expansion. Since medicine was dependent on research and since spectacular, tangible

results accrued from its investigations, the addition of a medical
faculty was an important event for the University.

It [medicine] had been the first profession based on the study of natural
sciences, and medical faculties were the first university departments to
teach them. For many years the only large-scale and permanent organizations where research was systematically conducted were the teaching hospitals. (72)

When Flexner visited the University in 1910 he praised the organization of its Faculty of Medicine:

The laboratories are in point of construction and equipment among the
best on the continent. Increasing attention has recently been devoted to
the cultivation of research. (73)

The powerful thrust to this position of excellence had occupied
some twenty years, but the foundations were laid during the 1890s.

Rapid physical growth was accompanied by qualitative changes.
In the sciences, professors conducted field trips and trained students
in laboratory methods. An American reviewer of a laboratory guide
for physics written by two Toronto demonstrators found that the
book was advanced and required "perfectly made instruments." (74)
By inference, the Toronto laboratory was well equipped. The University had a laboratory in psychology and from it came several experimental studies that received attention elsewhere. (75) In
Semitics, philosophy, and political economy, undergraduates were
encouraged to attend seminars.

In the climate created by the commingling of the various forces—
the general acceptance of research, the economic significance of the
scientific movement, the University's urban setting, and its growth
in physical size and curriculum—what was needed was a man who
would apply his energies to gathering together the supportive
strands in order to promote research and the doctorate. James Loudon assumed the presidency at a propitious time for this purpose.
He possessed both the energy and the single-minded preoccupation
with research that were required. A scientist, he had a lifelong interest in research; a nativist, he was determined to see Canadians able
to pursue advanced work in Canada; an expansionist, he intended
to have Toronto the intellectual center of such work. Fortunately, a
number of men shared his ambition for Toronto. Chancellor Blake
had worked to have him appointed president because he knew that

Loudon would press for innovative policies. (76) Many younger professors supported him and were ready to participate in his plans. (77)

In the matter of graduate studies and research, Loudon performed exemplary work in broadcasting the importance of this function. In 1893 he told Convocation:

It is not costly and attractive buildings, it is not mere numbers of students, but it is the work done by the staff in teaching and advancing literature and science which gives prestige to a University. (78)

He also encouraged the establishment of higher degrees. In 1894 Toronto established the Doctor of Paedagogy and in 1897 the Doctor of Philosophy, and in 1905 it revised the regulations for the Doctor of Music.

Like the large state universities, the University of Toronto had to shoulder growing responsibilities during the nineties. Moreover, it faced the same competition from the large, private, and mainly eastern universities that drained off the ambitious graduates who wished to study at an advanced level. With the opening of Clark and Chicago, competition was increased. Many students went on to graduate work in the United States and did not return to Canada. Supporters of Toronto could muster all the same arguments for their institution as could their counterparts in the American state universities. They could also appeal to a growing national sentiment. Canadians could not condone the loss of irreplaceable human talent. During Loudon's administration, the seductive appeal of American graduate schools loomed as a greater threat. It had become certain to promoters of the Ph.D. that Toronto could have no claim as an intellectual center unless it met the challenge and offered doctoral work.

Not everyone accepted the notion of an American threat or of the necessity to introduce the Ph.D. The government viewpoint, as expressed by Ross, was that the country was not faced with a "national calamity" because graduates went abroad for further education. (79) He was indifferent to the financial plight of the University. After the Federation Act it had grown rapidly, increasing enrollment from 381 in 1888 to 1,121 in 1898. (80) This expansion forced it to draw capital from its endowment to underwrite the cost of a building program. As a public institution, Toronto proved unable to tap private sources of wealth. Moreover, the government refused to consider annual grants from the Treasury. Ross explained, "That the State should provide the facilities for a higher education is not universally accepted as sound doctrine." (81) While he vaguely comprehended the value of higher education as an agency of national development, he was complacent about arrangements for universities in Ontario. In *The School System of Ontario (Canada): Its History and Distinctive Features,* a book designed for a North American market, Ross romanticized educational provisions in the province. (82) He proudly pointed to the inclusion of the University in the public system and its supervision by the government. The book was published in 1896. In 1897 the University was forced to budget for a deficit in order to meet its responsibilities. Ross boasted of the usefulness to the various departments of the "well-equipped laboratories"; yet the University complained of its inability to finance the sciences adequately. (83) The minister of education argued the excellence of the Ontario system by pointing to the success of its products in the United States. (84) F. L. Paton, President of Princeton, had passed through Ontario public schools and the University of Toronto, while William Osler, Professor of Medicine at Johns Hopkins, had attended Ontario public schools and had graduated from McGill. (85) President Daniel Wilson concurred with Ross in his attitude to the migration of students. On his own admission, he viewed "with complacency the resort of our students to other seats of learning." (86) He scorned those who professed concern about students aspiring to fellowships and degrees in foreign universities. (87)

Another problem for promoters of the doctorate was the slow rate of growth in higher education. Although Toronto was expanding, there was no significant growth among most Canadian colleges. As a consequence, the demand for researchers and professors was limited. Even Squair, who actively promoted the extension of graduate studies, admitted that the scarcity of positions made it unlikely that Canada could have absorbed many Ph.D.'s. (88) He was supported in this view by the *Varsity,* which appeared to sense no great need for the degree. Generally hostile to the innovation, it evinced concern that the introduction of the doctorate would have an adverse effect on the quality of undergraduate programs. (89)

Concern about the curriculum also motivated supporters of liberal culture to resist the introduction of professional scholarship. In 1890 Wilson summed up this position in a manner that was in direct contrast to that of the proponents of research:

Our aim in the Faculty of Arts is high culture in its truest sense; the pursuit of knowledge for its own sake and wholly independent of mere professional requirements. (90)

He presented this viewpoint at several convocations and was supported by many teachers in the colleges that comprised Toronto. These men advocated attention to discipline, the communal life of the residence, and the importance of teaching. (91)

The opposition was, however, unable to resist the determination of the promoters of the doctorate and the conditions that supported its inclusion in the curriculum. For a number of years they did effectively block the establishment of the degree; nevertheless they yielded to the piecemeal extension of its supporting apparatus through the institution of fellowships, laboratories, and seminars.

In 1897 the Senate established the regulations for the Ph.D. Actually, Loudon's motion of 1883 had never been revoked; consequently, since that date the University had favored the introduction of the degree in principle. The regulations activated the 13-year-old resolution. The two men who initiated a reconsideration of the question were Macallum and Alexander. Both were professors in the University, in physiology and English respectively. Both had earned the Johns Hopkins doctorate, Macallum in 1888 and Alexander in 1883. (92) Loudon attributed the implementation of the degree to Macallum's persistence in the face of opposition:

I may add that the chief credit for this step is due to Professor Macallum, whose persistent efforts on behalf of this statute were continued in the face of many obstacles until success was finally attained in 1897. (93)

On March 13, 1896, Macallum and Alexander introduced a motion to have a committee study the feasibility of offering the Ph.D. degree. Almost one full year later, on March 12, 1897, this committee laid before the Senate a set of regulations and a suggested list of disciplines in which the degree could be earned. On May 14, this body adopted a statute for the degree. The University, advertising the doctorate "for the purpose of encouraging research," listed seven departments as willing to supervise candidates: Biology, Chemistry, Physics, Geology, Philosophy, Orientals, and Political Science. English, History, Latin and Greek, Mathematics, and Modern Languages declined to participate in the program. (94)

The regulations (95) resembled those in many American universities. The candidate, who required the baccalaureate before admission to the program, had to attend the University for two academic years. He had to indicate a department of specialization in which he was required to pass an examination in a minor related to his major subject. Since Toronto did not arrange graduate courses, these examinations were at the undergraduate level. When attacked because the degree would necessitate the appointment of more professors to handle the teaching, Loudon replied:

No regular courses of instruction are provided for candidates for this degree, as it is assumed that they will be competent through previous training to proceed with their work with only occasional advice and assistance from their professors. (96)

The two major requirements for the doctorate were a dissertation embodying the results of an original investigation by the candidate and the submission of one hundred printed copies of this work. In form the Ph.D. did not match that of any particular American university, although individual requirements could be found at any number of the larger ones. (97) In all likelihood, the framers of the regulations examined a number of calendars and used these in deciding on a set of reasonable regulations for their own circumstances. In terms of organization, they selected the loose structure mentioned earlier, simply placing the degree at the end of the undergraduate program and under the supervision of an ad hoc Senate committee. Since this organization was less offensive than a graduate school to the opponents of the doctorate, it was more easily introduced than a graduate school.

By 1897 a set of interrelated conditions at Toronto prompted promoters of the Ph.D. to press successfully for its establishment. The City of Toronto was obviously undergoing continuing urbanization and industrialization. In that invigorating environment the future demand for specialists was patent to the promoters. Moreover, faith in the ability of science to resolve difficulties resulting from unplanned growth was general. Like the city, the University was expanding in physical size and complexity. Many of the teachers, including the president, realized the need to modify the curriculum and were determined to advance the institution on its research side. They were dazzled by the brilliance of American higher education, yet apprehensive of its lure for their graduates and the long-term effect on Toronto. They intended to emulate the best in American universities and to participate in the research movement. In this way, they hoped to establish a "Johns Hopkins" in Canada, and, by this fact, to stem the steady drain on Canadian talent.

NOTES

1. A. Bruce Macallum, who graduated in 1880 from the University of Toronto, taught there from 1883 to 1917. During the period 1896 to 1917, he actively promoted the establishment of the Ph.D. degree at Toronto, its extension to a larger number of disciplines, and the creation of a graduate school. In 1917 he resigned his position at the University to undertake the chairmanship of the newly formed National Research Council of Canada.
2. "The Johns Hopkins University Celebration," *University of Toronto Monthly* (April 1901): 176–80.
3. Ibid., p. 176.
4. James Loudon earned the B.A. degree from the University of Toronto in 1862. In 1863 he was appointed tutor in classics and mathematics and in 1875 he became the first Canadian to hold a professorship at the University when he assumed the professorship of mathematics and natural philosophy. He was also the first Canadian president of the University of Toronto, for which he provided dynamic leadership during a period of expansion. For a biography of Loudon see H. H. Langton, *James Loudon and the University of Toronto* (Toronto, 1927).
5. Johns Hopkins University, *Celebration of the Twenty-fifth Anniversary of the Founding of the University and Inauguration of Ira Remsen, LL.D., as President of the University* (Baltimore, 1902), p. 2 [hereafter cited as *Celebration of the Founding of the University*].
6. Ibid., p. 100.
7. Ibid., p. 45.
8. *University of Toronto Monthly* (June 1902): 254, and (June 1903): 309.
9. Elsie A. Hug, *Seventy-five Years in Education: The Role of the School of Education, New York University, 1890–1965* (New York, 1965), p. 30; Sidney Sherwood, *The Universities of the State of New York*, Contributions to American Educational History, ed. H. B. Adams, no. 28 (Washington, 1900), p. 67.
10. George W. Ross served Ontario as minister of education from 1883 to 1899, when he became premier—a position he held until his party

lost the election of 1905. He wrote a political autobiography, *Getting into Parliament and After* (Toronto, 1913).

11. R. R. Price, *The Financial Support of State Universities* (Cambridge, 1924); *University of Toronto Monthly* (March 1901): 203–20; Hon. George W. Ross, *Address Delivered on Moving the Second Reading of a Bill re. the University of Toronto in the Legislative Assembly of Ontario, April 1, 1897* (Toronto, 1897); W. J. Mulock to Ross, March 12, 1897, and S. H. Blake to Ross, May 10, 1901, Department of Education, University of Toronto and Upper Canada College Correspondence, Series D-7 [hereafter cited as Series D-7], Public Archives of Ontario [hereafter cited as P.A.O.]; see also *Varsity* and *University of Toronto Monthly* for 1900–1901.

12. A. B. Macallum, "The University Question in Ontario," *Varsity,* March 12, 1901; "The Presentation of the Portrait of Dr. Loudon," *University of Toronto Monthly* (November 1911): 36–37.

13. James Loudon, "Presidential Address: The Universities in Relation to Research," *Proceedings* of the Royal Society of Canada, 1902, app. A, p. lvii.

14. *The Strength of the University* (Toronto, 1968), p. 191.

15. A. B. Macallum, "The Foundation of the Board of Graduate Studies," *University of Toronto Monthly* (February 1916): 224.

16. Robin Mathews and James Steel, *The Struggle for Canadian Universities* (Toronto, 1970); the Executive and Finance Committee, Canadian Association of University Teachers, " 'Canadianization' and the University," in *Critical Issues in Canadian Society,* ed. Craig L. Boydell et al. (Toronto, 1971); the 1971–1972 Gerstein Lectures at York University, Toronto, were designed around the theme "Nationalism and the University."

17. Frederick Rudolph, *The American College and University: A History* (New York, 1965), pp. 333–52; S. Willis Rudy, "The 'Revolution' in American Higher Education, 1865–1900," *Harvard Educational Review,* 21: 155–74; Laurence Veysey, *The Emergence of the American University* (Chicago, 1965).

18. Quoted in Rudolph, *American College and University,* p. 333.

19. Ralph P. Rosenberg, "The First American Doctor of Philosophy Degree," *Journal of Higher Education* (October 1961): 387–94; Edgar S. Furniss, *The Graduate School of Yale: A Brief History* (New Haven, 1965).

20. Rudy, "The 'Revolution' in American Higher Education," p. 167; Hugh Hawkins, *Pioneer: A History of Johns Hopkins University, 1874–89* (Ithaca, 1960); Francesco Cordasco, *Daniel Coit Gilman and the Protean Ph.D.: The Shaping of American Graduate Education* (Leiden, 1960), pp. 54–115.

21. Rudolph, *American College and University,* pp. 346–48.

22. Ibid., p. 395.

23. *Celebration of the Founding of the University,* p. 80.

24. Veysey, *Emergence of the American University*, p. 330.
25. Joseph Ben-David and Awraham Zloczower, "Universities and Academic Systems in Modern Societies," *European Journal of Sociology* 3 (1962): 45–84. For their explanation of the diffusion of innovation, the authors of this article point to the interaction of a decentralized system of universities in a competitive environment. On pp. 71–76 they discuss the American situation.
26. Allan Nevins, *The State Universities and Democracy* (Urbana, Ill., 1962), p. 101.
27. Walter A. Donnelly, ed.; *The University of Michigan: An Encyclopedic Survey* 3 (Ann Arbor, Mich., 1953), quoted on p. 1043.
28. Winton U. Solberg, *The University of Illinois, 1867–1894* (Urbana, Ill., 1968), pp. 341–67.
29. Merle Curti and Vernon Cartensen, *The University of Wisconsin, 1848–1925* 1 (Madison, Wisc., 1949), pp. 448–49.
30. D. C. McHenry, "The Higher Education of Women," *Proceedings of the Ontario Educational Association, 1879*, p. 75; A. P. Coleman, "A Plea for More Science," *Canada Educational Monthly* (March 1880): 146; W.H.P., "German Science," *Varsity*, October 16, 1880.
31. "Canadian Institute—Occupation of the New Building and Opening Address of Prof. Loudon," *Toronto Mail*, January 29, 1877.
32. Minutes of the Senate, April 18, 1874; June 17, 1874; December 8, 1874; December 9, 1874; December 10, 1874, Office of the Registrar, University of Toronto [hereafter cited as U.T.R.].
33. J. H. Hunter, "The University Question," *Canada Educational Monthly* (January 1880): 1–9.
34. Ibid., p. 2.
35. Edward Blake, Chancellor of the University of Toronto, 1873–1900, graduated from the University, B.A. (1854) and M.A. (1858). He had a controversial career in politics in Ontario, Canada, and Britain. Between 1880 and 1892 he worked to forward Toronto as a national center for higher learning. For a biography see James Loudon, "Edward Blake," *University of Toronto Monthly* (May 1912) and C. T. Bissell, ed., *Our Living Tradition* (Toronto, 1957).
36. "Chancellor Blake's Address," *Canada Educational Monthly* (September 1880): 402–6.
37. Ibid., p. 405.
38. T. Wesley Mills, "The Johns Hopkins University of Baltimore, Maryland, U.S.," *Canada Educational Monthly* (January 1882): 1–6.
39. Johns Hopkins University, *Register of Johns Hopkins University, 1881–82*.
40. Minutes of the Senate, January 13, 1882, U.T.R.
41. The nine fellowships were offered in the following departments: French and German, Classics (2 awards), English, Physics, Chemistry, Mathematics, Mineralogy and Geology, and Natural History.
42. Cordasco, *Daniel Coit Gilman*, pp. 85–86.

43. For a biography of Daniel Wilson see H. H. Langton, *Sir Daniel Wilson, a Memoir* (Edinburgh, 1929).

44. *Globe,* May 18, 1883.

45. *Toronto Mail,* April 28, 1883; April 30, 1883; May 1, 1883; *Globe,* June 11, 1883. *Varsity,* April 21, 1883; October 6, 1883.

46. Minutes of the Senate, May 25, 1883; May 29, 1883; October 20, 1883, U.T.R.

47. *Varsity,* February 24, 1883; June 2, 1883; January 31, 1885.

48. Minutes of the Senate, 1883–1897, U.T.R.

49. Information on the fellows was compiled from three sources: H. J. Morgan, *The Canadian Men and Women of the Time, 1912* (Toronto, 1912); University of Toronto, *Register for the University of Toronto for the Year 1920* (Toronto, 1920); *Province of Ontario Gazetteer and Directory, 1907–08* (Ingersoll, Ont., 1908).

50. Macallum, "The Foundation of the Board of Graduate Studies," p. 220.

51. Hunter, "The University Question"; Mills, "The Johns Hopkins University"; Charles K. Adams, "University Education in the United States," *Canada Education Monthly* (April and September 1887): 131–35 and 268–73; J. P. Gordy, "Chairs of Pedagogy," ibid. (March 1891): 93–98; E. R. Sill, "Should a College Educate?" ibid. (January and February 1886): 10–13 and 57–62.

52. "Looking to Cornell," February 2, 1884; A. F. Chamberlain, "The University and the Government—*IV,*" November 7, 1894; H. R. Fairclough, "Stanford University," January 16, 1895.

53. *Varsity,* December 2, 1890.

54. In the Loudon Papers there is a number of letters in which Loudon and Koenig exchanged information about experiments, usually in acoustics; moreover, Loudon wrote a biographical sketch of Koenig (University of Toronto Department of Rare Books and Special Collections [hereafter cited as U.T.A.]).

55. Ashley to Ross, March 21, 1889, Series D-7, P.A.O.

56. Ashley to Ross, July 17, 1892, ibid.

57. Baldwin to Ross, November 17, 1890, ibid.; W. J. Baldwin "The Psychological Laboratory in the University of Toronto," *Science* 19 (1892): 143–44; G. Stanley Hall, *Life and Confessions of a Psychologist* (New York, 1924), p. 259.

58. Baldwin to R. Harcourt, Provincial Treasurer, October 4, 1892; Baldwin to Ross, n.d., Series D-7, P.A.O.; W. J. Alexander, ed., *University of Toronto and Its Colleges, 1827–1906* (Toronto, 1906), app. B and C.

59. Loudon to Ross, November 8, 1895, Series D-7, P.A.O.

60. James Loudon, "Post-Graduate Courses," *Canada Educational Monthly* (January 1898): 38–39.

61. Ibid.: 25.

62. "The Ph.D. Octopus," *Educational Review* (February 1918): 151 (reprinted from *Harvard Monthly* [March 1902]).

63. Boska to DeLury, February 24, 1895, DeLury Collection, U.T.A.

64. John Squair, who received the B.A. in 1883 from the University of Toronto, was among the first fellows appointed by the University. A Supporter of James Loudon's policies, he was appointed associate professor in 1892, shortly after Loudon became president.

65. "Post-Graduate Courses in the University of Toronto," *Proceedings of the Ontario Educational Association, 1894,* p. 67.

66. Alexander, *University of Toronto and Its Colleges,* pp. 57–70; G. G. McNab, *The Development of Higher Education in Ontario* (Toronto, 1925), pp. 83–91.

67. "The University of Toronto," *Canada Educational Monthly* (February 1897): 68.

68. V. C. Vaughan, "The Necessity of Encouraging Scientific Work," *Formal Opening of the New Building of the Biological Department, December 19, 1889* (Toronto, 1890), p. 20, U.T.A. (reprinted from the *Canadian Practitioner,* January 1, January 15, and February 1, 1890).

69. "The University of Toronto," *Canada Educational Monthly* (February 1897): 68.

70. D. C. Masters, *The Rise of Toronto, 1850–1890* (Toronto, 1947); J. Spelt, *The Urban Development in South-Central Ontario* (Assen, Neth., 1955).

71. Ontario, Legislative Assembly, 50 Victoria, ch. 43. This Act revived the University as a teaching body. (Between 1853 and 1887 University College was responsible for all teaching in the arts at the University of Toronto.) Under the new arrangement the colleges had their curriculum restricted to Greek, Latin, French, German, English, oriental languages, moral philosophy, and ancient history, while the University was authorized to teach all additional subjects, including history, political science, Spanish, Italian, mathematics, and the sciences.

72. Joseph Ben-David, "Scientific Productivity and Academic Organization in Nineteenth-Century Medicine," in *Sociology and History,* ed. W. J. Cahnman and A. Boskoff (New York, 1964), p. 518.

73. Abraham Flexner, *Medical Education in the United States and Canada,* Carnegie Foundation for the Advancement of Teaching, Bulletin no. 4 (Boston, 1910), p. 323.

74. *Science,* n.s. 3, January 17, 1896, pp. 103–4.

75. Alexander, *University of Toronto and Its Colleges,* app. C; H. H. Langton, "University of Toronto Studies," *Varsity,* March 14, 1907.

76. Edward Blake to Ross, July 27, 1892, and August 29, 1892, and Blake to Premier Oliver Mowat, September 2, 1892, Blake Papers, U.T.A.

77. J. G. Hume to Blake, August 22, 1892; J. F. McCurdy to Blake, August 29, 1892, ibid.

78. James Loudon, *Address at the Convocation of University College, Toronto, October 11, 1893* (Toronto, 1893), p. 8.

79. *University of Toronto Monthly* (March 1901): 213.

80. Hon. Edward Blake, *Address at the Convocation of the University of Toronto, June 10, 1892* (Toronto, 1892), p. 1; "Attendance at the Uni-

versity of Toronto and Victoria College, 1892–1899," Loudon Papers, U.T.A.

81. George W. Ross, *Address Delivered on Moving the Second Reading of a Bill re. University of Toronto in the Legislative Assembly of Ontario, April 1, 1897*, p. 11.

82. George W. Ross, *The School System of Ontario (Canada): Its History and Distinctive Features* (New York, 1896).

83. Ibid., p. 184, "The University of Toronto," *Canada Educational Monthly* (February 1897): 67; Langton, *James Loudon and the University of Toronto*, p. 17.

84. George W. Ross, *The Policy of the Education Department* (Toronto, 1897).

85. Osler had also attended a private school, Trinity College School, for part of his secondary education, although Ross did not mention this.

86. "Annual Convocation at University College," *Canada Educational Monthly* (November 1886): 342.

87. Sir Daniel Wilson, *Address at the Convocation of University College 1888* (Toronto, 1888), p. 17.

88. Squair, "Post-Graduate Courses in the University of Toronto," p. 67; John Squair, "Lessons from Lost Opportunities," *University of Toronto Monthly* (October 1904): 10.

89. *Varsity*, October 14, October 23, and November 11, 1897.

90. Sir Daniel Wilson, *Address at the Convocation of University College, 1890* (Toronto, 1890), p. 16.

91. In 1906 a Royal Commission was appointed to investigate the problems that Toronto faced as a provincial university. A number of briefs from the colleges and individuals argued the importance of liberal culture (Ontario, Royal Commission on the University of Toronto, *Report* [Toronto, 1906]).

92. Alexander was the first Canadian to earn the Ph.D. at Johns Hopkins.

93. University of Toronto, *Annual Report of the President of the University of Toronto for the Year Ending June 30th, 1902*, p. 6.

94. Minutes of the Senate, March 13, 1896; March 12, 1897; May 14, 1897, U.T.A.

95. Ibid., March 12, 1897.

96. Loudon, "Post-Graduate Courses," p. 38.

97. That the University of Toronto followed the general pattern that was emerging during the 1890s is confirmed by a comparison of the regulations for the Ph.D. at Toronto and at nine leading American universities: California, Chicago, Columbia, Harvard, Johns Hopkins, Michigan, Princeton, Wisconsin, and Yale. All nine were charter members of the Association of American Universities and, since they produced the majority of doctorates in the United States, were influential models.

Part IV

Approaches to Research

9. PATTERNS OF SCHOOL ATTENDANCE IN TORONTO, 1844–1878: SOME SPATIAL CONSIDERATIONS

Between 1844 and 1878 there were two waves of school construction in Toronto. This essay discusses the way in which the policy decisions about the location of the schools built at that time reflected educational purposes. The essay underlines the potential in the approach of the urban geographer for understanding the relation between social policy and institutional function.

I

WITH THE INTRODUCTION of free schools into Canada West in 1850, school attendance became, as it had for American educators, both the greatest obstacle to the successful implementation of the new system and the greatest justification for its future growth. Once the education of *all* school-age children became the primary goal of educational reform, the days of the district common school in the city were numbered. The district system had encouraged patterns of attendance attuned to the interests of the family and not those of the state. Schoolmen accused this more informal education of inefficiency and discrimination against the poorer classes and also objected to the large numbers of parents who kept their children out of school. (1) To its proponents, the extension of free schooling would not only ensure a higher rate of attendance, but would also serve to assimilate the "famine Irish" who had flocked to the cities

Mr. Bamman is a graduate student in the Ontario Institute for Studies in Education. This essay first appeared in The History of Education Quarterly *(Fall 1972).*

of Canada West in the late 1840s, and whose mere physical presence mid-nineteenth-century educators perceived as a direct threat to social order. To men like Dr. Egerton Ryerson, the Chief Superintendent of Education in Canada West, it was therefore doubly important to make operative as soon as possible the forces of social levelling, acculturation to work values, and diminution of crime inherent in universal primary education.

Free schools would make new arrivals into Canadians through moral suasion if possible, through coercion if necessary. The immigrant child would have to be separated from the influence of its parents between the ages of roughly five to twelve, and during that time taught the values of an expanding mercantile society. This view of the Irish in particular, and the labouring classes in general, was shared by educators at all levels of policy-making and proved to be remarkably prescient of the course public education would take in Canada West in the next quarter-century.

Yet, to understand only the intellectual underpinnings of the free school ideology, important as that may be, is not to grasp entirely how this system was impressed on the people of a city. That is to say, the problems schoolmen encountered in training the urban family to send its children to school interacted with social reality at a number of levels. We must not only ask what educators *said* about their school system; we must also ask what rationale there was to the spatial, organizational, and temporal ordering in urban free schools. The rapid expansion of cities, population movements, and changes in demographic characteristics all impinged on and became part of the perceptions of educational reformers. Such urban realities informed their policies, but they also thwarted some of the niceties of their elitist social theory.

The implications of a spatial-temporal approach to the analysis of school system growth are considerable. Historians have rarely used a spatial orientation as a setting for their narrative explanations, and when they have it is usually put in terms of some ecological imperative. (2) This paper hopes to make clear that both educators and their clientele played important roles in defining and shaping the physical environment of urban education. The implementation of the free school system represented more than just the ascendancy of one viewpoint over another—it meant as well that this viewpoint would be translated into school placement decisions and policies regarding spatial control of the population. At the same time, however, the lives of the working classes were bound by spatial patterns that essentially conflicted with those promoted by educators. An examination of these crosscurrents and how they affected one another will add a new dimension to our understanding of educational innovation in the nineteenth century.

The process of growth of the free school, then, was neither random nor preordained; rather it reflected much that was rational and amenable to ideological input. School placement is a case in point, for as one geographer has noted the location decisions of public bodies (such as school boards) reflect criteria vastly different from those used in locating commercial enterprises. The implication clearly is that "a new theoretical structure will be required to explain their [public facilities] distribution." (3) Part of that structure must take into account, as I shall argue later, how perceptions of the urban environment result in school placement. And as school placement is crucial to any analysis of the finer patterns of school attendance, educational historians will have to develop new research strategies to handle the immense amounts of spatial data on school attendance that nineteenth-century educators have left us. The core question is how do we explain increased school attendance, and any explanation that eventually emerges *must* include reference to the urban landscape in which the change occurred. (4)

In the city of Toronto, public education was transformed from a somewhat chaotic, loosely administered system of rate-paying common schools into a highly efficient, bureaucratic system between 1844 and the late 1870s. In the first period of growth, from 1844 to 1858, the section school system (equivalent to the district common school) was exchanged for free schools, centralization among the schools introduced, and a standardized internal economy established within each school. The elective status of the school board trustees was confirmed and the "public" nature of education made clear. The free schools were aimed specifically at the working classes, as was clear from educators' rhetoric and locational decisions. The planning that did occur during this period concerned itself with controlling residential mobility among the population and providing accommodation for school-age children in working-class areas of the city. In spite of the modern, centralized school plant constructed in the 1850s, it became clear that working-class parents were not to any large extent sending their children to these schools. At this juncture, a frustrated Board of School Trustees traded off moral suasion, that last remnant of noncoercive community life, for a more rigid view of education in an attempt to produce the desired attendance statistics. The free school system, although under fire for its lack of success, was reaffirmed in 1858. (5)

In the second period, from the late 1850s until the late 1860s, schoolmen in Toronto were confronted with a slowly growing school population. They did not appreciably enlarge the system, in part because of the adverse economic conditions of this time. Yet, they did refine its workings, in particular by increasing the number of teachers in an attempt to decrease the pupil ratio in the younger divisions. The transient quality of urban employment, however, forced parents (and their children) to move about the city rapidly, and as a result imbalances between accommodation and children in particular schools were not resolved. The large numbers of children not attending school came to be seen as "street arabs" by the conservative element of the Board of School Trustees, who then posited an institutional solution, i.e., reform school, to educate this portion of the school-age population. Yet, as a school census in 1863 showed, the numbers of these non-attending children were surprisingly low.

From the late 1860s onward Toronto, and the school system with it, began to expand again. The increase in population brought with it a large increase in the number of schools, as well as an increase in the scale of individual school buildings. The larger buildings were built to cater to pupils over twelve years of age. At the same time there occurred a hierarchical differentiation in school management, with the hiring in 1874 of an aggressive educator-bureaucrat as inspector. The inspector, James L. Hughes, brought with him notions on curriculum, grading, and school regulations quite "progressive" in tone, and within a few years he had overhauled most of the school system. Likewise, in the mid-1870s school attendance figures greatly improved: more children were attending than ever before and for longer periods of time. This was due neither to compulsory education legislation passed in 1871 nor to the increasing vigilance over the child while in school. Rather, an improved standard of living among the working classes probably explains in part this new pattern of school attendance. (6)

This brief outline might suggest that school development in Toronto was linear and somehow evolutionary. In fact, its growth was marked by peaks and troughs that corresponded much more closely to the transition of Toronto from a mercantile, preindustrial to a "modern" city than it did to coaxing the schoolmen. Yet, the decisions made by educators during these years went far in defining the relationship between the home and the school in this new order. Only the first period of growth will be explored in detail here; its conclusions will be presented as an explanatory hypothesis for the patterns of school attendance in the period 1858–1878.

II

The common school system in Toronto, organized in 1844, was comprised of fifteen school sections, each with one school house. The boundaries of each section, as well as the location of the school within it, were determined by the general distribution of the population. The schools were usually rented premises of frame construction, and school location could be changed on relatively short notice; new schools required only an adequate building and a teacher. In this period the common school board was not particularly interested in either land acquisition or permanent structures, perhaps because of the uncertain funding of education. When a parcel was donated to the board, for example, it was rented for the income. Suitable buildings could not always be found, of course, and areas of the city were periodically without any school. To this difficulty was added the disorganization inherent in fifteen semi-autonomous school sections and a common school board constantly at loggerheads with the city council. (7) Looking back from 1858, the Board of School Trustees reminded the public that

in the school times of 1844, the school buildings . . . were small, incommodious, badly ventilated, and ill adapted for the purpose of moral and social advancement, through the agency of popular education; children of both sex[es] assembled in one room, and mingled together in one common play-yard—in several cases as many as a hundred young persons were huddled together in a space not fit to accommodate—far less teach—two-thirds . . . of the number. . . . (8)

In spite of these alleged shortcomings, there were distinct advantages to the school section. It was shaped by its social and geographic environment, and was capable of responding quickly to changes in its constituency or public sentiment. The scale of the school section encouraged rate-payers to petition the common school board for new schools, new locations for existing schools, and additions or improvements to the section school house. In many cases such representations were successful; after all, the trustees could handle such affairs easily enough. (9) Parents, too, were more likely to send their children to school because of their own perception of the services the school might offer rather than from any sense of compulsion. A child could be removed at parental option, of course, but in difficult times the child as wage-earner was important to the survival of the family. When in school, children attended with regularity. While it was true that to a certain extent the ability to send a child to a school where the monthly fee equalled at least a day's wages was dependent on class, education had not yet become all-important in terms of life success.

In Toronto, the school section system appears to have served all classes equally. In section six, for example, the school was attended by children whose parents came from all the major occupational groupings (*see* Table 1). The section itself was located only slightly west of the city's expanding central business district (CBD), and between two of its busiest commercial streets. It is not surprising, therefore, to find a number of innkeepers sending their older sons to the school. Yet, the compactness of mid-nineteenth-century Toronto, as well as the characteristic preindustrial residential mix, also made the school a logical choice for considerable numbers of artisans and labourers. All the children linked to city directories in 1846 and 1851 lived in or quite near the school section, with one exception. An innkeeper's son in 1846 commuted to the school from a village north of the city—a journey requiring private transportation or the use of one of the omnibus lines in existence at this time.

The average ages of entering children in 1846, and of children in school in 1851, suggest that children from lower-class backgrounds were more susceptible to an irregular education than those from professional or business families. Residential mobility among the lower classes no doubt contributed to this phenomenon, but the decrease in numbers of lower-class children in 1851 suggests that

Attendance by Occupational Category
Toronto Common School District 6
1846 and 1851

Occupation		Number of Children Attending School		Number of Children				Average Age of Children			
				1846		1851		1846		1851	
		1846*	1851†	M	F	M	F	M	F	M	F
Professionals:	N	1	4	1	–	3	2	5.0	–	10.7	8.0
	%	2.3	11.1								
Businessmen:											
Sellers of Food and Lodging	N	7	3	5	5	4	–	10.2	8.3	7.0	–
	%	16.3	8.3								
Merchant/Shopkeeper	N	5	5	2	3	5	1	8.0	8.3	9.0	5.0
	%	11.6	13.9								
Business Employee	N	1	1	–	1	1	–	–	11.0	13.0	–
	%	2.3	2.8								
Artisans:											
Carpenters	N	3	5	4	1	5	–	7.7	12.0	10.0	–
	%	7.0	13.9								
Construction Trades	N	6	5	4	2	5	–	8.7	13.0	11.2	–
	%	14.0	13.9								
Other Artisans	N	4	8‡	5	1	8	1	9.2	9.0	9.4	14.0
	%	9.3	22.2								
Semiskilled	N	4	–	3	2	–	–	8.3	7.5	–	–
	%	9.3	–								
Labourers:	N	11	1	5	7	1	–	7.6	10.0	7.0	–
	%	25.6	2.8								
Miscellaneous:	N	–	1	–	–	1	–	–	–	7.0	–
	%	–	2.8								
Not Listed:	N	1	3	1	–	2	1	14.0	–	10.5	13.0
	%	2.3	8.3								
TOTALS	N	43	36	30	22	35	5				

*Based on all linkable entering children, 1846.
†Based on all linkable children in school, April-August 1851.
‡Includes a tinsmith and a watchmaker.
Source: Ontario Provincial Archives, R.G. 2, Education Records, General, "Toronto City School Register, District 10[6], 1844–1851," and Toronto City Directories, 1846 and 1851.

perhaps the influx of unskilled Irish labour into the city in the late
1840s depressed labourers' wages, thus forcing lower-class children
from the school. Artisans, however, were well represented in both
years; in each year one of them sent the largest number of children
to school from a single family: a carpenter in 1846 and a tinsmith
in 1851 each sent three. The smaller number of girls attending in
both years is probably due to the existence of a large number of
private schools in the city.

Yet there were problems with the section school system. It was
clearly inadequate to encompass the entire school-age population
of the city, since a single school house rarely held over one hundred
pupils. In fact, common schools in Toronto during the 1840s never
accounted for more than about two-fifths of all school-age children,
although they did achieve a daily attendance of about three-fourths
for those enrolled. (10) Additionally, the extent of the trustees'
powers was limited, and this meant that the quality of education
was uneven throughout the city. Finally, there were a number of
contentious issues between the common school board and the city
council—at one point the board simply closed down the city schools
for a full year (July 1848–July 1849) when the city refused to collect
taxes to support a free school system. (11) Thus, change in the
existing arrangement was seen as imperative by Toronto schoolmen, for there were thousands of children

who now loiter about the public streets, or frequent the haunts of vice,
creating the most painful emotion in every well-regulated mind; and, in
some degree involving the imputation that the social condition of the
body corporate, of which they form a part, cannot be of the highest
order. (12)

Dr. Ryerson could only agree, noting that "many children are now
kept from school on the alleged grounds of parental poverty. How
far this excuse is well founded, is immaterial to the question at
hand. . . ." (13) The answer to the question of how to deal with
the children of the working classes, the local superintendent was
convinced, would be found in a "sound, energetic, and uniform
school system, such as the Board of Trustees could readily carry
out." (14)

"System," then, would carry the day—and bring with it centralization and efficient organization. Ryerson had taken a step in that

direction in 1847 when he had given jurisdiction over the schools to municipalities, because "the peculiar circumstances . . . of cities and towns appear to . . . demand this modification of our school system." (15) In his drive for free schools, Ryerson disclaimed interest in compelling "the education of children by the terror of legal pains and penalties," but he was also convinced that to place "before parents the strongest motives for educating their children, and to provide the best facilities for that purpose, is alike the dictate of sound policy and Christian patriotism." (16) While it is true that the school section was inadequate to meet the educational needs of a rapidly expanding urban population, it also is clear that the passage of the Common School Act of 1850, the mechanism by which the tax-supported free school became a reality, provided educators with the structural opening they needed so desperately to implement their program for assimilating the children of the working classes. (17)

III

The perception of the Irish as a threat to the social order arose primarily from the manner in which they had arrived in Toronto. Poor Irish Catholics were herded into "immigrants sheds" to the southwest of the city as they landed, and thence shipped out to rural Canada to begin anew as farmers. Within a year, however, most of the Irish who had been processed in this manner returned to urban centers. Without funds or marketable skills, those who came to Toronto congregated in a shanty town on the flats of the Don River, on the eastern edge of the city. They "forced out the inhabitants of existing slums and some working class areas in such cities as Toronto," notes one sociologist, "and consolidated themselves as an urban proletariat." (18)

One of the underlying assumptions of Victorian thought, one unquestioned until recently, was that immigrant groups such as the Irish exhibited pathological social behaviour, and that the lower classes in general led chaotic, disorganized personal lives. Although this notion was used by educators as *prima facie* evidence that immigrants would have to be assimilated at any cost, it was based on a stereotype that, when analysed, bears little resemblance to social reality. As Lynn Lees, for one, has recently shown, "not only did structural regularities appear in supposedly random wanderings from slum to slum, but the physical movements of the poor paralleled those of the population as a whole." (19) Not only were residental moves of the Irish poor rationally ordered, but as one geographer has argued, we can no longer accept mistaken notions of the "mortal and socially pathological repercussions of congested and unsanitary housing conditions." These slums districts were "erroneously identified with high rates of infant mortality, crime, prostitution, drunkenness, and various other symptoms of social ills." (20)

Such evidence, although indirect for our case, nevertheless forces us to rethink educators' responses to the Irish. Where they saw only social and moral degeneracy, they should have seen a slow but steady assimilation of Irish into the larger economic and cultural patterns within the city, and a consciousness of social mobility that would have militated against any social disorder. Too, the immigrant was keenly aware of the benefits of schooling, not only for his children, but for himself as well. As we shall see, the Irish response to the denial of their rights to adequate separate school funds represents a remarkable show of cultural solidarity and a remarkable interest in schooling as well. (21)

By 1851, to judge from census returns, the Irish had already settled throughout the city—concentrations of the three major ethnic groups (English, Irish, and Canadian) were strikingly similar for all six wards. Distribution by religion indicated a somewhat higher proportion of Roman Catholics in the southeastern portion of the city near the Don River. Within each ward it is likely that the working-class settlements were concentrated where that ward was contiguous with the CBD; thus, it is probably not incorrect to assume that the Irish Catholics were moving from their shanty town on the Don Flats to work opportunities in the central area. In time, this process would result in a ring of working-class settlements encircling the CBD. Finer spatial distinctions than this, however, are beyond us, for as Peter Goheen has written of Toronto in this period, "the daily rhythm of lives and the patterns of association can no longer be recorded directly and . . . evidence of routine things has virtually vanished. . . ." (22)

Problems confronting the Board of School Trustees reflected the shifting residential pattern of the Irish. Once the Board's plan for the construction of modern school houses was approved at a public hearing in 1852, it took less than four years to build six new schools; within six years the outlines of the new educational bureaucracy had emerged. (23) The erection of these permanent structures highlighted two issues that were to prove particularly troublesome: (1) school placement—in terms of accurately gauging population densities, and (2) the control of population movements among the parents of school-going children. To complicate matters further, the Roman Catholics built a rival school system.

In 1858 the Board itself provided the best description of the first stage of development:

When the three new school houses first erected in 1852–53, came into operation, the teachers and pupils of three or four sections were drafted into the nearest school, and thus enabled the principles of centralization and classification to come at once into practical effect. And when the other three new school houses were ready for occupation in 1855–56, the same mode of proceeding was adopted to organize their commencement. From 1853 to 1856, therefore, the school section period gradually expired; and the period of centralization, and of separate divisions in each [class of boys and girls] graduated according to proficiency, from the child about to commence its A.B.C. to the grown-up lad or girl, completing their education, was completed in 1856, and has since been so continued. (24)

The schools were two-story brick structures that could be expanded to three stories, and capable of accommodating from 300 to 400 students each. The planned pupil-teacher ratio was 50 or 60 to 1. With two temporary school houses erected in 1858, there was room for 3,000 students—far more than the number actually in school at that time. The Board nevertheless planned to build at least three more large brick structures "in those locations where results have shown that even the imperfect provision now existing has been appreciated and largely profited by." (25)

Although Sam B. Warner has found for Philadelphia in the nineteenth century that "the municipal corporation dotted the grid with schools . . . as if it were salting an egg . . ." (26) it would be unfair to the ideological astuteness of Toronto's educators to accuse them of having no rationale for school placement. The new school houses were not located simply to efficiently account for pupils from the older sections. Of the six new schools, five were in close proximity of one another and quite near the CBD, while the sixth was located in St. David's Ward (which had the highest Roman Catholic population in the city and was contiguous on its eastern boundary with the Don River). Of the two temporary schools established in 1858, one was located in a traditionally working-class neighborhood. These new, larger, and more formal schools, the Board made clear, were intended to serve the working-class population near whose homes they had been erected, for

as nearly as all the children who attend the city schools come from the industrial classes, the system of instruction pursued in the schools has been based upon the practical considerations of utility so as to impart to the pupils such a sound and useful English education as shall fit him or her to enter upon the daily pursuits of industrial or domestic life. . . . (27)

Planning, both for the schools built between 1852–1856 and those of the later 1850s, also reflected this concern with reaching the greatest number of working-class children. Much effort went into anticipating or correcting imbalances among the pupil population in various parts of the city. For example, the Park School (in St. David's Ward) had been the object of a Board resolution in 1851, a year before its construction, to the effect that:

Whereas there are great numbers of children residing in . . . St. David's Ward . . . who are prevented from attending the public schools of this city owing to the great distance from the school houses from that neighborhood . . . And whereas it is necessary in order to secure to them the blessing of education and thus prevent their growing up in idleness and ignorance, [it is hereby resolved] that a school be established in said locality as early as possible. (28)

The Committee on School Sites and Buildings likewise reacted to severe overcrowding in the younger classes in another school by planning a new structure in the northern part of that ward. (29)

In these and other decisions, several criteria for the selection of school sites became evident. Whatever influence the people had wielded over school placement through rate-payer petitions was gradually eroded as the expertise of the commitee of trustees developed. Given the free school preoccupation with efficiency, the trustees were committed to centralized education achieved through large-scale, permanent structures placed in working-class neighborhoods. Beyond this, the Board of School Trustees avoided proximity between public and private school houses to prevent the inevitable "collision" between the pupils of the two systems. (30) Finally, there was the criterion of economy in site acquisition and construction of the schools, to assuage a cost-conscious polity. The Board could hardly afford land in the CBD, but it could purchase lots at reasonable rates not far outside it.

After they removed the inherent geographical limitations on school attendance found in the school section system and effectively enlarged the individual school area, educators expected the availability of school facilities to produce radically improved patterns of attendance among the lower classes. Quite to the contrary, what did emerge was only a stabilized version of the rate-paying common school pattern (*see* Table 2). Although the figures for city and school-age population were admittedly guesses, those for children

TABLE 2

School Attendance in Toronto
1851– 1858
(Each Column as a Percent of Preceding Column)

		City Population	Population* Ages 5–16	Ages 5–16* on Roll	Average Registered Attendance	Average Daily Attendance
1851	N	30,762	7,773	3,059	1,845	1,366
	%		25.3	39.4	60.3	74.0
1852	N	35,000	7,805	3,791	1,872	1,346
	%		22.3	48.6	49.4	71.9
1853	N	40,000	9,000	3,413	1,886	1,402
	%		22.5	37.9	55.3	74.3
1854	N	41,500	9,000	4,557	1,971	1,459
	%		21.7	50.6	43.3	74.0
1855	N	42,500	11,000	4,058	2,066	1,570
	%		25.9	36.9	50.9	76.0
1856	N	43,250	N/A	4,238	2,318	1,747
	%		–	–	54.7	75.4
1857	N	45,000	10,000	5,630	2,480	1,863
	%		22.2	56.3	44.0	75.1
1858	N	47,500	11,000	6,484	2,522	1,987
	%		23.2	58.9	38.9	78.8

*Annual Report of the Chief Superintendent of Schools, 1851–1858.
Source: Report of the Past History, and Present Condition, of the Common or Public Schools of the City of Toronto, p. 126.

enrolled were taken from school registers. Overall, they indicate that about 50 percent of those enrolled at some time during the year still attended on the average each month, and of these about 75 percent attended daily. In terms of days attended, more than 50 percent of the children enrolled attended less than 100 days (about five school months). The question immediately arises as to how educators could have so badly misjudged the working classes of the city.

One possible answer must be that they had built their system from ideological design, and although they implemented it in rough geographic proximity to their intended clientele, that alone was insufficient to encourage people to send their children to school. The threat of social disorder had been met in a typically bureaucratic fashion, which represented

a rational, if rigid, response to social complexity and political exigency. Primarily, the complexity of administering a sprawling, loosely organized school system in a growing and heterogenous city highlighted the necessity for rationalization and efficiency. . . . (31)

Too, the internal economy of the classroom, with its skein of para-military regulations covering the relationships between parent, child, and teacher, could only have alienated many people. One typical rule was that "no pupil who is irregular in attendance, punctuality, or conduct, will be permitted the privilege of the school libraries, or be eligible for reward of any sort." (32) These explanations are plausible, but they fail to take into account more dynamic causes of nonattendance, namely, the counter-cultural response of Irish Catholics and population mobility. (33)

The Common School Act of 1850 was no sooner in effect than Catholics approached the Board of School Trustees for their share of the public school fund. Catholics had supported a separate school since 1843, but their needs had grown enormously by 1851, and they would continue to grow throughout the 1850s. (34) In January 1851, the Board tabled a request for seven separate schools; other individual requests were also put aside. (35) Although the Board did agree to support three separate schools, it would go no further, in part because that course would lessen the public, i.e., Protestant, school fund, and in part because it considered *all* children as coming under its purview. (36)

At this point the Catholic community turned to its own resources to build the necessary schools, at the same time continuing its drive for public funds under the leadership of the controversial Bishop Charbonel. In 1852 Catholic rate-payers from each of the wards separately petitioned the Board for separate schools. "This Board," replied the trustees,

cannot too strongly deprecate the demand for separate schools, and regret it as utterly indefensible upon the ground either of justice, wisdom, or patriotism, inasmuch as it involves the entire ruin of any sound system of public instruction. (37)

In its reply, the Board's anti-Catholicism coincided with its fear that the fledgling public school system might not be legitimized by the presence of sufficient numbers of children to make it an efficient enterprise. Legislation in 1853 and 1855 designed to clarify and strengthen the Catholic position vis-à-vis separate schools did little to soften the Board's attitude. (38) Relations between the trustees and Catholic spokesmen continued to deteriorate, until in 1858 the Lord Bishop of Toronto and four church wardens presented a petition to the Board asking that:

the parochial schools connected with said churches respectively may be declared to be schools of the city and as such that adequate funds be set apart for the support of the same. (39)

Despite opposition from the Board and from Ryerson, the separate school system continued to grow. A Board of Separate School Trustees was elected in 1853, and between 1851 and 1854 the number of separate schools increased from one to seven. In these schools, located near the city's Catholic churches, the pupil-teacher ratio was always high and the number of pupils grew rapidly (*see* Table 3). Not only did the separate school total enrollment grow more quickly relative to that of the public schools, but fragmentary evidence indicates that the rates of attendance were at least competitive. (40)

Educational reformers failed not only to encourage the working classes to enter the schools, but also in their attempt to claim socialization of the Catholic child as a "public" task. The assertion of community by Toronto's Irish Catholics, however, need not imply a radical political or cultural consciousness. In fact, by the early 1860s public educators came to understand the essential similarity of the two systems and applauded the success of the Catholic clergy

TABLE 3

Toronto Roman Catholic Separate Schools
1855–1860

Year	No. of Schools	No. of Pupils	As a % of Public School Enrollment	No. of Teachers
1855	7	1,162	56.2	16
1856	6	1,268	54.7	16
1857	6	1,431	57.7	17
1858	6	1,807	71.6	18
1859	6	1,886	68.8	16
1860	6	2,200	67.7	20

Source: Annual Report of the Chief Superintendent of Schools, 1855–1860.

at a time when their own schools were achieving only indifferent results. Ryerson's journal admitted in 1861 that,

the good sisters of St. Joseph and the Christian Brothers deserve our gratitude, for the manner in which they are educating our Catholic youth. They are a blessing to the city of Toronto. They are pointing out to the youthful mind the way to virtue, religion, morality, and useful knowledge. (41)

Even if Catholics had not subtracted themselves from the free school equation, however, it is doubtful that the pattern of school attendance would have changed significantly in the 1850s. What schoolmen only partially understood—and what historians are now only rediscovering—was that their city was a vortex of movement. The residential mobility of the working classes, so essential to their survival, thoroughly undercut the purposes of a rigid, centralized school system.

Among the problems of school attendance under the free school system, and they were legion, irregularity of attendance and pupil transiency best illustrate the interdependence of movement among the school population and the working classes. (42) As early as 1851 the Board became alarmed by the large number of school transfers among pupils:

We have in our city, in round numbers, no less than six hundred pupils, who have been for the last year migrating from school to school, or attending just as it suited their convenience or caprice. These migratory habits on the part of the school-going population have been productive of serious disadvantages to the educational interests of the community, and of discouragement and annoyance to the teachers.

To correct these "evils," a new regulation was passed making

the written consent of the local directors of the ward, and the certificate of the teacher of that school which the pupil desires to leave . . . necessary for his transfer to another. This consent will of course never be withheld, *when the parent can assign any just or rational cause . . . for the transfer of his child;* but the very fact of such consent being necessary, will act as a salutary check upon that inordinate desire for change which has hitherto but too much characterized . . . parties most interested in the common school education of this city. (43)

The Board's response to pupil transfer presents in crystalline form several neglected currents of the free school movement. Schoolmen implicitly understood that the success of their program hinged on tying children to one school long enough to insure that the proper values were inculcated. Aware of the connexion between pupil and parent mobility, they sought to influence this larger pattern. When residential movements among the parents of schoolgoing children became predictable, orderly, and rational, assimilation could be assured.

This attempt of the Board to impose spatial as well as social control on the population constituted an overt threat to the very people it was trying to serve, and its charge of "capricious migration" conveniently overlooked the painful truth that the residential mobility of the working classes was not of their own making. As David Rubinstein has shown in his study of school attendance in nineteenth-century London, mobility among the poor was hardly voluntary. On the contrary, pressures caused by the economic failure of the family, the desire for anonymity, and the destruction of slum housing for CBD expansion kept the lower classes on the move at least until they could secure a toe-hold in the lower middle class. (44) As members of a casual labour force, however, the poor were forced by their occupational status to follow shifting work opportunities in a fairly defined arc corresponding to the cheapest available housing. (45) But high population turnover, as Peter Knights has shown, occurred throughout the social structure in urban areas. (46)

Data gathered by the board from school registers on pupil transfers during the 1860s (and probably applicable as well to the 1850s) illuminate the educational component of residential mobility (*see* Table 4). By 1858 the regulation covering transfers had been

TABLE 4

Rate of Pupil Transfer
for Six Toronto Common Schools
1863–1872

(Percent of Total Enrollment for Each School)

		George St. School	Park School	Victoria St. School	Louisa St. School	John St. School	Phoebe St. School	Total Transfers	As % of Total Enrolled	Number of Schools
1863	N	44	22	93	88	69	83	459	5,298	8
	%	6.4	4.1	10.4	7.4	12.1	10.5		8.7	
1864	N	24	56	60	59	35	51	362	5,550	9
	%	3.3	9.5	7.5	5.2	7.0	6.3		6.5	
1865	N	28	32	27	78	34	28	300	5,726	9
	%	3.6	5.3	3.5	7.0	6.1	3.6		5.2	
1866	N	45	30	57	90	56	50	362	5,488	9
	%	5.7	5.6	7.6	8.1	9.0	6.9		6.6	
1867	N	13	17	49	43	55	19	236	5,611	9
	%	1.5	3.1	6.2	4.1	7.9	2.4		4.2	
1868	N	41	23	60	59	66	41	371	6,108	9
	%	5.0	4.4	7.4	6.3	8.1	4.7		6.1	
1869	N	41	23	32	63	64	46	323	6,434	9
	%	5.0	4.0	3.7	6.7	7.5	4.6		5.0	
1870	N	46	14	55	42	62	50	395	7,098	9
	%	5.7	2.0	5.6	4.5	7.1	4.6		5.6	
1871	N	44	30	46	61	116	50	498	8,018	10
	%	4.4	4.0	4.1	6.6	12.7	3.9		6.2	
1872	N	44	29	26	46	126	36	1,638	9,639	13
	%	4.9	3.7	2.8	5.3	12.7	3.0		17.0	

Source: Annual Report of the Local Superintendent, 1863–1871; Annual Report of the Inspector, 1872.

refined so that now "no pupil shall be transfered from one school to another except on account of the change of residence of his or her parent or guardian. . . ." (47) Thus, the rate of transfer is roughly equivalent to the annual rate of residential mobility, with the notable exception that parental moves within a few blocks of the former residence (or even within the same ward) would probably not require children to change schools.

The relationship between workplace and residence for the lower classes is shown by comparing the school with the highest average rate of transfer (John Street) and that with the lowest (Park School). One would have expected a much higher rate at the Park School, given the rationale for its original placement which, as we have seen, stressed its proximity to a large working-class population. The reason for the low rate of transfer can be found in a statement made by the local superintendent in 1860, reporting

a diminuation of the number of residents in the section of the city in which the Park School is situated, as indicated by the reduced attendance . . . at that school; and . . . the increased attendance at the Junior Division of the John Street school may be, in part, accounted for by the fact that a large number of persons in the employment of the railway companies have taken up their residence in that particular neighborhood. (48)

The employment characteristics of its surroundings, then, gave the John Street school a consistently high rate of pupil transfer, paralleling the mobility endemic to railway labourers. At the same time it controlled the pattern of attendance in terms of regularity of attendance and average length of stay. The rate of transfer, although high in this case, was probably even higher than reported, since transfers were counted in terms of the listing of the same child in more than one school register, and those children who left school to reregister but never actually did would still be officially entered on the books. In an early twentieth-century study, for example, it was found that only about 70 percent of the children who left school with transfer permission ever reentered. (49) The high rate of transfer in 1872 (when three new schools were opened), which is only partially reflected in the six schools considered, indicates that many children had been attending schools inconvenient to their residence and had redistributed themselves to schools closer to home.

The most interesting pattern, though, is that between the schools. For any year, the interrelation of transfer rates among all six schools comprise a year-to-year measure of certain kinds of intra-urban, or circulatory, mobility. Although the absolute figures for school mobility seem small by comparison with those which must have prevailed in the city as a whole, they are significant when measured against the proportion of school-age youth the Board actually reached. The varieties of information about mobility that can be derived from school transfer rates and rates of attendance from a single school seem to parallel those for the population as a whole.

Controlling attendance through transfer rates, at least during the 1850s and 1860s, was beyond the Board. The working classes, caught in the vicissitudes of a floating labour market, could hardly assume stable residential patterns. Nor could the middle classes until public transportation became generally available. The upper classes, of course, had always had access to transportation, and their children attended private schools in the city. Yet, as late as 1875, the year attendance drastically improved, the inspector had by no means solved the problems of student transfers. (50)

IV

It is much easier to suggest why school attendance did not increase in the 1850s than why it did in the mid-1870s (*see* Table 5). Certainly, the traditional explanation leaves something to be desired. The Board's historian suggests that "the all-embracing reason . . . is found in the improved management of the schools under a progressive and energetic young inspector and a body of trained teachers." (51) Yet Inspector Hughes, hired in 1874, could only impose his draconian regimen on those children whose parents had already decided to send them to school, and to do so for longer periods of time. And although the pattern of attendance remained much the same in 1875 as it had been in 1858, the number of children entering the schools was increasing markedly. This increase in students, it might be argued, was only the result of compulsory education legislation passed in 1871. In that case one can only offer the observation that both the legislation and the truant officer hired to enforce it were quite limited in their powers. At any

TABLE 5

School Attendance in Toronto 1869–1878

Year		Number of Days Attended						Total Enrolled	Average Registered Attendance	Average Daily Attendance	Average School Days in Year	Number of Schools
		<20	20–50	50–100	100–150	150–200	200 >					
1869	N	785	1,051	1,549	1,146	1,255	648	6,434	3,907	3,132	214	9
	%	12.2	16.3	24.1	17.8	19.5	10.1		60.0	80.2		
1870	N	901	1,177	1,648	1,351	1,310	670	7,098	4,107	3,288	217	9
	%	12.7	16.6	23.2	19.0	18.5	9.4		57.9	80.1		
1871	N	1,006	1,457	2,023	1,481	1,478	573	8,018	4,616	3,646	212	10
	%	12.5	18.2	25.2	18.5	18.4	7.1		57.6	79.0		
1872	N	1,306	1,973	2,796	1,890	1,428	246	9,639	5,101	4,071	202	13
	%	13.5	20.5	29.0	19.6	14.8	2.6		52.9	78.7		
1873	N	1,018	1,706	2,430	1,751	1,922	646	9,473	6,040	4,453	210	13
	%	10.7	18.0	25.7	18.5	20.3	6.8		63.8	73.7		
1874	N	1,216	2,020	2,692	1,876	1,921	654	10,379	5,924*	4,791*	208	17
	%	11.7	19.5	25.9	18.1	18.5	6.3		57.1	80.9		
1875	N	794	1,328	2,313	1,800	2,543	889	9,667	6,477	5,397	208	18
	%	8.2	13.7	23.9	18.6	26.3	9.2		67.0	83.3		
1876	N	547	1,079	2,069	1,715	2,541	1,848	9,799	6,912	5,919	213	18
	%	5.6	11.0	21.1	17.5	25.9	18.9		70.5	85.6		
1877	N	596	1,171	2,487	1,979	3,787	990	11,010	7,606	6,822	203	23
	%	5.4	10.6	22.6	18.0	34.4	9.0		69.1	89.7		
1878	N	548	1,058	2,334	1,963	5,019	565	11,487	8,276	7,474	201	23
	%	4.8	9.2	20.3	17.1	43.7	4.9		72.0	90.3		

*Averages of the Average figures for each month are given for 1874–1879.
Source: *Annual Report of the Local Superintendent, 1869–1871; Annual Report of the Inspector, 1872–1878.*

rate, the Board of School Trustees, literally overwhelmed by the crush of pupils entering the schools they had so assiduously avoided in the past, encouraged Hughes to concentrate on those children willing to attend.

The increase in attendance could be seen simply as a response of the people to the increase in school accommodation. To be sure, throughout the 1860s hundreds of children were turned away for lack of space, and as a result the Board embarked on a vigorous building program in 1871. In his report for 1875 alone, Hughes reported the construction of two new schools, the doubling in size of two others, and the addition of nine rooms in eight other schools. He also planned the addition of thirty-six rooms in new and existing buildings for 1876. Great as this increase in school accommodations was, however, Hughes had to admit that "it has not kept pace with the increase in the average attendance." (52) Hughes, at least, was candid enough to admit that the cause of the increase in numbers of children preceded and was beyond him. Nor did he ever claim that the drastic improvement in length of schooling was entirely the result of his school reorganization. After 1874 the daily average attendance did increase, but only by about 10 percent. The percentage of children remaining in school for more than one hundred days, however, rose dramatically: from 32.9 percent to 65.7 percent between 1874 and 1878. To some extent these two improvements can be ascribed to Hughes, but again it must be emphasized that he was only exploiting a phenomenon that rested on some prior decision by parents. Finally, I think we must reject any explanation supported solely by evidence of population mobility, because that is roughly equivalent to accepting a description of an event as its explanation.

Why were more people suddenly willing to send their children to school, and for significantly longer periods of time? Could there have been some rapid change in parents' perception of the school either as a socializing agent or avenue of social mobility? If so, how can we explain a finding of an 1863 school census that 82.8 percent of the city's school-age population had attended some school during the first six months of that year? The next such census, taken in 1875, showed that 94.8 percent of all school-age children had attended some school during the course of the year, but much of the increase was due to a higher enrollment in private schools. (53) Apparently, long before compulsory education the majority of people had accepted schooling.

In point of fact, all of the above undoubtedly contribute to the explanation of changes in patterns of school attendance. Yet, unless we enter into a different sort of analysis we are only left with recondite speculation. What is needed at this point is a thorough-going analysis of many kinds of school populations, in isolation and in relation to their family characteristics. The context of such an analysis must be the social and spatial interstices of the home-school-work matrix throughout the industrialization process. Then we can begin to understand the success of common schooling in the nineteenth century. Some ways in which this research can be carried out are suggested in the essay by Michael Katz which follows.

In the absence of precise data about these interrelationships between family, work, and school, we may now offer the following speculations of the increase in school attendance in Toronto in the 1870s. As we have seen, the working classes, especially the Irish Catholics, wanted education for their children in the 1850s, but the exigencies of urban life prevented the formation of regular patterns of attendance. Casual labour conditions entailed frequent change of residence and workplace, causing children to either remain in school for only short periods of time or move from school to school. The lack of school facilities altogether in the northern and western portions of the city exacerbated this situation in the 1860s, and as these areas were developed physically, large numbers of children were in effect being discriminated against educationally. Existing transportation lines, even when taking into consideration the nickel fare, were out of the question for the working classes.

These disutilities of urban life had been largely removed by the 1870s, when school attendance increased so drastically. In fact, as Peter Goheen has argued, Toronto assumed the social landscape of the "modern" city in the decade from 1870 to 1880. The components of this modernity include a real segregation by class, increased transportation facilities, and the separation of residence from work-place. The latter, especially, would seem to enhance the possibility of long-term school attendance. (54) When the school plant began to expand in the 1870s, many working-class children undoubtedly attended school for the first time, especially in the extremities of the city. This more stable urban environment coincided with the ever-present promise of social mobility through educational persistence, then, to produce lengthened school attendance.

Of course, class played an important part in determining who could participate in this newly rationalized city life. The poor, residing in marginal housing along the waterfront and in a few densely populated slum areas, were still disfranchised educationally, for school regulations did not permit the attendance of children who were not properly dressed or did not possess the correct textbooks. On the other hand, the creation of centralized common schools for the age group 12–16 ideally suited the educational needs of the middle classes. In fact preliminary analysis of city school registers from 1877 shows that these upper common school classes were almost devoid of the children of labourers. Thus, the working classes filled the lower divisions of certain schools while the middle and upper classes patronized educational facilities leading eventually to business and professional positions. Inspector Hughes's reorganization of the schools and curriculum in 1875 along more "progressive" lines theoretically served all the people of Toronto, but it seems to have served some better than others.

The study of the spatial patterns of school attendance serves to emphasize the interdependence between decisions made by Canadian educators and their physical consequences. The values of the free school movement were not peripheral to the development of the school system, but in many respects guided its growth. Ideology became embedded in the landscape in the form of an educational bureaucracy geared to efficient organization and the handling of large numbers of school children. The labouring classes could, on occasion, successfully counter the schoolmen, but as a whole their lives were too splintered by work and residential mobility to mount an effective alternative to the centralized free school system. Largely unchecked in its development, the educational bureaucracy in Toronto came to fruition at a time when the labouring classes were finally able to afford, in every sense of that term, to send their children to school. The people had no choice but to accept an educational environment that they had not created and over which they exerted little, if any, control.

NOTES

1. See, for example, Chief Superintendent Ryerson, *Annual Report of Normal, Model, and Common Schools in Upper Canada, for the year 1847* (Montreal, 1849), p. 10, as well as his *Journal of Education for Upper-Canada* 1, no. 10 (October 1848): 300.

2. John A. Jackle, "Time, Space and the Geographic Past: A Prospectus for Historical Geography," *American Historical Review* 76, no. 4 (October 1971): 1087; see also Cole Harris, "Theory and Synthesis in Historical Geography," *Canadian Geographer* 15, no. 3 (Fall 1971): 157–72.

3. James W. Simmons and Victor H. Huebert, "The Location of Land for Public Use in Urban Areas," *Canadian Geographer* 14, no. 1 (Spring 1970): 45–56. See also Michael B. Teitz, "Toward a Theory of Urban Public Facility Location," in *Internal Structure of the City: Readings on Space and Environment,* ed. Larry S. Bourne (New York, 1971), pp. 411–20.

4. J. Donald Wilson also comes to this conclusion in "The Ryerson Years in Canada West," in *Canadian Education: A History,* ed. J. Donald Wilson, Robert M. Stamp, and Louis-Philippe Audet (Scarborough, Ont., 1970), p. 216.

5. The local superintendent advocated abolishing free schools and returning to the rate-paying system when it became clear that free schools had failed. The Board of School Trustees voted 8-3 against such an abolition, and the superintendent resigned (Toronto Board of Education Historical Collection [hereafter cited as TBEHC], *Minutes of Board of School Trustees,* vol. 2, May 12, 1858.

6. My model of bureaucracy owes much to David Tyack, "Bureaucracy and the Common School: The Example of Portland Oregon, 1851–1913," *American Quarterly* 19, no. 3 (Fall 1967): 475–98, and Michael B. Katz, "From Voluntarism to Bureaucracy in American Education," *Sociology of Education* 44 (Summer 1971): 297–332.

7. TBEHC, *Minutes of Board of School Trustees,* vol. 1, November 1847–January 1851, passim.

8. Board of School Trustees, *Report of the Past History, and Present Condition, of the Common or Public Schools of the City of Toronto* (Toronto, 1859), p. 73.

9. Cf. Joseph F. Kett, "Growing up in Rural New England, 1800–1840," in *Anonymous Americans: Explorations in Nineteenth-Century Social History,* ed. Tamara K. Hareven (Englewood Cliffs, N.J., 1971), pp. 3–4, 7–9, where an essentially similar pattern of home-school relationships is discussed.

10. The city's school-age population (5–16 years) from 1845 to 1850 was

reported in the Annual Report of the Chief Superintendent of Schools. It ranged in these years from 2,033 to 6,149. That given for 1846—4,450—seems accurate enough, as it differs only slightly from that found in *Brown's Toronto City and Home District Directory, 1846-7* (Toronto, 1846), p. 22, which reports the 1846 census figure for children ages 5–16 as 4,626. The total enrollment for 1846 was estimated to be 1,600, which is 34.5 percent of the age group 5–16. The average daily attendance was 75.8 percent of the total number registered.

11. Peter N. Ross, "The Free School Controversy in Toronto, 1848-1852," (research paper, Ontario Institute for Studies in Education, Spring 1971), pp. 1–2.

12. TBEHC, *Minutes of Board of School Trustees,* vol. 1, December 6, 1847.

13. *Annual Report of the Normal, Model, and Common Schools in Upper Canada, for the Year 1848* (Montreal, 1849), p. 35.

14. TBEHC, *Minutes of Board of School Trustees,* vol. 1, November 23, 1847.

15. The Act of 1847, 10th & 11th Vic., Cap. 19, was the topic of a circular sent by Ryerson to the heads of city and town corporations, *Journal of Education for Upper Canada* 1, no. 1 (January 1848): 16–17.

16. *Annual Report of the Normal, Model, and Common Schools in Upper Canada, for the Year 1848,* p. 36.

17. The impact of urban population growth on educational change was early appreciated by Ellwood P. Cubberley in his *Public Education of the United States* (Boston, 1919), chap. 4.

18. Kenneth Duncan, "Irish Famine Immigration and Social Structure in Canada West," in *Canada: A Sociological Profile,* ed. W. E. Mann (Toronto, 1968), "Population and Immigration," p. 5.

19. Lynn H. Lees, "Patterns of Lower-Class Life: Irish Slum Communities in Nineteenth-Century London," in *Nineteenth-Century Cities,* ed. Stephan Thernstrom and Richard Sennett (New Haven, 1969), p. 383. This is also the conclusion of David Ward, *Cities and Immigrants: A Geography of Change in Nineteenth-Century America* (New York, 1971), p. 117. For the older view see Barbara Miller Solomon, *Ancestors and Immigrants: A Changing New England Tradition* (New York, 1956), p. 152, where she states that "these ethnic stereotypes often derived from literary associations of the past, were comic in tone; even when related to real life, they lacked ulterior purpose of malice or insult."

20. Ward, *Cities and Immigrants,* p. 106; see also his article, "The Internal Spatial Structure of Immigrant Residential Districts in the Late Nineteenth Century," *Geographical Analysis* 1, no. 3 (October 1969): 337–53.

21. The conclusions of the Canadian Social History Project's study of nineteenth-century Hamilton, Ontario, powerfully reinforce this line of reasoning, and largely agree with those in Stephan Thernstrom,

Poverty and Progress: Social Mobility in a Nineteenth-Century City (New York, 1970).

22. Canada, Board of Registration and Statistics, *Census of the Canadas, 1851–52* (Quebec, 1853), 1: 30–31, 66–67; Ward, *Cities and Immigrants,* pp. 107–9; Derwyn S. Shea, "The Irish Immigrants' Adjustment in Urban North America," (B.A. honours essay, Laurentian University, 1970), pp. 42–43, 45; and Peter G. Goheen, *Victorian Toronto, 1850– 1890: Pattern and Process of Growth,* University of Chicago, Department of Geography, Research Paper No. 127 (Chicago, 1970), p. 75.

23. Ross, "The Free School Controversy in Toronto, 1848–1852," pp. 27– 35; it should be noted that both the educational reformers and their opponents on the free-school issue held anti-Irish views.

24. *Report of the Past History . . . ,* p. 56.

25. Ibid., p. 58.

26. Sam Bass Warner, Jr., *The Private City: Philadelphia in Three Periods of Growth* (Philadelphia, 1968), p. 54.

27. *Report of the Past History . . . ,* p. 58; cf. Gillian Sutherland, *Elementary Education in the Nineteenth Century* (London, 1971), p. 3, where he notes that the inspector of schools in Great Britain accused educators in 1846 of breaking off "a fragment from the education we suppose necessary for our own children—its mechanical and technical part—and give it to the poor man's child. . . ." Joseph Kay, an English educational reformer whom Ryerson greatly admired, made the function of this utilitarian education perfectly clear when he wrote that the purpose of educating the lower orders was "to diminish our number of criminals, to lessen the dangers of social convulsions, and to unite the different classes of society by bounds of common interests, mutual confidence and satisfaction," in *The Education of the Poor in England and Europe* (London, 1846), p. xix.

28. TBEHC, *Minutes of Board of School Trustees,* vol. 1, November 5, 1851.

29. Ibid., March 23 and May 25, 1853.

30. *Report of the Past History . . . ,* p. 48.

31. Michael B. Katz, "Education and Social Development in the Nineteenth Century," in *History and Education: The Educational Uses of the Past,* ed. Paul Nash (New York, 1970), pp. 103–4.

32. *Report of the Past History . . . ,* p. 67.

33. Thernstrom, *Poverty and Progress,* p. 51, sees popular education in mid-nineteenth-century Newburyport as "not popular enough . . . to be a powerful instrument of social control," in part because of "the compelling economic considerations which kept the sons and daughters of laborers out of school."

34. D. C. Masters, *The Rise of Toronto, 1850–1890* (Toronto, 1947), pp. 33–38, 79–83; cf. Goheen, *Victorian Toronto, 1850–1890,* p. 75, who simply counts the Irish population as being "English." By 1861 the Irish were the second largest ethnic group in the city, following only

those born in Canada (which must have included large numbers of children of Irish parentage). The residential and religious mixes were roughly similar to those of 1851. Canada, Board of Registration and Statistics, *Census of the Canadas, 1860–61* (Quebec, 1865), 1:48–49, 128–29.

35. TBEHC, *Minutes of Board of School Trustees,* vol. 1, January 3, 1851.
36. Ross, "The Free School Controversy in Toronto, 1848–1852," pp. 27–28.
37. TBEHC, *Minutes of Board of School Trustees,* vol. 1, July 7, 1852.
38. 16th Vic., Cap. 186, Sec. 4 (1853), and 18th Vic., Cap. 131 (May 1855); for a discussion of this and other separate school legislation, see C. B. Sissons, *Church and State in Canadian Education* (Toronto, 1959), pp. 25–41.
39. TBEHC, *Minutes of Board of School Trustees,* vol. 2, June 2, 1858.
40. Ontario Provincial Archives (POA), Education Department Records, RG 2, F-3-F, Box 1, "Half-Yearly Return of the Roman Catholic Separate Schools in Toronto, from the 1st January to the 30th June, 1855."
41. *Journal of Education for Upper Canada* 14, no. 9 (September 1861): 144. That anti-Irish opinion had hardly vanished is shown by the comment of one of the Board of School Trustees at the annual convocation for school awards in 1865. In introducing an English commissioner of education to the audience, the trustee related how "the other day the Bishop of Chicago . . . told him [the commissioner] that one priest was as good as a hundred policemen in keeping in order the Germans and turbulent Irishmen in that city. (Applause)" (ibid., 18, no. 9 [September 1865]).
42. David Rubenstein's excellent monograph, *School Attendance in London, 1870–1904: A Social History,* Occasional Papers in Economic and Social History, no. 1 (Hull, England, 1969), and the early but still very valuable study by Edith Abbott and Sophonisba P. Breckenridge, *Truancy and Non-Attendance in the Chicago Schools* (Chicago, 1917), constitute virtually the entire literature on the topic.
43. *Annual Report of the Normal, Model, and Common Schools in Upper Canada, for the Year 1852* (Quebec, 1853), p. 123 (italics added).
44. Rubinstein, *School Attendance in London, 1870–1904,* pp. 64–68; David Ward, "The Emergence of Central Immigrant Ghettoes in American Cities, 1840–1920," *Annals of the Association of American Geographers* 58, no. 2 (June 1968), pp. 343–59, examines the effect of the expanding CBD on immigrant housing opportunities.
45. Ward, *Cities and Immigrants,* p. 119; Thernstrom, *Poverty and Progress,* p. 134. For an excellent analysis of the casual labour market see Gareth Stedman Jones, *Outcast London* (Oxford, 1971).
46. Peter R. Knights, *The Plain People of Boston, 1830–1860: A Study in City Growth* (New York, 1971), pp. 65–66, and with Stephan Thernstrom "Men in Motion: Some Data and Speculations About Urban Population Mobility in Nineteenth-Century America," *Journal of In-*

terdisciplinary History 1, no. 1 (Autumn 1970): 7–35. Work in progress on aged female welfare recipients in mid-nineteenth-century Hamilton, Ontario, indicates that even this unlikely group changed residence on the average of once a year. A recent discussion of residential mobility in nineteenth-century Toronto can be found in Michael J. Doucet, "Sherbourne Street, 1875–1888; A Study in Urban Residential Mobility," (geographical research paper, York University, 1971).

47. *Report of the Past History* . . . , p. 68.

48. *Second Annual Report of the Local Superintendent of the Public Schools of the City of Toronto, for the year ending December 31st, 1860* (Toronto, 1861), p. 5.

49. Abbott and Breckenridge, *Truancy and Non-Attendance in the Chicago Schools,* p. 101; disturbed by the mobility of students, these progressive social workers reported that "especially difficult are the cases of immigrant children who drift in from other cities and many who have lived in several towns without attending school in any one of them. Unless some system of transfers between cities can be worked out, there is not much hope of catching these more migratory families" (p. 278).

50. *Annual Report of the Inspector of the Public Schools of the City of Toronto, for the year ending December 31, 1875* (Toronto, 1875), p. 14.

51. Honora M. Cochrane, ed., *Centennial Story: The Board of Education for the City of Toronto, 1850–1950* (Toronto, 1950), p. 71.

52. *Annual Report of the Inspector of the Public Schools for the City of Toronto, for the year ending December 31, 1875,* p. 16.

53. *Fifth Annual Report of the Local Superintendent of the Public Schools of the City of Toronto, for the year ending December 31st, 1863* (Toronto, 1864), pp. 6–8, 46–47; *Annual Report of the Inspector of the Public Schools for the City of Toronto, for the year ending December 31, 1875,* pp. 12, 63–64.

54. Goheen, *Victorian Toronto, 1850–1890,* pp. 1–2, 219–21.

10. TOWARDS A MEANING OF LITERACY: LITERACY AND SOCIAL STRUCTURE IN HAMILTON, ONTARIO, 1861

In this social structural analysis of literacy in a nineteenth-century city methodological considerations are stressed, particularly the utility and use of the 1861 urban manuscript census. The essay discusses the relationship of this approach to other methods of studying literacy historically. Substantively, the essay establishes rates of adult literacy and, more importantly, discusses the characteristics of illiterates. The discussion places literacy in a comparative context and shows its intimate relations to the social structure of a nineteenth-century city.

Despite its relevance to many kinds of historical study, literacy does not feature very often in historical discussion, and when it does appear a certain vagueness surrounds its meaning. (1)

APPROACHES TO THE PROBLEM

THESE PEOPLE resided in Hamilton, Ontario, in the year 1861, and were duly recorded in the census:

Richard Sorrick, third ward, Emerald Street, age 45, sex—male, born in the United States, religion—Episcopal Methodist, married, no children, occupation—minister, "colored."

B. E. Charlton, third ward, Rebecca Street, age 26, sex—male, born in Canada, religion—Presbyterian, married, no children, owned a carriage for

---

H. J. Graff is currently a faculty member of the University of Texas, Dallas.

pleasure and a horse, occupation—manufacturer (vinegarmaker) with $5,000 invested in the business and an annual product valued at no less than $10,000.

James Morgan, fifth ward, age 40, sex—male, born in Ireland, religion— Roman Catholic, married, four sons and two daughters, occupation— laborer.

Francis Lane, fifth ward, age 29, sex—male, born in the United States, religion—Anglican, married, no children, occupation—laborer, "colored."

Mary Walsh, first ward, age 51, sex—female, born in Ireland, religion— Roman Catholic, widowed, one son, occupation—dairy maid.

These five citizens, diverse as they may seem, had one characteristic in common. They were all illiterate. They were members of a core of 895 adults who had recorded on their census form an inability to read or write. The appearance of such a group in a commercial city of 19,000 points to a very important yet frequently overlooked historical problem—that of literacy.

Little is known about the quantitative dimensions of literacy in either the preindustrial era or the Age of Industrialization, and, in fact, even less is known about what it meant to be literate or illiterate. Recently, a new interest has been shown in the problem, through the works of Lawrence Stone, Carlo Cipolla, and Roger Schofield, (2) and the ongoing studies of Kenneth Lockridge, Egil Johansson, and Sune Ackerman, while critical questions are being asked by others. Gillian Sutherland, discussing Schofield's work with the Cambridge Group for the History of Population and Social Structure, asks,

Apart from the immediate and enormous question why, there is also the question, crudely, so what? Does this mean they behaved differently? If so, how? . . . In general, how much does it matter that some people, more people, can read, go to school, go to university? . . . These may sound banal and familiar questions, but for most societies at most periods they have yet to be adequately answered. . . . Just because the relationship between education and social structure "are various, involve structural discontinuities and are singularly lacking in symmetry," there is a whole new important field for exploration in the history of education. (3)

Literacy is one such important field for exploration in the history of education, and central research in this area must revolve around the question of how much it mattered that some people could read or go to school. Literacy may not have held all the advantages that one might have assumed, and life for an illiterate may not have been as poor and simple as previous literature has portrayed.

The study of literacy can become a first step for the historian of education in transcending statements that maintain that the relationships between education and social structure are "various, involve structural discontinuities. . . ." He can clarify these relationships, illuminating such problems as the ways in which educational systems functionally discriminate against individuals and groups along lines of nationality, class, religion, and race. In this way literacy's sociological relations may be discovered and understood by isolating those who were illiterate, discerning their place in the social order, and assessing the effects of illiteracy on their behavior as it contrasted with those who were literate.

It is apparent that past means of investigating literacy offer little to such a pursuit. Literary sources at best reveal little more than how literate or illiterate those on the upper rungs of society were, and perhaps what was available for them to read. Traditional histories of education largely ignore the problem of literacy. However, quantitative methods can be utilized to advantage in studying literacy, using such sources as census manuscripts, assessment rolls, and city directories. Qualitative sources, particularly the contemporary writings on education, are also valuable in giving a fuller picture. (4)

There is an important body of literature on literacy that may be divided into three principal areas: the measurement of literacy, (5) its relationship with the social structure, (6) and its social-psychological meaning. (7) In this essay we are primarily interested in two aspects of this writing, the methodological points that it raises and interpretative insights that it suggests.

Robert K. Webb, in two articles devoted to the study of literacy and the working classes in nineteenth-century England and Scotland, provides several methodological suggestions. He introduces the concept of differential rates among various occupational groups, a notion fruitfully utilized by E. J. Hobsbawm in his work on the "labor aristocracy." Webb states that this situation "must mean as well that the illiterate groups were those most affected by immigration and by the depression of the lower levels of the working classes." (8) Webb indicates the importance of regional variations as another consideration. Additionally, he points to the gap between male and female literacy, finding males slightly more literate.

Finally, in an important caveat, Webb reminds us that reading could be learned in many situations, removing the discussion from solely a concern with formal educational institutions, a point well developed by Edward Thompson in *The Making of the English Working Class.* Thompson adds that the ability to read is only the elementary technique; the ability to handle abstract and consecutive argument is by no means inborn. (9)

Lawrence Stone has offered a framework for interpreting relationships between literacy and elementary education and society. (10) These factors, social stratification, employment opportunities, religion, theories of social control, demographic and family patterns, economic organization and resources, and political theory and institutions serve well as a checklist for approaching the question on a local scale and as a history of the growth of literacy.

It is helpful to briefly examine these factors. Social stratification, Stone finds, determines the general framework for the growth of elementary education; each of the educational levels is normally designed to meet the need of a different social grouping, serving to reinforce class distinctions and to reduce social mobility. This of course, is a reciprocal process. As well, economic laws of supply and demand of job opportunities dictate levels of literacy and secondary education. Thirdly, religion was a critical element in the rise of literacy, through Protestantism's demands for a Bible-reading public and post-Reformation religious pluralism. Religion functions in various, complex ways to spread or inhibit the growth of literacy. The key is to seek out the differential literacy rates and economic ranking among various sects.

The fourth factor to consider is social control, the effects on education of ideas held by those who possess wealth and political power. Stone suggests that the struggle against illiteracy has been indistinguishable at times from the increased power exerted over the individual by the central authorities. Obviously, the relationship between literacy training and social control is complex; it has been perceived, and indeed has operated, as both a positive and a negative factor towards the spread of education. The role of social control is closely tied to the factors of social stratification and religion; this situation has often led to confusion regarding its contribution to the development of elementary education.

The effects of demographic patterns must not be ignored. Stone maintains that until the end of the eighteenth century, high rates of childhood mortality militated against investment in education; modern demographic conditions were needed for the rise of mass education. The emergence of primary education as a large-scale activity is often associated with a surplus of women in the population. As well, a rapid rise in population and urbanization puts heavy strains on existing educational facilities. Too, the family structure plays an important, if not completely understood, role in determining the character of education. Clearly, it provides early instruction in values and skills as in the introduction of the child into society, as well as determining the mode of formal or informal education.

Another factor Stone includes is the role of purely economic relationships. These, of course, are inseparable from most of the other factors, and are often determined by human will rather than by blind economic forces (i.e., decisions of investment in education, war, or conspicuous consumption). However, the often supposed link between literacy and economic development must be questioned, both historically and contemporarily. For as John Talbott suggests, "in the first decades of industrialization, the factory system put no premium on even low-level intellectual skills. Whatever relationships existed between widespread literacy and early industrial development must have been quite roundabout." (11) There is now some evidence that mobility as well as literacy initially declined with the onset of large-scale industrialization in England. (12) R. P. Dore has gone further in suggesting that "at the very best literacy constitutes a training in being trained." (13)

The seventh factor is the result of political considerations, such as the support given by the state to the development of the schools. These factors are very general, but they easily may serve as a springboard to detailed study of the problem on the local level.

There is, finally, the question of the meaning of literacy. This must be considered in larger, more abstract socio-psychological terms, and this area is perhaps more barren than the others surveyed. However, Jack Goody, Ian Watt, and G. H. Bantock have made significant suggestions that are as thought-provoking as they are frightening. They have pointed to the great changes wrought by the rise of literate society, with its creation of a new means of communication between men. The range of human intercourse has been greatly extended over time and space, and the potentialities for this affect the entire spectrum of human activity: political, economic, and religious.

The effects of the rise of literacy on man have been profound. Goody and Watt suggest that writing provides an alternative source for cultural transmission that favors an awareness of inconsistencies. This has brought a sense of change and of cultural lag and a split between fact and fiction, for the activity of writing and reading is infinitely more abstract than that of speaking and hearing. The wide use of printed material has fostered a new reliance on sight and an increasing dependence on visualization creating greater social distances between individuals. This has resulted in a narrowing of experience, as the individual has little chance of participating in the cultural traditions in any kind of patterned whole. Thus literate societies are characterized by a high level of cultural conflict, which may produce anomie. As well, Bantock maintains that high levels of literacy contribute to states of psychic rootlessness.

Jack Goody, an anthropologist, suggests that one way of exploring the problem is to research the ethnography of literacy in traditional or preindustrial societies by analyzing in detail the uses made of reading and writing in a particular social setting. This is a far simpler matter for the anthropologist than the historian. Indeed, anthropology in recent years has made significant progress in this area, while history shows scant awareness of the problem. (14) Nevertheless, perhaps quantitative research into the social structure may provide historians with a methodology from which to write their own ethnographies, entailing a cultural approach to history. Perhaps we may then understand how literacy or illiteracy affected the behavior of those in the past, and discover how the possible psychic results of illiteracy related to poverty, immigration, and urbanization in the nineteenth century.

THE CASE OF HAMILTON

METHODOLOGY

In light of both past and present attempts to study literacy, it is essential to understand the utility of the data employed in any such research. As indicated above, this work is based on the evidence from a Canadian city that underwent rapid industrialization in the late nineteenth century. We are presently considering the city in one year, 1861, when it remained a commercial but rapidly growing area of 19,000 people. This study rests on an empirical basis, principally the census of 1861, which has been coded and key punched in its entirety with no sampling or editing of the available information. (15)

By the 16th Section, 3d and 4th subsections of the Act 22, Victoria Cap. 33. Consd. Stats., it was enacted that "every occupant of any House, or of any distinct story, apartment, or portion thereof, with or for whom, any such schedule is left as aforesaid, shall fill up the same to the best of his or her knowledge or belief and sign the same. . . ." On each form, question 25-M and 26-F directed the head of household to indicate, "persons over 20 who cannot read or write." This information forms the basis for this essay and the wording of the question acts as a definition of literacy. The standardized format provides us with a firm basis for comparative study, directly with any city in Canada or the United States.

Let us consider this definition of literacy. First, it helpfully limits us to a study of adult literacy by virtue of the cut-off point at twenty years of age. Second, we are operating within the framework of those "who cannot read or write." Stone, Webb, and Schofield, among others, have put well the case that one would, throughout English history, learn to read before learning to write. They have argued soundly that by counting signatures one may obtain a measure of a minimum level of literacy. This fact will not be argued here, for there seems to be no contradictory evidence, and present-day education certainly seems to function in a like manner.

There is a certain ambiguity in the phrase "cannot read or write," as to whether it defines an either/or situation or would include an inability to carry out both operations. But in any case, it does serve to give a measure of a minimum standard of literacy, certainly a safe method of quantitative historical procedure.

We must now confront the questions of the utility and accuracy of the data. It does meet Roger Schofield's two conditions for literacy research. It is "applicable throughout the country to people of a wide range of ages and economic and social conditions and

over a long period of time." It is also "a standard as a measure
from one person to the next, from one group to the next, and from
one historical period to the next." Although Schofield does not
define the phrase "historical period," he does state that the English
marriage registers utilized for literacy studies are available for about
85 years. Schofield finds these requirements to be stringent and we
are pleased to accept them.

He also maintains that a measure of literacy should "therefore
not only be universal and standard, it should also be direct," that
is, by signature. It might be contended that measuring literacy
from census manuscripts does not meet this stricture. But, random
sampling indicated that a direct test could successfully be applied
to census material. The status of fifty illiterates, chosen at random
roughly in proportion to the number of illiterates residing in each
ward, was checked with their original manuscript. Of this group,
48 had had their forms signed by another individual, presumably
he who had completed the schedule, and the illiterate had countered with his mark. The manuscripts of the remaining two were
unsigned. Literacy levels could thus be derived from the census
by counting marks, but this gives us no check on other members
of the household scored as illiterate. However, there is little reason
to doubt the accuracy of the data, as will be shown.

It is important to note the advantages of the manuscript census
for literacy studies. Previously historians have approached the problem through lists of publications and size/number of printings of
published materials, criminal records, reports of statistical societies,
petitions, wills, allegations, bonds for marriage licenses, depositions
of witnesses in ecclesiastical courts, and, most importantly, parish
marriage records. The census is only one of several sources from
which researchers are currently studying literacy and its correlates.
Schofield is engaged in the analysis of a national-sample of marriage
registers for the eighteenth and nineteenth centuries in Great
Britain. Swedish scholars are in the process of preparing a study
of literacy in the nineteenth century based on the extraordinarily
rich and detailed parish catechetical examination registers, which
exist for the whole of the country from the seventeenth-century to
the end of the nineteenth. Egil Johansson and Sune Ackerman will
soon be able to establish the determinates of various levels of reading comprehension as well as to relate the levels of achievement to

the ability to sign one's name, providing guidelines for other students of literacy. Finally, Kenneth Lockridge is utilizing wills from the colonial period in United States history to analyze the attitudes and attitudinal changes of literates and illiterates, isolating types of bequests as charitable behavior and the recipients as a key problem. Wills, when they remain in sufficient numbers, may be used as a supplement to census or other indicators of literacy serving as a signatory check on the documents' accuracy.

However, information from the Canadian urban Census of 1861 possesses certain virtues which marriage registers and wills do not. One is dealing with a total population, rather than a sampling, and also, one may choose his locale and period to be studied, not being dependent on what records survive. (16) The researcher does not have to extrapolate from a sample population, for example, those who married or those who left wills, to the rest of the population within a certain age, occupational, or ethnic grouping—although such problems are surmountable. For studying literacy from such a census, one collected by distribution of individual schedules to each household rather than by enumeration, is an easier yet potentially more accurate method. One is dealing with the entire adult population of an area, not with varied samples. The census enables the researcher to conduct his study of selected groups, ethnic, religious, and occupational, with a control body of the rest of the group and population. This is a simpler matter than constructing the controlling parameters for the study of parish material. The census, though, has the limitation of one geographical place. However, enumerative censuses exist for much of North America, which once joined with other types of records such as wills, depositions, etc., make their use possible. Finally, the census gives a far greater amount of direct information on such variables as occupation, sex, age, marital status, religion, place of birth, family size and school attendance, type of dwelling, amounts of property owned than do other records, thus eliminating some of the difficulties of nominal record-linkage. However, it is indeed essential to link census-type records to such sources as assessment rolls to give a more complete and accurate picture of literacy.

The Canadian urban census exists in this form only for 1861, while that of 1851 and those of the United States (from 1841) must be used with caution and checked with wills. Parish registers and wills allow research for the seventeenth and eighteenth centuries as well. The English marriage registers, the basis for systematic study in that country, are available on a national basis from 1754, while the Swedish registers go back to the seventeenth century. Studies from all these sources must, and will, be combined to give a full understanding of the meaning of literacy in the past.

A final question remains, that of the accuracy of census data. Two objections may be raised to it; one may generally question its reliability and one may contend that the role of social stigma would act as a counteracting force to the accuracy of census reports. Several points must be made in regard to these objections. First, there is the factor of legal sanctions against giving false information. The directions on each form declared that: "any false return of all or any matters specified in any such schedule shall hereby incur a penalty of not less than EIGHT, nor more than TWENTY DOLLARS. The several Enumerators have express orders to rigidly enforce the observance of the foregoing clauses." Little research has been carried out on attitudes to legal strictures and none on nineteenth-century Canada, so this is an uncertain factor. But, it is not valid to argue from present-day norms that such sanctions would carry no force.

The Hamilton *Spectator* in January 1861 provides additional support. In the issue of January 5, the newspaper called for accuracy and general compliance in completing the census schedule. On January 6, it called for attention to the instructions included with the forms and provided detailed explanations. On January 10, the *Spectator* announced that the Catholic Bishop urged his parishioners to comply and on the 15th it was reported that the Anglican Bishop followed suit.

Secondly, the fact that an illiterate head of household would be unable to fill out his own form adds another dimension. The question becomes, would another party, a relative, boarder, neighbor, or census enumerator, perjure himself for the benefit of an illiterate, especially in light of the fact that he would usually affix his own signature to the form?

Thirdly, the role of social stigma is countered by two arguments. R. K. Webb found that "a good many people would admit to illiteracy." In addition, there were well-to-do and, indeed, rich Hamiltonians who would admit to illiteracy, perhaps exhibiting a pride in their accomplishments. This brings the role of social stigma into question.

As a final check, the literacy rates derived for Hamilton in 1861 were compared with figures from the aggregate census for Hamilton, Kingston, London, and Toronto for the same year. In the case of Hamilton, the register-general reported that there were 871 illiterate men and women who were over the age of 20. Figures on population by age showed a cohort of 9,338 over 20, giving a literacy rate of 90.7 percent. My figures, however, indicate 895 illiterates producing a rate of 90.4 percent. Comparatively, the rates are:

Hamilton (my figures)	Hamilton	Kingston London (census figures)		Toronto
90.4%	90.7%	92.2%	92.2%	91.3%

The close agreement among these four cities serves as a final and conclusive argument for the accuracy of the data, for these cities were in a similar state of development as shown by research for the Canadian Social History Project. It is probable that illiteracy was underestimated in the aggregated statistics for the other cities as it was for Hamilton; in that case the rates would correspond more closely.

Let us now turn to the results of research into literacy in Hamilton. The most important question is, who were the illiterates? Table 1 shows a preponderance of Irish illiterates, over two-thirds of the total with immigrants from the United States and from England and Wales far behind. This is instructive of the immigration patterns of the 1840s and 1850s, of course, and the high percentage of Irish illiterates is hardly surprising. Certainly, the 1848 potato famine was an impetus to a massive Irish immigration to Canada. Unfortunately, the literature on immigration in this period is meager; indeed, it tells us little more than that many Irish immigrated and that their passage was made in conditions of squalor.

Of 4,148 Irish in Hamilton in the year 1861, 3,092 were twenty years old or more, and 20.4 percent of these adults were illiterate.

Comparatively, this is a low figure, for Webb reported that of the Irish in one London area, 55 percent of parents could neither read nor write. (17) This sheds some light on who would emigrate across the Atlantic. Carlo Cipolla reported that in 1871, 60 percent of Ireland's Catholics were illiterate and that in 1880, 69 percent of

TABLE 1

Place of Birth of Illiterates

Place	No. of Illiterates (n = 895)	Per- centage	No. of Adults in Population (n = 9338)	Per- centage
England and Wales	66	7.4	2125	22.8
Scotland	32	3.6	1699	18.2
Ireland	630	70.4	3092	33.1
Canada (French)	1	—	—	—
Canada	45	5.3	1268	13.6
United States	101	11.2	601	6.4
Nova Scotia and Prince Edward Is.	2	—	—	—
New Brunswick	1	—	—	—
West Indies	3	—	—	—
Germany and Holland	10	—	—	—
Italy and Greece	1	—	—	—
Sweden and Norway	1	—	—	—
Russia, Poland, Prussia	2	—	—	—

brides and 74 percent of grooms were illiterate—rates higher than those found among Hamilton's Irish Catholics. Literacy, with the somewhat greater opportunities for wealth and mobility it may have provided, may well have acted as a spur to some. If Webb's figures may be trusted, literacy may well relate to the length of voyage, as those who crossed the ocean were proportionally far more literate. However, a large number of illiterate immigrants made the voyage —perhaps they had little to risk in such a venture.

Mention must be made, too, of the over-representation of those born in the United States. Significantly, sixty-seven percent of the 101 were blacks, presumably freedmen or escaped slaves who had emigrated to Canada via the Underground Railroad. (18)

The religious breakdown of illiterates is shown in Table 2.

Again, there are few surprises; the number of Catholics roughly corresponds to the Irish population, and Anglicans to English and Canadian. What are suggestive, however, are the figures for Methodists and Baptists, for these Protestant sects were generally marked by low economic standing and high membership of United States born blacks.

Analysis by household status of all illiterates proves very illuminating. A majority, 75 percent, were either heads of a household or

TABLE 2

Religion of Illiterates

Religion	No. of Illiterates (n = 895)	Per- centage	No. of Adults in Population (n = 9338)	Per- centage
Church of England	138	15.4	2727	29.2
Church of Scotland	17	–	804	8.6
Church of Rome	568	63.5	2266	24.3
Free Church Presbyterian	16	–	889	9.5
Other Presbyterian	6	–	591	6.3
Wesleyan Methodist	56	6.3	1190	12.7
Episcopal Methodist	36	4.0	82	0.9
New Connection Methodist	1	–	–	–
Other Methodist	6	–	–	–
Baptist	45	5.0	287	3.1
Unitarian	1	–	–	–
Jewish	4	–	–	–

their wives. In a society with many boarders, few seem to have been illiterate, and few of the illiterates were servants. However, the paucity of servants does not reflect their age distribution, as 53 percent of female servants were twenty or more years old. It seems unlikely that serving demanded literacy; perhaps the heads of household were unaware of their lack of educational attainments.

Demographically, one discovers:

TABLE 3

Sex of Illiterates

Sex	No. of Illiterates (n = 895)	Percentage	No. of Adults in Population (n = 9338)	Percentage
Male	324	36.2	4897	52.4
Female	571	63.8	4441	47.6

A gap between males and females is to be expected, but its dimension, women outnumbering men almost two to one, is surprisingly high in light of figures reported for England and for rural areas in Ontario. In these areas, female illiteracy rates were only slightly higher. The wide differentiation may well have been a product of the effects of urbanization and immigration on women, giving them less chance to acquire literacy skills. This also explains why boarders, most of whom were men, were not often recorded as illiterate.

The age distribution of illiterates is striking as it indicates a pronounced tendency for illiteracy to increase with age. Several hypotheses are possible; either age caused individuals to forget how to read or write, or perhaps the spread of elementary education is directly related to the lower percentage of illiterates in the lower age brackets. The latter seems more probable, as the illiterates show a skewness toward the older age brackets when compared with the adult population.

Of the illiterates, though, women outnumbered men by ratios of 1.5 to 2.3 until the age of fifty, when the numbers become near equal, pointing again, perhaps, to the effects of immigration and the city on women.

Analysis of family size indicates that the mean number of children for illiterate-headed families was 2.33 children. The comparable figure for the total population was 2.61—making illiterate families smaller by 0.28 children, a startling difference. Could these families have been practicing some form of family limitation technique, was this part of the family pattern of the poor, or did illiterates merely marry later? One detailed reconstitution may answer this intriguing question. Finally, it is also clear that the illiterates were not huddled together in early forms of tenement housing for 86 percent of the families resided in single-family dwellings.

Economic data is available for 53 percent of the illiterate heads of household and for 70 percent of all heads who were linked with the City Assessment rolls of 1861. Twenty-five percent of the illiterate heads of household were free-holders, owning their own home, compared with 28 percent of all heads of household in the city. Of those who reported rental value (158), six percent paid annual rentals of over $100, and of those reporting income (36), 15 percent showed an income in excess of $300 a year. The data "for total annual value, including both real and personal property and income" are more complete and allow for greater generalization (see Table 5).

Here we find that the illiterate heads of household were predominantly poor, 71 percent falling below a poverty line drawn at the

TABLE 4

Ages by Sex of Illiterates

	Male				Female			
	Illit-erates	%	Adults	%	Illit-erates	%	Adults	%
20–29	64	19.8	1703	34.8	153	26.9	1798	40.5
30–39	92	28.4	1472	30.1	150	26.4	1233	27.8
40–49	64	19.8	980	20.0	146	27.5	788	17.7
50–59	58	17.9	430	8.8	70	11.9	394	8.8
60–69	30	9.3	224	4.6	33	5.8	144	3.2
70–79	11	3.4	69	1.4	9	1.6	63	1.4
80–	5	1.5	19	0.4	7	1.2	21	0.5
	324		4897		568		4441	

fortieth percentile. (19) But they held their own place in the 40–59 percentile group and, indeed, are only slightly underrepresented in remaining groupings, up to the 94th percentile of the population.

Occupationally, the illiterates fell overwhelmingly into laboring and manual trades (70 percent), but there were significant exceptions. (20) Two percent of Hamilton's illiterates were high status proprietors and professionals, including an innkeeper, a clergyman, and two merchants. Another five percent were in the white-collar range: a broker, high bailiff, customs collector, wagon maker, mariner, manufacturer, and several tavern keepers. These individuals were generally aged in their fifties, however, one fourth were younger than thirty-six. The question remains did it require a longer period for an illiterate to achieve success? Twenty percent were skilled laborers. (See Table 6.)

Some of these men possessed considerable wealth and property as fifteen had investments of over $500 in real or personal estate. This group included a manufacturer with $5,000 invested in his business, a customs collector with $8,000 invested, and an innkeeper with investments of over $10,000.

These figures reveal that while most illiterates were poor, some were possessors of moderate and even great wealth. Such evidence questions the traditional viewpoint that illiteracy is a definite roadblock to economic success. As we have seen, it was not necessary

TABLE 4—Continued

	Illit-erates	%	Total Adults	%
20–29	217	24.2	3501	37.5
30–39	242	27.0	2705	28.9
40–49	210	23.5	1768	18.9
60–59	128	14.3	824	8.8
60–69	63	7.0	368	3.9
70–79	20	2.2	132	1.4
80–	12	1.3	40	0.4
	892		9338	

to be able to read or write in order to hold high economic or high status employment. Generally, it would have been helpful, but one could still become a gentleman, merchant, superintendent of an asylum, or even a clergyman without literacy skills. Most were poor and laborers as one would expect, but that so many held higher positions and great wealth is surprising. Illiteracy does not seem to have prevented the talented or fortunate man from rising in Hamilton.

Geographically, the illiterates were mixed throughout the five wards and fifteen districts (21) of the city. This information is very suggestive of both patterns of settlement and of economic development. One finds that the fifth ward is greatly overrepresented, containing 22 percent of all illiterates, 23 percent of the illiterate heads of household, and almost 30 percent of the households with a resident illiterate, with a predominance of Irish, while only 13.53 percent of the total adult population resided there. Apparently, changes in urban development began in the mid-1850s as the Great Western Railway was connected to Hamilton in 1854 and the first locomotive engine shop was opened in 1856. A number of foundries, machine shops, and boiler works were built. This area bordered on the fifth ward, suggesting that the availability of manual labor kept those illiterates who had settled in an Irish Catholic ward in that area. As well, there was economic development in the third

TABLE 5

Economic Ranking

Total Annual Value	Number of Illiterates (n = 197)	Percentage	Percentile of Total Assessed Population
$ 0–9	20	30.9	0–19
10–19	41		
20–29	40	40.1	20–39
30–39	39		
40–49	21	15.7	
50–59	4		40–59
60–69	6		
70–79	4		
80–89	3	6.1	
90–99	1		60–79
100–149	4		
150–199	5		
200–249	5	6.1	
250–299	1		80–89
300–399	1		
400+	2	1.0	90–94

ward with a correspondingly high percentage of illiterates in districts 2 and 9. Let us remember, though, that the nineteenth-century commercial city was spatially a complex place.

Finally, it is valuable to consider if these illiterates were sending their children to school. The census shows that 4,591 children in the 5–16 age group were attending school in 1861; a rate of 85.75 percent of the eligible children. However, analysis by individual child reveals that only 57.8 percent, or 2,310, were in attendance. Boys and girls seem to have gone to school in almost equal percentages. (22)

Among the children of illiterates, we discover that 97, or 46.8 percent, of eligible males and 66, or 40.2 percent, of the girls were being sent. In all, 44 percent of children aged 5–16 were regarded as attending school. This would point to the fact that in the mid-century city, male educational opportunity exceeded that of the female. In Hamilton, this was true for the children of illiterates,

TABLE 6

Occupational Classification

	Economic Standing				Status	
	No.	Percentage			No.	Percentage (n = 380)
I (high)	8	2.1	I Proprietors, Professionals		9	2.3
II	17	4.4	II White Collar		19	5.0
III	80	21.1	III Skilled Manual		75	19.7
IV (low)	265	69.7	IV Semi- and Unskilled		265	69.7

by a full one-third, if not for the rest of the population. The attitude of illiterate parents toward the schools seems to turn on the question of sex; they permitted their sons some formal education while withholding the girls more often. This picture contrasts sharply with the school attendance patterns of the total population, with the children of illiterates almost fifteen percent behind, while leaving the school a full three years earlier. In addition, this information, joined with Ian Davey's analysis of the Central School, calls for important qualification of Stephan Thernstrom's study of Irish Catholic laborers in Newburyport, Massachusetts. It appears that post-primary education was the crux of the issue; secondary education was often withheld from the child of the laborer and from the child of the illiterate, while these children attended school in large numbers through the primary years. So, it seems that the quest for property mobility to which Thernstrom points, certainly does take place without removing all educational opportunity to the children. Indeed, there may be an important class differential associated with the secondary school as Davey has suggested. (23) The school attendance of the illiterates' children closely follows that of the Irish and Catholic; so as Katz has shown, in the differential between groups the illiterates suffered.

Having examined the ethnic, religious, demographic, economic, geographic, and educational dimensions of literacy, it is also necessary to place Hamilton in comparative perspective. Hamilton's 90 percent literacy rate was not at all high for Canada West, but over 10 percent greater than the aggregate figure for all of Canada. The

TABLE 7

School Attendance of Children of Illiterates

	Males				Females			
Age	Children of Illiterates Attending	Number Eligible	Percent	Percent of All Children	Children of Illiterates Attending	Number Eligible	Percent	Percent of All Children
5	2	2	100.0	19.1	1	1	100.0	14.0
6	6	23	26.1	41.1	3	17	17.6	41.8
7	13	18	72.2	65.0	8	22	36.4	58.4
8	14	24	58.3	71.2	14	22	63.6	73.3
9	11	18	61.1	72.8	10	18	55.6	75.5
10	12	20	60.0	79.5	8	14	57.1	77.7
11	13	21	61.9	75.9	8	13	65.1	72.3
12	7	18	38.9	75.0	5	14	35.7	72.1
13	8	12	66.7	80.3	2	5	40.0	69.2
14	5	16	31.3	57.6	5	13	38.5	65.9
15	3	17	17.6	40.5	2	13	15.4	42.3
16	3	20	15.0	28.9	0	12	.0	29.7
5–16	97	209	46.8		66	164	40.2	

majority of rural counties in Canada West were more literate than the urban regions. Perhaps home education was more widespread in the countryside; but the presence of a larger number of Irish immigrants in the city certainly seems to be the cause, pointing to the influence of immigration.

A preliminary study of Elgin County, Canada West, an over-whelmingly rural area, highlights some comparisons between literacy in rural and in urban areas in the nineteenth century. Elgin had an extremely high literacy rate in 1861, over ninety-five per-cent, and the few illiterates differed in significant ways from those of Hamilton. (Though the rate is inflation by the enumeration process.) The correspondence between literacy, wealth, and social stratification seems to be less rigid than in the city; illiterate farmers were often poorer than the distribution of all farmers, but corre-sponded more closely to the median. The number of exceptional illiterates—those with large farms, high values, capital investments—was higher too. Indeed, in an economy which seemingly required less familiarity with literacy skills, there were fewer illiterates and

TABLE 7—Continued

	Totals		
Children of Illiterates Attending	*Number Eligible*	*Percent*	*Percent of All Children*
3	3	100.0	16.5
9	40	22.5	42.2
21	40	52.5	61.4
28	46	60.9	72.2
21	36	58.3	74.4
20	34	58.8	78.7
21	34	61.8	74.3
12	32	37.5	73.6
12	32	58.8	73.6
10	17	34.5	61.5
5	30	16.7	41.3
3	32	9.4	29.2
163	373	43.7	57.8

they proved less unique. Too, the sex ratio of illiterates was much closer.

However, the rural illiterates also had smaller families and were not clustered in any one area of the county. But the religious and ethnic distribution was much finer, with no predominance of any one birthplace or sect. Age and immigration patterns point to the significant differences in a well-settled and prosperous rural area. Finally, the illiterates in Elgin were sending their children to school in greater numbers. Thus, it would seem that the allocation of the abilities to read and write relates less to economic needs and opportunities than to social stratification as a result of immigration and the allocation of economic resources, as an explanation of the variation between the city and the countryside.

Finally, making an international perspective, we find that Hamilton's literacy was high indeed. Available figures show only Scotland, Denmark, Sweden, and the United States to be close rivals. (24) These nations all possessed widespread educational systems and near universal levels of literacy by the end of the eighteenth century.

(Caution must be exercised on using these figures, as Cipolla notes; methods used for each enumeration and the level of accuracy vary widely, so they must be accepted only as general indicators.) (See Table 8.)

The importance of this study must be assessed in its larger context. This has been one attempt to investigate literacy in a non-tribal area, based upon 895 illiterate adults in one mid-nineteenth-century city, in one year. Indeed, this is the only way for meaningful studies of this nature to commence, but this research must not be considered more than a beginning if a "meaning of literacy," at least in the social structure, is to be ascertained. In assessing the evidence and arguments presented herein, one must look for those

TABLE 8

Estimated Adult Literacy (percentages)
(1861 unless otherwise noted)

	Adult Popu- lation	Males	Grooms	Fe- males	Brides	Army Recruits
Hamilton	90.4	93.9	—	87.1	—	—
France	—	—	71	—	66	68
England and Wales	—	—	75	—	65	—
Scotland	—	—	89	—	79	—
Denmark (1859–60)	—	—	—	—	—	97
Russia (c. 1850)	5–10	—	—	—	—	—
Prussia (1849)	80	—	—	—	—	—
Sweden (1850)	90	—	—	—	—	—
Austrian Empire (1851)	55–60	—	—	—	—	—
Belgium	50–55 (1856)	—	—	—	—	61 (1860)
Italy	20–25	—	—	—	—	—
Spain (1857)	25	—	—	—	—	—
Europe (c. 1850)	50–55	—	—	—	—	—
United States (1850)	85–90 (whites)	—	—	—	—	—

Source: Carlo Cipolla, *Literacy and Development in the West,* 14, 72, 88, 89, 91, 99, 115, 119, 122, 124.

clues, insights, hypotheses, that may be helpful in guiding further research on this problem.

The primary purpose of this essay has been to show that literacy and thus elementary education are intimately related to the social structure of the nineteenth century city, a preindustrial center undergoing change. There are many connections and relationships to be developed, including the economic standing of illiterates, immigration and residential patterns, and demographic patterns.

The illiterate adults of Hamilton, presumably, were those with the least opportunity for any kind of elementary education. As they were in the vast minority among the total adult population, they are important exceptions to the social processes that allocated some form of education to the majority of their cohorts. What was different about these individuals, and what permitted some of them to become successful without literacy skills? The school attendance patterns for the children of illiterates are important to the history of education—how did their attendance differ, as it did in Hamilton, why was this so, and what was the subsequent effect on future generations? These questions must be confronted in future studies.

The question of the qualitative and psychological meanings of literacy must soon attract attention. The matters of the consequences and implications are of profound importance to the social historian. The question of what it meant to be literate is equally difficult, but it must be confronted for a true understanding of the condition of an illiterate or even of many literates in the nineteenth century, or at any other point in modern history. Research on this matter has begun, however. The Harvard Project on Social and Cultural Aspects of Development has attempted to comprehend the role of literacy in adaptation to modernization. Alex Inkeles, project director and a sociologist, has reported that literacy correlated with modern attitudes and that a distinctly modern personality type exists: activist, change-oriented, aware of larger forces, optimistic. (25) Kenneth Lockridge is engaged in testing this in a historical setting: colonial United States and eighteenth-century England. Lockridge's preliminary findings, based on a sampling of wills, show no difference in attitudes from literate charitable-givers to illiterate givers. The isolation of a change in attitudes, to more "modern" ones and their relationship to the acquisition of literacy is a central concern of research in this area.

This is but one of many questions awaiting the historical student of literacy if a "meaning of literacy" is to be discovered. The key, I would suggest, is to ascertain if the society in question was a functionally literate one. Certainly, the adult literacy rate was high: ninety percent. But what were the uses of reading and writing in one's daily life? Who needed to read to carry out his job? How often was it necessary to sign one's name? What were the forces which resulted in a highly literate society and were these significantly related to material needs? To do so, research must take several tacts: the quantitative and the comparative in order to discern if illiteracy had a behavioral dimension; an examination of the teaching of reading to discover how well and successfully literacy skills were imparted; and the possible spectrum of uses for the skills—was it a functional or a nonfunctional literacy? We must discover if literacy offered real advantages, was an agent of modernization, or was simply, as J. F. C. Harrison has stated, "a process of acculturation, of assimilation to the norms and goals of middle-class society." (26)

This is part of a larger and continuing study, "Literacy and Social Structure in the Nineteenth Century City." See H. J. Graff, "Towards a Meaning of Literacy: Literacy and Social Structure in Hamilton, Ontario, 1861" (M.A. thesis, University of Toronto, 1971), "Notes on Methods for Studying Literacy from the Manuscript Census," *Historical Methods Newsletter,* 5, 1 (1971), "Approaches to the Historical Study of Literacy," *Urban History Review,* 3 (1972), and "Literacy and Social Structure in Elgin County, Canada West, 1861," *Histoire Sociale,* 6 (1973).

NOTES

1. Roger Schofield, "The Measurement of Literacy in Pre-Industrial England," in *Literacy in Traditional Societies,* ed. Jack Goody (Cambridge, 1969), 312.
2. See Lawrence Stone, "Literacy and Education in England, 1640–1900," *Past and Present,* no. 42 (February, 1969): 61–139; Carlo Cipolla, *Literacy and Development in the West* (Hammondsworth, 1969); and Schofield, "The Measurement of Literacy."
3. Gillian Sutherland, "The Study of the History of Education," *History* 54 (February, 1969): 59.
4. For example, such sources as the Papers of the Central Society of Education of London, contemporary English volumes, Mary Carpen-

ter's *Reformatory Schools,* Edward Baines' *The Social, Educational, and Religious State of the Manufacturing Districts,* Thomas Pole's *A History of the Origin and Progress of Adult Schools* (all reprinted: New York, 1969), the *Journal of Education for Ontario,* and the Annual Reports of the Chief Superintendent of Education for Upper Canada.

5. R. K. Webb, "Working Class Readers in Early Victorian England," *English Historical Review* 65 (July, 1950): 333–51, and "Literacy Among the Working Classes in Nineteenth Century Scotland," *Scottish Historical Review* 33 (February, 1954): 110–14; Cipolla, *Literacy and Development;* Schofield, "The Measurement of Literacy"; Stone, "Literacy and Education."

6. Stone, "Literacy and Education"; Philippe Aries, *Centuries of Childhood* (New York, 1962); R. P. Dore, *Education in Tokugawa Japan* (London, 1967); Michael Sanderson, "Social Change and Elementary Education in Industrial Lancashire," *Northern History* 3 (April, 1968): 131–53; Stephan Thernstrom, *Poverty and Progress* (Cambridge, 1964); E. P. Thompson, *The Making of the English Working Class* (New York, 1963); E. J. Hobsbawm and George Rude, *Captain Swing* (New York, 1969); D. C. McClelland, "Does Education Accelerate Economic Growth?" *Economic Development and Cultural Change* 14 (April, 1966): 257–78; C. A. Anderson, "Literacy and Schooling on the Development Threshold," in *Education and Economic Development,* ed. C. A. Anderson and M. J. Bowman (Chicago, 1965), 347–62.

7. Jack Goody and Ian Watt, "The Consequences of Literacy," *Literacy in Traditional Societies,* ed. Jack Goody (Cambridge, 1969) and G. H. Bantock, *The Implications of Literacy* (Leicester, 1966).

8. R. K. Webb, "Literacy Among the Working Classes in Nineteenth Century Scotland," *Scottish Historical Review* 33 (February, 1954): 114.

9. Thompson, *The Making of the English Working Class,* p. 394; see also pp. 350–400.

10. Stone, "Literacy and Education," 71, passim.

11. John E. Talbott, "The History of Education," *Daedalus* 100 (Winter, 1971): 141.

12. Michael Sanderson, "Literacy and Social Mobility in the Industrial Revolution," *Past and Present* 56 (August, 1972): 75–104.

13. R. P. Dore, *Education in Tokugawa Japan* (London, 1967), p. 292.

14. See Jack Goody, ed., *Literacy in Traditional Societies* (Cambridge, 1969).

15. These cards form part of the data bank in preparation for the Canadian Social History Project under the direction of Michael B. Katz of the Ontario Institute for Studies in Education and the University of Toronto.

16. Rather, one is dependent on the existence of an accurate census that inquired about the possession of literacy skills.

17. Webb, "Working Class Readers," 344.

18. For a general report, see Robin Winks, *The Blacks in Canada* (New Haven, 1971). Ninety percent of North American-born blacks resident in Hamilton were illiterate, but they led the Irish—and the rest of the illiterate families—in seeking education for their children, sending over 45 percent of school-age children. On the serious problem of census-underrenumeration of blacks in Canada, see Winks, 484–496.

19. Analysis of those assessed by total annual value in 1851 indicates that those falling below the fortieth percentile could be considered poor. There is no apparent reason to suggest a large degree of change in the decade that included a depression; see Michael B. Katz, "Social Structure in Hamilton, Ontario," in Stephan Thernstom and Richard Sennett, *Nineteenth-Century Cities* (New Haven, 1969), 212.

20. See Michael B. Katz, "Occupational Structure and Occupational Rank," Working Paper No. 14, September 1970, for an explanation of the scheme, and H. J. Graff, "Towards a Meaning of Literacy: Literacy and Social Structure in Hamilton, Ontario, 1861" (M.A. thesis, University of Toronto, 1971), 51 for complete detail on the ranking of Hamilton's illiterates.

21. The city of Hamilton was divided into five administrative wards in 1861, but fifteen subdivisions (districts) were created by the Canadian Social History Project for analytic purposes as the larger areas may conceal differences.

22. Michael B. Katz, "Changing Patterns of School Attendance 1851–1861," Working Paper No. 26, May 1971, and "Who Went to School?" in this volume.

23. Stephan Thernstrom, *Poverty and Progress* (Cambridge, 1964), 22; Ian Davey, "School Reform and School Attendance: The Hamilton Central School, 1853–1861," unpublished M.A. Thesis, University of Toronto, 1972. His article in this volume summarized his findings. See also, Katz's article.

24. Cipolla, *Literacy and Development,* passim.

25. See especially, Inkeles, "Making Man Modern," *American Journal of Sociology,* 75, 2 (September, 1969): 208–225, and Inkeles, Howard Schuman, and David H. Smith, "Some Social Psychological Effects and Noneffects of Literacy in a New Nation," *Economic Development and Cultural Change,* 16, 1 (October, 1967), 1–14, among that Project's publications.

26. J. F. C. Harrison, "Education in Victorian England," essay review, *History of Education Quarterly* 10 (Winter, 1970): 490.

MICHAEL B. KATZ

11. WHO WENT TO SCHOOL?

*School attendance is one of the most important and least
studied aspects of the history of education. This essay shows
its importance, outlines methods by which it may be
studied, and presents the findings of one empirical investigation into the relation between school attendance, the
family, and social structure in a mid-nineteenth century
Canadian city. The conclusions of the analysis support the
interpretation that the expansion of educational facilities
reflected rather than altered the relations between social
and ethnic groups.*

I

"CALMLY, deliberately, and advisedly, I give it as my opinion that
no one other anti-progressive agent exercises so pernicious and clog-
ging an influence on the educational growth and prosperity of
Canada as irregular attendance of children in school." (1) The aura
of profundity and revelation with which the author of this statement surrounded his remarks surely was unnecessary; by 1861, when
it appeared, virtually no one associated with schools would have
disagreed. Nearly all of the writers on educational problems during
the last two decades had made the same point. After all they believed, as Mr. G. A. Barber, the superintendent of schools in Toronto, put it in 1854, that "a numerous and regular attendance of
scholars" was "the keystone of successful popular education." (2)
If that were the case, the success of popular education remained
problematical. Judge Haggarty might have substituted the name of
almost any other North American city when he told a grand jury
that "the streets of Toronto, like those of too many other towns, still
present the miserable spectacle of idle, untaught children, male and
female—a crop too rapidly ripening for the dram-shop, the brothel
and the prison—and that too under the shadow of spacious and

271

admirably kept school houses, into which all may enter free of cost." (3)

To schoolmen throughout North America securing the regular and punctual attendance of all children at school was the central educational problem of the nineteenth century. In fact they wrote about attendance with such monotonous regularity that their complaints comprise a litany within educational documents whose significance, by its very frequency, it has become easy for the historian to underestimate. Despite the fact that attendance was the principal problem and preoccupation of late Victorian schoolmen, there is only one modern monograph in English on the topic. (4)

It is certainly the case that from first impressions the history of school attendance seems a narrow and dry subject of little general interest. But, appearance aside, its analysis provides a fresh and provocative lead into problems central to social and intellectual development. To paraphrase Mr. Barber, school attendance is the keystone of educational history. A few examples should make that point clear.

First of all, the literature of school attendance both reflects and illuminates important topics in the history of social thought. One of these is the controversy concerning the role of the state in the promotion of social welfare. The critical decisions about school attendance policy rested on contentious assumptions about the obligations, limitations, and style of the state and its relationship to essentially private groups such as the family. Three kinds of decision illustrate this point: should the provision of school facilities assume the attendance of all or a portion of the eligible children; what, if any, degree of coercion should be applied to bring recalcitrant children into school; what sanctions should be levied against parents who refused to send their children to school?

It is at the point that it intersects with and overlaps the histories of the family and social structure that the study of school attendance acquires broadest significance for the social historian. Patterns of school attendance may be redefined as the record of family decisions about formal education. Seen as artifacts of the nineteenth century family, shifting percentages of school attendance provide important clues into elusive areas such as: relationships between social class and parental attitude; the impact of economic fluctuation and technological advance on family fortune and behavior; or changes in the length and nature of dependency in different sorts of families over time.

Finally, school attendance is at the center of educational history. Its literature abounds in explicit and relatively uninhibited statements about the purposes and powers of formal schooling. At the same time, it reveals the major everyday problems which confronted schoolmen. Thus the history of school attendance uncovers an important aspect of the day-to-day history of schools. In the process, it wrenches us loose from our easy contemporary acceptance of universal schooling as a fact of life. For we learn the magnitude —and presumption—of the attempt to insure the receipt of an elementary education by every child. (5)

The systematic analysis of school attendance in history is a vast and intricate undertaking. However, there are several quite straightforward approaches with which one may begin. One, using traditional historical sources, is to analyse with care and discrimination the statements about school attendance in educational writing and to assess their broad social and cultural significance. This sort of analysis requires a consideration of what was said about at least the following topics: (*a*) why people should go to school; (*b*) who should go to school; (*c*) how long people should go to school; (*d*) what should be done about people who refuse to go to school; (*e*) for what reasons some people resist schooling. The study of *activities* undertaken to promote school attendance complements the analysis of the sentiments expressed in educational literature. It is possible, for instance, to study the history of truant officers, or the passing and implementation of legislation bearing on attendance, or to follow the efforts of school authorities as they experimented with one device after another to overcome the enormous social and economic handicaps that hampered their efforts to bring every child into school. David Rubenstein's fascinating monograph, *School Attendance in London, 1870–1904,* is a model of this approach to the topic.

Even if we knew all that was necessary about the thoughts and activities of people concerned with school attendance, we should still be left with at least three critical and unanswered questions: who actually went to school? What factors determined the level of school attendance within a community? How and why did levels of school attendance differ between communities? Through the use of quantitative sources it is feasible to attack these problems systematically. To begin with the last question—the differentiation between communities—a variety of documents provide evidence about levels of school attendance, defined as the percentage of children of a given age group attending school during some period of time. Using these sources, which are available at the least from quite early in the nineteenth century, one can assemble statistics which show how the level of school attendance in a given place fluctuated over time and how that level differed from place to place. The technical problems involved in assembling statistics of this sort should not be minimized, for problems of arriving at comparable rates and of assessing reliability can be very great. In this endeavor the educational historian has much to learn from the historical demographer, who has developed sophisticated techniques to handle similar problems. There would seem to be no reason why these techniques cannot be adapted to provide reasonably reliable series of statistics on school attendance over long periods of time.

Whenever it is possible to find figures for school attendance, other social, economic, and demographic information about the same place can almost always be located as well. Censuses, assessment rolls, vital statistics, educational reports and other sources may be combined to produce a composite picture of individual communities that includes school attendance, social structure, demographic character and relative prosperity. This information may be used to construct and test hypotheses about the relation of school attendance, considered as a dependent variable, to its social context. Here are examples of a few of the many hypotheses that might be explored in this way: school attendance varied inversely with the proportion of Irish immigrants in a community; school attendance varied directly with the proportion of the workforce employed in professional and commercial occupations; school attendance decreased as the proportion of children employed in factories increased; school attendance increased directly with per capita wealth; school attendance increased most during periods of industrial and technological change; school attendance varied inversely with the birth rate; and so on. The list could be extended for pages. It is not a list, and this is the crucial point, that contains questions of merely passing interest. Each hypothesis that I have stated is vital to understanding the actual functions of schooling. But there is *not one of them* which historians can say, with any confidence, is true.

The search for evidence that bears on hypotheses which attempt to explain differences in school attendance between communities should not obscure the importance of differences *within* the same community. As Haley Bamman shows in his essay in this collection, there were frequently striking variations in school attendance between the districts of a city. One of the most fruitful ways to approach these differences, he has shown, is to study the timing of the provision of educational facilities. His essay demonstrates that the geography of school building is central to the interpretation of attendance patterns as well as to the study of educational purpose. The fact that a city chose to build schools in certain places and not in others reflects in part the uses which those schools were to serve, for it defines, in advance, to whom education would be most accessible.

Finally, there is the question of who it was that went to school. This may be studied in two ways: one is through school registers. Surprisingly many nineteenth-century registers (lists of children attending a school) still exist. It is an intricate, lengthy, but nonetheless entirely feasible procedure to trace the students whose names appear in registers to other sources, especially to the manuscript census. This in effect locates the student in the context of his family; it shows the occupations, religion, and birthplace of his father and mother, the ages of his brothers and sisters, and, as well, a good deal about the structure and economic status of his household. This is the way in which to examine the social background of students who attended different sorts of schools. If the registers are good, the questions may be refined; for it may be possible to examine not only the fact of attendance but its regularity and duration as well. Consider just a few of the possibilities that may be tested in this way: perhaps there was little social class influence on who went to school at some point during the year but very much on the regularity and length of that attendance. There may have been a marked difference in social origins between children *entering* and children *graduating* high school. It could be the case that common schools have been common in name only, since early in their history the realities of residential segregation may have kept the range of social status in most of them quite narrow. Once again these are sample questions that are both unanswered and vital to interpreting the history of education.

The other method of finding out who went to school is to begin with the manuscript census itself. Usually the census schedule contained a column which was supposed to be filled in if a person had attended school during the previous year. Beginning with this column, the gross fact of school attendance may be related to a host of other variables about the status and structure of the family and household. This procedure has one obvious and serious disadvantage; it confounds attendance at all types of schools and it permits no conclusions about regularity or length of attendance during the year. It is the grossest possible measure. Nonetheless, it has the great merit of including the entire population. Nowhere have I ever seen a complete set of school registers for a community in the middle of the nineteenth century. Thus the study of registers, vital though it is, is almost always the analysis of attendance at a particular school, whereas by starting with the census one may study the gross patterns of attendance among the children of any group, religious, ethnic, occupational, or any other into which the census material can be arranged. In the rest of this essay I shall demonstrate how that may be done. In part that discussion should serve as an illustration of what may be learned through a quantitative approach to the history of school attendance; it should also point to a number of significant and intriguing suggestions about just who it was that went to school.

II

In the remainder of this essay I shall discuss patterns of school attendance in Hamilton, Ontario, in 1851 and 1861. The information comes from the manuscript censuses of those years, which have been coded in entirety as part of the Canadian Social History Project, which I direct. (6) In 1851 Hamilton, a lakeport about forty miles west of Toronto, was a commercial city with a population of slightly over 14,000. It was largely an immigrant city; fewer than ten percent of the heads of household had been born in what is now Ontario. Most had come from Scotland, England, and Ireland, and about six percent had emigrated from the United States. Although

Hamilton's population had increased to more than 19,000 in 1861, industrialization had hardly begun, and the city retained many of its earlier features. Throughout the decade the ethnic composition of the population remained remarkably similar and its household and family structures altered very little. Patterns of school attendance, on the other hand, changed dramatically.

The manuscript censuses contained a column headed "attended school during the past year." In more than 85 percent of the cases this column was completed for individual children within the household; in the remaining cases the head of the household merely stated the number of people living with him who had attended school but did not specify which particular individuals they were. There is no reason to believe that as a general rule this column was filled in unreliably. The aggregate figures for school attendance correspond reasonably to the reports of the superintendent of schools with some allowance for attendance at private schools. They are also comparable to figures for other cities. (7) It is therefore possible to analyze the patterns of attendance they reveal with some degree of confidence.

At mid century school attendance remained far from universal; within families the mean percentage of children aged 5–16 who had attended school during 1851 was 40.8 (Table 1). On the whole rather more boys than girls attended at every age level, from 3 to 20 (Table 3). However, very few of either sex—0.4 percent of the three year olds, 3.9 percent of the four year olds and 17.7 percent of the five year olds—entered school before the age of six when school going became relatively common with nearly a third of the children in attendance. The years of heaviest school attendance were seven through thirteen; only then did the proportion of children exceed forty percent. The peak years for attendance were nine through eleven, the only ages at which more than half of the children went to school. After age 13, attendance dropped rapidly: only 28.9 percent of the 14 year olds went to school, a figure which dwindled to 8.7 percent of the 17 year olds.

In addition to age, religion, ethnicity, wealth, and family size all affected school attendance. The least likely ethnic group to send its children to school was the Irish; less than one-third of the children aged 5–16 whose fathers had been born in Ireland went to school in 1851 (Table 1). By contrast those fathers who had been born in

Scotland and in Canada each sent more than one-half of their school-age children to school. Statistics for religion reinforce those for ethnicity (Table 1); less than thirty percent of Catholic children attended school compared to more than one-half of the children of members of the Church of Scotland and Wesleyan Methodists and over 60 percent of those whose fathers were Free Church Presbyterians. The obvious conclusion is that Irish Catholicism and Free Church Presbyterianism, respectively, retarded and promoted school attendance. However, this explanation takes no account of other factors; it could be that Irish Catholics were poor and Scottish Presbyterians prosperous, and therein lay the difference. The point is of some importance, for it raises the question to what extent school attendance was a product of cultural and to what extent a result of economic factors.

There was no direct measure of wealth on the census. The closest indicator is number of servants, which in fact provides quite a reliable way of separating the moderately prosperous and the wealthy from the rest of the population. There were three categories into which people could be divided on the basis of servants: those who employed none, about 70 percent of the household heads in 1851; those who employed one, about 21 percent; and those who employed two or more, about 9 percent. The precise social meaning of these distinctions is not clear. However, Eric Hobsbawm has argued that the employment of a servant signified class status in mid-nineteenth century Britain, and another historian recently claimed that the employment of two or more servants distinguished the affluent or upper class in the same period. (8) The data from Hamilton support these contentions; there is a direct association between the employment of servants and economic rank when census and assessment records are joined, and, additionally, the three groups differ from each other on almost every measure that we have devised. (9) School attendance is no exception. The proportion of children attending school generally increased with the number of servants in a family (Table 1): from slightly more than one-third in families with none to more than one-half in families with one and even higher in those with two or more servants.

Thus far two quite commonsensical patterns emerge from the statistics: poor Irish Catholics sent relatively few children to school and prosperous native and Scottish families sent proportionally many. However, the relations between attendance and both occupation and family size complicate this tidy picture. The practices of men in different occupations differed widely with respect to sending their children to school, and these differences cut across status lines in a sometimes inexplicable way (Table 1). Lawyers, for instance, sent relatively few, 28.6 percent, of their school age children to school. It is entirely possible that they hired private tutors. Yet their practice was not typical of all professionals, for doctors sent substantially more of their children, an average of about 58 percent, to school, and merchants fell somewhere in the middle, with generally about 45.6 percent of their children in attendance. Craftsmen in some trades sent more of their children to school than did some professionals and businessmen. Tinsmiths, for instance, sent 84.7 percent of their children to school, a figure exceeded only by the teachers, 91.7 percent of whose children had attended. Nonetheless, there were striking differences between trades: an average of 37.7 percent of the children of shoemakers had attended compared to 53.9 percent of those of cabinetmakers, to take one example. The figure most consistent with other findings is the one for laborers, who sent the fewest children of any group, less than one quarter, to school.

Factors particular to individual trades undoubtedly influenced school attendance patterns. The high attendance of tinsmiths may have been a product of their wealth, for they were the wealthiest of the craftsmen, wealthier by and large, in fact, than people in some commercial callings, such as clerks. (10) On the other hand, the relatively high attendance among children of cabinetmakers and carpenters may have reflected the demands of their crafts, which called for a knowledge of mathematics; certainly in England men in both groups were noted for sending their children to school for just that reason. (11)

Family size is the other factor that operated independently of wealth on school attendance. Contemporary research emphasizes the connection between a small family size and educational achievement, and that finding accords well with popular stereotypes of ambitious and aspiring parents restricting the size of their families. Thus we might expect that in the nineteenth century small families sent proportionally more of their children to school than large ones. This, however, was decidedly not the case. Among the wealthiest families, those with two or more servants, it was those with the most children, five or more, that generally sent the greatest proportion of children of all ages to school (Table 6). In fact within each economic rank it was the families with the fewest children which sent proportionally least number of children to school. The explanation of these patterns is not at all clear; it is a problem to which we shall have to return when we consider the degree to which the same patterns persisted ten years later.

However, before we examine the changes in school attendance patterns that came about in the next decade, it is useful to point out that the same relationships which I have described appear even if different statistical measures are used. One different measure is the percentage of families in which more than half of the children aged 5–16 attended school (Table 2). Here, once again, the Irish and the Catholics score low, people with servants very high, and the occupations present a mixed picture.

Likewise, with one or two important refinements, the same results emerge from the study of attendance among specific age groups (Table 4). Catholics once more are the lowest of any group at each age: they sent their children to school later, they sent fewer at each age, and they removed them earliest. At the other extreme the Free Church Presbyterians still appear the most education conscious of any denomination. Similarly, among ethnic groups the Irish had the lowest percentage of attendance at every age, except the very youngest, a point to which I shall return. The people sending fewest very young children were the native Canadians, who more than compensated for this by keeping their children in school longer than men who had been born anywhere else, although the Americans were a reasonably close second. For most occupations the numbers, when children are divided into age groups, are too small to make very many meaningful statements. Nonetheless, children of laborers do appear at the bottom in every age group, except the very youngest. Merchants kept about two-thirds of their children in school through the age of fourteen, which was exceptionally high. Not surprisingly, people without servants sent fewer of their children to school at each age, with the exception of the very youngest, and removed them soonest. Among the very wealthy, it was, as in other measures, those men with the largest families who sent the most children at each age.

Some of these relations are puzzling. Why, for instance, did the poor Irish Catholic laborers send a relatively high number of their youngest children to school when they sent so few of their older ones? Perhaps the explanation is simple; schools served as baby-sitting agencies for poor working mothers. It is likewise difficult to understand why, among the wealthy, a large family size promoted school attendance so sharply. Could it be that the relations between family size and school attendance represent random happenings, peculiar to that year and not to be trusted? One way to answer that question, quite obviously, is to examine the same relationships at another point in time.

A major change in social behavior occurred between 1851 and 1861, for school going increased dramatically. Within families the average percentage of children aged 5–16 attending school rose 17 percent, from 40.8 percent to 57.8 percent (Table 1). What was the source of this increase? Who was in school that had not been there a decade earlier? In the most general terms there are two possible answers to this question. First, the increase was disproportional; one group of people increased their rate of school attendance very much more than the others. One variant of this possibility is that the increase came from people who had not used the school very much before. In other words, it represented a mass invasion of the common schools by the poor. Another variant is that the increase might represent a drive by a group already education conscious. The middle class may have provided most of the increase, thereby extending its lead over the poor, simply by sending all rather than the majority of its children to school. The second major possibility is that the increase was proportional; everybody sent more children to school and the differences between groups remained as they were before. Obviously, the interpretation of the rise in school attendance depends upon which of these possibilities was in fact true.

The first fact of importance about the increase is that it spread itself quite evenly among all age groups (Table 3). There was a slight decline in the proportion of very young children, those aged 3–5, attending school, but by the age of seven the rise was marked. The age at which school attendance peaked was ten; nearly 80 percent of the ten year olds attended school during 1861, an increase of about 25 percent during the decade. In 1851 most children left school between the ages of 11 and 12; by 1861 the average school life had increased by about three years, for most students now left between the ages of 14 and 15. Likewise, the attendance of students older than 15 also increased sharply.

Despite the increase in the proportion and length of school attendance, differences between groups remained mostly unaffected. Each economic, religious, and ethnic group sent proportionally more children to school, and the gaps between them remained about as wide as ever (Table 1). For instance, the average percentage of children from families with no servants attending school rose about 20 percent, from families with one servant about 9 percent, and from families with two or more servants, about 24 percent. Similarly, although the mean percentage of Irish children attending rose from 31.3 to 40.1 percent, and although the proportion of Catholic children rose in a like manner, both the Irish and the Catholics remained lowest because other groups also increased at such a sharp rate. Once more laborers sent fewer children than men in any other occupations, but, with that exception, relations between occupation and school attendance are as fuzzy as ever. Percentages of attendance continued to vary widely from one specific kind of job to another.

Some interesting patterns do emerge from a study of specific age groups (Table 4). Among the 7–13 year olds Catholics made the greatest gain; their proportion of attendance rose from 31.3 to 60.1 percent, a greater increase than any other group. At the same time, among ethnic groups, Americans now sent fewer of their 7–13 year-old children to school than did the Irish, a shift reflected in other figures as well and one which may reflect an influx of exslaves into the city. As in 1851, wealthier children stayed in school considerably longer than poorer ones, and at every age the children of laborers went to school least often. It is important to stress this point because the laborers sent fewer children to school than either the Catholics or the Irish. This points to two conclusions: first, it was probably the more prosperous Catholic families, ones in which the father was not a laborer, that accounted for the particularly pronounced increase in Catholic school attendance. Perhaps the settlement of the separate school question in the 1850s removed a barrier between aspiring, upwardly mobile Catholic families and the schools. The first Roman Catholic separate school in Hamilton was established in 1854; by 1861 it enrolled 841 pupils (Table 7). (12) The second and related conclusion is that class, defined here as wealth, counted more than either religion or ethnicity in school attendance. It was the poverty that accompanied laboring status and not Catholicism or Irish birth that did most to keep children out of school.

The one factor that remains to be examined is family size. The relations between family size and attendance, interestingly, are even sharper in 1861 than in 1851, but their direction is similar (Tables 5 and 6). The fact that a large family size did nothing to inhibit, and to the contrary frequently promoted, school attendance is clear. One place where family size was of particular importance was among very young children. Of the children aged 3–5 from small families (1–2 children), 3.1 percent attended school, compared to 6.5 percent from families with three or four children and 10.0 percent from families with five or more. Controlling for wealth modifies the findings slightly, for it appears that the relation between early attendance and family size was most pronounced among families with no servants; large families of this rank sent nearly 19 percent of their young children to school. Among the more prosperous families the relations between family size and attendance are sharpest for six year olds, for large families with servants were more likely than smaller ones to send children of that age to school.

These persistent patterns reinforce, first of all, my earlier suggestion that schooling played an important role for large poor families. It provided the mother with someplace to send young children when she had to work. For large prosperous families schooling may have served a somewhat different but equally important role. Education conscious parents may have commonly begun their children's education at home at about the age of six as a way of preparing them for entry into school the next year. However, in very large families this may have been difficult to do because there would simply be too many distractions. In these circumstances parents might have felt that it was important to start their children in school a year earlier than usual if they were not to lag behind the children from smaller families.

With these relationships in mind, we may turn to the general question with which this section began: the significance and in-

terpretation of the increase in school attendance between 1851 and
1861. Consider the following hypothesis: the economic and occupational benefits that school provides come primarily from the
differential, rather than the *absolute,* amount received. It is, very
simply, an advantage to receive more schooling than someone else.
It follows from this that for any group to gain an advantage from
prolonged school attendance it must decrease the differential between itself and other groups. Its gain must be relative as well as
absolute. In Hamilton this did not happen. Despite the dramatic
rise in school attendance among every group, the affluent were as
far ahead at the end of the decade as they had been at its beginning. Insofar as schooling affects social mobility, the life-chances
of a poor boy had not increased very much, if at all. Extensions of
educational facilities (such as those suggested by Table 7) served
primarily to enable the affluent to retain their favored position.
The poor had to run harder than ever just to keep from falling
farther behind. (13)

Some factors modified the relations between wealth and school
attendance. School going served important economic and psychological functions for large, poor families and important educational
ones for large, rich ones. At the same time men in some trades
which relied peculiarly on formal learning encouraged their children to attend school more than other artisans did. Still, for the
most part schooling reflected and reinforced the class structure of
this mid-nineteenth-century Canadian city.

TABLE 1

Mean Percentage of Children Age 5–16 Attending School
by Selected Variables
Hamilton, Ontario, 1851 and 1861

| | *Children 5–16 Attending School* | | | |
| | *1851* | | *1861* | |
	%	N	%	N
Number of Children 5–16 in Family				
One	29.1	288	55.3	187
Two	41.9	318	53.2	339
Three	47.5	230	52.4	459
Four	66.7	155	59.8	339
Five	60.8	60	62.8	240
Six	58.1	22	66.2	157

TABLE 1 — Continued

	Children 5–16 Attending School			
	1851		1861	
	%	N	%	N
Seven	61.7	18	68.7	68
Eight	66.7	1	73.8	32
Nine	80.0	1	70.1	23
Age of Parent				
20 – 29	36.5	78	40.6	106
30 – 39	41.4	464	55.0	688
40 – 49	42.6	460	60.7	650
50 – 59	40.7	178	61.9	321
60 and over	28.0	58	61.5	98
Birthplace of Parent				
England	45.1	336	61.3	484
Scotland	51.6	184	68.5	342
Ireland	31.3	519	49.1	694
Canada West	53.3	90	65.8	134
United States	45.9	88	55.3	102
Religion of Parent				
Anglican	45.8	310	59.1	566
Church of Scotland	53.0	31	63.3	142
Catholic	29.8	334	42.6	483
Free Church Presbyterian	60.3	35	69.8	148
"Presbyterian"	47.4	119	62.8	100
Wesleyan Methodist	55.4	64	67.8	252
"Methodist"	41.3	113	49.7	15
Baptist	38.3	38	57.8	61
"Protestant"	38.3	115	60.0	1
Number of Servants				
None	35.3	885	55.3	1,481
One	51.1	255	60.2	281
Two	60.1	52	84.1	61
Three	58.1	31	85.1	26
Four	105.3	11	78.5	11
Five	0.0	3	100.0	3
Six	100.0	1	100.0	6
Seven	100.0	1	—	—
Eleven	—		100.0	1
Fourteen	—		100.0	1
Occupations				
Baker	40.6	8	63.9	18
Lawyer	28.6	7	58.0	22
Blacksmith	43.2	23	46.1	42
Cabinetmaker	53.9	15	56.1	20
Carpenter	45.8	46	62.4	128

TABLE 1 — Continued

	Children 5–16 Attending School			
	1851		1861	
	%	N	%	N
Clergyman	85.7	7	86.8	12
Clerk	50.1	26	50.1	29
Constable	41.7	4	61.7	5
Engineer	25.0	11	73.1	12
Innkeeper	58.0	23	86.1	6
Laborer	24.0	261	40.0	378
Merchant	45.6	28	63.5	44
Physician	57.9	11	81.5	13
Tailor	31.0	39	56.5	42
Teacher	91.7	5	70.0	5
Tinsmith	84.7	10	67.6	15
Gentleman	64.8	29	90.5	27
Shoemaker	37.7	56	57.4	53
Watchmaker	41.7	7	86.1	6
Mean for Whole Population	40.8		57.8	

TABLE 2

Percentage of Families with More Than 50 Percent
of Children Age 5–16 Attending School
by Selected Variables
Hamilton, Ontario, 1851 and 1861

	More Than Half Attending			
	1851		1861	
	%	N	%	N
Number of Children 5–16 in Family				
One	23.6	288	47.6	187
Two	35.2	318	45.7	339
Three	39.6	230	46.0	459
Four	57.4	155	53.6	339
Five	58.3	60	61.3	240
Six	50.0	22	64.4	157
Seven	66.7	18	70.6	68
Eight	100.0	1	68.8	32
Nine	100.0	1	82.6	23
Age of Parent				
20 – 29	27.0	78	35.9	106
30 – 39	36.2	464	49.9	688
40 – 49	36.8	460	57.8	650

TABLE 2 — Continued

| | More Than Half Attending | | | |
| | 1851 | | 1861 | |
	%	N	%	N
50 – 59	32.0	178	54.9	321
60 and over	22.4	58	48.0	98
Birthplace of Parent				
England	38.7	336	58.4	484
Scotland	45.2	184	64.0	342
Ireland	25.8	519	68.9	694
Canada West	42.3	90	60.7	134
United States	38.6	88	46.2	102
Religion of Parent				
Anglican	38.4	310	54.1	566
Church of Scotland	61.5	31	59.8	142
Catholic	23.3	334	39.0	483
Free Church Presbyterian	48.6	35	64.1	148
"Presbyterian"	44.6	119	53.0	100
Wesleyan Methodist	48.5	64	61.9	252
"Methodist"	32.8	113	66.7	15
Baptist	34.2	38	55.7	61
"Protestant"	31.2	115	—	1
Number of Servants				
None	29.6	885	50.5	1,481
One	44.4	255	56.2	281
Two	50.0	52	75.4	61
Three	51.6	31	61.5	26
Four or more	58.7	11	82.3	11
Occupations				
Baker	25.0	8	66.7	18
Lawyer	28.6	7	50.0	22
Blacksmith	43.5	23	40.5	42
Cabinetmaker	46.6	15	55.0	20
Carpenter	39.2	46	61.8	128
Clergyman	57.1	7	91.7	12
Clerk	42.3	26	55.1	29
Constable	50.0	4	60.0	5
Engineer	18.2	11	75.0	12
Innkeeper	60.9	23	83.4	6
Laborer	21.5	261	35.2	378
Merchant	39.3	28	59.2	44
Physician	45.4	11	69.3	13
Tailor	25.6	39	57.1	42
Teacher (male)	80.0	5	40.0	5
Tinsmith	70.0	10	73.3	15
Gentleman	48.3	29	74.0	27
Shoemaker	28.6	56	56.6	53
Watchmaker	42.8	7	45.6	6

TABLE 3

School Attendance by Age
Hamilton, Ontario, 1851 and 1861

Age	Males in School 1851 %	N	Males in School 1861 %	N	Females in School 1851 %	N	Females in School 1861 %	N	Males and Females in School 1851 %	N	Males and Females in School 1861 %	N
3 years old	0.9	229	0.4	277	0.0	226	0.7	295	0.4	455	0.5	572
4 years old	3.5	170	2.7	291	4.2	192	1.8	271	3.9	362	2.3	562
5 years old	22.7	211	19.1	257	11.4	167	14.0	271	17.7	378	16.5	528
6 years old	32.9	149	41.1	231	32.6	138	41.8	227	32.6	287	42.2	458
7 years old	52.2	186	65.0	186	45.9	135	58.4	226	49.5	321	61.4	412
8 years old	53.9	154	71.2	205	42.4	165	73.3	176	48.0	319	72.2	381
9 years old	61.5	161	72.8	169	46.8	154	75.5	188	54.3	315	74.4	357
10 years old	47.8	138	79.5	200	54.9	152	77.7	166	45.1	290	78.7	366
11 years old	58.3	132	75.9	170	50.9	106	72.3	137	55.0	238	74.3	307
12 years old	46.8	126	75.0	176	40.6	138	72.1	172	43.6	264	73.6	348
13 years old	41.3	138	80.3	142	38.5	109	69.2	130	40.1	247	75.0	272
14 years old	30.3	122	57.6	144	27.2	113	65.9	126	28.9	235	61.5	270
15 years old	22.0	91	40.5	153	22.0	100	42.3	111	19.2	191	41.3	264
16 years old	16.9	89	28.9	142	12.5	104	29.7	118	14.5	193	29.2	260
17 years old	6.9	72	23.1	108	10.1	89	19.1	115	8.7	161	21.2	223
18 years old	6.4	63	13.5	104	11.2	85	6.1	115	3.5	148	9.6	219
19 years old	6.6	61	4.2	95	3.1	68	4.9	82	5.0	156	4.5	177
20 years old	7.1	42	3.6	83	0.0	48	0.0	91	3.3	90	1.7	174

N = Total number in school and out.

TABLE 4

Percentage of Children of Various Age Groups
Attending School by Selected Categories
Hamilton, Ontario, 1851 and 1861

	Age Groups											
	3–5 %		6 %		7–13 %		14 %		15–16 %		17–20 %	
Category	1851	1861	1851	1861	1851	1861	1851	1861	1851	1861	1851	1861
Religion of Head of Household												
Anglican	6.6	7.1	30.3	41.9	51.1	74.0	42.2	59.5	27.4	35.7	7.1	12.1
Church of Scotland	2.9	6.3	62.5	48.3	73.8	77.5	28.6	76.2	36.4	32.5	0.0	6.9
Catholic	6.4	4.5	24.1	27.7	31.3	60.1	15.5	43.3	8.1	22.0	1.7	2.8
Free Church Presbyterian	10.2	7.6	50.0	51.3	52.7	84.9	57.1	63.3	37.5	56.2	14.3	9.6
"Presbyterian"	6.5	5.5	35.5	47.8	66.9	80.9	25.0	83.3	24.3	52.2	6.1	18.8
Wesleyan Methodist	14.0	7.9	36.4	50.0	67.6	75.9	38.5	74.4	31.3	42.7	8.3	16.1
"Methodist"	5.2	5.9	50.0	40.0	48.4	60.0	35.3	55.6	7.1	50.0	7.7	9.1
Baptist	8.9	3.9	20.0	52.9	55.4	65.1	0.0	—	10.0	55.6	0.0	0.0
"Protestant"	6.9	—	40.0	100.0	56.7	100.0	15.0	100.0	7.6	—	3.3	—
Whole Group	6.9	6.2	32.6	41.4	48.7	72.4	28.9	61.5	18.2	35.2	5.3	10.0
Birthplace of Head of Household												
England	9.6	6.9	33.3	49.6	54.5	75.2	20.6	72.2	16.8	36.5	5.4	8.7
Scotland	6.6	7.5	40.0	53.8	65.2	82.8	40.0	64.4	27.1	52.1	9.1	12.3
Ireland	6.5	4.8	31.0	32.6	37.6	65.3	22.7	51.9	12.4	24.8	2.4	5.4
Canada West	4.1	6.6	29.4	34.4	53.1	77.7	52.9	66.7	44.0	56.8	5.9	18.3
United States	2.8	5.7	34.8	45.2	53.5	61.2	50.0	60.0	21.7	27.3	16.7	26.3
Number of Servants in Household												
None	5.8	5.6	20.8	39.8	43.0	70.2	22.4	59.4	14.0	33.0	3.5	7.9
One	9.3	6.4	34.5	42.7	58.7	77.2	42.1	60.6	20.5	39.1	5.9	18.8
Two	7.9	10.0	60.0	50.0	79.8	90.0	81.8	100.0	45.0	57.9	28.0	12.1
Three	3.4	19.4	50.0	54.5	63.6	86.1	20.0	60.0	54.5	83.3	0.0	26.7
Four or More	18.2	6.2	83.3	66.7	76.0	88.2	100.0	100.0	50.0	33.3	66.7	33.3
Number of Children in Family												
One	3.8	2.3	18.2	38.9	52.9	57.9	55.6	47.4	8.3	41.4	9.4	12.2
Two	3.2	3.3	28.6	50.9	54.9	69.8	30.8	55.6	17.5	18.3	4.8	8.8
Three	6.1	4.6	27.4	40.2	43.9	73.8	24.1	68.3	12.8	36.4	1.5	9.2
Four	6.8	8.3	42.4	37.6	46.9	72.9	19.5	55.6	21.5	35.1	4.7	11.5

TABLE 4 – Continued

| | Age Groups | | | | | | | | | | | |
| | 3-5 % | | 6 % | | 7-13 % | | 14 % | | 15-16 % | | 17-20 % | |
Category	1851	1861	1851	1861	1851	1861	1851	1861	1851	1861	1851	1861
Five	9.5	10.0	31.0	46.7	52.7	69.7	34.8	63.4	22.8	40.2	7.6	8.3
Six	13.6	8.5	23.8	35.4	42.7	73.9	19.2	59.1	12.8	32.1	4.3	7.8
Seven	8.6	7.3	44.0	48.3	52.5	78.4	25.0	63.0	16.3	35.4	4.5	8.7
Eight	13.0	6.1	75.0	25.0	61.7	80.5	85.7	83.3	25.0	50.0	4.2	17.6
Nine	8.3	11.8	40.0	33.3	61.8	83.8	42.9	81.8	22.2	44.4	21.4	3.6
Ten	0.0	0.0	0.0	0.0	23.1	40.0	50.0	0.0	0.0	50.0	9.1	0.0
Eleven	–	–	0.0	–	37.5	–	0.0	–	50.0	–	0.0	50.0
Twelve	–	0.0	–	–	0.0	100.0	0.0	–	0.0	–	–	–
Occupation												
Baker	0.0	6.7	100.0	40.0	63.6	86.7	0.0	66.7	0.0	50.0	0.0	28.6
Lawyer	0.0	12.5	16.7	25.0	44.4	80.6	–	100.0	–	10.0	0.0	11.1
Blacksmith	13.3	2.5	40.0	41.7	57.9	67.2	50.0	50.0	0.0	23.5	0.0	0.0
Cabinetmaker	0.0	0.0	50.0	50.0	65.6	83.9	75.0	75.0	0.0	60.0	12.5	0.0
Carpenter	8.5	8.1	42.9	44.1	54.0	75.0	27.8	80.0	26.9	40.0	7.7	7.8
Clergyman	0.0	0.0	50.0	66.7	35.3	93.8	0.0	100.0	50.0	66.7	0.0	40.0
Clerk	16.7	5.4	50.0	42.9	63.6	76.2	0.0	80.0	0.0	60.0	0.0	0.0
Constable	0.0	0.0	–	50.0	42.9	100.0	0.0	100.0	0.0	50.0	0.0	0.0
Engineer	0.0	20.0	20.0	50.0	40.0	75.0	–	0.0	0.0	33.3	0.0	30.0
Innkeeper	8.7	4.4	100.0	100.0	84.2	75.0	20.0	100.0	25.0	50.0	16.7	33.3
Laborer	4.7	4.4	17.9	26.9	30.5	56.4	11.8	43.4	9.5	15.8	4.2	0.0
Merchant	6.5	6.3	33.3	40.1	62.7	73.4	66.7	44.4	16.7	44.4	25.0	33.3
Physician	0.0	23.1	–	100.0	47.6	85.2	0.0	50.0	75.0	100.0	50.0	16.7
Tailor	4.3	11.8	0.0	40.0	40.8	82.5	25.0	71.4	0.0	60.0	0.0	10.0
Teacher (male)	20.0	0.0	100.0	50.0	83.3	75.0	100.0	100.0	66.7	–	25.0	–
Tinsmith	22.2	0.0	0.0	25.0	69.2	92.6	100.0	100.0	66.7	50.0	0.0	0.0
Gentleman	6.3	0.0	0.0	44.4	57.1	94.9	57.1	60.0	33.3	44.4	7.7	15.2
Shoemaker	2.0	6.3	15.0	44.9	40.3	72.4	33.3	87.5	18.8	35.3	8.0	11.5
Watchmaker	0.0	25.0	33.3	–	40.0	90.9	–	–	0.0	50.0	0.0	0.0
Widow	6.3	8.0	20.0	35.7	43.6	63.7	29.4	43.3	15.4	23.2	2.8	2.8
TOTAL NUMBER	1,195	1,662	287	458	1,994	2,443	235	270	384	524	555	793

TABLE 5

Number of Children in Family and Percentage of Children Attending School Hamilton, Ontario, 1861

Number of Children in Family	Age Group					
	3–5	*6*	*7–13*	*14*	*15–16*	*17–20*
1 – 2 Children	3.1	47.9	66.2	52.2	33.8	10.4
3 – 4 Children	6.5	39.1	73.3	61.6	35.8	10.4
5 – 12 Children	10.0	41.6	73.8	65.2	38.2	9.8

TABLE 6

School Attendance at Different Ages by Family Size, Controlling for Wealth Hamilton, Ontario, 1851 and 1861

Family Size		Mean % Attending Age 5-16		Mean Percentage														Families With More Than 50% Attending	
				Age 3-5		Age 6		Age 7-13		Age 14		Age 15-16		Age 17-20					
		1851	*1861*	*1851*	*1861*	*1851*	*1861*	*1851*	*1861*	*1851*	*1861*	*1851*	*1861*	*1851*	*1861*	*1851*	*1861*		
No Servants																			
1 – 2 Children	M	35.7	53.4	7.0	5.3	24.7	41.0	43.2	65.2	17.4	51.8	15.9	29.8	4.9	8.3	27.4	42.1		
	N	489	989	227	459	77	178	326	607	46	85	82	188	89	221	134	416		
3 – 4 Children	M	38.6	61.0	8.7	7.6	25.9	42.9	45.1	72.6	26.6	65.3	19.1	35.1	5.6	6.4	37.7	64.4		
	N	284	458	157	268	81	134	283	454	64	95	89	178	90	181	107	295		
5 or More Children	M	24.9	55.5	5.5	18.6	44.4	26.3	38.8	71.6	24.4	61.7	10.0	36.9	0.0	15.8	18.9	63.2		
	N	111	98	73	74	27	38	111	98	45	47	75	65	48	38	21	62		
One Servant																			
1 – 2 Children	M	52.3	56.4	8.0	3.3	30.3	36.3	65.8	69.4	57.1	69.2	21.7	29.2	4.0	27.9	42.0	47.4		
	N	155	196	79	105	33	51	95	108	7	13	30	24	25	34	65	93		
3 – 4 Children	M	54.9	67.6	17.0	15.2	33.3	50.0	62.4	78.5	41.2	60.0	26.1	41.7	20.0	23.5	53.9	72.6		
	N	76	80	49	56	18	20	75	79	17	10	23	24	15	17	22	58		
5 or More Children	M	31.4	59.7	5.3	6.3	40.0	53.8	46.9	78.8	40.0	58.3	15.4	50.0	0.0	7.9	29.2	63.6		
	N	24	22	19	16	5	13	24	22	10	12	13	18	10	13	7	14		
Two or More Servants																			
1 – 2 Children	M	59.4	84.5	7.4	22.0	44.4	60.0	67.4	84.7	50.0	66.7	12.5	60.0	18.2	15.7	45.8	58.6		
	N	48	58	27	25	9	10	23	36	4	9	8	10	11	18	22	34		
3 – 4 Children	M	66.9	76.9	6.2	7.9	80.0	42.1	66.4	84.4	50.0	100.0	62.5	50.0	30.0	50.0	66.7	88.8		
	N	36	48	24	38	5	19	36	48	6	5	11	18	10	11	21	39		
5 or More Children	M	68.2	99.3	33.3	18.8	50.0	71.4	85.0	100.0	90.0	100.0	62.5	50.0	30.0	50.0	66.7	88.8		
	N	15	9	9	8	4	7	15	9	5	6	8	4	5	4	10	8		

TABLE 7

Educational Statistics
Hamilton, Ontario, 1851 and 1861

| | | | In Attendance | | | | Total Number of Teachers | | Trained in Normal Schools |
	No. of Schools	Number of Free Schools	Children Between 5–16	Children Between 5–16	Pupils Over 16	Indigent Pupils	Total Attending School	M	F	
1852	7	0	2,971	1,271	19	36	1,290	7	0	0
1861	8	0	4,200	3,937	N/A	106	3,963	7	30	19

| | Roman Catholic Separate Schools | | | Grammar Schools | | Academies and Private Schools | |
	Number of Schools	Number of Teachers	Number of Pupils	Number of Schools	Number of Students	Number of Schools	Number of Students
1852	0	0	0	1	93	27	1,003
1861	1	7	841	1	80(approx.)	8	250

Source: Chief Superintendent of Schools, Annual Report of the Normal, Model and Common Schools in Upper Canada for the Year, 1852 (Québec, 1853).
Chief Superintendent of Schools, Annual Report of the Normal, Model and Common Schools in Upper Canada for the Year, 1861 (Québec, 1862).

NOTES

1. *Journal of Education* (May 1861): 68.
2. Quoted ibid. (July 1854): 198.
3. Ibid. (April 1860): 56.
4. David Rubenstein, *School Attendance in London, 1870–1904: A Social History*, University of Hull, Occasional Papers in Economics and Social History No. 1 (Hull, England, 1969).
5. I have dealt with some of these problems in *The Irony of Early School Reform* (Cambridge, 1968) and in *Class, Bureaucracy and Schools: The Illusion of Educational Change in America* (New York, 1971); I have collected some nineteenth-century documents that bear on the topic in *School Reform: Past and Present* (Boston, 1971).
6. The Canadian Social History Project is described in my *The Canadian Social History Project: Interim Report No. 3,* an informal publication of the Department of History and Philosophy of Education. The Ontario Institute for Studies in Education, November 1971, and in two earlier interim reports.
7. See "How 'Representative' was Hamilton?" Working Paper No. 23 in Interim Report No. 3.
8. Eric Hobsbawm, *Industry and Empire* (London, 1969), p. 157; John Foster, "Nineteenth-Century Towns—A Class Dimension," in *The Study of Urban History,* ed. H. J. Dyos (London, 1968), p. 299.
9. See "Conspicuous Consumption," Working Paper No. 5, Interim Report No. 2, November 1969.
10. By my calculations, in 1851, 25 percent of tinsmiths were reasonably well-to-do, compared to 11 percent of clerks.
11. E. P. Thompson and Eileen Yeo, eds., *The Unknown Mayhew* (London, 1971), pp. 338, 367.
12. The separate school issue refers to the settlement of the Catholic demand for a share of public money to run Catholic schools. See *Report of the Royal Commission on Education in Ontario* (1950).
13. The 1850s was a decade of educational reform in general throughout the province. In Hamilton it was most notable for the establishment of the central school but evident in other respects, too (*see* Table 7).

IAN E. DAVEY

12. SCHOOL REFORM AND SCHOOL ATTENDANCE: THE HAMILTON CENTRAL SCHOOL, 1853–1861

The attendance patterns at one deliberately innovative nineteenth-century public school form the subject of this essay, which demonstrates the use of school registers in the analysis of the relation between education, social class and family background. Specifically, the essay compares the population of the school to the population of the entire city and analyses in detail the demographic and socio-economic characteristics of its student body. It explores the role of tax-supported centralized school systems in changing attendance patterns in the community and demonstrates the different use made of schools by the various social classes in midnineteenth-century Ontario.

MODERN PUBLIC EDUCATION officially began in Hamilton, Ontario, on May 2, 1853, when the Central School first opened. More than a local institution in importance, the Central School was the first "representative institution" in Canada West to classify students properly, to grade classes systematically and to introduce "the most approved methods" of instruction. (1) Despite its self-conscious progressivism the Central School failed to meet all of the purposes for which it was founded. For the social composition of the students who entered the new school did not reflect the egalitarian aims expressed by its promoters, as an analysis of its early attendance records reveals.

The register for the Hamilton Central School contained the name, age, sex, address, occupation of parent and date of entry of all students who had enrolled since its inception in 1853. I have

---

I. E. Davey is a graduate student at the University of Toronto.

used this information to determine the demographic and social background of the students who attended the school in 1853 and 1861; where possible I have linked the information about individual students to the 1851-2 and 1861 manuscript census and assessment records of their parents. The data permit, first, an assessment of the success of the school in reaching its perceived clientele. Second, they provide important insights into the role of the institution in the community. The study is complementary to Michael Katz' "Who Went to School?" which approaches the empirical study of school attendance from the information available on the manuscript census. (2) Katz' study of Hamilton in 1851 and 1861 investigates the behaviour of all groups in the community but the nature of the census information makes it impossible to differentiate between the types of school the children attended. This study focusses on those groups who took advantage of the public school facilities.

The centralized school system came into existence after a battle lasting more than five years. Its advocates—a coalition of educators, businessmen and professionals in the young but growing city— argued for a centralized, tax-supported, universal, graded system of public education. The influx of Irish immigrants and the emergence of an unruly class of urban poor, they believed, threatened the established moral and social order. The ward schools, which had been in existence since 1843, were ineffective: at mid-century, approximately one-half of the school-age children did not attend school and, of those that did, the majority were in private institutions. Within the ward schools, less than half of those listed on the rolls attended daily and the physical conditions in the one-room, rented schoolhouses were, some thought, actually injurious to the health of both pupils and teachers. What was even more alarming to the reformers, was the non-attendance of the "poorer classes" of the city, whose only exposure to the redeeming features of education was confined to attendance at the various sabbath schools. The new system was to improve this situation radically by ushering in the era of universal school attendance, thereby uplifting the social and moral condition of the community through removing the consequences of ignorance—vice and crime. Through the attractions of an efficient and systematically graded education, furthermore, the new system was to promote community cohesion by luring the "more respectable classes" away from private schools.

Despite the reformers' persuasive rhetoric the community was anything but unanimous about the benefits the new school system would confer. Both churchmen who considered its non-sectarian basis "ungodly" and people who objected to the property tax necessary to pay for it stridently opposed the Central School, planned originally as a large, permanent structure drawing students from primary feeder schools.

The opposition delayed the construction of the school for years. Its opening, in fact, had so deeply divided the community and predictions of its failure were so widespread that Archibald Macallum, principal-designate, refused to take up his position because he felt the contending factions would bring about its ruin. When it finally opened in 1853, its early effect, nonetheless, appeared in some ways to justify the claims of its champions. For, to the jubilation of the reformers, the new system of public education effectively destroyed the city's educational alternatives, with the exception of Roman Catholic separate schools which opened in 1856. Furthermore, the proportion of school-age children enrolled in the city's schools increased dramatically after the establishment of the reformed system in 1853; in fact by 1861 almost all of the potential students were enrolled.

Notwithstanding these achievements the new system failed to fulfill critical elements of reformist aims. It did not act either as an agent of social control or community cohesion because important social groups never sent their children and attendance patterns within the school reflected the economic problems and cultural diversity of the city's population.

THE MEASURE OF SUCCESS

At its inception the Central School was the public common school system in Hamilton because the primary feeder schools did not open until 1854. Thus, its students represented all of those families who availed themselves of the public education facilities in 1853.

On the first day, May 2nd, 451 students enrolled and by the end of the year some 1,294 had registered, of which 721, or 56%, were

TABLE 1

The Age Structure of the Students by Sex, 1853

	5	6	7	8	9	10	11	12	13	14	15	16	17	Total
Boys	23	54	72	84	83	99	97	69	65	40	15	6	9	721
Girls	46	57	52	63	67	67	60	48	51	25	13	14	4	573
Total	69	111	124	147	150	166	157	117	116	65	28	20	13	1,294

Source: The Central School Register, 1853.

boys. The advent of the Central School did not alter the age structure of school attendance in the city. Although the school contained students ranging in age from five to nineteen, the vast
majority of them, nearly 85%, were between six and thirteen years
of age with a peak at age ten.

Counsell, the superintendent of schools for Hamilton, had reported in 1850 that the "greater number of those who attend our
common schools are between the ages of 7 and 12; that most of
them, when they arrive at 14, are put to some useful employment." (3) Katz reports similar findings in the preceding chapter. (4)
The 1,294 students represented about 40% of the school-age children, a proportion similar to that attending the ward schools in
1852. Thus, initially, the new school did not radically alter attendance patterns in Hamilton, a finding confirmed by an analysis of
the parents' occupations.

Approximately 20% of the working population of Hamilton were
professionals, proprietors or gentlemen, 8% white collar workers,
40% skilled artisans, 23% unskilled labourers and about 5%
widows. The comparison of these figures with those listed on the
register for the parents of the students makes it possible to gauge
the "common-ness" of the school in 1853.

As in the whole population, about 20% of the students' parents
were professionals or commercial proprietors. But importantly,
lawyers, doctors and clergy were all under-represented, the merchants and lesser proprietors accounting for most of the group.
The professionals were obviously somewhat wary of the new school.
Students from white collar backgrounds (which in this paper means
mainly clerks and some public employees), about 6.4% of the total,
were slightly under-represented. However, the most disproportionate figures were those for children of the skilled and unskilled

manual workers. Almost half (48.1%) of the students' fathers were skilled craftsmen; this was about 8% more than their proportion of the total workforce. Clearly, the artisans of Hamilton found the school attractive as a place to educate their children. Conversely, the only group greatly under-represented in the school was the children of the unskilled manual workers of whom most were labourers. Their representation was less than half what it was in the workforce—10.9% as compared with 23%. This is not surprising, although it is of great significance. Katz found that it was the labourers who sent the least number of children to school prior to the opening of the Central School. (5) It was the urban poor, most likely to be found in the unskilled occupations, that the reformers were attempting to attract to the new school. They failed to achieve this aim in its first year.

An analysis of the economic rank of the students' parents—derived from linking the manuscript census and assessment information about each person—reinforces this conclusion. (6) Some 272, or 30.7%, of the 887 families represented in the Central School were linked; these were distributed quite normally throughout the major occupational categories (20.8% professionals and proprietors, 7.2% white collar workers, 53.8% artisans, 13.3% unskilled workers and 3.4% widows).

The low proportion of the families linked reflects the extraordinary mobility of the populations of nineteenth-century cities. Katz has found that Hamilton's population was turning over rapidly in the early 1850's: of the 2,552 people listed on the 1852 assessment, only 1,995 had been there three months earlier when the census was taken and a similar number listed on the census were not to be found in the assessment. Moreover, less than half of those on the census and assessment were to be found in the City Directory for 1853. Katz discovered one critically important fact about the transients in 1851. Although those who moved in and out did not differ from the remainder of the population in terms of age and occupation, within every occupational category these people were poorer than those who stayed. Thus, it must be assumed that those household heads linked to the children on the register were more wealthy than the parents of the children who had left the city. (7)

Table 2 shows the parents' wealth (measured by the assessed value of total annual real or personal property and income). Even

TABLE 2

Wealth of Parents of Students, 1852 [a]

Income £ p.a.	Gentleman, Proprietor, Professional	White Collar	Skilled Manual	Unskilled Manual	Widow, Etc.	Total	Total for City
1–5	0.0	5.3	4.2	8.6	11.1	4.2	20.0
6–11	1.8	5.3	10.6	37.1	22.2	12.1	20.0
12–18	14.5	21.1	30.3	37.1	22.2	27.3	20.0
19–37	25.5	63.2	27.5	5.7	33.3	26.5	20.0
38–78	27.3	0.0	14.1	8.6	11.1	14.8	10.0
79–143	9.1	5.3	8.5	2.9	0.0	7.6	5.0
144–488	18.2	0.0	4.2	0.0	0.0	6.4	4.0
488+	3.6	0.0	0.7	0.0	0.0	1.1	1.0

[a] As defined in text.
Source: Assessment roll, City of Hamilton, 1852.

allowing for the bias that was characteristic of the persisters, wealth was a major unifying characteristic of the parents. Only 4% of them earned less than £6 per annum compared to 20% of the assessed population and over 15% of those linked from the census to the assessment. Furthermore, over 15% were in the top ten economic ranks in Hamilton while over 68% of them fell within the middle (40–90 percentile) range. Clearly, this was not a school populated by the children of the urban poor. Moreover, the same relationship between wealth and school attendance was equally apparent two years earlier in 1851, as Katz' analysis of the census information shows. (8)

As a whole, the parents of children in the Central School owned a great deal of property. Whereas 28% of the assessed population owned property, over 47% of the students' parents did. Interestingly, more parents who were unskilled workers owned property—51.5%—than any other occupational group.

These unskilled parents were atypical of all labourers in the city, about 20% of whom owned property. Thus, they were not representative of the urban poor. The unskilled parents' propertied position is of special interest because of Thernstrom's findings about labourers in Newburyport, Massachusetts. He discovered

TABLE 3

Assessed Status of Parents of Students Who Were Heads of Household, 1852

	Gentle-man, Pro-prietor, Profes-sional	White Collar	Skilled Manual	Unskilled Manual	Widow, Etc.	Total
Freeholder	40.0	33.3	27.5	42.9	33.3	32.7
Householder	52.7	50.0	50.7	45.7	44.4	49.8
Both Freeholder & Householder	7.3	11.1	19.0	8.6	11.1	14.8
Boarder	0.0	5.6	1.4	0.0	0.0	1.1
Statute Labourer	0.0	0.0	1.4	2.9	11.1	1.5

Freeholder means owner and Householder, renter.
Source: Assessment roll, City of Hamilton, 1852.

that labourers who remained in the city were often able to accumulate property. But in the process they had to make considerable sacrifices, not the least of which, especially among the Irish, was the education of their children who were sent to work to contribute to the family income. (9) To the contrary, the linked Central School parents were a geographically stable and occupationally immobile group with a disproportionately large number of Irish who had accumulated property and were sending their children to school. As the unskilled parents were older, on the average, than the other parents, they may have initially sacrificed their children's education and later arrived at a position where they could afford to send them to school.

Apart from this anomaly, the parents exhibited most of those characteristics associated with wealth in mid-nineteenth century Hamilton, although there were two important exceptions. The nationalities of the parents reflected the immigrant nature of the city except that the Irish were under-represented as, among religious denominations, were the Roman Catholics (most Irish Catholics were poor). Furthermore, similar to Katz' findings, the students were more likely to come from larger families although by far the greatest number of them were the only representative of their family at the school. (10) However, two groups who might have been expected to send their children were conspicuously under-represented among the parents: the native Canadians, a very wealthy group who were more likely than most others to send their children to school in 1851, and the Anglicans, a large and wealthy segment of the city's population. (11)

The relatively small number of children from these wealthy religious, ethnic and occupational groups indicates that the most affluent parents did not send their children to the Central School initially, presumably keeping them in the private institutions. (12) In short, the typical students in 1853 were between six and thirteen years old and came from large, middle-income white Anglo-Saxon protestant families headed by a skilled craftsman or a proprietor.

The Central School survived its first year despite the community's apprehension and its own failure to attract the children of the poor. In the years to 1861 the new public system expanded and consolidated its position as it opened primary feeders and greatly increased the number of students enrolled. Four primary feeders opened in 1854, two more in 1855 and another in 1857 as the Central School took on the function of higher elementary and secondary education. This expansion reflected increased community confidence in the new system as well as a rapid increase in Hamilton's population in the fifties. Major trends in enrollment can be gauged from the aggregate figures supplied annually by the superintendent of schools for the city, even though the accuracy of his figures is questionable because the number of students listed as enrolled each year included each new student regardless of his length of stay. Given the rapid population turnover in the 1850's, there must have been many students who stayed less than a year.

Three events affected enrollment and attendance at the public schools in the fifties. First, the district grammar school was incorporated into the public school system in 1856. The grammar school appears to have operated previously as a "mere common school for the wealthy," hence, its incorporation indicated both the acceptance of the new system by the wealthier residents and the completion of the gradation of classes within the public schools. Second, two Roman Catholic separate schools were also opened in 1856. They removed over 1,000 actual and potential students from the centralized school system, lessening the chances of incorporating the poor into the mainstream of public education as a disproportionate number of the poor were Irish Catholics. The third event was the onset of a severe depression in the late fifties. The depression strangled Hamilton's growth and the population dropped from an estimated 27,000 in early 1858 to 19,000 in 1861. The loss of school-age children forced the Board of Trustees to retrench and it closed primary schools in a series of money-saving ventures. But the figures for school enrollment continued to increase proportionately throughout the depression, suggesting that the shortage of jobs may have encouraged parents to keep their children in school.

The trends in school enrollment in Hamilton throughout the period illustrate clearly the expansion of the public school system. After a shaky start in 1853, the proportion of school-age children attending the public schools increased rapidly to 1856, dropped with the opening of the separate schools after 1856 and then rose to almost three-quarters of those eligible to attend in 1861. Obviously, the establishment of the central school system had considerable impact on the other schools in Hamilton, drawing its first students from the old ward schools and the private institutions—from those already in school—rather than attracting the unschooled children. The opening of the separate schools ushered in the era of almost universal school enrollment by providing educational facilities for the previously unschooled Irish poor. The successful establishment of these schools confirmed both the protestant nature and middle-class bias of the public system which had been evident in its first year. At the same time, many more girls were sent to school after the new system was established. As Table 5 clearly shows, the percentage of female students increased dramatically after 1853 and girls accounted for almost one-half of the students in public and separate schools by the end of the decade.

However, even though by 1861 the schools had spread their educational tentacles throughout the city, gathering in and enrolling most children, the reformers still faced one major problem. Average daily attendance had not proceeded apace with enrollments.

After the opening of the centralized system average attendance rates rose sharply but in the latter part of the decade the rate dropped back, approaching the lowly average in the old ward schools. It seems that the initial increased attendance rates reflected the new system's expansion at the expense of the private schools and its incorporation of those students already in schools. The subsequent decline resulted from the geographic mobility of the school

TABLE 4

The Number of Students Enrolled in Hamilton Schools, 1852–61

	1852	1853	1854	1855	1856	1857	1858	1859	1860	1861
No. of Children 5–16 in Hamilton	2971	3400	3700	4000	4400	5500	6335	5000	5000	4200
No. Public Schools	1290	1373	2333	3926	3234	3307	3713	3560	3709	3122
%	43.4	40.4	63.1	75.7	73.5	60.1	58.4	71.2	74.1	74.3
No. Grammar Schools	110	21	77	80	80	–	–	–	–	–
%	3.7	0.6	2.1	2.0	1.8	–	–	–	–	–
No. Separate Schools	–	–	–	–	–	1,395	1103	1137	970	841
%	–	–	–	–	–	25.4	17.2	22.7	19.4	20.0
No. Private Schools	1003	600	601	600	600	N.A.	N.A.	N.A.	N.A.	250
%	33.8	17.6	16.2	15.0	13.6	(11.0)	(8.0)	(6.0)	(6.0)	6.0
No. Total	2403	1994	3011	3706	3914	4702+	4816+	4697+	4679+	4213
%	80.9	58.6	81.4	92.6	89.0	85.4	75.6	93.9	93.6	100.3
						(96.4)	(83.6)	(99.9)	(99.6)	

The figures in parentheses are estimates of the percentage of school-age children in private schools from 1857 to 1860 as the actual numbers were unavailable.

Source: Superintendent of Schools for Hamilton, Annual Report, 1852–1861.

TABLE 5

Percentage of Students of Each Sex Attending Public and Separate Schools, 1852–61

		1852	1853	1854	1855	1856	1857	1858	1859	1860	1861
Public Schools	Boys	72.8	56.7	58.6	62.1	61.4	57.9	53.6	55.2	51.8	53.3
	Girls	27.2	43.3	41.4	37.9	38.6	42.1	46.4	44.8	48.2	46.7
Separate Schools	Boys	–	–	–	–	–	43.9	60.6	51.5	55.2	52.7
	Girls	–	–	–	–	–	56.1	39.4	48.5	44.8	47.3

Source: Superintendent of Schools for Hamilton, Annual Report, 1852–1861.

TABLE 6

Average Daily Attendance at the Public Schools, 1852–61

		1852	1853	1854	1855	1856	1857	1858	1859	1860	1861
Summer	No.	483	823	1409	N.A.	1469	1425	1668	1361	1532	1688
	%	37.4	59.9	60.4	–	45.4	43.1	44.9	38.2	41.3	54.1
Winter	No.	425	–	1571	N.A.	1692	1475	1627	1537	1502	1675
	%	32.9	–	67.3	–	52.3	44.6	43.8	43.2	40.5	53.7
Total	No.	454	823	1490	1569	1581	1450	1648	1449	1517	1682
	%	35.2	59.9	63.1	51.0	48.9	43.8	44.4	40.7	40.9	53.9

Source: Superintendent of Schools for Hamilton, Annual Report, 1852–1861.

population (attendance was calculated from all students on the rolls) and the public schools' success in reaching those who were not used to regular attendance, if they were used to attending at all. Obviously, in the depression years in particular, schooling was not considered a full-time activity for the majority of students.

Thus, the reformers' system expanded in the fifties so that some 75% of eligible children were enrolled in the public schools by 1861. But the expansion was not without its problems. While the new system had virtually destroyed the private institutions and greatly increased the number of girls in attendance, the Roman Catholic separate schools attracted the urban poor, thus making universal enrollment possible. Moreover, average daily attendance rates remained depressingly low. The public schools, therefore, neither enrolled large numbers of their target clientele—the children of the poor, nor succeeded in ensuring regular attendance of those students who had registered. The Central School itself had become a higher elementary and secondary institution after 1853 and its enrollment in 1861 reflected the system's failures.

Some 346 students were enrolled in the Central School in 1861, of whom 189 or 54.6% were boys. In keeping with the changed nature of the school, the students were, on the average, older than in 1853. Students ranged in age from seven to thirty with the largest single group the thirteen year olds. The bulk of them (75%) were between ten and fifteen years, as compared to six to thirteen in 1853, and there were no five and six year olds and only one seven year old. However, the number of students over sixteen had increased from thirteen to twenty-six. This supports Katz' findings that not only were more children attending school than in 1851, but that the average age of leaving had increased from between

TABLE 7

The Age Structure of the Students by Sex, 1861

	7	8	9	10	11	12	13	14	15	16	17	18	19	20	21 & Over	Total
Boys	1	11	14	17	16	23	26	23	22	15	5	3	5	4	3	189
Girls	—	9	5	30	19	24	28	16	13	4	4	—	2	—	—	157
Total	1	20	19	47	35	47	54	39	35	19	9	3	7	4	3	346

Source: The Central School Register, 1861.

eleven and twelve to between fourteen and fifteen with a marked
rise in the number of students over fifteen. (13)

As the Central School became primarily a place of secondary
education, the class divisions within it intensified. In this way the
social composition of the school reflected the trends in the city's
social structure during the decade. Although the distribution of the
workforce into various occupations remained quite similar, class
divisions became somewhat more sharply etched. (14)

By 1861, the professionals' and proprietors' children accounted
for one-third of the school's enrollment compared to one-fifth in
1853. The proportion of white collar workers' children also had
increased slightly. On the other hand, the proportion of students
whose parents were skilled tradesmen dropped 13% to 35.1%, the
children of unskilled manual workers accounted for less than 8%
and no widow's children were enrolled in 1861. In fact, the representation of proprietor and professional parents in the school had
increased even though their proportion in the total workforce fell
three percent to 17% in the decade. (15) By comparison, the children
of skilled artisans, who had accounted for nearly half of the students in 1853, were now under-represented and proportionately
even fewer labourers' children were in attendance. Interestingly,
however, some 11% of the students were orphans, suggesting that
the system supported some under-privileged groups.

Certainly, as a higher elementary and secondary school, the Central School was even more of a haven for the well-to-do of the city
than it had been when it opened as a common school in 1853. As
in 1853, the occupational dividing line among the parents lay between the skilled and unskilled workers rather than between the
manual and the non-manual groups but the class divisions were
more emphatically drawn. Universal common school enrollment
may have been achieved by 1861 but enrollments in secondary
education indicated the continued existence of inequalities in
educational opportunities.

Some 102, or 34.9%, of the 292 families in the school were linked
to the 1861 census and assessment. With the exclusion of the forty-
four orphans and non-residents of Hamilton, those linked represented over 41% of the families in the school. The smallness of the
total number linked and an over-representation of the skilled workers among them must be borne in mind in the following analysis.

TABLE 8

Wealth of Parents of Students, 1861 [a]

$ p.a.	Gentle-man, Pro-prietor, Profes-sional	White Collar	Skilled Manual	Unskilled Manual	Total	Total for City
0–23	3.3	11.1	0.0	38.6	3.9	20.0
24–42	0.0	44.4	24.0	42.9	19.6	20.0
43–71	13.3	11.1	26.0	0.0	18.6	20.0
72–168	20.0	22.2	28.0	28.6	24.5	20.0
169–374	20.0	0.0	12.0	0.0	12.7	10.0
376–700	6.7	11.1	4.0	0.0	5.9	5.0
701–2366	26.7	0.0	4.0	0.0	9.8	4.0
2367 & Over	10.0	0.0	2.0	0.0	4.0	1.0 [a]

Source: Assessment roll, City of Hamilton, 1861.

(In 1861 people who left the city between the time the census and assessment were compiled do not seem to have been any poorer than those who remained.)

As a group, the parents of 1861 differed from their counterparts in 1853 only by being more wealthy. Over 20% of the parents were among the wealthiest 10% of the population, compared to 15% in 1853. The increase reflected the greater acceptance of the new public system in the fifties by the wealthy professionals and proprietors of the city. No fewer than thirteen of the twenty-one wealthiest parents were from this occupational category. Conversely, the poor of the city were virtually excluded from the Central School in 1861 as they had been in 1853. Whereas 20% of the heads of household in Hamilton earned less than $24 per annum, only 3.9% of the Central School parents did. The bulk of the students' parents fell in the middling economic ranks of the city, as they had in 1853, but the under-representation of the poor was more evident because of the increase in the number of wealthy families with children in the school.

The parents were mainly immigrants, disproportionately English, with the Irish slightly under-represented. Significantly, the most affluent group, the native Canadians, were still grossly under-represented indicating that some wealthy parents continued to send

their children to the private schools. The proportion of Roman
Catholic parents had declined markedly (to less than 5%) even
though their proportion in the city had increased, reflecting both
their lack of wealth and the opening of the separate schools. (16)
However, in contrast to 1853, the Anglicans were over-represented
in 1861, illustrating that they had come to accept the new system and
had taken advantage of its upper school facilities. The relationship
between large family size and school attendance was more pronounced in 1861, a fact that concurs with Katz' findings. (17) Over
32% (compared to 22% in 1853) of the parents had families with
more than five children while in both years over 80% of the parents
had more than three children. As family size remained stable in
the decade, it must be concluded that parents of large families were
more likely to send their children to school than those with small
families.

In short, the Central School in 1861 was more the preserve of the
large and wealthy white Anglo-Saxon protestant families than it
had been in 1853. The most important social difference between
the school as the harbinger of the centralized common school system
in 1853 and as the most significant higher elementary and secondary
institution in 1861 was its increased internal stratification: the
increase in the proportion of upper class students and the decrease
in the proportion of labourers' children. It is clear that with the
approach of universal common schooling, the class differential in
education was maintained by the relative absence of the poor from
the secondary school. As Katz has concluded, "the affluent were as
far ahead at the end of the decade as at the beginning." (18)

THE COMPOSITION OF THE STUDENT BODY

The demographic composition of the student body partially reflected its class structure. Insofar as conscious decisions have to be
made by parents as to when, where and for how long their children
will attend school, variations in the enrollment patterns indicate
behavioural discrepancies within and between community groups.

One of the most important effects of the establishment of the
new public system was that the number and proportion of girls
attending school increased dramatically (see Table 5). Katz found

TABLE 9

The Percentage of Students of Each Sex by
Major Occupational Categories of Parents, 1853

Age Groups		Gentle- man, Pro- prietor, Profes- sional	White Collar	Skilled Manual	Un- skilled Manual	Wid- ows, Etc.	Un- known	Total Number
5	Boys	13.0	13.0	47.8	13.0	8.7	4.5	23
	Girls	6.5	8.7	56.5	8.7	2.2	17.4	46
	Total	8.7	10.1	53.6	10.1	4.3	13.2	69
6	Boys	22.6	7.5	45.9	10.8	6.7	6.5	623
to	Girls	17.8	4.3	49.9	11.7	7.2	9.1	461
13	Total	20.6	6.2	47.9	11.2	6.9	7.2	1,084
14	Boys	25.0	5.9	48.5	5.9	3.0	11.7	68
&	Girls	17.9	7.1	44.6	12.5	3.6	14.3	56
Over	Total	21.8	6.5	46.8	8.9	3.2	12.8	124
Total	Boys	22.5	7.6	46.2	10.4	6.4	6.9	714
	Girls	16.9	5.0	50.4	11.5	6.4	9.8	563
	Total	20.0	6.4	48.1	10.9	6.4	8.2	1,277

Source: The Central School Register, 1853.

that in 1851 there were more boys attending school in every age group. (19) This was not the case in the Central School in 1853. Although there were more boys than girls in most age groups, there were three groups—five, six and sixteen—in which a majority of students were girls (see Table 1). In the older age group this distribution was probably random as the numbers were very small but the divergence in the two youngest age groups is significant, particularly among the five year olds, two-thirds of whom were girls. Perhaps there was a tendency to send girls to common school at a younger age.

Table 9 shows the relationship between students' age, sex and the occupation of their parents. Three age groups are represented: the five year olds, the six to thirteen year olds, who comprised most of the students, and those fourteen and over. Not surprisingly, the proportions for the largest group show little variation from those for the total student body. Similarly, the proportions for the older children conform roughly to the total even though there was some tendency toward over-representation of the non-manual groups. However, the proportion of five year olds whose parents were professionals or proprietors was markedly less than among the student population as a whole—8.7% in comparison to 20%. At the same time, the children of white collar and skilled manual workers were over-represented. Since two-thirds of the five year olds were girls, the variations in their parents' occupational structure are most significant. Among them, the small number of girls from the homes of professionals and proprietors, 6.5%, and the large number from skilled manual backgrounds, 56.5%, is especially striking. Thus, it appears that artisans sent their children, especially girls, to common school earlier than did professionals and proprietors.

This discrepancy between the two major occupational groups within the five-year-old cohort reflects most sharply a situation true for the whole school population in 1853. The professionals and the proprietors sent consistently larger numbers of boys than girls to the school in each age group. Conversely, the skilled workers (and the labourers) sent as many girls as boys, their daughters accounting for proportionately more of the girls because of the smaller total number enrolled. Obviously, there was a class differential operative in the determination of parental attitudes to the new common school system. The absence of younger upper-class children, especially girls, may have resulted from the presence of governesses in the homes of the more affluent. The dominance of boys from these families may also indicate that the girls were educated in the home or at private institutions. It was the artisans who accounted for the relative increase in the proportion of girls attending the common schools after the establishment of the new system. There is no obvious reason for the different behaviour of upper class and artisan parents. However, it may have reflected the fact that most artisan activity was still carried on in the home, a circumstance which may have made it desirable to have the children away from the house as early as possible. This would apply particularly to the girls since the boys were more likely to have remained at home to learn their father's trade.

The same difference in behaviour between artisans and professional/proprietors remained in 1861. By that time, girls dominated at ages ten through thirteen even though there were more boys enrolled overall (see Table 7). Although girls entered secon-

TABLE 10

The Percentage of Students of Each Sex by Major Occupational Categories
of Parents, 1861

Age Groups		Gentle-man, Pro-prietor, Profes-sional	White Collar	Skilled Manual	Unskilled Manual	Widow, Etc.	Orphan	Un-known	Total Num-ber
7–9	Boys	40.0	12.0	28.0	8.0	—	4.0	8.0	25
	Girls	28.6	7.1	35.7	7.1	—	14.3	7.1	14
	Total	35.9	10.3	30.8	7.7	—	7.7	7.7	39
10–15	Boys	30.5	11.7	34.4	10.2	—	9.4	3.8	128
	Girls	29.5	4.7	41.1	5.4	—	14.6	4.7	129
	Total	30.0	8.2	37.7	7.8	—	12.1	4.2	257
16 &	Boys	55.6	—	22.2	5.6	—	8.3	8.3	36
Over	Girls	30.0	—	30.0	10.0	—	20.0	10.0	10
	Total	50.0	—	23.9	6.5	—	10.9	8.7	46
Total	Boys	36.5	9.5	31.2	9.0	—	8.5	5.3	189
	Girls	29.4	4.6	39.9	5.9	—	15.0	5.2	153
	Total	33.3	7.3	35.1	7.6	—	11.4	5.3	342
% in City		17.0	7.0	38.0	24.0	10.0	—	—	—

Source: The Central School Register, 1861.

dary school as frequently as boys, the latter remained much longer; over 75% of the students fourteen years and over were male. (20) As Table 10 indicates, it was the divergent occupational backgrounds of the boys and girls which accounted for the peculiarities of the age-sex structure.

The most significant feature of the breakdown was the disproportionately large number of boys sent by professionals and proprietors, and of girls sent by skilled artisans. This was true for each of the three categories and is particularly significant because the number of students sent by each major occupational group was approximately the same in 1861. The numerical dominance of girls age ten through fifteen resulted entirely from the fact that artisans dominated among the parents of students at these ages. Conversely, the dominance of boys among the older students reflected the fact that most of them were sons of professionals and proprietors. Twenty-three of the forty-six students over fifteen came from upper class families and of these twenty were boys.

Clearly, the parents from the two major occupational groups had divergent attitudes about the function of the Central School. Either the professionals and proprietors were more concerned with the education of their male children and sent more to school for longer, or they entrusted their daughters to private institutions. Artisans, on the other hand, were more likely to send their girls to the public schools and keep them there longer while their sons left to work at the father's trade or to seek other employment. This pattern is understandable, given the fact that opportunities for female employment, outside of domestic service, were severely limited.

CONCLUSION

The new centralized, tax-supported public system of education had not fulfilled the extravagant claims of the reformers, even though its achievements were very impressive. The restructuring of public education had been effected in the face of initial determined opposition from conservatives and indifference from the working class. In a mere eight years, the public system had grown from the one central school to a complex of graded primary and secondary schools which enrolled most of the protestant school-age children in the city. In the process it had incorporated the district grammar school and cut a swathe through the private schools which had flourished prior to 1853. But the composition of the student body illustrates that the new system did not serve all groups in Hamilton, nor did those who sent their children share common aims.

The reformers had claimed that the new system would act as an agent of social control and social cohesion. As a means of social control it was of dubious value for in 1853 the students were largely from artisan, white collar, and proprietor backgrounds. Their parents were more wealthy than the norm and overwhelmingly Anglo-Saxon and Protestant. Unskilled workers who did send their children were inordinately propertied compared to the rest of their class. The children of the poor were not to be found in the school initially and if later enrolled, their daily attendance was far from regular. Clearly, in the fifties the public system could not have eradicated the social ills associated with ignorance and urban poverty because they were slow to bring the poor children into the schools.

In addition, the new system did not foster social cohesion. Even though it brought the children of the wealthy into the public schools, the educational differential between the poor and the rich remained wide. Before the advent of the new school system the differential existed because of the virtual absence of the children of the poor from any form of school. After its expansion, the differential was maintained by the virtual absence of the poor from the upper level of the elementary and the secondary school. Only a minority of students stayed at school beyond the primary level and those that did were largely from the wealthier families of Hamilton. In fact, the Central School as a higher elementary and secondary institution in 1861 differed from that in 1853 only insofar as more of the wealthy families of the city had children there.

The differing conceptions of the school's function emphasized the class bias of the new system. For the wealthy proprietors and professionals, the Central School was primarily a place to educate their sons, presumably in preparation for clerical and professional occupations. For the artisans, it was mainly a place to send their daughters in the absence of occupational opportunities in the fledgling city. The new school system both reflected and further entrenched the social inequalities in mid-nineteenth century Hamilton.

NOTES

1. J. H. Smith. *The Central School Jubilee Reunion: An Historical Sketch* (Hamilton: Spectator Printing Company, 1905), p. 7.
2. Michael B. Katz. "Who Went to School?" This article also contains a discussion of the possibilities and methodology of the historical analysis of school attendance.
3. Upper Canada. Department of Public Instruction. *Annual Report of the Normal, Model, Grammar and Common Schools in Upper Canada,* 1850, p. 184.
4. Katz. "Who Went to School?"
5. Ibid.
6. The linkage of the students to their parents has been made possible by easy access to the data of the Canadian Social History Project. My thanks are due to the director, Michael Katz, and research assistant, John Tiller.
7. Michael B. Katz. "The People of a Canadian City." For further information about the transiency of urban populations see Peter Knights,

"Population Turnover, Persistence and Residential Mobility in Boston, 1830–1860," in Stephan Thernstrom & Richard Sennett (Eds.), *Nineteenth Century Cities* (New Haven: Yale University Press, 1969), pp. 258–274 and Stephan Thernstrom & Peter Knights, "Men in Motion: Some Data and Speculations about Urban Population Mobility in Nineteenth Century America," in Tamara K. Hareven (Ed.), *Anonymous Americans* (Englewood Cliffs, N.J.: Prentice-Hall, 1971), pp. 15–47.

8. Katz. "Who Went to School?"
9. Stephan Thernstrom. *Poverty and Progress* (New York: Atheneum Paperback, 1970), especially pp. 152–157.
10. Katz. "Who Went to School?"
11. Ibid.
12. For the tables from which this and the following summary information is derived see Ian E. Davey, "School Reform and School Attendance: The Hamilton Central School, 1853–1861." Unpublished M.A. Thesis. University of Toronto, 1972.
13. Katz. "Who Went to School?"
14. See Michael B. Katz. *Canadian Social History Project: Interim Report.* No. 3 (Toronto: OISE, Dept. of History & Philosophy, 1971), p. 100ff.
15. A part of this increase resulted from the presence of thirteen students from townships surrounding Hamilton, of which eleven were the children of professionals and proprietors, particularly farmers.
16. Katz found that the Roman Catholics proportionately made the greatest gain in school attendance between 1851 and 1861 in the age group seven to thirteen. See Katz, "Who Went to School?"
17. Ibid.
18. Ibid.
19. Ibid.
20. Older girls from wealthy families probably attended private schools. The Wesleyan Female College, which opened in 1861 and operated for many years, enrolled 136 girls in its first year of which sixty-four were from Hamilton.

INDEX